THE POLITICS OF ATTRACTION

FOUR ⊠

MIDDLE ⊠

POWERS AND ⊠

THE UNITED STATES ⊠

1977

ANNETTE BAKER FOX

THE
POLITICS OF
ATTRACTION

COLUMBIA UNIVERSITY PRESS   NEW YORK

ANNETTE BAKER FOX is a research associate with the Institute of War and
    Peace Studies of Columbia University and lecturer
    in political science at Barnard College.

LIBRARY OF CONGRESS CATALOGING IN PUBLICATION DATA

Fox, Annette Baker, 1912–
    The politics of attraction.

    Includes bibliographical references and index.
    1. United States—Relations (general) with Canada. 2. Canada—Relations
(general) with the United States. 3. United States—Relations (general) with
Mexico. 4. Mexico—Relations (general) with the United States. 5. United
States—Relations (general) with Australia. 6. Australia—Relations (gen-
eral) with the United States. 7. United States—Relations (general) with
Brazil. 8. Brazil—Relations (general) with the United States. I. Title.
    E744.F78   327.73   76-27291   ISBN 0-231-04116-0

COLUMBIA UNIVERSITY PRESS   NEW YORK   GUILDFORD, SURREY

TO

THE

MEMORY

OF

ANNETTA GRIMM BAKER

PREFACE

THIS IS A STUDY OF interpenetration and responsiveness between the United States and each of four friendly middle powers, two of the four being next-door neighbors to the superpower. To what extent and in what ways did one country respond to the needs of the other, and how did the policies of one country affect those of the other? The study was started in 1966, when excitement about European integration still was high; it continued through a period of intense scholarly interest in the phenomenon of "international community." What has gradually emerged, however, is less a pattern of partially integrating neighbors than one in which a special kind of power—neither great nor small—is attracted to and attracts the western superpower.

During these years, I spent several months at one time or another in all of the countries involved, Canada, Mexico, Brazil, and Australia. I was able to supplement more formal field work by taking advantage of the opportunity to sense the difference in behavior and attitude towards the United States which seemed to depend upon distance. On these visits and at other times, numerous officials and private citizens in all of the four countries offered invaluable aid. To single them out would be unintentionally discriminatory and might even be unwelcome. Particularly close associations with some Canadians helped me to appreciate the significance of "the Canadian identity" without accepting that Canadians were truly foreign to an American.

Especially helpful were academic persons at Carleton University, Australian National University, the Colegio de Mexico, and the Instituto Rio Branco. At Columbia University, several graduate students assisted in data collecting, including Donald Bakker, Jeffrey Mayer, John Rounsaville, John Tabori, Roger Cohen, Leonard Levine, Richard Pagano, and Stephen Marsh. I am grateful to Peter Schoettle and Noel Kaplowitz for digesting much periodical material from Australia and Canada, respectively. Professor Donald J. Puchala was an invaluable consultant along the way, and his stimulating suggestions after reading the completed manuscript put me further in his debt. I also would like to thank Professor Richard L. Merritt of the University of Illinois for proposing fresh and very useful ways to improve the presentation. Once again, I am greatly obliged to Jane P. M. Schilling for her perceptive and meticulous editing. Like others in the Institute of War and Peace Studies, I am eternally grateful to the administrative assistant, Anna Hohri, for aid above and beyond the call of duty.

The ways in which my husband and colleague, William T. R. Fox, contributed to whatever might be worthwhile in this study are too innumerable to mention, except for one. Without him, I would not have been able to live in the four very interesting countries whose relations with the United States are the subject of this book. With him I was fortunate to be able to contemplate and discuss the results of my study at the Rockefeller Foundation's Villa Serbelloni.

ANNETTE BAKER FOX
Institute of War and Peace Studies,
  Columbia University
September, 1976

CONTENTS

INSTITUTE OF WAR AND PEACE STUDIES
OF THE SCHOOL OF INTERNATIONAL AFFAIRS OF
COLUMBIA UNIVERSITY

The Politics of Attraction: Four Middle Powers and the United States is one of a series of studies sponsored by the Institute of War and Peace Studies of Columbia University. Recent publications by those who have been associated with the Institute are *The Politics of Policy Making in Defense and Foreign Affairs* by Roger Hilsman; *Dominance and Diversity: The International Hierarchy* by Steven L. Spiegel; *Planning, Prediction and Policymaking in Foreign Affairs* by Robert L. Rothstein; *The Origins of Peace* by Robert F. Randle; *Foreign Affairs and the Constitution* by Louis Henkin; *European Security and the Atlantic System,* eds., William T. R. Fox and Warner R. Schilling; *American Arms and a Changing Europe: Dilemmas of Deterrence and Disarmament* by Warner R. Schilling, William T. R. Fox, Catherine M. Kelleher, and Donald J. Puchala; *The United Nations in a Changing World* by Leland M. Goodrich; *The Cold War Begins: Soviet-American Conflict Over Eastern Europe* by Lynn E. Davis; *The Crouching Future: International Politics and U.S. Foreign Policy—A Forecast* by Roger Hilsman; *Germany and the Politics of Nuclear Weapons* by Catherine M. Kelleher; and *The ICBM Story* by Paul Edmund Beard. Earlier works relating to the conduct of foreign policy prepared under Institute auspices are *Foreign Policy and Democratic Politics* by Kenneth N. Waltz (jointly with the Center for International Affairs, Harvard University); *NATO and the Range of American Choice* by William T. R. Fox and Annette Baker Fox; and *Alliances and Samll Powers* by Robert L. Rothstein.

PREFACE

THIS IS A STUDY OF interpenetration and responsiveness between the United States and each of four friendly middle powers, two of the
four being next-door neighbors to the superpower. To what extent and in
what ways did one country respond to the needs of the other, and how did
the policies of one country affect those of the other? The study was started
in 1966, when excitement about European integration still was high; it continued through a period of intense scholarly interest in the phenomenon of
"international community." What has gradually emerged, however, is less
a pattern of partially integrating neighbors than one in which a special kind
of power—neither great nor small—is attracted to and attracts the western
superpower.

During these years, I spent several months at one time or another in all
of the countries involved, Canada, Mexico, Brazil, and Australia. I was able
to supplement more formal field work by taking advantage of the opportunity to sense the difference in behavior and attitude towards the United
States which seemed to depend upon distance. On these visits and at other
times, numerous officials and private citizens in all of the four countries offered invaluable aid. To single them out would be unintentionally discriminatory and might even be unwelcome. Particularly close associations with
some Canadians helped me to appreciate the significance of "the Canadian
identity" without accepting that Canadians were truly foreign to an American.

Especially helpful were academic persons at Carleton University, Aus-
tralian National University, the Colegio de Mexico, and the Instituto Rio
Branco. At Columbia University, several graduate students assisted in data
collecting, including Donald Bakker, Jeffrey Mayer, John Rounsaville, John
Tabori, Roger Cohen, Leonard Levine, Richard Pagano, and Stephen
Marsh. I am grateful to Peter Schoettle and Noel Kaplowitz for digesting
much periodical material from Australia and Canada, respectively. Professor
Donald J. Puchala was an invaluable consultant along the way, and his stim-

ulating suggestions after reading the completed manuscript put me further in his debt. I also would like to thank Professor Richard L. Merritt of the University of Illinois for proposing fresh and very useful ways to improve the presentation. Once again, I am greatly obliged to Jane P. M. Schilling for her perceptive and meticulous editing. Like others in the Institute of War and Peace Studies, I am eternally grateful to the administrative assistant, Anna Hohri, for aid above and beyond the call of duty.

The ways in which my husband and colleague, William T. R. Fox, contributed to whatever might be worthwhile in this study are too innumerable to mention, except for one. Without him, I would not have been able to live in the four very interesting countries whose relations with the United States are the subject of this book. With him I was fortunate to be able to contemplate and discuss the results of my study at the Rockefeller Foundation's Villa Serbelloni.

ANNETTE BAKER FOX
Institute of War and Peace Studies,
Columbia University
September, 1976

THE POLITICS OF ATTRACTION

ONE

THE GIANT NEXT DOOR AND FAR AWAY

DOES LIVING NEXT DOOR TO the giant United States involuntarily entangle even such large and vigorous states as Canada and Mexico in ways they would prefer to avoid? Or can their relationships with the giant neighbor be so managed as to provide mutual benefits? Are powers of like magnitude farther away likely to experience similar risks to their freedom of action? Can they enjoy similar opportunities for reciprocal advantage through a comparable system of attraction? Perspectives differ, partly as a result of location.

While the Mexican dictator Porfirio Diaz was lamenting, "Poor Mexico, so far from God, so near to the United States," he nevertheless was making use of proximity in a way that revolutionary leaders who overturned his regime would not. More objective, perhaps, was Canada's Minister of External Affairs Mitchell Sharp, who commented that "conflict is a function of contact" in explaining the great number of controversies between Canada and the United States.[1] A different view was advanced by an Australian historian, Geoffrey Blainey, who called his book on Australia's fate *The Tyranny of Distance*.[2] The daughter of the Brazilian dictator Getulio Vargas, referring to a faraway political rival of her father, declared untrue the aphorism, "far from the eyes, far from the heart." [3] She could have made the same observation about relations with the United States, and the contrast would be equally true: that the nearby competitor arouses more criticism and complaint. Opinions evidently vary as to how and to what extent distance affects relations with the United States. How do these opinions accord with the historical record?

In relations between the American superpower and middle powers like Canada, Mexico, Australia, and Brazil, geographical distance may be less important than other factors that affect the behavior of their leaders, such as cultural affinity. Yet location is surely one element in determining the weight of a superpower's influence on the less powerful state and the chances that the latter can influence the actions of the giant. Examining the interactions of the United States with the four non-European middle powers cited above should tell something about who can influence whom, and when, and about what. Such influence can be seen both in efforts to cooperate and to act independently.

Each of the four middle powers examined in this study could be said to constitute with the United States a "security community," in the sense that the use of violence or the threat of violence in any of the four relationships has become inconceivable. Canada and Australia, Mexico and Brazil constitute two culturally similar pairs of states, and one in each pair has a long common border with the United States. Whether those issues arising from proximity have had noticeable effects on other aspects of their relations with the United States may be ascertained by comparing neighboring Canada and distant Australia, two Commonwealth and more industrially advanced countries, with neighboring Mexico and distant Brazil, two Latin American and less developed countries. Distance can be either cultural or geographic; thus the four countries can be paired in two different ways.[4]

The use of the term middle powers in this study differs from the recent tendency of some scholars to apply the term to the second-tier powers of Europe—Britain, France, Germany—and to Japan. In the terminology of this study, these would be great powers, second only to the United States and the Soviet Union. The states that are the subject of this study are clearly less powerful than the second-tier powers and differ from them in several ways. One difference is that Canada, Australia, Mexico, and Brazil do not engage the continuing attention of top-level policy makers in Washington but rather are only intermittently the focus of concern. Although in the aggregate less influential than the second-tier powers, these four countries, on certain issues, at certain times, under certain circumstances, can be at least as influential, if not more so. This will become evident in the course of the study. Another difference will be observed: that the middle powers' leaders often exhibit towards the United States an attitude of something like awe, if not respect or apprehension, unknown among greater powers. The middle powers in turn are marked off from smaller states by their importance to the United States in more issue areas and by the importance of their roles on the world political scene. All four of the countries included in this study are sufficiently significant to the United States that the latter cannot afford lightly to jeopardize good relations with them. Thus there is an attraction exerted in both directions.

Considering the great disparity in military and economic power, one might expect that the potential of the United States for influencing the behavior of its close neighbors would be enormous, much greater than in the case of countries farther away. Yet the actual exploitation of this supposed potential has been relatively small; incentive, opportunity, and skill in application variously have been lacking. Even when the two neighbors move in the same direction as the giant United States, that they would not have done so if their great neighbor had not pressed them is difficult to assert.[5] Where the United States and a neighbor disagree over an issue, which makes what concessions does not correlate closely with their respective positions on some generalized scale of power. If power lies in not having to give in, it may be exerted in a particular situation somewhat independently of the ranking of two contending governments in someone's power calculations.

When cooperation rather than competition or conflict is the focus, proximity has offered many favorable occasions for mutually advantageous collaboration between the United States and its neighbors, who, like it, are at some remove from the European realm of political competition. Some of the cooperative enterprises, such as policing the border and regulating radio transmission, have been almost inescapable. Others, particularly the management of water resources, grew out of necessity but expanded to exploit opportunities which nature offered when a boundary could be more or less ignored. These contacts are peculiar to countries bordering on each other; there is no equivalent for countries which are not contiguous.

Other ways in which Canada and the United States and Mexico and the United States cooperate with each other, however, do not depend on their being next door to each other. By definition, none of the many comparable cases in Australian-American and Brazilian-American relations depend on propinquity. Ties between the United States and Australia have been facilitated by cultural affinity and between the United States and Brazil by long historical association. Australia and Brazil, like Canada and Mexico, might be said to belong to the "outer world," a system different from that traditionally centered around Europe. Neither Asian nor African, these are four countries whose kind of relationship with the United States is seldom examined by scholars except in world-conflict terms.

None of the cooperative activities between the United States and one or the other of its neighbors was undertaken as a conscious step toward ceding responsibility for the particular function to any kind of centralized authority. The very notion of formal integration would be anathema to most Canadians and probably all Mexicans and is unlikely to arise in the minds of contemporary Americans. For proponents to label these cooperative patterns as potential breeders of closer political association would likely doom the cooperation.

Intent aside, observation of the Canadian-American and Mexican-American experience in collaborating to achieve a common objective may reveal some kind of spillover and an incremental process in which one task jointly performed leads to another, depending upon the circumstances of each case and issue.[6] With the relationships between Canada and the United States and Mexico and the United States conceived in terms of Karl Deutsch's communications systems, observation of particular instances of communication will identify feedbacks which alter the system, if only slightly, whether in the direction of greater autonomy or that of greater interdependence.[7]

Being good neighbors or good, if geographically distant, friends means responsiveness to each other's needs, that is, as in Kal Holsti's definition, "a disposition to receive another's requests with sympathy, even to the point where a government is willing to sacrifice some of its own values and interests in order to fulfill those requests . . . the willingness to be influenced" and, as he later adds, "to consult broadly regarding issues of common interest."[8] As he and others have noted, capacity and willingness to respond do not depend on joint institutions. Thus some of the good effects expected from membership in the European Economic Community might conceivably be experienced by countries without formal community ties. Nor need the responses be purely governmental, for private groups may have transnational interests. The frequency, intensity, casualness, and informality of contacts between Americans and Canadians, as well as between Americans and Mexicans (although such contacts between the latter and Americans are less marked), could not be maintained in the case of Australia and Brazil. Thus the occasion for and examples of responsiveness should be much more numerous between the United States and Canada and the United States and Mexico. Readiness to respond is significant, whether viewed as an essential link in the communications network of friendly countries cooperating with each other or as an indispensable element in the exercise of influence.

As will be shown in subsequent chapters, readiness to respond on particular questions has varied markedly through time and the momentous changes accompanying its passage. This study begins with World War II; the nearly four decades which are covered have seen tremendous shifts in international relations, shifts that have affected the position of the United States and of the four middle powers in relation to other participants in world politics. Some of these shifts have brought one or more of the four countries closer to the United States; others have made them more autonomous. One of the changes is in leadership. Any generalization about foreign relations of the countries involved must take account of the personal impact of individuals such as Franklin D. Roosevelt, Lester B. Pearson, Robert Menzies, Adolfo López Mateos, or Juscelino Kubitschek, to name a nontypical few.

Another change is in the significance of various kinds of distance. Some writers, notably Albert Wohlstetter, have pointed out that "shrinking" the globe has had some unrecognized effects on international relations. They contend that not only has "diminishing" distance meant speedy, easy communication and a radically increased circulation of its inhabitants but that this technological revolution renders doubtful the very notion of regionalism.[9] Wohlstetter has suggested that mere proximity is a poor criterion for association. Others have derided myths based on the idea that "water divides, land connects" and the fallacy that "significant interests are not shared with those outside the land borders."[10] Still others, such as Richard Merritt, have pointed out the difference between noncontiguity and distance.[11] Herbert Goldhamer has ridiculed the conventional notion that "a 'neighbor' . . . can be any country between which and oneself there is no intervening land mass."[12] Two scholars interested in "international community" pointed out in 1970 that there were few empirical studies of the effects of proximity on interaction, although geographical factors were assumed to be important variables.[13] Many years ago Quincy Wright tried to rank great powers on various distance scales: technological, strategic, legal, intellectual, social, political, psychic, war-expectant.[14]

Most of Quincy Wright's ways of looking at distance will be utilized in this study, but geographical contiguity and its relation to responsiveness will be stressed. Although Bruce Russett's definition of what constitutes a "region" (not proximity but close ranking on scales of many social and economic indicators) does not accord with common usage, he did try to discover empirically to what extent contiguity was related to other factors often used in identifying region.[15] In this examination of the United States and its immediate neighbors a special relationship between the United States and Canada and the United States and Mexico is simply assumed and its components described. The next step is to ask which of these components could be duplicated with countries somewhat similar to these two but far away.

Basic to the study is the by no means novel assumption that relations between any two states differ issue area by issue area.[16] The ensuing chapters will examine various national-security issues, several different kinds of economic issues, some foreign-policy orientations on world politics, and neighborhood issues. Although the major focus will be on Canada and Mexico as they have interacted with the United States in these different issue areas, appropriate comparisons will be drawn with Australia's and Brazil's relations with the United States. A look at issues which arose during World War II will initiate the examination, since this period was a turning point in the relations of the United States with each of the four countries, bringing them into intimate contact in many fields. The study will describe and interpret experiences largely in terms of responsiveness, proximity, cooperation, and capacity to influence. For each of the issue areas the following questions will be asked of the four relationships with the United States:

¶Were there **joint enterprises** in which the two governments mingled their efforts or resources in some relatively symmetrical fashion? Joint enterprises involving a partnership of roughly equal shares in costs and benefits are rare among sovereign states. Their existence suggests an unusual degree of responsiveness to a commonly felt need and a willingness to rely to some extent on the actions of another government.

¶Did the two governments **reciprocate** by exchanging benefits, each incurring some sacrifice for a common objective? Far less uncommon than joint enterprises, reciprocal arrangements attest, nevertheless, to an acceptance of the implications of interdependence. When the need itself, recognition of the need, and readiness to meet it in a mutual fashion all are present, those involved have forged one link—even though limited—between their two countries.

¶In a particular case, how **specific** was the request and the response? As will be shown later, one government's general response to the need of another is less significant—except for psychological purposes—than specific acts which may be sought. Specificity is sometimes a touchstone in determining how seriously the actors view their relationship with each other.

¶What part did **distance,** viewed as remoteness or inaccessibility, play in the relationship? There may be geographical or cultural impediments which, despite technical possibilities, are difficult to overcome even if the two countries have a common need which they could meet together. These obstacles to recognition and response are weightier when the governmental systems and the underlying political myths already interfere with easy communication.

¶Did the governments learn from their responses, did feedbacks result from **cumulated experience** in cooperation (negative or positive) or in **spillover** into other areas? If the results of a cooperative venture were favorable, they might be followed by further ventures, which could grow by accretion into clear patterns of interdependence, especially if cooperation spread into other issue areas. If the participant's experience in cooperation was unsatisfactory for some weighty reason, on the other hand, that government might reject further collaborative ventures. Even if satisfactory, however, a participant could feel sufficiently strengthened to contemplate going it alone in the future.

¶What **channels of communication** or institutions have been involved in a relationship? The creation of particular channels or agencies through which to deal with a common problem usually signified a special link between the two countries and indicated a serious purpose. Yet informal or unofficial channels, when effective, often tied the two countries together in a stronger fashion than if purely formal agencies alone were relied upon. Although this study focuses on bilateral relations, many of the problems and issues had multilateral aspects and could better be dealt with multilaterally. When this occurred, the patterns of interdependence broadened out to include other states and to that extent reduced the significance of the bilateral relationship in that issue area.

¶Were questions treated in an **administrative** (or bureaucratic) fashion, were problems to be solved dealt with on a relatively technical level, or did the issues become **politicized?** In the latter cases, were issues handled by the principal national authorities through diplomatic bargaining in which concern for the "state" (or for other political interests) took precedence over substantive matters? One sign of some kind of special relationship between two states is the routine handling of certain common problems on their merits, without the intrusion of national considerations unrelated to the specific task. Such an apolitical approach is rather rare and always tentative and subject to a shift in emphasis. When issues have required the attention of the principal political leaders of two of the countries, they sometimes have become entangled with considerations unrelated to the substance of the issue, often threatening the special relationship. On the other hand, sometimes only the top authorities have been able to put a discussion back on the administrative track, demonstrating the will to remove the political overtones from an issue in a cooperative spirit.

¶Were there connections between an issue and **domestic politics,** and how sensitive were leaders to each other's internal political needs? Most of the issues to be considered below have their roots in domestic politics, and their handling must in turn affect political competition inside the countries involved. This complicates the task of those who deal with common problems across national borders. Although responsible officials may take cognizance of the domestic concerns of their counterparts, such sensitivity may not overcome the internal impediments to the cooperation that seemed desirable to those immediately faced with the common problem. On the other hand, transnational ties between domestic interests in the United States and in each of the four countries examined here are growing and thereby demonstrating a mutual attraction worthy of study.

Sections of later chapters correspond to these questions.

Finally, during what periods and under what circumstances did two neighbors disparate in power readily collaborate and about what? What tended to bring them together and how? What tended to drive them apart and why? Were comparable forces operative for the more distant pair of states?

Prior to the analysis of the various issue areas, some relevant characteristics of the four middle powers are set forth. Noted briefly are the change in American attitudes toward Mexico from hostility and low esteem to considerable admiration, the manner in which the United States view of Brazil has constituted a kind of unspoken (and unequal) alliance except for one brief period, and the fact that United States perceptions had hardly formed about Australia until World War II but later became very friendly in certain issue areas. Also examined is the growth of American regard for Canada, as the Canadians struggle to assert their identity, a struggle which has always been ambivalent: complaints about being taken for granted alternate with demands to be left alone, and expectations of special consideration alternate with the desire to be treated like any other foreign power. Inevitably, the largest proportion of this study concerns Canada. By its closeness to the United States it provides a touchstone for other middle powers both in the capacity to be heard by the western superpower and in the ability to act autonomously. That the politics of attraction represents a mutual relationship must always be kept in mind.

TWO

INSIDE THE FOUR MIDDLE POWERS

To EXPLAIN THE BEHAVIOR OF any state in foreign affairs, one needs to have some grasp of the kind of actor involved, despite the risks encountered when trying to define the social and political conditions in that country. Some characteristics can be quantified; others must remain more or less impressionistic, phrased in just such terms as "more" or "less." One defense for the qualitative approach is that the individuals who conduct relations between one country and another usually see things in this fashion, although their vision may be obscured by prejudices or lack of information. One of the obstacles to describing accurately the actors involved is that they change over time, as even in the thirty-five years covered by this study. Some of the internal changes are directly related to changes in the external world, including that part of it which is the United States.

With such caveats, this chapter presents a broad-brush painting of domestic conditions in the four middle powers, stressing those characteristics which may affect their relations with the United States. Table 1 provides some pertinent quantitative data.

CANADA AND AUSTRALIA

Both Canada and Australia have immense territories, for the most part sparsely populated. There are about 13 million Australians, about 22 million Canadians; both countries' citizens are highly conscious of these disparities with the more than 200 million Americans. Australians live mostly along the eastern and southern seaboards; Canadians concentrate along the border with the United States. Australia is one of the world's most urbanized countries,

TABLE 1   POPULATION, AREA, GROSS NATIONAL PRODUCT, AND DERIVATIVES
OF FOUR MIDDLE POWERS AND THE UNITED STATES

	Population 1973	Area (square miles)	Population per square mile
Australia	13,000,000	2,974,581	4
Brazil	104,670,000	3,286,170	32
Canada	22,560,000	3,851,809	6
Mexico	56,380,000	760,373	74
USA	213,460,000	3,615,211	59

Gross National Product
(millions of US dollars)

	1967	1968	1969	1970	1971	1972
Australia	39,600	41,100	44,500	47,000	49,000	50,500
Brazil	31,060	33,960	37,010	40,340	44,900	49,570
Canada	80,300	84,900	89,400	91,600	97,000	102,600
Mexico	29,695	32,100	34,150	36,510	37,800	40,670
USA	986,400	1,032,300	1,060,100	1,055,600	1,089,000	1,155,200

Per Capita Gross National Product
(US dollars)

	1967	1968	1969	1970	1971	1972
Australia	3,385	3,451	3,670	3,793	3,879	3,924
Brazil	357	380	402	426	461	495
Canada	3,929	4,088	4,240	4,299	4,490	4,696
Mexico	649	679	698	722	724	753
USA	4,964	5,143	5,230	5,152	5,260	5,532

Sources: Agency for International Development, *Gross National Product: Growth Rates and
Trend Data by Region and Country* (May, 1974); *Hammond Medallion World Atlas* (1969).

for most of its population lives in a few large cities (the capitals of the
states). Vast areas of both countries are hardly habitable because of the in-
hospitable climate but contain rich natural resources which are beyond the
means of their peoples to exploit alone and which would be difficult to
defend by their peoples' own efforts if a hostile and determined greater
power were ever to threaten them with aggression. The remoteness of Australia from the centers of world power, once a kind of protection, disappeared with developments in World War II. After the war, Canada's northern regions also lost the protection provided by the remoteness and assumed

strategic significance because they lay between the more temperate parts of North America and the Soviet Union. More recently, the Canadian North has lost its economic insignificance with the discovery of exploitable natural resources, particularly oil and natural gas. Meanwhile, the outside world, especially the United States in the case of Canada and Japan in the case of Australia, developed an intense demand for the resources awaiting exploitation in the two Commonwealth countries. Although there are good ports for international trade on the southern and eastern coasts of Australia, they are 12,000 to 13,000 miles away from industrial centers (except those in Japan, which are about 4,000 miles distant). The western coast is only slightly closer to the industrial centers of Europe, farther still from the United States, and has only one good port, Perth. Canada, on the other hand, is next door to the world's greatest industrial power and not more than 3,500 miles from the industrial centers of Europe; it has adequate port facilities on both coasts and the St. Lawrence Seaway.

Despite areas of poverty, the per capita income of Canadians has been among the highest in the world, while that of the Australians, though lower, puts them among the affluent countries. The economies of both countries are highly dependent upon foreign trade, since their internal markets are relatively small. Both countries are striving to industrialize further and to reduce their dependency upon the sale of certain basic agricultural products for which their physical conditions are ideally suited, but Canada is farther along this road. Unlike Canada, Australia belonged to the sterling bloc while that bloc was important.[1]

Most Australians are of European descent (the Aborigines are a much smaller minority than the Indians and Eskimos in Canada), and their society is far more homogeneous than that of either the Americans or the Canadians. Although all three countries share the political and cultural heritage of England, not all Canadians stem from it. In addition to the roughly 30 percent of the population comprised of French-speaking Canadians, the majority of whom live in the huge province of Quebec, there are large numbers of other originally non-British Europeans in Canada. They form a distinctive mosaic pattern in contrast to the American ideal of the melting pot. Canada, like Australia, has welcomed immigrants from Europe, who have played a vital role in the development of both countries.[2]

The desire of the Quebecois to maintain their own culture antedated the renaissance of Quebec; but it took on new dimensions in the 1960s in the form of demands for greater participation in national life, for special treatment, or for an independent state. Canadian leaders for generations have been exquisitely sensitive to the dangers of a nation sundered if the French-speaking portion of it was acutely dissatisfied with public policy. This preoccupation with national unity shares the forefront of political concern with that flowing from being next door to the United States, and the two preoccupations are occasionally linked. Nothing like the French-Canadian problem assails Australian leaders as they deal with the United States or any other country. Meanwhile, the white-Australia policy gradually has been eroded since World War II and had almost disappeared by 1973.

Like the United States, Canada and Australia are affluent societies with industrialized economies, and the three share a common language. In many ways English-speaking Canadians and Americans are more alike than are Canadians and their fellow members in the Old Commonwealth, the Australians. This similarity has given rise to the fear of many Canadians that they are being culturally enveloped. Large numbers of Canadians have migrated to the United States, and some Americans have gone north: The southward migration, so easy until recently, gave rise to the assertion that "Canadians to an extraordinary degree are Canadians by choice." [3] In many of their associations, Canadians are linked to Americans: not only in business enterprises but also in "international" labor unions, church affiliations, and other social and professional groups. In some parts of Canada north-south ties are almost as strong as east-west ties.

Regardless of some Canadian efforts to find a distinctiveness, in all three countries there is a somewhat similar kind of attachment to democracy and to the rights of citizens, as well as an egalitarian attitude not so commonly found among their forebears in Europe or among people elsewhere in the world. On this point even the extreme nationalists in Canada are likely to agree.

The parliamentary systems which Canada and Australia inherited from Britain distinguish them politically from the United States in no very striking way except to make difficult Canadians' or Australians' appreciation of the role of Congress or how it operates. The truly important political contrast between them and the United States is the tremendous disparity in the size of their governments; not all the advantages by any means accrue to the large one. In the United States, despite its size or the fact that like Canada and Australia it has a federal system, power has tended to gravitate toward the center. By contrast, Australian states and Canadian provinces are much more independent of their national capitals. This has implications for the capitals' foreign policy, especially in respect to trade and economic-development matters, for in these areas the states and provinces send their own representatives abroad.

In both Australia and Canada the party in control of one or more state or provincial governments is often different from the one forming the national government, thus accentuating national-regional tensions. Both countries have what could be called a two-and-one-half party system, since a third party (the conservative Country party in Australia, the socialist New Democratic party in Canada) may hold the balance in the national government. This factor contributed to the long tenure of the Australian Liberal party in national office and, to a much lesser extent, to the customary Liberal party's hold on the Canadian federal government. It is usually easier for American officials to deal with counterparts to whom they are accustomed; changes in the Australian and Canadian governments have caused problems for the Americans as party shifts altered the tone of the countries' external relations. The transfer of power in Australia from the Australian Labor party in the late 1940s and back again to Labor in 1972 marked the end and a new beginning, respectively, of much more independent behavior internationally and a somewhat defiant posture towards the United States. In Canada, the Progressive Conservative government of John Diefenbaker, 1957–1963, also strove for "independence," and its relations with the United States were rocky. Prime Minister Pierre Trudeau, although a Liberal, was a new kind, one who tried to break with traditional Canadian foreign-policy stands. He did so even before his hold on the national government depended (temporarily) on support from the New Democratic party, a party always more nationalistic and ideological than the Liberals.

Although foreign-policy issues usually have played only a minor role in Canadian and Australian electoral campaigns, parliamentary party opponents seldom have missed an opportunity to keep their rivals on the defensive regarding current international questions, among which relations with the United States have been foremost. Lack of wide public interest in or understanding of foreign policy and the habit of secrecy in policy making has given the Australian government a freer hand in foreign affairs than is available to the Canadian government. By the mid-1960s, however, important changes had made people in both countries more conscious of the world outside, and their leaders have had to take note of this new awareness.

In both Canada and Australia the foreign ministries are relatively new and have had to struggle for a place beside the older, more powerful ministries, Treasury and Trade.[4] Both governments have, in effect, four foreign services; the other three deal with migration, trade, and defense. A move began in 1971 to bring the Canadian services closer together; management of the elements of foreign policy seems to remain more diffused in Australia. In Canada and Australia the cabinet plays an important role in foreign policy, but only certain members have observable influence on particular policies, and then only through their association with the prime minister either as political rivals or aides. In each country the prime minister has tended to play the part of foreign minister from time to time; in fact, there was no separate minister of external affairs in Canada until after World War II, when Louis St. Laurent became secretary of state for external affairs and right-hand man to Prime Minister Mackenzie King. Not External Affairs but the prime minister's office has been the main coordinator of foreign policy in Canada as well as in Australia, so far as this function has been performed. Although the corps of senior civil servants in both countries are influential in determining public policy and provide among themselves very important personal coordination, prime ministers such as Robert Menzies and Pierre Trudeau have ignored them or built up their own offices in a manner not dissimilar to the Executive Office of the President in the United States. The American custom of the in-and-outer is only beginning in Canada and has not made its appearance in Australia to provide a personal kind of coordination between officialdom and private groups.

The parliaments in both countries are not well equipped to enter into the foreign-policy process to even the extent that the American Congress does. They lack independent committees with staff and powers comparable to those in the United States Senate and House, which can check on the executive, although each has a committee which ostensibly deals with foreign-policy questions.[5] The system of responsible parties means that in both countries members of parliament who belong to the government party are expected to give assent to the government's proposals, while the function of the opposition is to oppose the prime minister's policy even though there is no effective means of blocking it.

In contrast stands the American government, notoriously composed of noisily competing quasi sovereignties. This multitude of government actors complicates relations with the middle powers while providing occasional opportunities for the smaller governments to prevail on an issue. This picture, as will be seen later, oversimplifies the way business is actually conducted between the countries concerned, since much of it, especially in the case of Canadian-American relations, is handled by officials low in the political hierarchy of the administrations of the two countries or far removed from what is perceived as foreign affairs. Only a few, politically sensitive questions rise to the top for decision by the main actors.

MEXICO AND BRAZIL

"North America" ends at the Rio Grande. One aspect of the cultural difference between north and south is that identification of the real foreign-policy makers in Latin America is difficult for the North American. But the differences between Mexico and Brazil on the one hand and the two Commonwealth countries on the other hand are in many ways also the differences between the Latin American countries and the United States.

Although Mexico and Brazil are still "developing countries," each has made gigantic steps toward industrialization and toward diversified production. Their growth rates have been much higher than Canada's and Australia's. But they started from a very low base. In 1965, the per capita gross national product of Mexico was $427 and of Brazil, $175.[6] By 1972, Mexico's per capita GNP was still only $753, while Brazil's was only $495. Although these two countries had the largest GNPs in Latin America (Brazil's was about $50 billion; Mexico's was about $40 billion), on a per capita scale Mexico ranked fifth in Latin America, and Brazil ranked ninth.[7] Feudalism in some primitive parts of Brazil, subsistence farming in both countries, modern factories, and multinational corporations exemplify the complicated economic structure of these two Latin American states.

Like Canada and Australia, these two Latin American countries possess extensive territories. Although the smallest of the four countries, (only one-fifth the size of Canada), Mexico ranks thirteenth in size among all countries and is five times the size of the large Western European countries. Brazil is almost as large as Canada or the United States. The two Latin American countries are also like the two Commonwealth countries in possessing valuable natural resources in areas which make their exploitation extremely difficult. Brazil is made up of very large, diverse, and distinctive regions, which because of the terrain and their historical development have made national unity difficult and a remarkable achievement. Unlike Brazil's, Mexico's arable area is relatively small, with topography and centuries of erosion presenting serious obstacles to efficient agricultural production. Furthermore, for most of Mexico the climate, though equable, is too dry. The same is true for parts of Brazil, while exactly the opposite problem affects much of the rest of that huge country, a land so immense that almost every kind of climate characteristic of the tropical and temperate zones can be found there. Hard work is necessary in Mexico to exploit its agricultural potentialities, while in the tropical parts of Brazil the climate militates against such industry. The gap between perceived potential and current achievement is irksome to Brazilian and Mexican alike and tempts them to find external causes for it, especially American-induced ones.

Approximately two thousand miles of border are shared by Mexico and the United States, roughly two-thirds the length of the main boundary between the United States and Canada (disregarding the Alaskan border). As on the Canadian boundary, great inland water systems are a feature of the Mexican border, made more significant because of the need for water in the southwest of the United States and northern Mexico. Because of the astigmatism produced by use of certain kinds of maps (e.g., with Mercator projections), Brazil seems closer to North America than it actually is. As part of the New World and in the Western Hemisphere, it usually is in Americans' minds when they think of their "neighbors" of Latin America, even though they are less likely to encounter Brazilians than the "remote" Australians in the United States. Brazil is also remote from Mexico; the visit of López Mateos on his 1960 tour of South America was the first time a Mexican president had paid a call on that country. But Brazil is "close" for American tourists and government officials in a way Australia surely is not. Time zones separate on an east-west basis, not on a north-south line, and Australia will always have night when it is day in continental United States, regardless of telephonic communications far superior to Brazil's.

Partly because of the large size of their territories, neither the Brazilian government nor the Mexican government until 1972 took seriously the problem of overpopulation; they regarded their demographic growth rates (among the highest in the world) as beneficial, ignoring the serious consequences in terms of dependency ratios. While Canada—and Australia, too, though less so—have aging populations (but with the bulk of their people still in the productive years), the largest age groups of Mexicans and Brazilians are moving into increasingly younger categories, with adverse effects upon their countries' efforts to modernize. Social and political tendencies have impeded these Latin American countries from facing the economic consequences of uncurbed population growth, and outsiders' suggestions have not been well received. Of great significance, therefore, was the belated but marked change in the Mexican government's attitude towards family planning. There were signs of change, too, in Brazil in 1974. Growth rates aside, Mexico and Brazil, with populations of somewhat more than 54 million and 101 million, respectively, are in an entirely different category from the two truly underpopulated Commonwealth countries.

As in Australia and Canada, agriculture plays a vital role in the economies of Brazil and Mexico. Despite noteworthy agrarian reforms in Mexico and increasing productivity in both Latin American countries, farming offers so inadequate a livelihood that rural inhabitants are flocking to the cities. This massive movement creates serious social and economic problems, but in neither Brazil nor Mexico does it form a basis for militant rebellion. As befits so huge and variegated a country, Brazil has several very large urban centers: Rio de Janeiro numbers around 4 million and São Paulo around 6 million. The only truly big metropolitan center in Mexico is Mexico City, with about 8 million, although Guadalajara and Monterey are growing rapidly. (The preeminence of Mexico City is indicative of the much more centralized political system of Mexico, compared to Brazil.) Yet even in Mexico the difficulties of managing rapid urbanization make the political leadership uneasy and increasingly sensitive to external events. American officials have been among the victims of the political terrorists who became active in both countries during the 1970s (and who came from the middle class).

That Mexicans speak Spanish and Brazilians Portuguese, while Australians and the majority of Canadians are with Americans part of the English-speaking world, barely suggests the cultural contrasts. The diverse strands which compose Brazilian society—old Portuguese, West Africans who came as slaves, nineteenth- and twentieth-century infusions of white Europeans, especially Germans and Italians, and the somewhat later introduction of the Japanese—make Brazil unique in Latin America. (Unlike Mexico's, Brazil's indigenous Indians are almost obliterated, the remnants having no significance in foreign affairs). The diversity of Brazil's peoples makes the task of governance more difficult. Less distinctive in Latin America, yet in very marked contrast to that of the United States, Mexican culture combines in somewhat fragmented fashion institutions from pre-Columbian civilizations, from more modern Indian sources, and from European (predominantly Spanish) roots. Since the revolution of 1910 (though in line with the earlier reforms of Benito Juarez), Mexicans have stressed the Indian aspects, as part of their nation-building symbolism. Noticeably absent are important modern migrations from Europe, except for some Republicans from Spain. Both countries fascinate artists and anthropologists, while they continue to perplex the political scientist, whether he is concerned with orderly governmental procedures or the locus of decision making. There are well-recognized differences between the two Latin American countries on the one hand and the three English-speaking nations on the other in respect to attitudes towards formal organizations and legal authority and the distinction between theory and practice. These differences in attitude do not need to be kept in mind by Americans who deal with Australians or Canadians. They do complicate relations with Latin Americans, whether the Latin Americans are the stern and proud Mexicans or the easy-going, resilient Brazilians for whom "gringo" means any foreigner (usually an Argentine), not just the Yankee.

Between Brazil and Mexico, however, there are marked differences in political regimes.[8] Brazil's governmental system has developed erratically. The populist "revolution" of Getulio Vargas took various forms, becoming an almost pure dictatorship in the late 1930s, after an earlier, more liberal rule which he inaugurated by his coup of 1930. Following World War II came a modified kind of democracy, and even Vargas, in his second incarnation, was a duly elected president. A fairly democratic regime characterized Juscelino Kubitschek's period—perhaps too democratic and certainly with too many competing parties. In any case, parties have a different significance in Brazil, and the political loyalties of the minority of Brazilians who participate at all in the system cut across party lines.[9] When Jânio Quadros gave way to João Goulart, who seemed too friendly towards leftist forces, the military launched their coup of 1964. After a somewhat benign beginning, including the authorization of a single opposition party, the later manifestations of General Humberto Castelo Branco's successor, General Arturo da Costa e Silva, became those of an unprecedentedly ruthless dictatorship, in a country where political change has usually been much less violent than in most of Latin America. General Emelio Garrastazú Médici continued these practices, but some amelioration was anticipated after General

Ernesto Geisel was inaugurated president in 1974; the improvement has not been very great.

The trend in Mexico's political system generally has been in the opposite direction, although rigidities in the political process aroused protest and some repressive counteraction by the late 1960s. To outsiders, Mexico has in the past few decades been a model of constitutional stability in Latin America. The revolution became "institutionalized" by the 1930s, after the many frightfully violent years following the era of Porfirio Diaz. Earlier fears of assassinations and coups began to disappear, and eventually presidents succeeded each other peacefully for a six-year term and according to the constitutional rule, "no reelection." By the end of the 1930s, the military, although not inactive politically, were firmly under civilian control. However, one almost all-encompassing party, now called the PRI (Partido Revolucionario Institucional), is so identified with the regime that its supremacy is hardly more than symbolically challenged by opposing parties— chiefly the PAN (Partido Acción Nacional). Bolstered by the mystique of the revolution and by some of its concrete accomplishments, the ruling party has shown itself relatively invulnerable to attack from more extreme opponents on the right or left, although political terrorism began to create problems in the 1970s. The Communist party, once of some political importance in Mexico, as well as Brazil, in recent decades has greatly declined in strength, especially through schism. Neither in Mexico nor Brazil have the means by which governing groups maintain themselves been in accord with the general principles of political conduct in Australia or Canada. Both Mexicans and Brazilians tend to view their governments with distrust but also with resignation. For the United States government, the main question in Latin America has generally been: can a country's government maintain control, rather than how does it succeed in doing so.

Despite a sizable and growing middle class in both countries and the existence of a variety of voluntary associations and journals of news and opinion, no direct line seems to run between interest articulation by these potential pressure groups and government responses. Those interests which can be identified usually do not relate to foreign policy except with respect to demands about foreign direct investment. An important exception appeared in the early 1960s, when an articulate intellectual group in Brazil began to argue for an "independent foreign policy" and secured a spokesman in Goulart's government.[10]

Congress in Mexico has usually rubber-stamped executive initiatives. When the Brazilian Congress became unruly and posed a threat to the executive, it was either prorogued or muzzled, and the government, whether under Vargas or Castelo Branco and his more dictatorial military successors, ruled by decree.[11] Once the Mexican presidential aspirant has been designated *"el tapado"* by the party leadership, his power has grown until, on assuming office, he has been able to wield unassailable political authority, whatever the mysterious forces which play upon him from the small elite around him. There have been weak as well as strong presidents in Brazil, but their strength has been measured by their ability to cope with competitors for office, upon whom the president's attention has tended to be focused rather than upon the outside world.

In both countries an impressively increasing body of *técnicos* are available to implement policies, on which they may have some influence because of their expertise. They are to be found in the foreign ministries as well as in the more obvious departments, and the foreign minister himself is likely to be among the most astute members of the government, whether in Brazil or Mexico. Unlike the Mexican president, who has long presided over a government in which rival state leaderships have been tamed into submission, the Brazilian president until fairly recently has been confronted by competitors in the powerful state governments—governments powerful enough to have their own armies and to take actions, even with respect to foreign affairs, not in line with those of the federal government. Vargas in the 1930s met this challenge to his power by appointing *interventores* to govern some states. The rise of urban demagogues and the establishment of a military dictatorship after the 1964 coup apparently have reduced drastically the power of the state bosses, a result satisfying to American officials, who prefer to deal with one central government. Today, rivals threatening the power of Brazilian presidents are likely to be found within the national military forces.

Both Mexican and Brazilian leaders customarily have employed impressive declarations for the outside world which suggest rather formal doctrines underlying their rule and which formulate their policy in lofty language. The 1964 military coup in Brazil, for example, was officially denominated a "revolutionary movement," while Mexico's reigning Party of the Institutionalized Revolution appears to present a semantic paradox. Both governments make special claims to leadership of the less developed countries. Nevertheless, underneath this verbal surface the actions of leaders in both countries have been remarkably pragmatic, as befits practiced and sophisticated politicians who present a real challenge to American and other foreign negotiators. (The discrepancy between a government's declaratory and action policy is not unknown in the Anglo-Saxon world, but the contrasts are far less sharp and the contradictions more frequently assailed by the governed.)

Popular among Latin American scholars is a set of theories, subsumed under the term *dependencia,* which attribute the malfunctioning of economies, the bifurcation of social classes, political repression, and the skewing of development in directions both inequitable and denationalizing to the dominance of the United States (and other industrialized countries).[12] Without evaluating these hypotheses, this study takes as given the social and political conditions in Brazil and Mexico. It is true that directly and indirectly Americans have influenced life in these countries, not only by government policies but even more by private action, and that expressions of suspicion, envy, bitterness, and recrimination are not uncommon there. Rather than seeking some direct connection between American penetration and the structure of Mexican and Brazilian societies or inquiring into how those in the elites came to their position, this study will focus on what they sought from the United States and the responses secured, as well as on their recognition of American requirements.

Domestic contrasts presented by the four countries illustrate that the psychological or cultural distance in foreign affairs is not necessarily directly related to geographical distance. Although the American officials who deal with officials from these four countries may know and understand their special national characteristics, official conduct is to some extent modified by the perspectives of citizens outside the government. It makes some difference, for example, that ordinary Americans tend to think of Canadians as more or less interchangeable with Americans, of Mexicans in terms of underprivileged laborers, of Australians mostly in terms of gallant comrades in arms, and of Brazilians hardly at all. Though scarcely noticed by Americans, about three million Canadians were living in the United States in 1970. Much more noticeable are the approximately eight million American citizens of Mexican origin, who occupy a low economic level and who are beginning to find a voice to express their discontent. These Mexican-

Americans are concerned for their position in the United States, not for the plight of Mexicans living in the United States or in Mexico.

Regardless of popular stereotypes which offer policy makers little direction, government authorities in the United States and the four middle powers have been attracted to each other throughout the thirty-five years of this study in numerous areas of common concern, most of them growing out of internal requirements. To the extent that they have responded to each other the political distance between their countries has diminished.

THREE

RELATIONS WITH THE UNITED STATES: THE INTER-WAR YEARS

DISTANCE IN TIME MAY make events which occurred forty years ago seem somewhat irrelevant to relations of the United States with its neighbors and faraway middle powers in the postwar period. Yet the influence of experiences in the years between the two world wars was not blotted out completely, even though World War II proved to be a watershed for Canada, Australia, Mexico, and Brazil in their respective relations with the United States. Historical memory plays a part in the behavior of public officials, even when new conditions require new ways of thinking. It also points up the differences attributable to geographic distance from the great power, distance which technology diminished markedly in later years. Until World War II loomed on the horizon, neither with Canada nor with Mexico were United States relations particularly amicable, especially on economic issues. With Australia and Brazil the United States was not sufficiently involved to have many controversies, to say nothing of cooperative enterprises.

Unlike their counterparts far from the United States, both Canada and Mexico had experienced American threats to their territorial integrity during an earlier period. Mexico in fact lost a huge portion of its patrimony to the United States in 1848 through conquest. The Canadians, spared this experience, nevertheless felt on numerous occasions that they could be swallowed up by an expansionist power to the south and were party to several border disputes. War with the United States had been a part of their colonial history. By the First World War, however, threats to Canadian territory were a thing of the past.[1] During the Mexican Revolution, more than one American military intervention took place, the most serious being that of General Pershing in pursuit of Pancho Villa, but following the entrance of the United States into the First World War none was again attempted. Controversies arising from the protracted Mexican Revolution continued to exacerbate Mexican-American relations until the United States entered the Second World War, but they did not involve Mexico's territorial integrity.

During the interwar years, the neighbors of the United States feared the Americans for different reasons. In the north, the Canadians were concerned for their "identity," a constant (and almost unique) anxiety. In the south, the revolutionary objectives pursued by various Mexican leaders that ran counter to deeply imbedded American economic interests created concern on the part of Mexicans about United States reactions. The demand for "nonintervention," the lodestar of foreign policy followed by all Latin American countries, was most sharply espoused in Mexico, where independence from the domination of American capitalists was an integral part of the revolution. In contrast to the Canadians, the Australians were never in any doubt about who they were, even though they might have had difficulty had they tried to call attention to their nation, so far from the great powers' capitals. In contrast to the Mexicans, the Brazilian dictator Getulio Vargas, having brought about a semirevolution, called for independence from foreign capitalists only when it suited his more immediate political purposes.

FOREIGN POLICY

Not just separateness from the United States but isolation from the world in general marked the foreign policy of the four countries. World War I left almost no lasting effects on relations between the United States and the four middle powers, once hostilities ended. That the Canadians and Australians were cobelligerents with the Americans was soon forgotten on all sides.[2] The major consequence of Mexico's reputation for being somewhat pro-German though neutral was that it was coldly regarded by the victors after the war had ended.[3] Brazil, on the other hand, abandoned its formal neutrality once the United States entered the war; it declared war on Germany a few days after the American action. No military consequences but a sudden surge of economic prosperity accompanied this effort to align Brazil with the United States.

During the interwar period, the visible sign of participation in world politics was membership in the League of Nations. Canada played a half-hearted role as part of the British Commonwealth bloc, although resistant to being bound by obligations to collective security. When the Canadian representative "presumptuously" spoke in favor of league sanctions during the Ethiopian crisis, he was publicly repudiated by Prime Minister Mackenzie King.[4] Brazil started boldly, intending to be the most important Latin American member, but withdrew in a huff in 1926, having failed to get a permanent seat on the League Council as the leader from Latin America when the council was reorganized to adjust to German membership.

Mexico originally was not invited to join the league, partly because of American opposition to its inclusion in view of certain of its revolutionary actions. The Mexican government refused a later invitation, in 1923, but sent an observer in 1929 and formally joined in 1931. For Australia, membership meant entrance into the society of independent states, but it followed the British lead for the most part, even when lukewarm about the desirability of specific actions, such as sanctions against Italy. To all these countries the league's orientation seemed European and its work not immediately relevant to their own foreign-policy or security problems, which in any case were less pressing than domestic concerns. Fear of getting entangled in others' quarrels was also strong. The isolationist example set by the United States provided support for similar leanings in Canada and Mexico; the American attitude had less impact on Australia and Brazil, concentrated on their own concerns.[5]

Besides the league, two combinations of states, the Commonwealth of Nations and Latin America, affected relations with the United States of the two pairs of countries. Commonwealth meant to both Canadians and Australians chiefly Britain; that Canada was less attached to this relationship than was Australia was due partly to the fact that the United States was Canada's sole (and powerful) neighbor. The tensions in the "North Atlantic triangle" provided more opportunities for Canada to shape an image apparently independent of Britain—when Americans happened to notice their northern neighbor—than were available to the Australians, so aware of their dependency upon "imperial defense," that is, upon the British navy. Neither was wholly successful in its effort to be treated as a country fully separated from Britain, so gradual and recent was the severing of the various constitutional and governmental ties to the mother country.[6] Canada began to assert its individuality in foreign affairs when in the Siberian intervention it sided with the Americans against the British and Japanese and, despite British pressure, withdrew its troops from Vladivostok.[7] Prime Minister Arthur Meighen successfully strove in 1921 to turn the British away from renewing the Anglo-Japanese alliance, arguing that it should be replaced by some multilateral arrangement which above all would include the United States.[8] In 1923 (three years before the Balfour Declaration which defined Canada and the other dominions as autonomous), the Canadian government on its own negotiated and signed the halibut treaty with the United States.[9] Always concerned that nothing impair the friendship between Britain and the United States, Canadian leaders also were on guard that they not become the puppets of either. Alleged partiality to one or the other at various times was charged by opposition parties in domestic competition, as the government strove not to be called the colony of one or the satellite of the other great power.

Australia, in contrast, clung much longer to a status defined by the Commonwealth. For it, not only did Commonwealth really mean the British tie but foreign relations until World War II chiefly meant relations with or conducted through Britain. Where the Canadian government at the time of the Chanak incident in 1922 refused to commit itself to aid Britain, the Australians did promise, although reluctantly.[10] So dependent upon the British connection was Australia that, prior to World War II, the officers commanding the Australian air force and navy were seconded from the Royal Air Force and Royal Navy, respectively.[11]

Like the Canadians, the Australians in the late 1930s appeared to want peace at almost any price, but they were much more concerned than were Canadians about security. Two problems in particular worried them: freedom of passage to and from the Mediterranean and the expansionism of Japan. While Canadians began to look eastward to Europe, Australians began to look northward to Asia; the former continued to be Atlantic-oriented, while the latter became oriented to the Pacific. For the United States foreign and defense policy, these two countries soon acquired unusual importance because of the roles they could play in their respective spheres of concern, the Atlantic and the Pacific.

Relations with the United States played a part in the development of both the Canadian and Australian departments of external affairs. Although Canada's department can be traced to 1909, it was not important until after World War II, and the prime minister until 1946 filled the role of foreign minister.[12]

Long before this time Canada's special need for dealing with the United States through Canadian rather than British officials was responsible for the expansion of the ministry. Separate representation in Washington was established in 1920, and Canada's first regular diplomatic mission as a sovereign state was sent to the United States in 1927.[13] Australia's Department of External Affairs is much younger, having been established only in 1935. Although Prime Minister Joseph Lyons had broken precedent in 1932 by giving the East Asian portfolio to a minister other than himself, Australia had no diplomatic missions, only trade commissioners, until 1940. In that year, it sent out its first diplomatic minister, accredited to the United States government as Canada's had been; 1940 also saw an Australian high commissioner established in Ottawa and a mission in Tokyo. Both Commonwealth countries had high commissioners in London, who functioned in lieu of diplomatic representatives for their respective governments.[14] (All Commonwealth countries continue the practice of denominating their representatives to each other "high commissioner.")

Long antedating Canada and Australia as sovereign states, Mexico and Brazil had much older foreign ministries. The illustrious chancellor of the Brazilian Ministry at the turn of the century, the Barão de Rio Branco, linked his country with the United States in his intricate diplomacy. Mexico and Brazil have played different roles in Latin America largely because they differed in their relationship to the greatest power of the hemisphere. From the 1920s, Mexico was a leader among the Latin American countries in their joint efforts to nullify the Monroe Doctrine, in pressing the United States to modify its diplomatic recognition policies, and in otherwise obtaining international declarations that opposed American practices in the Western Hemisphere, especially those related to intervention.[15] Although Brazil was ready to cosponsor such efforts, its rivalry with the large Spanish countries in South America (not with Mexico) created a basis for an "unwritten alliance" with the United States. The complementarity of the two countries' interests was symbolized many years ago by Foreign Minister Lauro Mueller's advice to move along "with the United States but not as a dinghy in tow."[16]

Historical memories of a larger domain long affected Mexican leaders' perspectives on a hegemonial position in Central America, while the great size and resources of Brazil had from time to time caused its leaders to think of it as a world power, in embryo if not yet born. Yet internal conditions kept these two countries in a status of lesser powers in the Western Hemisphere system dominated by the United States. This system, not including Canada, was loosely organized by successive inter-American conferences and by the Pan American Union. (Mexico was a not too enthusiastic participant at one period, partly because of its failure to be eligible for the governing board of the Pan American Union when the United States had not recognized its government.[17]) For many purposes the Americans lumped Mexico and Brazil together as part of the Latin America which they had to keep in mind even when treating individually with these two leading members. But for the Mexicans security meant safety from American intervention, while for Brazil it meant safeguards against other South American countries. Like some leaders in Australia, certain Brazilian officials became more aware as World War II approached that their country might need protection from faraway threats, protection which the Mexicans and Canadians took somewhat for granted.

Although the leaders of all four middle powers were far more concerned with domestic problems than with foreign policy until World War II approached, internal issues had repercussions on their respective relations with the United States. Politics in Canada and Australia only indirectly affected these relations and then mostly in the economic sphere. In contrast, revolutionary movements in the Latin countries inevitably involved the United States, far less in Brazil, however, than in Mexico. The various manifestations of Getulio Vargas's leadership were ideologically distasteful to the United States. But this aversion was far overshadowed by genuine hostility arising from Mexican leaders' attacks on interests closely identified with those of some Americans, including attacks on the powers of the Catholic church. Of the four states, only in Mexico's case did the United States government's policies regarding that country become an issue in American election campaigns. When Mexico backed the opponent of the leader favored by the United States during the Nicaraguan political crisis of 1926, American critics charged Mexico with seeking to spread bolshevism. A brief war scare arose.[18] This was but one example of heavy pressure on successive American administrations to intervene to protect interests of various American groups. With President Roosevelt's New Deal, however, the Mexican government began to feel friendlier toward the United States, partly because of an apparent convergence in official social philosophies. The government of General Lázaro Cárdenas in the 1930s was not above telling American diplomats that unless Mexican government views were more favorably accepted his regime would be imperiled, and if it fell, so would the Good Neighbor policy.[19]

ECONOMIC POLICY

For all four middle powers, the questions which most affected their relations with the United States were economic. Canada's economic health has long been so closely associated with that of the United States that there are few (though important) exceptions to a parallel movement of the economies. One exception was Canada's departure from the gold standard in 1928. During the depression of the 1930s, however, the same types of reaction, official and private, can be discerned in the two countries, although Canada lagged behind. One example was the belated somewhat blurred carbon copy of the New Deal eventually promoted by Prime Minister Richard B. Bennett. His efforts in this direction did not prevent his electoral downfall, and they were later disavowed by the Privy Council, action rather reminiscent of the behavior of the United States Supreme Court in the mid-1930s. Because the Canadian economy was much smaller and much more vulnerable, the consequences of the depression were more severe. To deal with them, an earlier Bennett tactic diverged from the parallel development of the North American economies: he tried to tie Canada's economy closer to Britain's. These efforts culminated in the Ottawa imperial-preference agreements of 1932, a reaction to the ruinously high Smoot-Hawley tariff of the United States. For a time, the United States was the principal non-Commonwealth sufferer from these agreements. Bad examples of efforts to beggar thy neighbor could be seen in both countries' abrupt changes in their immigration policies. New restrictions ended for some time the easy movement back and forth of workers on the two sides of the border, and each repatriated its own citizens.[20] On the other hand, President Roosevelt's devaluation of the American dollar precipitated a boom in Canadian gold mining.

Adoption of the imperial-preference scheme, which built a high protectionist wall around Commonwealth countries, was followed the next year by a reduction in the level of Canadian trade with the United States to 31 percent of the 1929 figure.[21] The system did not deliver to Canada the benefits that had been anticipated. It was not long before the Canadian government was importuning Secretary of State Cordell Hull to consider Canada quickly

as a partner for one of his reciprocal trade agreements, an effort not unrelated to Prime Minister Bennett's efforts to stay in office. Canada, however,
had to get in line with others also eager for trade agreements; American
resentment of the Ottawa agreements was clear. Eventually, after Bennett's
departure from office, an agreement was negotiated in which the United
States got rates midway between the British preference and the general tariff. This was followed, in 1938, by a series of agreements of a triangular nature between Canada, the United States, and Britain. For, in truth, many of
Canada's important exports competed with American exports, particularly
wheat and some other agricultural products, thus requiring British participation to make a complementary deal.[22]

Even more than in Canada's case, Commonwealth preference and agricultural competition produced friction in Australian-American economic relations. A serious impediment to harmonious commerce between the United
States and Australia developed when the latter government suddenly announced a new policy in May, 1936, in an effort to increase trade with Britain. To stem the flood of Japanese textiles and slow the importation of
American automobiles in favor of British interests, restrictive measures were
decreed which naturally caused very strong reactions in the two countries
adversely affected. Within two years the restrictions were abandoned, having secured no tangible benefits to Australia. The discrimination, further
widened in January, 1937, had led the United States, for example, to withdraw the most-favored-nation concession earlier granted to Australia. [23]
Prior to this "trade diversion" episode, the Australian minister for trade in
1934 had tried to take advantage of the new reciprocal-trade-agreement legislation in the United States by seeking free entry for some wool, butter,
beef, and mutton and asking the United States to restrict to European markets its exports of certain commodities also produced in Australia, actions
which would help Australia to overcome an extremely unbalanced payments
situation. (The depression was so severe in Australia that at one time one-
third of the labor force was unemployed.) Nothing came of this overture,
and further, somewhat maladroit, efforts to increase Australia's trade, tied
so closely to a preference system abhorred by Secretary Hull, resulted in no
reciprocal trade treaty being signed before the war. However, as in Canada,
a changed government and the approach of war caused the Australians to
become more eager to conciliate the United States.[24]

Although Brazil's economy also depended heavily on the export of
primary, principally agricultural, products, most of these did not compete

with American exports and, being tropical or semi-tropical, were able to find a market in the United States. During the depression of the 1930s, however, this market was not a sufficiently large one nor were prices at a level to make the trade profitable. The various devices by which the Brazilian government tried to bolster the coffee industry, including even the burning of stocks, were of no avail to a country whose economy was based on the export of this product above all other activities. As a result, Vargas defaulted on interest payments for Brazil's foreign debts in 1938 and 1939 and instituted numerous controls on trade, adversely affecting many Americans.[25] While other countries were eager for a reciprocal trade agreement with the United States in the earlier part of the decade, the Brazilian government was cautious, partly because it feared duty-free coffee might be at stake and partly because its tariffs and other trade restrictions on American imports were heavy. The Brazilian government dragged its heels, using such delaying tactics as trying to get American officials to come to Brazil to discuss trade questions. Its hesitation to send negotiators to Washington to bargain seriously was overcome by information that some South American competitors were doing so and by increased concern for coffee's continued duty-free status. A treaty was signed in February, 1935, the second reciprocal trade agreement, the first having been negotiated with Cuba. This near primacy signified Secretary Hull's eagerness to have Brazil set an example.[26] The agreement was controversial in Brazil in part because of domestic political rivalries, German approaches for barter trade, and the financial plight of the government.

Mexico, on the other hand, apparently was eager in 1934 to get discussions on a reciprocal trade agreement started, for some of the reasons which eventually moved Brazil—in particular, getting ahead of competitors. Like the Canadians', the Mexicans' plea for early consideration was supported (privately) by references to a prospective change in their government.[27] A treaty was not signed, however, until more than a year after the United States entered the war. A drastic increase in Mexican tariffs at the end of 1937 (to stabilize the peso) had angered Secretary Hull. He upbraided the Mexican ambassador particularly on the manner and timing of the increase, made when he was trying in other parts of the world to ensure peace through increased trade. After a certain amount of evasiveness about the locus of authority, the Mexican government did reduce the tariff schedule, except for a few items.[28]

Trade questions were, however, of minor importance compared to the great issue of expropriation of property owned by Americans in Mexico, most of which was agricultural land but some of which was oil-producing property. (There were also unsettled claims of foreign bondholders.) Agrarian claims had troubled relations between the two countries since the earlier days of the revolution, resulting in prolonged negotiations over who was entitled to what kind of compensation in what amounts and when. These issues were complicated by demands of some Americans to be compensated for damages resulting from revolutionary violence and by counterclaims of Mexicans against American property holders. European agrarian claimants eventually accepted settlements amounting to about three percent of the value they had put on their losses. Longer and more acrimonious negotiations between Mexico and the United States ended with an accord in 1934, worked out in detail by 1936. Under it, through a lump-sum settlement to be paid in installments, American claimants received about the same amounts as those which Europeans had obtained.[29] Although these "special claims" were thereby settled, discussions of other claims for expropriated agrarian property continued until 1941, when another lump-sum settlement to be paid in installments was negotiated. The Mexican government declared that its assent to the agreement was a generous concession, not an affirmation of an obligation.[30]

Agrarian reform, signaled in the constitution of 1917, was energetically renewed by President Cárdenas in the 1930s; he not only believed in Mexico for the Mexicans but also in the virtues of a state based on a thriving rural population. At issue was the historical conflict between the American interpretation of the obligation to compensate foreigners according to international law and Mexican interpretations of that obligation in terms of the Mexican government's sovereign right to carry out social programs in accordance with Mexico's constitutional principles. Also at issue was Mexico's insistence on treatment of foreigners like citizens, their only legal recourse lying in appeals to domestic tribunals (the Calvo doctrine).[31] Even if Mexico had agreed in principle to pay the claims demanded by foreigners whose property had been expropriated, it had not, in fact, the means to do so. But the Mexican government did not emphasize this practical limitation, except in referring to worthier social claims, and Secretary Hull for many years stuck by his insistence that the legal questions had to be decided, not just "the facts." [32]

Political pressures generated by American agrarian claimants eventually were overshadowed by those coming from the large oil companies. The economic issue which most embittered Mexican-American relations before World War II grew out of the expropriation of foreign-owned oil properties. Here again the principles of the Mexican Revolution as implemented by General Cárdenas ran straight into United States views of Mexico's legal obligations, and eventually over them. During the earlier years of the revolution, the oil properties were not seriously threatened, and American owners understood through certain voluntary decisions made by Mexican officials in the 1920s that they could retain possession if they were actively working the concessions they had been granted earlier in the century. Yet the American (and British) oil companies constituted in Mexican eyes the most conspicuous symbols of foreign exploitation. Thus in 1936, after small plant unions of oil workers (embracing only about 13,000 employees) had struck for higher wages, their demands were taken up by the National Petroleum Workers Syndicate (into which they had been consolidated) and in turn by the expanding Confederacion de Trabajadores Mexico (CTM). The British and American companies combined to confront the union demands, especially those which the owners claimed infringed on the rights of management. President Cárdenas ordered a six-month cooling-off period after the Syndicate's strike call, but at the end of this period the government recognized the Syndicate's claim that the strike was in fact an "economic conflict." Such a conflict required government arbitration, which resulted in a decision that the companies refused to accept, appealing to the Supreme Court. When the court upheld the earlier ruling, the companies offered a compromise but made the mistake of challenging Cárdenas's honor by demanding a formal document to seal an arrangement that the Mexicans were ready to accept as reasonable. When the period of grace permitted for bargaining was up, the companies refused to abide by certain parts of the arbitration board's decision. At this point Cárdenas suddenly ordered the expropriation of the American and British oil properties by nationalizing the petroleum industry. March 18, 1938, is to Mexicans a critical date in their progress towards economic independence; tremendous popular acclaim immediately greeted the act. A public collection was undertaken to help reimburse the oil companies, the amount raised being a tiny percentage of their claims. Yet it was highly significant, for it symbolized the growing pride of Mexicans that their government could stand up for its principles.[33]

There was clamor in Washington, too. For the Roosevelt administration, the challenge was difficult to meet. So intense was the commitment to the Good Neighbor policy that, despite wavering but continued diplomatic representations on behalf of the oil companies' right to adequate compensation, the prickly conflict eventually ended with the Mexican government's position more or less validated, yet not before World War II was under way. Until the actual expropriation, the State Department had not been active in the case, being content to permit Mexican constitutional procedures to take their course. (The United States government informed the British of this position in February, 1938). Ambassador Josephus Daniels, however, earlier had tried mediating between the companies and the Mexican government. Not at issue was the legality of the expropriation, merely the compensation to be paid (the British challenged as well the right to expropriate).[34] For about two years after the expropriation, the United States experimented with different ways of concluding the controversy and then proposed arbitration, which Mexico rejected. At this point, Sinclair broke the united front of the oil companies and accepted a settlement. Another year and a half of negotiations ensued. Then, in November, 1941, three weeks before the attack on Pearl Harbor, the United States accepted a Mexican counterproposal for a commission composed of two experts (one Mexican, one American) to settle all issues. The State Department had failed earlier to get the remaining oil companies to accept this procedure but finally went ahead with the intergovernmental agreement. After the decision of the two experts was issued in the spring of 1942, the companies at last acquiesced.

During the controversy, the State Department did not interfere one way or another in certain sanctions imposed by the oil companies.[35] The American government did briefly suspend the monthly purchase agreement under which the United States Treasury bought Mexican silver at a price slightly higher than the world price, an arrangement which the Treasury Department earlier had instituted to help stabilize the Mexican currency. In fact, even in the absence of the monthly agreement, purchases continued on a day-to-day basis. A large proportion of Mexican-silver producers were Americans, and without the silver sales Mexico would have been even less able to pay its foreign debts. No loans from United States government lending agencies were made to Mexico from August, 1937, to November, 1941. However, even before the final agreement on disposition of expropriation claims, Mexico and the United States, as the war came closer to the New World, began to discuss defense cooperation and the establishment of a joint defense commission. Joined to the public announcement of the oil settlement were statements concerning plans for adjusting agrarian and other claims and promises of continued purchase of Mexican silver, of credits from the Export-Import Bank, of help in stabilizing the Mexican currency.[36] Clearly, the coming of the war speeded up the settlement with the Americans, always more the focus of antiimperialist feeling in Mexico than were the Europeans, but also more potentially helpful. Security needs induced the United States government to accept more readily than it might otherwise have accepted an expropriation which, as many recognized, set an important precedent. The Mexicans, however, did agree to pay the sum to be determined by the two experts, and they faithfully met each installment.

Until the late 1930s, then, it is hard to discern evidence of convergence, to say nothing of attraction, in the foreign policies pursued by the United States and each of the four middle powers. At least, they were not actually hostile to each other. For all four, however, there were already signs of inevitable attraction to the United States in the economic sphere, despite the efforts of each of the middle powers to move against the trend. Still, compared to succeeding periods, contacts were minimal and not notably friendly or cooperative.

Although most striking in the case of Mexico, in all four countries the threat of a second world war and its eventual outbreak began to dissolve the prewar patterns of diplomatic and economic relations with the United States. No longer could any of the five countries remain in isolation. Inexorably, developments in world politics were driving them together, and soon in all four cases the middle power and the great power would be learning to respond to each other's needs in unprecedented fashion. Some of the looming changes will be examined in the next chapter, which centers on the wartime experience, which offered opportunities for dramatic examples of cooperation between each of the four countries and the United States.

FOUR

WORLD WAR II COLLABORATION

WHAT DID PROXIMITY OR remoteness mean to those officials actually conducting foreign relations in Washington or in the capitals of the four middle powers, all destined to be allies in World War II? Canadian Prime Minister Mackenzie King, in deriding the idea that Canada could be invaded, said in May, 1938, that it "ignores our neighbours and our lack of neighbours." [1] Australian Prime Minister Robert Menzies admitted that Australia depended on its "great and powerful friends." [2] When the Brazilian government supported President Roosevelt's appeal to Italy and Germany in April, 1939, it said, "Far from Europe [*longa da Europa*] and without any connection with the grave political problems which perturb their life, but on whose solution depends universal tranquility, we cannot remain strangers [*estranhos*] to the President of the U.S.A." [3] To the United States Ambassador Josephus Daniel's concern about Mexico's current attitude towards Germany in the light of Mexico's behavior during World War I, President Cardenas responded, "That was another and distant day." [4]

Asked by Australian Minister R. G. (later Lord) Casey on March 5, 1940, about the United States's policy regarding Australia's security, President Roosevelt replied that his cabinet had agreed that (in Casey's words)

the United States could not be indifferent to Canada, and had authorized him to make a public statement to that effect. In consequence, he had said in effect that the United States would spring to the aid of Canada if she were attacked. In respect of the Latin American republics, the element of distance began to enter in, but the certainty of American intervention might be said to increase in respect of the Central and South American republics . . . geographically close to the United States. So far as Australia and New Zealand were concerned, the answer was that the element of distance denoted a declining interest on the part of the United States. [5]

The course of hostilities modified some of these reactions. In certain ways the period 1939–1945 marked a high point in responsiveness and cooperation between the United States and the four middle powers that would not be equaled thereafter; in other ways it set patterns for continued or further responsiveness after the fighting ended.

The wartime partner with whom the United States developed the most responsive relationship, however, was none of these countries but Great Britain. It was often in the framework of Anglo-American cooperation that the Americans viewed collaboration with Canada and Australia. In a somewhat similar though less specific way, the need to be sensitive to the requirements of Mexico and Brazil was frequently seen in the framework of that overall Latin American policy called "inter-American solidarity."

During World War II, unlike some later periods, American power was very attractive. The middle powers, far from being repelled by it, strove to take advantage of the strength of the United States for their own purposes. Furthermore, their purposes and those of the United States were broadly similar and often the same. Bargaining took place around the edges of interests perceived to be only roughly congruent, not fully so.

During the period when the United States was officially neutral, Canada and Australia already had become active belligerents. Some difficulties appeared, but fewer than would have been the case had not American leaders been wholeheartedly on their side. Furthermore, neutrality did not bar military arrangements with Canada for continental defense, despite the problems posed by American efforts to maintain neutral status.

The way in which each of the four middle powers and the United States regarded the other varied greatly as their roles changed at successive stages of the war. The shifting role of the United States from 1938 onward is familiar; it changed from one-sided neutrality to partnership with two other great powers in prosecuting the war in Europe and to paramount leadership in the Pacific war. Australia was in the war from the day Britain declared war, and its troops first fought in North Africa, Greece, and Crete. After Singapore fell, most Australian units were brought back for duties closer to their homeland—in apparently imminent danger of invasion—and to help wage the war in the Pacific. Meanwhile, Australia became a major base for Allied operations. Canada declared war a week after Britain did, stationed troops in Britain early in the war, had a major role in the abortive Dieppe raid of 1942, participated actively in the invasion of Europe, and, at the time of the Japanese surrender, was preparing for a smaller role in the Pacific. Second only to the United States, Canada was a principal supplier of "mutual aid" to the Allies. Mexico and Brazil were, initially at least, as eager as the United States to preserve neutrality and to prevent the spread of war into the Western Hemisphere. They were gradually drawn into war with the Axis powers; in both cases the loss of their ships to German submarines was a crucial turning point. Meanwhile, they played leading roles among the Latin Americans in hemisphere defense. Brazil eventually sent an expeditionary force to Europe, the first of its kind in Latin American history, having meanwhile provided an aerial bridge to North Africa and Europe. In an action unprecedented for Mexico, that country sent an air squadron to the Philippines very late in the Pacific war.

By virtue of the breadth of its interests and resources, the United States more often took the initiative in seeking cooperation from the four middle powers than vice versa. How responsive these states were depended on how threatened by the Axis powers their leaders felt their countries to be. Exactly who it was who first had the idea or moved to put it into effect is not always easy to determine; there were some cases where similar desires arose spontaneously on both sides. President Roosevelt and Prime Minister King were each much concerned about the vulnerability of certain strategic points on the North American continent and quickly responded to each other in historic statements and meetings between 1938 and 1941 concerning their readiness to participate in continental defense.[6] Continental defense (protection of the area between the Arctic Ocean and the United States–Mexican border) and hemisphere defense (protection of the area between the United States–Canadian border and the bulge of Brazil) were the first of a large number of policies that provided the occasion for cooperation between the United States and one or more of the four countries. Others especially prominent while the United States remained neutral involved declarations of policy and support regarding relations with and embargos on goods to Axis countries, both of which applied mostly to the Latin American states. Next came delicate negotiations about bases or joint facilities for United States air, naval, and ground forces, sought from each of the four at one time or another with only limited success. Somewhat similar bargaining for transit and staging routes for airplanes ensued. The United States looked to the Latin American countries for actions to ensure that they preserved internal political security against Axis infiltration. Even before the United States entered the war, cooperation with Canada in sea patrol began, and arrangements for protecting nearby territories in the Atlantic and Caribbean, in which Brazil also collaborated, were devised. Once the United States became a belligerent, questions arose concerning military forces, involving cooperation in providing, directing, deploying, and combining them. Of great importance to the United States was the provision of scarce raw materials by each of the four countries and, in Mexico's case, of labor. Meanwhile, the four middle powers were seeking industrial supplies and war materiel; the Latin American countries also sought technical aid, both military and industrial. The United States received appeals for help in military training, and especially from the Latin American countries came pleas for financial, trade, and fiscal assistance. Canada was a junior partner in the development of the atomic bomb. One form of cooperation was denied the four lesser powers: consultations on strategy. All were left out, despite strenuous efforts by Canada and Australia to be participants along with the great powers in the grand discussion of those areas in which their forces were involved.

JOINTNESS

Only a few of the above types of cooperation could be called truly joint in the sense that the two governments pooled resources to conduct a common enterprise. Outstanding were the continental defense arrangements between the United States and Canada; the fact that Canada became a belligerent within a week after war broke out initially forced American leaders to become concerned about dangers to the north. After the shocking German successes in the spring and summer of 1940, President Roosevelt on August 18, 1940, made with Prime Minister King the unprecedented declaration of Ogdensburg. This was followed by another landmark announcement at Hyde Park on April 20, 1941. The first culminated in the Permanent Joint Board on Defense (PJBD) and the second in an advanced degree of economic integration for war-production purposes. Although the United States was still a nonbelligerent, this acknowledgment of joint responsibilities for continental defense helped bridge the gulf between it and its future allies. Thus several months before the attack on Pearl Harbor the PJBD had drawn up, and the two governments had approved, a joint plan for defending North America— in effect, Canada, Newfoundland, and adjacent portions of the United States, including Alaska.[7] Although the coastal areas were of primary concern, cooperation extended to the locks of the Sault Ste. Marie, in guarding which more than one thousand United States soldiers were stationed on the

Canadian side and where during 1942–1943 a Canadian battery was under control of a United States commander.[8]

Until the United States and Canada had each expanded its own war production, such enterprises in either country could obtain materials and technical help where needed, regardless of the national boundary, since they were treated alike by the two governments' control agencies or at least with special consideration not given to others. But the two countries did not specialize their functions, instead eventually producing the same kinds of materiel. Furthermore, since price levels in Canada were lower, its government put stringent controls on exports to prevent the flight of especially scarce goods.[9] Nevertheless, in the last two years of the war Canada furnished the United States with 14 percent of Canadian total war production.[10]

A unique example of integration was the United States–Canadian First Special Service Force, composed of Americans and Canadians serving without regard to nationality. It saw action in Italy in December, 1943. Handpicked and highly trained for mountain and desert warfare as it was, its actual combat experience scarcely exploited its capabilities.[11] Although Canadian forces were far more closely intertwined with the British, there were numerous instances of Canadian and American forces "mixed up together."[12] Even before the United States entered the war, there were Canadian-American contingency plans (linked with Anglo-American plans) which envisaged movements of the forces of one country into or across the other's territory to defend the continent, movements to be coordinated yet not to be under a unified command.[13] When the Japanese were about to penetrate the Aleutians, some Canadian air-force squadrons entered American territory to help defend it, following joint recommendations from the American and Canadian commanders of their respective adjacent regions; the squadrons remained until the end of 1943. To regain Japanese-held Kiska, a Canadian brigade group of 4,800 men, organized along United States Army staff patterns, using much American equipment, and transported in United States ships, joined American ground forces for a massive assault. But they found that the last enemy garrison in North America had been evacuated just prior to their arrival in August, 1943. The First Special Service Force took part in this operation, too, before being used in Italy.[14]

For the Canadians, the question of who was to command joint forces was a more touchy issue than for the other countries; it was most easily alleviated in naval operations, which took place mostly on the high seas, rather than on the territory of one of the participants.[15] The question dwindled in importance when the forces joined were overseas and part of a larger allied operation. Joint operations also were impeded by differences in organization and in equipment and training, some of which were standardized (on the American model) for particular forces later in the war.

In the nuclear research which produced the atomic bomb, Canada joined Britain and the United States; its capacity to provide a safe area, the necessary uranium, and some qualified scientists interested the two great powers. After two years (1942–1944) of frustration in accommodating to American requirements, the Canadians nevertheless were glad to be a partner, even if a junior one, in this wartime collaboration.[16]

In some ways the Australians were joined more completely to American military operations than were the Canadians, whose territory appeared less endangered by invasion. Australia was an important base of operations and an indispensable source of supplies and services for the Pacific war, which was directed for the most part by Americans, with the supreme commander's headquarters in Australia. There was a three-way tension here, however, since Australia began wartime activities joined to Britain for most purposes.[17] Winston Churchill had great difficulty conceiving of Australia as an independent actor, and the British intensely resented the statement of Menzies' successor, Prime Minister John Curtin, who after Pearl Harbor declared:

The Australian Government . . . regards the Pacific struggle as primarily one in which the United States and Australia must have the fullest say in the direction of the democracies' fighting plan. Without any inhibitions of any kind, I make it clear that Australia looks to America, free of any pangs as to our traditional links or kinship with the United Kingdom. . . . Australia can go and Britain can still hold on. We are, therefore, determined that Australia shall not go, and shall exert all our energies towards the shaping of a plan, with the United States as its keystone.[18]

Even without advance notice, the Australians rejoiced in the coming of General Douglas MacArthur and readily went through the requested form of asking that he be named supreme commander for the newly designated South-West Pacific Area. The jointness of combined Australian-American military operations thereafter was somewhat lopsided. An Australian, General Thomas Blamey, was designated commander of Allied Land Forces, the other two force commanders under MacArthur being American.[19] Not only did the Australians' pressure to be at least consulted in the general strategy

of the Pacific war fail, but except for coordination on general proposals between MacArthur and the prime minister, the supreme commander preferred
that details of the two countries' operations in the South-West Pacific be
dealt with by the regular departments and agencies of their respective governments.[20]

The Australians' readiness to accept forms of joint operations in the
South-West Pacific, where they felt most threatened, contrasted markedly
with their largely successful efforts to disentangle a large part of their
ground forces which had been fighting in the Middle East and bring them
back home. They did so despite the most frantic pressures from Winston
Churchill, seconded by Roosevelt, to divert some of the forces to the Neth-
erlands East Indies, or at least to Burma, after the fall of Singapore. The
Australians stuck to their intentions despite offers of American forces to protect Australia while its own forces were farther afield, although the Australian government did leave one division in Egypt and permitted two brigades
to pause in Ceylon.[21] Meanwhile, the Royal Australian Navy, which also
had operated in the Mediterranean and the Indian Ocean as well as around
Singapore, began in 1942 to collaborate with the Americans in the South-
West Pacific as part of the Allied Naval Forces under an American vice admiral, ultimately responsible to General MacArthur.[22]

For the Latin American allies, asymmetry was inevitable when units of
their forces were joined with those of the United States during the last year
of the war. Although the initiative for the Brazilian Expeditionary Force apparently came from Brazilians who had discovered that by the summer of
1942 United States defense officials had shifted their attention from hemisphere defense to Europe, the Brazilian force was trained and equipped by
United States military authorities, organized along American lines, and
transported under United States auspices to Italy. The Brazilian minister of
war had asked that it serve under the American theater commander.[23] By
June, 1944, a formation which eventually totaled 25,000 men moved overseas, the first Latin American force ever to do so.[24]

Within a year after the Brazilian force went to Italy, one of Mexico's
three air squadrons moved to the Philippines. Squadron 201, trained and
equipped in the United States, served with the Americans in the Pacific until
the end of the war against the Japanese.[25]

Regardless of the jointness of the wartime cooperation of any of the
lesser powers with the United States, something was held out. The Cana-

dians and Australians excepted from the authority of an American commander of their forces such matters as servicemen's discipline and the right
to appeal directly to their home governments an order for deployment or
other questionable orders. Differences in pay also complicated the service of
Canadian and Australian armed forces in proximity with Americans. Important symbolically was the right of Canadians and Australians to wear their
own uniforms.[26] Although the Brazilian government was willing to merge
its small air and naval forces with those of the Americans, it withstood for
several years heavy United States pressure to permit large numbers of American ground units to be intermingled with its own totally inadequate ground
forces in the defense of Brazil's northeastern bulge. It parried all horse-and-
rabbit stew proposals; finally the Americans lost interest in the area in view
of more demanding tasks elsewhere.[27] The Mexican government could not
bring itself to agree upon as much as a joint plan with the Americans for the
defense of their adjoining regions, although it willingly entered into protracted negotiations over what such a plan might contain. Questions of who
should exercise command when forces of one country were within the territory of the other and who should control and operate the airfields and radar
stations built by the Americans in Mexico created the most intractable problems. Despite considerable collaboration locally, only a statement of general
principles proved acceptable to the Mexicans as late as November, 1944.[28]

RECIPROCITY

If there were few instances of genuine jointness, there were many instances
where the United States and one of the middle powers took reciprocal actions in pursuit of their war aims to their mutual benefit. For such an
exchange, it was not necessary to have a common need (or for each to give
the highest priority to a common need); the requirements could be complementary. The line between a joint program and reciprocal action is not
always easy to draw, as in the case of Canada's permitting the development
of transit facilities on its territory for specifically American use (although a
use in the interest of both) or the case of Canada's and Mexico's each agreeing to take measures on its side of the border to defend the general region
about which it and the United States were concerned.

CANADA

So long as one country was neutral, only reciprocal actions between the United States and Canada rather than joint projects were feasible. Not only belligerency status but also differences in expectations constrained cooperation and minimized responsiveness. During the period when American military planners were intent on keeping war far from the United States they looked to the south as the most vulnerable region, particularly the Panama Canal and Caribbean areas. Thus they were not particularly receptive to Canadian initiatives in the spring and summer of 1940 for joint military discussions.[29] That Americans and Canadians felt different defense needs and had unequal capacities to respond to each other was somewhat covered over by the Canadian-American defense plans which they eventually made. In these plans each country sought aid from the other to protect its territory, but in fact only the northern borders of the United States, not the whole country, were involved in the preparations.[30]

As a belligerent, Canada was much concerned about the fate of Greenland after the Germans occupied Denmark in 1940. Canadian efforts to involve the United States in defending Greenland were not only unsuccessful, but the Americans, confusedly clinging to their neutrality, effectively opposed Canadian or British occupation. Under further pressure from Canada and Britain either to let Canada construct defenses, to help Greenlanders to build them, or to do so itself, the United States government finally arranged with the Danish governors of Greenland in April, 1941, the setting up of defense installations in the name of the "American nations." The Canadians welcomed this movement, but their subsequent offer to aid the United States in garrisoning Greenland was politely turned down by the Americans.[31] Closer still to Canada but not then part of it was Newfoundland. Without the participation of Canadians, despite their vigorous efforts to take part, British and American leaders arranged the leasing of bases in Newfoundland in September, 1940. Canada had already begun its own defense installations in Newfoundland; eventually the Canadians and Americans coordinated their separate facilities.[32]

Despite such failures to respond more favorably to each other, the United States and Canada shared an intense concern in the period before the attack on Pearl Harbor that Britain not be forced to its knees, and a three-way reciprocal relationship began to grow up. This relationship put Canada in a unique position, as it acquired an unusual importance to the United States, yet was assigned a subordinate position as part of the British machinery for dealing with the United States.[33] As the United States became more completely involved in the war, Canada's special role diminished, while collaboration with the United States increased.

Although President Roosevelt, when he met Prime Minister King in August, 1940, referred to the possibility of an American base in Nova Scotia, no American request for a base in Canada was actually made.[34] Canada, however, readily made improvements in and permitted American use of naval facilities in the Nova Scotian ports of Halifax, Shelburne, and Sydney after July, 1941, when the United States Navy began actively convoying ships as far as Iceland, and also agreed to make facilities available for some American air squadrons, although the Americans did not take advantage of the latter.[35]

Large numbers of Americans, military and civilian, eventually went to Canada to carry out projects in which the two countries shared responsibility for development, building, operation, and maintenance costs, according to varying formulas. These projects included the Northwest Staging Route to Alaska, used for protecting that outpost of the continent, for delivering planes to the Soviet Union, and for transport of materiel to the Pacific war theater. Another project was the Alaska Highway, built through Canada, the most important function of which was to back up the air route. There was also the incomplete northeastern staging route, to ferry planes to Europe.[36] The Canadians made at least two concessions to American wishes, in spite of doubts as to desirability and their own unwillingness to share the task. As the Canadian section of the joint defense board put it, they accepted the Alaskan Highway project and agreed to facilitate it but without participation "for reasons of general policy," and they permitted the Americans to go ahead with the controversial Canol project, which was to develop oil for Alaska at the Norman Wells field in the Mackenzie Valley.[37] In dividing up responsibilities for airfields in Canada, the two governments followed the principle that the country which chiefly used a particular facility should provide for its defense, maintenance, and control, so long as all the defense measures met the standards of the Canadian chiefs of staff.[38]

Besides Canadian-American cooperation in air staging and ferrying to the battlefronts, probably the most important type of reciprocity was in manpower training. This got off to a slow start, for when the Canadians organized their special contribution to the conduct of the war, the Commonwealth air training plan, they unsuccessfully sought planes, training facilities, and instructors in the United States. However, large numbers of individual Americans were already teaching or being taught as volunteers in the Canadian air force. When the earlier scarcity was overcome, the Canadians proposed in December, 1941, a coordinated air-training scheme for North America. Despite discussions held the following April, nothing came of it, because the United States Army Air Force opposed it.[39] Eventually, however, numerous instances of reciprocal training assistance developed, including Canadian parachutists at Fort Benning, Georgia, and American cold-weather tests at Camp Shilo, Manitoba.[40]

From Canada to American war industries came such especially scarce and strategic raw materials as lead, zinc, nickel, aluminum, and uranium. The Canadians also supplied manufactured war materiel such as small arms. Eventually Canada was able to produce enough aircraft for its own needs; earlier, aircraft was one of the types of war materiel most urgently sought from the United States. For Canada as for the other middle powers, the problem was that the American cupboard of munitions and war materiel did not contain enough even for American forces during the first two years the war was being waged. The Canadians, however, were able to secure President Roosevelt's assurance in November, 1940, that they and the British would share equally in America's output of aircraft.[41] Under the cash-and-carry neutrality law, Canada had an advantage in purchasing war materiel in the United States, much of which then went to Britain. After December, 1941, since so much of Canadian war production was going abroad, the United States exempted Canada from the severe restrictions imposed on foreign purchasers and permitted Canadian producers to obtain materials and equipment in short supply on the same basis as that on which they were available to American producers.[42]

The only actively fighting ally not to be a partner to lend-lease agreements (except indirectly, through Britain's own agreement), Canada began in 1943 to provide "mutual aid" directly to other allies. After passing through a phase of extreme dollar scarcity because of its war purchases from a neutral United States, Canada later had to make arrangements with the United States Treasury Department to reduce the huge holdings of American dollars acquired once the Hyde Park agreement began to take effect and the United States became a belligerent. These arrangements included the right to buy the permanent installations made by the United States in Canada.[43] Both countries made numerous adjustments in customs duties and other taxes to facilitate their war-related cooperation. They also developed a coordinated overseas export and import policy, including shipping controls.[44]

AUSTRALIA

Even before the attack on Pearl Harbor, the Australian government had agreed to the preparation of airstrips for heavy American bombers in several localities, both in New Guinea and on the mainland in the North, although no work had yet begun on them.[45] Short of manpower and fearful that the rapid advance of the Japanese would culminate in the invasion of Australia, Australian leaders felt reassured by the unprecedented presence of a powerful ally's forces on their soil. (The Japanese had invaded New Guinea in January, 1942, bombed Darwin in February, 1942, and later even made a small effort to attack Sydney harbor by minisubmarines.) The Australian government hoped that the American forces based in their country would garrison Australia, as well as prepare for offensive operations; they were pleased that General MacArthur put his headquarters in Brisbane. By June, 1942, there were, excluding naval personnel, approximately 88,000 members of the American armed forces in Australia, a number which rose rapidly to 200,000 within a year, while the peak of naval personnel reached 14,300 in December, 1943.[46] As the war progressed, Australia became more important as a base of supplies for the Allied forces than for its fighting forces. Meanwhile, the Americans made huge demands on the country for construction, accommodations, and provisioning. Yet no serious disagreement regarding bases developed until after the war, when controversy arose over American installations at Manus Island in the Admiralties.

Not only for American forces in Australia was that country a main source of supply, but also for Allied forces throughout the South-West Pacific, who received food and munitions and those products for which transport from countries farther away was especially scarce. At the final accounting, Australia had supplied in reciprocal lend-lease to the United States more than 60 percent of what it had received from the United States under the same program.[47]

Of all the middle powers, Australia responded most readily to American requests and offered the most reciprocal advantages to American forces; it also later complained the most that its active role was not adequately appreciated. It was not a question of a low capacity to help; from the beginning Australia was a valuable ally. General Dwight D. Eisenhower made clear in December, 1941, when preparing his advice to General George C. Marshall, that as the nearest base to the Philippines which the United States could hope to establish and maintain for the war in the Pacific, Australia's safety had to be assured.[48] But the Australian and American governments had differing perspectives on what were the worst dangers. Because the crises facing them were not always in the same phase, each was not always ready to respond with everything the other desired. The Australians, for much of the war, were struggling against the current, because their great allies, the United States and Britain, had determined on beating Hitler first. Global considerations made the Americans and British attend less to the needs of the South-West Pacific and, when made aware of them, less willing to respond affirmatively to Australian desires.

Whereas earlier the Australians had tried unsuccessfully to get more Allied aid and war materiel for what they regarded as a country under siege, later they began to have differences of another kind. By 1943, the manpower squeeze caused by provisioning the Allies produced a strong demand to get soldiers discharged to fill the production gap. If their forces were to be continued to be used, as MacArthur moved northward, Australians did not want them employed merely in mopping up bypassed Japanese remnants in New Guinea and nearby islands but instead to participate in the offensive.[49] Australians in and out of public office objected to MacArthur's covering up the role of their forces in the war by equating "Allied" with "American." The Australians learned that as their usefulness to their American allies decreased, so did their bargaining power for reciprocal action.

MEXICO

Feeling far less threatened than did inhabitants of the two Commonwealth countries, at least prior to the attack on Pearl Harbor, the Mexicans were ready to bargain very hard to get equal value for any concessions made to the United States in furtherance of what the Americans envisaged as mutual aims. Before December, 1941, and more especially until German submarine activity in the Caribbean began, Mexicans were far less concerned than Americans about the defeat of the Nazis and could even hint that if Americans would not provide oil tankers, they could get them from the Germans.[50] Once Mexico entered the war, however, its government's objectives complemented American goals and in some cases began to approximate them.

As previously noted, the overall oil settlement with Mexico was not reached until just before the attack on Pearl Harbor. Prior to the agreement, the Mexicans had indicated a willingness to be accommodating on defense matters, but concrete progress was hardly visible until the settlement cleared the decks. Although the settlement was not directly linked with wartime cooperation, it included terms very useful to Mexico's economic development and thus laid a favorable foundation for defense negotiations. It also included a statement of the intention to negotiate a reciprocal trade agreement, not feasible earlier. Negotiations ran on for more than a year and provided Mexico with most-favored-nation treatment.[51]

With the logjam thus broken, Mexican concessions in addition to one granted in April, 1941, for transit of United States military planes to Panama, became possible.[52] Adamant against permitting the United States to acquire naval or air bases, even by lease, the Mexicans did eventually allow the use of their own facilities, which were enlarged and improved by Americans. They agreed to the construction of three radar stations in Baja California, eventually to be operated and owned by the Mexican army, and to the development of a heavy-bomber airdrome at Tehuantepec to permit patrol of the Pacific. Mexicans were to build it at American expense, and United States forces could then use it. For operations in the Caribbean against German submarines, from which Mexican trade was suffering, the government agreed to the use of facilities to be developed in Yucatan. By the time these installations on the peninsula were ready, they were no longer needed except for emergency use. A network of airfields in Baja California, agreed to in 1942 after much negotiation, never was constructed.[53]

In granting the use of their territory for carefully defined purposes, such as temporary stays in their ports by United States naval vessels, the Mexicans regularly insisted that such concessions be called "reciprocal" and that they be available to all Latin American countries in the name of hemisphere defense (although in fact only the United States made use of them). More important, the Mexicans secured agreement in principle that the United States should provide the military supplies and equipment to build up their defensive capacity. At first, there was little the American military could part with, but eventually Mexico became, with Brazil, the most favored Latin American recipient.[54] Although Mexico unsuccessfully sought air training for its pilots in 1940, by 1942 the United States did institute training programs for members of the Mexican armed forces at various American service schools.[55]

On the economic front, Mexico won appreciation from United States officials for banning oil exports to Japan in 1940–1941, when its newly nationalized oil industry was struggling for markets.[56] After discreet American hints, it restricted other exports to Axis countries.[57] Raw materials vital to war industries, including copper, lead, zinc, and nickel, went from Mexico to the United States; from the United States came industrial materials and technical aid for building up basic industries related to the war, including the rehabilitating of Mexican railroads. Credits under lend-lease and from the Export-Import Bank provided the necessary financial aid, although until 1942 the Mexicans were reluctant to sign a lend-lease agreement.[58] Probably the most important Mexican contribution to the United States war effort— and it was unique—was the labor which went north. Under carefully defined conditions laid down by the Mexican government, tens of thousands of workers were supplied to fill a vital need for food production and to work on railroads in the United States.[59]

Rather remarkably, the Mexican government agreed with the United States in January, 1943, that citizens of one country subject to the draft could be required to serve in the armed forces of the other country if residing there. More than 15,500 Mexicans served in the United States armed forces.[60] During the previous year the Mexican government decreed that in case of clear need the Mexican executive could authorize armed forces of other hemisphere countries to cross its territory.[61]

Less remarkable was the Mexicans' readiness to undertake measures to combat subversion by Axis agents, an action much desired by the Americans, who expressed greater concern than the Mexicans about this danger.[62] After the German government had "insulted" Mexico because the latter acquiesced in the American blacklisting of traders, Mexico closed the German consulates and took some Axis ships into custody. Prior to breaking relations with the Axis countries, the Mexicans imposed further controls on Axis nationals to prevent espionage, agitation, and sabotage.[63]

BRAZIL

As war approached, in addition to concern for the Panama Canal, American military planners were greatly worried that the northeastern bulge of Brazil would be the most likely and vulnerable place for armed penetration by Axis powers into the western hemisphere. (The planners had a similar fear about the island of Fernando de Noronha, far out in the South Atlantic towards Africa.) Judging by their actions, though not by their words, the Brazilians hardly reciprocated these fears and were reluctant to move their forces to these unguarded areas from their traditional concentration along the southern border. Resisting strong American pressure to permit American help in guarding the Northeast, they successfully held out for protection by their own forces, which were to be armed and trained by the Americans. However, even prior to the attack on Pearl Harbor, Brazil agreed to the construction or reconstruction by Pan American Airways of airfields in the Northeast, to be used by the military, and after December, 1941, eventually permitted the stationing of United States Army specialists at these airfields.[64] By June, 1941, surface vessels of the United States Navy were allowed to use the ports of Recife and Bahia, and its planes instituted South Atlantic patrols from Recife and Belem immediately after the United States entered the war.[65] Brazil first permitted ferrying of transport planes by way of its northeastern region to British forces in Africa and the Middle East in June, 1941.[66] After the attack on Pearl Harbor, three fifty-man American marine groups were allowed to guard the airfields. Although this scarcely satisfied United States Army planners, they were much gratified that following the signing of a lend-lease agreement in March, 1942, which contained far more generous provisions than Brazil had received the previous year, Brazil quickly accepted the new Ferry Command program.[67] With enlargement and improvement of the airfields in the Northeast and unrestricted transit arrangements, "the airway to Brazil, planned for hemisphere defense, became in 1943 the air funnel to the battlefields of the world." [68]

Bargaining hard before granting these concessions, the Brazilians held out for much larger quantities and more sophisticated types of military equipment than the Americans were originally willing to provide, although less than the Brazilians originally sought.[69] Their obvious incapacity to build up, with their own resources, facilities usable by United States military forces, to say nothing of modernizing their own defense forces, was a persuasive argument if any was needed.

A similar argument could be (and was) made for assistance to the chronically ailing Brazilian economy. As war approached and until mid-1940, President Vargas was able to extract economic advantages from the rivalry between the United States and Germany. Brazil was slow to impose embargoes on exportation of strategic materials to the Axis, and Brazilian leaders hinted to the Americans that not only for arms but for trade and credits they might have to turn to the Germans.[70] The war provided President Vargas with a fine opportunity to press forward his industrialization projects, the most noteworthy a state-owned steel mill to be built at Volta Redonda. This project was launched by means of an Export-Import Bank loan of $20 million made in September, 1940, the original loan being followed by additional large credits later.[71] Previously, in 1939, the United States had helped Brazil to put its foreign exchange on a better footing by liquidating frozen credits and adjusting interest payments due on Brazilian debts to Americans.[72]

Other large credits were made available to develop production of strategic materials such as rubber, to refurbish communications facilities, and to promote food growing for "hemisphere defense." A United States technical mission to help plan Brazil's war mobilization was sent in 1942, and extensive technical aid was rendered in addition to the granting of credits.[73] The United States also assisted Brazil to adjust to the cutting off of its traditional markets elsewhere. This was mutually advantageous; the Americans wanted strategic raw materials from Brazil, such as tungsten, cobalt, and nickel, which they preemptively purchased, while Brazil needed industrial goods.[74]

Even for its antisubversion measures, Brazil received substantial economic aid from the United States, whose leaders were concerned about Axis agents (including those of Japan) tilling fertile political soil in Brazil. Not only were there large, unassimilated German and Italian colonies in Rio Grande do Sul and Santa Catarina, but also German and Italian airlines, CONDOR and LATI, were operating in Brazil. After the attack on Pearl Harbor, the government eventually closed out the airlines by taking them over, an action facilitated by specific United States financial and technical aid and urged by Americans the previous year when they had promised help. By this time also, Americans finally had persuaded Brazil to suppress coded radio messages sent by transmitters owned by CONDOR and LATI and others, messages which could communicate information about military traffic. And the government began to curb Axis activities by closing Axis countries' news agencies and freezing credits of nationals of Axis countries.[75]

With respect to Brazil as well as Mexico, the United States position was that in view of the strategic military and naval advantages received from

Latin American states, "it would be impolite, unwise, and improper to expect or ask for an additional contribution" under lend-lease.[76] On their parts, both Latin American countries, although very touchy about sovereign rights when it came to bases, were willing to do considerable eye winking in meeting American requests in practice, while not making concessions formally. The controversy about who was to guard facilities in northeastern Brazil eventually become moot; their defense in the end was provided mainly by British, Soviet, and American arms far away in other theaters.[77] Meanwhile, however, Brazilians could regard their bargains with the United States as useful in protecting and elevating them in their relations with their rivals, the uncooperative Argentines.[78]

SPECIFICITY

The two Latin American countries often responded warmly in general terms to an American request for some broad form of military cooperation. They then seemed to drag their feet, offered distracting substitutes, suggested a change in venue, pointed out technicalities preventing full compliance, made what seemed to the Americans exorbitant counterclaims, and generally failed to concede in practice more than a relatively small fraction of what the United States asked for, and then well surrounded by conditions.[79] True, American military authorities often were importunate and not very sophisticated about Latin American politics, were in fact encroaching on sensitive concerns about sovereignty, and were in the beginning unable to make good on their own promises of delivering war goods quickly and fully.

Much more readily the Latin American countries responded to United States desires that they provide diplomatic support against the Axis. At successive inter-American meetings, Mexico and Brazil were leaders in promising mutual consultation if the hemisphere was threatened from outside, in making United States neutrality policy collective, in providing for potential trusteeships over European possessions in the Western Hemisphere endangered by transfer, in giving assurance of reciprocal assistance if an American state was attacked from abroad, and in resolving to combat internal subversion by foreign (Axis) powers. Brazil was host to a meeting of foreign ministers after the United States was attacked. At this conference, Mexico and Brazil again played leading parts in promoting resolutions that called for breaking off relations with Axis powers, affirming the principles of the Atlantic Charter, and organizing an Inter-American Defense Board.

Following this conference, Brazil did break relations with Axis countries; Mexico had broken with Japan directly after the attack on Pearl Harbor, and three days later it severed relations with Germany and Italy. Declarations of war against Germany did not take place until after the two countries had had ships sunk by the Nazis, Mexico declaring war in May, 1942, and Brazil, in August of that year. (Two months before the attack on Pearl Harbor, Mexico renewed relations with Britain, broken during the oil controversy, and later, partly responding to American urging, reestablished ties with Soviet Union, severed in 1935.) [80]

For different reasons, the United States on occasion also tended to rely on symbolic measures; implementation of general promises was hindered by lack of capacity, the incoherent organization of the United States government, and the need to coordinate its actions with its British ally. Thus the Australians (and Canadians, too) discovered that the Pacific War Council set up in Washington to answer their desires to participate in war planning was mainly windowdressing.[81] This discovery prompted the Australians' continual complaint that they were expected to carry out specific actions to fulfill general plans in the making of which they had no part.[82]

DISTANCE

Although distance and strategic location helped explain American leaders' interest in Australia, distance was a great handicap to the Australians in gaining a favorable response. Australia was clearly at the end of the line for scarce war equipment. When the Australian government pleaded for materiel in early 1942, it was told by President Roosevelt that the global situation had to be taken into account in assessing its needs, a different response from that received by the other three Middle powers.[83] Far away from the European theater, to which Churchill and Roosevelt gave priority, the Australian government heard only months later of the Allies' intention to concentrate their efforts against Hitler first.[84] When decisions regarding the Far East were made at the Cairo conference of 1943, again the Australians learned only later and in fragments matters of direct concern to them.[85] The foreign minister, Herbert Evatt, expressed his resentment during a conference with

New Zealand in January, 1944, which culminated in a declaration on the future of the Pacific area; this statement was regarded as presumptuous by some American officials, especially Secretary Hull, so distant from the antipodal point of view.[86]

Brazil, too, was interesting to the United States because of its distance from North America—and its relative closeness to North Africa. To some extent, American planners compensated for both geographical and cultural distance by preparing ahead of time, since their first military soundings with the Brazilians came very early (1939) and laid a foundation for later negotiations.[87] Distance did not prevent Washington from hearing and worrying about a controversial speech of President Vargas, made after the fall of France. Seeming to indicate a wide gap between his and American loyalties, he used the language of European fascists and apparently was leaning in their direction. The speech was later rationalized by Brazilians and some Americans as one intended to secure public support within Brazil.[88] A shift in the Allies' fortunes reduced the distance markedly.

CUMULATION AND SPILLOVER

CANADA

Defense cooperation began with economic measures which gradually tied the economies of Canada and the United States close together; they were followed by collaborative military projects to defend the continent and strengthen those fighting abroad. Within the military field, one project often led to another; thus the Alaska Highway project followed from requirements for the Northwest Staging Route. Collaboration with Britain called for Canadian-American collaboration. As the war went on, Canadian armed forces came less and less to use British equipment and organization and methods, as they increasingly depended on certain kinds of American war materiel and engaged in joint operations with the Americans. Cooperation both in defense and production required the two countries to impose similar standards of performance, a kind of partial incorporation of one country's rules into those of the other country.

The cumulative effect of continental-defense planning and activities eased the transition of the United States from neutrality to active belligerency. The growth of self-confidence that resulted from Canada's being an important belligerent early in the war and the increased mutual trust between Canadians and Americans that flowed from successful cooperation did not prevent Canada from taking precautions against postwar continuation of wartime concessions. Uneasy about the large numbers of American personnel, uniformed and civilian, in Canada, Canadians took care to specify conditions for their presence and requirements for disposal of wartime facilities.[89]

Canada's military collaboration was not permitted by Britain and the United States to spill over into the councils of the leading allies when they were considering global strategy. Officials in the Mackenzie King government cited Canada's exclusion from the planning when they refused to take a role in the postwar occupation of Germany. Instead, Canada quickly withdrew its forces from Europe.[90]

AUSTRALIA

Although also barred from high-strategy councils and not permitted to participate in working out Japanese-surrender terms, Australia did seek and win a role in the occupation of Japan. Its was the last non-American force to be present there and thus was available to participate in the Korean War in 1950. On the economic front, the Australians, in resistance to "learning"— that is, in resistance to applying wartime practices to postwar foreign economic relations—did what they could to prevent cooperation under lend-lease from compromising continuation of the imperial-preference trade system.

BRAZIL AND MEXICO

If the Latin American states were to contribute to hemisphere defense or to engage in other forms of military cooperation with the United States, the capacity to do so inevitably required economic assistance from the great power. The ultimate effect was a tremendous boost to their industrialization, qualitatively more significant than similar economic effects in the two Commonwealth states. Within the military sphere, building up the defenses of Brazil and Mexico, however, inevitably made them highly dependent upon the United States for spare parts, repairs, and replacements. In the economic sphere, their trade became increasingly skewed in the direction of the United States, not entirely through American efforts but also through being cut off from other markets during the war and because of the economic weakness of their old European trading partners in the immediate postwar period.

Starting with hemisphere defense, both Latin American countries broadened their wartime military cooperation to sending an armed force abroad. Although this unprecedented collaboration was not followed by very active participation in the peace negotiations, both countries experienced numerous Good Neighbor actions taken by the United States. The actions made them somewhat less suspicious and more responsive to American requests, at least in spirit, and this carried over into the postwar period. Yet, even more than the Canadians, the Mexicans took great care to keep the American camel's nose from pushing into the tent under the guise of mutual defense assistance.

In all four countries, some United States military men were slow learners about operating in the territory of lesser powers. They tended to ignore the contributions of their hosts even after securing concessions for which they had strongly pressed. They preferred performing the necessary military tasks themselves, and their publicity failed to give satisfactory credit to their collaborators.[91]

CHANNELS OF COMMUNICATION

CANADA

Military representatives were combined with civilians and the chairmen were civilians on the outstanding agency for Canadian-American defense cooperation, the Permanent Joint Board on Defense. This agency dealt almost exclusively with continental defense, although in its later stages it was concerned also with actions which supported the war in the European and Pacific theaters. Despite being formally an advisory body, it occasionally acted in an administrative capacity, overseeing, expediting, and facilitating the carrying out of projects it had earlier promoted. It provided for exchange of information, improved the supply of materials and services, and helped to coordinate activities in both Canada and the United States, although the projects with which it was concerned were located only in Canada or Newfoundland.

The success of the board lay less in its formal structure than in the style of its functioning. Possessing distinguished civilian chairmen and representatives from the Department of State and the Department of External Affairs meant that the military recommendations made by one of its national sections were tailored to the domestic political and economic situation in the country of the other section. The Canadian military members had a dual responsibility, since they also functioned as staff officers dealing with the same types of problems in the staffs of their respective services; the American military members were formally separate from their staffs but operated close to them. The American section reported directly to the president and the Canadian section to the Cabinet War Committee, presided over by the prime minister. Meetings were conducted in private, informally, and in an atmosphere of frankness combined with cordiality, with decisions on joint recommendations made only after all had assented. Nearly every recommendation the board made was later approved, either tacitly or expressly. Members of the board, realizing that the success of their recommendations depended in practice upon acquiescence, if not support, from the agencies in the two countries dealing with foreign and military affairs, maintained liaison with the appropriate offices so as to reflect as far as possible the views of the latter.[92]

Among innumerable other wartime agencies of communication was the Canadian Joint Staff Mission in Washington.[93] This mission was established in 1942 after lengthy Canadian pressure and against the resistance of the United States armed services and the British, both of whom held that the British mission could serve adequately for Canada and Australia.[94] Canadian efforts to be separately represented on the combined boards set up by the British and Americans were successful in only two cases, those dealing with production and resources and with food.[95] Nevertheless, the Canadians were more numerous in Washington than were any other foreigners and were in much more frequent contact informally; they even occupied offices closer to their American counterparts, which facilitated interchanges at the working level.[96]

AUSTRALIA

Since the Canadians were looking to Europe rather than to the Pacific, they had an advantage not enjoyed by the Australians, who felt they had to work against the priorities set by the great powers. The distant Commonwealth country did not obtain membership on a single combined board in Washington. Roosevelt would have accepted Australia on at least one of them, but Churchill overruled this.[97] The Pacific War Council turned out to be chiefly a device for learning what was on President Roosevelt's mind and for permitting an Australian voice to be heard.[98]

There was an Australian voice in the British War Cabinet, an arrangement upon which the Australian government relied for exercising some influence.[99] However, such a footing indicates the nature of their problem. It suited Churchill to insist on speaking for the whole Commonwealth as a unity, and for his own reasons Roosevelt preferred to deal with Australia through the British connection.[100] While R. G. Casey was Australian minister to the United States, he made the most of his opportunities to acquaint Americans with his country's situation and advantages as collaborator; then in March, 1942, he accepted Churchill's appointment as British secretary of state for the Middle East.[101] Others in the official Australian entourage in Washington followed in his path to develop personally close relations with American officials, similar to the Canadians' but necessarily on a smaller scale. In Australia, General MacArthur's close working relationship with Prime Minister Curtin helped to provide Curtin's government with access where it might count, but to that extent Australia's fortunes were tied to those of MacArthur. MacArthur himself had to compete with others in Washington. Among them, however, Admiral Ernest J. King helped the Australian cause by pressing for more attention to the war against Japan.[102]

BRAZIL

Since the Brazilians, like the Australians, knew that Washington was the place where the important decisions were made, they preferred holding military talks there.[103] The problems confronting their principal representative (advisory) to the Joint Brazil–United States Defense Commission, General Leitão de Carvalho, during 1942 were mainly with his own government and military superiors, not with the Americans. He recognized that implicitly it was the strategic views of the United States chiefs of staff that framed the recommendations of the commission.[104] But Washington was a good place for information gathering, and his presence there enabled Brazilians to discern quite early the shift in interest of the American military planners to the North African theater.[105]

In Brazil itself, a Joint Brazil–United States Military Commission was established in Rio de Janeiro in December, 1942, to work with the existing United States military and naval missions to improve the combat readiness of Brazilian forces.[106]

The various inter-American conferences provided a method acceptable to the Brazilians (and Mexicans) by which the United States could stimulate

cooperation. The conference held in Rio de Janeiro during the month following the Pearl Harbor attack proved especially useful in laying foundations
for later collaboration. However, one agency proposed by the Department of
State (and opposed by United States defense officials), the Inter-American
Defense Board, turned out to be window dressing. United States military officials went through the motions of working with it, but in fact the questions
with which it dealt were peripheral to the important military policies adopted
by the United States government. Even the State Department expected that
the board would neither have real responsibilities nor interfere in bilateral
military arrangements made by the army and navy.[107]

MEXICO

Regardless of the subsequent practical ineffectiveness of such agencies
as the Inter-American Defense Board, Mexicans preferred an inter-American
framework for wartime collaboration with the United States.[108] Unlike Brazilians, Mexicans often appeared to prefer an arms-length although courte-
ous dialogue with Americans; they apparently were not eager either to be on
the inside of important decision making or to get as many concessions as
possible from the United States.

The Mexican government did eventually agree, in 1942, to the establishment of a Joint Mexican–United States Defense Commission. Although some Americans originally envisaged it as operating somewhat like
the board set up with Canada earlier, this was not to be the case, for a
number of reasons. There were no civilians on it because their inclusion was
opposed by the United States Department of War and Department of the
Navy. The scope of the commission was confined to very specific technical
details relating to military and naval cooperation. One national section
would draw up an action to be formally presented for approval by the other;
if this was secured, the recommendation was then submitted to the appropriate military authorities in the two countries.[109] One of the commission's
tasks was to review all Mexican lend-lease requests, and it also worked to
speed war materiel to Mexico and to facilitate projects for the manufacture
of such materiel in Mexico.[110]

Another agency of limited life was the Mexican Industrial Commission,
set up in September, 1943, in which the American members were government officials, but the Mexicans were an industrialist, a banker, and a government official. Its task was to study and recommend actions that would

bring about industrialization in Mexico. Like similar commissions established for Brazil, these were joint in the sense that they served as useful channels for information moving in both directions.

ADMINISTRATIVE TREATMENT VERSUS POLITICIZATION

BRAZIL

For the United States to establish joint agencies for handling technical problems with Brazil or with Mexico required diplomacy, and the agreements had to be formally accepted by the respective governments. Even when military staff talks occurred between Americans and Brazilians (or Mexicans), they were, in addition to being fact-finding or fact-disseminating sessions, also occasions for hard bargaining to solve problems only partially technical; national sensitivities could be very strong. Questions which were mainly military in the eyes of the American officers became high politics to their Latin partners and had to be referred to the highest government authorities.

Numerous impasses required intervention by the American president to reopen them. On occasion, President Roosevelt in effect overruled the War Department. For example, he put his desire to make the Rio de Janeiro conference of January, 1942, a "success" above a projected move to help the army gain permission to put American forces in northeastern Brazil.[111] President Roosevelt, recognizing that Brazilian cooperation required the active support of Brazil's shrewd and cautious dictator, had numerous personal communications with Getulio Vargas. It was only after he met with President Vargas at Natal on his way home from the Casablanca conference in January, 1943, that Brazil formally joined the Allies.[112]

Brazil occupied such a strategic spot both militarily and diplomatically, however, that wartime collaboration with it became not only a matter of high politics but also produced mundane bureaucratic politics between agencies within the United States government. On the American side, the army contended with the navy and both with the State Department on such matters as putting American ground forces in Brazil and on supplies of war materiel.[113] Instead of a gradual depoliticizing of bilateral military dealings once the general policy had been set, allied cooperation sometimes intensified bureaucratic politics inside one or both governments.

AUSTRALIA

The main sources of conflict between Australia and the United States were on the plane of high politics, and once the policy was accepted, administration became fairly routine. In Australia an elaborate and constantly evolving system of administrative committees on which American military representatives sat along with the responsible Australian officials worked out details of cooperative ventures and determined priorities for specific requests. Only occasionally toward the end of the war did the Australian government feel strong resentment, arising from the tendency of United States military authorities to retain equipment that the Australians thought should be allocated to them or from the apparently ever expanding American demands under lend-lease arrangements.[114]

CANADA

In the early stages of Canadian-American wartime collaboration, the easy friendship between President Roosevelt and Prime Minister King facilitated the basic shift of policy which was to place the two countries' relations on a new cooperative footing.[115] On later occasions, this personal relationship gave the final touch necessary to convert a projected collaboration into a reality. For example, presumably nonpolitical negotiations between scientists from the United States, Canada, and Britain regarding nuclear research were about to founder on the nationalist demands of that part of the United States Army which became responsible for atomic-bomb development; they were saved when the president repeated his earlier pledge to Winston Churchill that the bomb be a cooperative venture.[116] President Roosevelt was given to describing Canadians and Americans in such terms as being members of the same family, and he acted accordingly.[117]

The informality with which the two leaders announced the creation of the Permanent Joint Board on Defense set the tone for its later style of operations.[118] More than in any other wartime relationship between the United States and a lesser ally, the functioning of this board was on a technical or bureaucratic level rather than on the level of high politics (or state policy), and problems were handled as technical questions. For example, divisions often occurred along service lines rather than national lines. A kind of informal unanimity rule prevailed, testifying to the parties' dependence on consensus. Although formally the board was advisory only, many of its decisions ultimately had executive effect. This was due partly to the type of liaison provided by overlapping appointments of some members, who also had official responsibilities in their own services or departments. The board considered problems coming from other agencies but also took up some on its own initiative and in general acted as a catalyst. Extensive correspondence not only between the two national sections but also between members of one section and their counterparts in the other section provided an alternate channel of communication between the political and military departments of the two governments. American members sometimes dealt directly with the appropriate operating agencies in the United States, civilian as well as military, in seeking to facilitate joint actions.[119]

DOMESTIC POLITICS

When defense questions reached President Roosevelt and Prime Minister King, each revealed a feel for the domestic political problems the other faced, and from the time when they conferred privately before making their reciprocal promises of defense support in August, 1938, each often responded in accord with the other's domestic political requirements.[120] The prime minister's consciousness of the president's need to tread carefully while the United States was neutral left him open to some adverse criticism for not pushing harder to get American aid.[121] However, both he and his American counterpart were sitting firmly in the saddle after their respective reelections in 1940, and their increasingly close ties could eventually be given more publicity. The Ogdensburg declaration met with public acclaim on both sides of the border. After the passage of the Lend-Lease Act, Mr. King broke his silence to answer both Canadian and American criticism concerning Canadian aid to Britain, a silence he earlier had kept in order not to interfere in the American debate.[122] Minor intrusions of rivalries among American producers and government agencies occasionally occurred in carrying out the Hyde Park agreement, as when the two countries' export controls had to be coordinated.[123]

Americans, especially, needed to be sensitive to their partner's domestic politics, and even more so after the United States became a belligerent. American war planners wanted secrecy when acceding to the first military talks, in 1940, but it was later necessary for other reasons. The numbers of

Americans engaged in joint projects in Canada rose to heights alarming to Canadians aware of them in their communities, even though much of the actual construction work was done by Canadians. Only after the war had ended could the Canadian government feel free to reveal that there had been more than three thousand United States servicemen in the Northwest (some in places where they were not seen by Canadians) and hundreds in several other areas.[124] It was not just their presence but also their behavior and assumptions which bothered many Canadians, such as their acting as if unconscious of the fact that they were not on United States soil. Military requirements seem to have been the sole factor considered in stationing American troops on Canadian territory; American defense authorities showed no concern for the political risks necessarily incurred by the Canadian government in assenting to an action so certain to be unpopular.[125]

Problems with the presence and behavior of uniformed Americans on their territory could not arise in Mexico or Brazil because, with minor exceptions, these governments refused to accept them.[126] It was inconceivable for a politician who wished to remain in office in Mexico to have done otherwise, and this was only slightly less true in Brazil, facts that took a long time to penetrate the thinking of United States Army planners, even after they had been warned about difficulties by American negotiators. As with his Canadian counterpart, President Roosevelt himself, however, was sensitive to the difficulties the Latin American presidents faced in making concessions of a military nature, and so were officials in the Department of State. The Americans recognized that they could not push too hard while the Mexicans were going through an election and probably were unduly impressed with the alleged dangers of an insurgent group which might prevent President Manuel Ávila Camacho's inauguration if he appeared too cooperative with the United States.[127] After the cordial words of Ávila Camacho's inaugural address and the disappearance of any real or alleged threats to the regime, not all the American negotiators could understand why secrecy and further delays were imposed for almost another year.

Getulio Vargas did not have a Congress whose recalcitrance he could refer to when disinclined to accede to a request, an occasional negotiating ploy of Mexican presidents. Yet despite his position as dictator of the Estado Novo, he had to keep a wary eye on competitors for leadership in a far more unstable situation than that facing the Mexican Cárdenas and Ávila Comacho, especially since elements of the Brazilian military forces were pro-

Axis. Concentrating on his political position and domestic program, Vargas was inclined to give Foreign Minister Afrânio de Melo Franco and his successor, Oswaldo Aranha, a relatively free hand in foreign policy, so long as it did not interfere with Vargas's primary concerns.[128] Both foreign ministers were strong supporters of Pan Americanism, and Aranha developed a close relationship with President Roosevelt, who may have been somewhat misled about Brazilian domestic politics by Aranha's fervent pro-Allies position.[129]

Not surprisingly, the Australians, feeling under attack and eager to maintain good relations with a strong and helpful ally, did not exhibit political sensitivities to which the Americans were obliged to respond with care. Prime Minister Curtin did have some important domestic concerns that were affected by the war effort, such as the areas in which conscripted soldiers could serve, the allocation of scarce supplies, coal-mine labor conflicts, and discontent over unwonted regulation of private lives. Except for domestic problems flowing from the strain on manpower, United States war policy was not directly involved.[130]

SUMMARY

In World War II, the United States and its four middle-power partners had to work together in two main areas, military affairs and the allocation of goods and services under conditions of wartime scarcities. These areas were separable in theory and practice but so closely intertwined in their effects on each other that cooperation in one area called for cooperation in the other. To an unprecedented extent, wartime decisions of the United States and its lesser allies became intermingled, but the particular arrangements for cooperation or coordination, with one exception, did not endure (for practical purposes) beyond the war's end and the release from acute insecurity. The exception, the Canadian-American Permanent Joint Board on Defense, suggests that a specific institution for a joint activity may make such collaboration become more routinized, less political; yet the defense boards in Mexico and Brazil, which in some ways were copied from the Canadian-American board, did not function in the same way nor continue to be active after the war.

Meanwhile, however, each of the four middle powers contributed usefully and successfully to the common war effort. While accepting the leadership of the United States, each determined the boundaries of its participation. The power of each of these countries to set the conditions for collaboration in any particular enterprise depended, among other considerations, on its location, its own and the Americans' capacity to be useful to each other in particular matters, the intensity of the threat, and the absence of other alternatives. Only *willing* collaboration could serve the needs of the United States; coercive methods theoretically available to any great power were ruled out. Bargaining was primarily about the terms of cooperation already accepted in principle, and the lesser powers had an advantage in that what they asked of the United States was primarily to make good their capacity to aid it and the other major belligerents. When the Latin American states, which were less immediately involved in the war and less capable of direct military participation, were pressed to make a difficult concession, they sometimes procrastinated until the timeliness of the desired action had passed.

In scope and intensity, Canadian and Australian collaboration with the United States was far greater than Mexican or Brazilian. What were the factors that distinguished Canada and Australia from the Latin countries in their readiness to respond and their capacity to evoke an American response? They both had strong, democratically based governments which were secure from serious domestic political attacks on their relations with the United States, although Liberal governments in Canada have always been fair game for opponents who wanted to attack their record of cooperation with the Americans one way or another. Their modern economies were easier to mesh with that of the United States, and their peoples shared a common language and were culturally similar. Government leaders in the United States, Canada, and Australia felt a comparably intense concern about the war, and there was a degree of mutuality in the give and take of their wartime relations wholly lacking in relations with the Latin American allies. Furthermore, the United States, Canada, and Australia were bound together with Britain in its hour of supreme trial, a relationship which occasionally complicated their bilateral relations but most of the time made them teammates psychologically and gave flexibility to their direct relationships. Distance or proximity would seem to be the main explanation for the differences between the wartime relations of the United States with Australia and with Canada.

Not only was collaboration with Mexico and Brazil on an entirely different basis, but also Latin Americans behaved as if they were not quite sure that the metamorphosis of the Colossus of the North into the Good Neighbor was yet complete. Despite the economic and military aid that the United States provided, what it wanted of them seemed to Mexicans and Brazilians to be closer to the needs of an imperialist than to the mutual concerns of a friend. Nevertheless, the United States acted with enough restraint that by the end of the war a more trusting relationship existed than at its beginning.

The reciprocal arrangements characteristic of the United States cooperation with the Latin countries were in effect package deals and did not have the staying power of the type of arrangement more common with Canada and Australia, where each bargain could stand on its own merits. Even when one of the latter governments was not entirely happy with a concession, it sometimes made the concession in the interests of the common cause, a cause the United States could promote more vigorously as a result of the concession. The Mexicans and Brazilians could less afford to make concessions and also were less inclined to do so. That Mexicans and Americans treated each other differently during the war than did Brazilians and Americans could be explained by Mexico's proximity, absence of the long tradition of friendship existing between Brazil and the United States, and Mexico's greater internal political cohesion.

How easy it was to respond affirmatively to a wartime proposal for cooperation depended on its nature. The easiest response, in terms of sacrifice, was the declaration of solidarity. Only moderately difficult were economic concessions and the supplying of industrial and war materials or scarce raw materials. Training projects probably ranked next in difficulty; they were troublesome because of American military authorities' fear that there would be insufficient training facilities for their own men if the program was extended to others. More vigorous bargaining ensued over the use of territory for transit, except for Australia. And only Australia permitted its territory to be used for American military bases; the other countries insisted on retaining control of military facilities afforded the United States. It was almost equally difficult for a middle power to agree to put its forces under another's commander. Even in Australia, its army was under an Australian general who was the Allied commander for ground forces in that region. Hardly any of the cooperative projects took place on American soil, except for training and the production of war materiel. The less conspicuous the concessions, the readier were the other governments to respond; in most cases, secrecy was an ingredient for success.

The more distant countries, Australia and Brazil, appeared readier to respond and less likely to examine all angles of an American request. However, the deed lagged far behind the declaration in Brazil's case, and the Australians eventually learned to be circumspect in the face of expanding American claims. The most cautious was Mexico, especially prior to the settlement of the oil controversy. However, Canadian-American and Australian-American collaboration was more substantial than was the case with the Latin countries, which suggests that during the war cultural distance was more of an obstacle to cooperative activities than was geographical distance.

Wartime cooperation in most cases was a matter of high politics, involving much diplomatic negotiation and requiring the attention of the political leaders in the various countries, even in the United States. The outstanding example—and it was a rare one—of cooperation which became substantially bureaucratic and permitted problems to be dealt with as technical questions, was the Canadian-American Permanent Joint Board on Defense. Another was the administrative arrangements for construction and local supplies needed by American forces based in Australia. President Roosevelt's personal intervention both at home and with leaders in the foreign capitals often seemed indispensable to getting a cooperative project over national hurdles, including those thrown up by affected administrative officials. Yet trust between the United States and its middle-power allies visibly increased with their collaboration during the war. In no case did a government "learn" by saying "this time we did join an enterprise but never again."

No matter how cooperative, however, none of the middle powers won a place at discussions of global strategy and post-war planning, even when their own forces were involved. Asymmetry showed itself also in the essence of the bargains, namely, politically difficult concessions made by the smaller allies in return for American protection of their territory and, for the Latin American countries, implicit United States support for their regimes. With so much to offer, the Americans could usually call the tune in such exchanges, but the others were free to limit their responses and did so when they did not consider their interests close to those of the United States.

FIVE

POSTWAR COLLABORATION IN DEFENSE

WITH THE END OF World War II and the advent of a very different global power configuration, practices of defense cooperation which had developed during a period of intense danger and national insecurity were unlikely to persist. Yet the onset of the cold war revived some of these practices, as the various governments each responded to its own interpretation of the threat of Russian and/or Communist expansion and to the proposals of the United States as leader in various coalitions to compete militarily with its superpower rival. Despite the easing of cold war tensions after the defusing of the Cuban missile crisis, the rivalry has persisted. In the thirty years since the end of World War II, however, this often quasi-military conflict has taken different forms, and other changes in the external environment, as well as in domestic leadership, have occurred. Military cooperation of each of the four middle powers with the United States has flowed and ebbed accordingly.

By far the closest defense cooperation throughout this period is to be found between Canada and the United States, although in a variety of ways Australians also collaborated closely with Americans in defense matters. In the case of both Commonwealth countries, experiences during World War II taught United States officials to perceive them as countries quite independent of Britain and quite ready to uphold their own national views. A comparison of the North Atlantic Treaty Organization (NATO) with the Southeast Asia Treaty Organization (SEATO) or of the North American Air Defense Command (NORAD) arrangements with those of the Australian–New Zealand–United States alliance (ANZUS) shows that the Australian connections with the United States were more attenuated. So were Australian domestic repercussions from defense-related controversies with the United States during most of this period.

There were real differences between the two Commonwealth countries' behavior in the Korean theater; in contrast to Australia, the Canadians rather unwillingly joined the Americans in this "United Nations" action, which soon took a turn the Canadian government would have avoided. In another area the two countries diverged; Australians helped carry out the Berlin airlift, while Canadians took no part. (Nor did Canadians directly after the war appear eager to participate in the occupation of Germany, while Australia pressed hard and successfully for a role in the occupation of Japan.) [1] Two decades later Australians staunchly (even stubbornly) reinforced Americans in Vietnam, while the Canadians, exempted from pressure to participate by membership on the International Control Commission, eventually became critics of United States policy in that war. Canadians, however, have actively engaged in United Nations peacekeeping operations, while the Australians for various reasons have taken relatively little part.

In part because of domestic considerations in the two Latin American countries, the story of their postwar defense cooperation with the United States is brief or, in Mexico's case, almost nonexistent. Always uneasy in working closely with Americans in the area of defense, Mexicans confined their contacts, for the most part, to sending some military officers to the Inter-American Defense College (the establishment of which they had earlier opposed) and to some American professional-military training schools. (A minor type of cooperation, carried over from World War II, was some mapping of a limited part of their territory, near the United States border.) The Mexicans continually stressed that the Rio pact of 1947 and the Organization of American States charter had no military-alliance implications, and they were strong opponents of the American proposal in the 1960s to set up an inter-American peacekeeping force. A few years after the Chapultepec conference (where Mexico favored a regional approach), Mexicans began to emphasize the superior juridical role of the United Nations, without taking part in any United Nations peacekeeping operations. Unlike almost all of the other Latin American countries, Mexico accepted no American military mission of any sort and was unwilling to participate in the bilateral United States military-aid programs for Latin America set up in 1951. The Mexican government emphasized that the satellite tracking station at Guaymas was an entirely civilian, scientific joint enterprise for the exploration of outer space through Project Mercury. [2] Mexicans realized that their country formed part of a zone which American military strategists considered a "mainline of national defense,'' and they counted on potential enemies to share this perspective.[3] In contrast to the Canadians, they felt no compulsion to share in the burden.

Unlike the Mexicans, with their steadily held attitude of aloofness (which was related to their desire to maintain civilian supremacy over their military), Brazilians alternated between warmly responding to American defense overtures and dragging their feet on military cooperation. These shifts depended almost entirely on the domestic political balance, although the current government's view of Brazil's appropriate international role was also a factor. President Vargas's efforts to keep all factions satisfied required caution in responding to the Americans. Mutual suspicion between Brazilians and Americans during the leftist regimes of Quadros and Goulart contrasted with reciprocated cordiality when the military were in the ascendant. Brazilian–American defense ties included military training of Brazilian officers in the United States, joint naval maneuvers, a missile tracking station on Fernando de Noronha, United States military missions in Brazil, and American grants-in-aid for procuring military equipment for Brazilian forces. (Brazil also took part in some United Nations peacekeeping operations.)

Compared to those in other parts of the world, the ratios of defense expenditures to gross national product in Latin America are low. Mexico's is unusually low, even for Latin America, while Brazil's is high for the region, reflecting concern for internal security and for Brazil's uncertain relations with its South American neighbors, especially Argentina. Armed forces in proportion to population were low also for both countries, representing about .2 percent in 1967.[4] Although higher than the ratios in Latin American countries, Canadian defense expenditures as a percentage of GNP declined markedly throughout the 1960s. Australia's rose as a result of the Vietnam war but started from a base much lower than that of Canada's in the early 1960s. At no time was either country's defense expenditures–GNP ratio close to that of the United States, and the same was true for the ratio of men under arms to total population.[5] These contrasts should be kept in mind in noting ways in which the superpower and the four middle powers responded to each other's security needs following World War II. In tables 2 through 5, data on defense expenditures and numbers of men under arms in the giant power and the middle powers can be compared.

TABLE 2   DEFENSE EXPENDITURES OF FOUR MIDDLE POWERS AND THE
UNITED STATES, 1969–1973 (millions of US dollars)

	1969	1970	1971	1972	1973
Australia	1,294	1,226	1,250	1,451	1,873
Brazil	803	1,054	1,127	1,241	1,328
Canada	1,763	1,975	2,111	2,257	2,391
Mexico	205	220	250	296	344
USA	81,433	77,854	74,862	77,638	78,462

TABLE 3   DEFENSE EXPENDITURES AS A PERCENTAGE OF GROSS NATIONAL
PRODUCT FOR FOUR MIDDLE POWERS AND THE UNITED STATES, 1969–1973

	1969	1970	1971	1972	1973
Australia	4.4	3.8	3.5	3.5	3.2
Brazil	2.4	2.7	2.6	2.5	2.1
Canada	2.4	2.4	2.3	2.2	2.0
Mexico	0.7	0.7	0.7	0.7	0.7
USA	8.8	8.0	7.1	6.7	6.1

TABLE 4   PER CAPITA DEFENSE EXPENDITURES OF FOUR MIDDLE POWERS
AND THE UNITED STATES, 1969–1973 (constant US dollars)

	1969	1970	1971	1972	1973
Australia	133	118	113	112	106
Brazil	10	12	12	12	12
Canada	103	106	104	103	102
Mexico	5	5	5	5	5
USA	458	411	374	372	353

Source for tables 2, 3, and 4: Arms Control and Disarmament Agency, *World Military Expenditures and Arms Trade, 1963–1973* (1975).

JOINTNESS

BRAZIL AND MEXICO

The only joint defense activity engaged in by the United States and either of the two Latin American countries was Brazilian participation in *Unitas,* naval maneuvers which the United States periodically carried out with

TABLE 5   MEN UNDER ARMS, NUMBER AND PERCENTAGE OF MEN OF MILITARY
AGE, FOR FOUR MIDDLE POWERS AND THE UNITED STATES, 1972–1975

	1972		1973		1974		1975	
	Number	*Percent*	*Number*	*Percent*	*Number*	*Percent*	*Number*	*Percent*
Australia	88,100	3.5	73,300	2.8	68,851	2.6	88,300	2.6
Brazil	198,000	1.1	208,000	1.2	208,000	1.1	195,000	1.3
Canada	84,000	2.0	83,000	1.8	83,000	1.8	85,000	1.7
Mexico	73,200	0.8	71,000	0.8	82,000	0.9	a	a
USA	2,391,000	6.1	2,252,900	5.8	2,174,000	5.5	2,130,000	5.1

Source: International Institute for Strategic Studies, *The Military Balance, 1972–73* through
1975–76.
[a] Figures for 1975 are not entirely comparable to earlier figures.

Brazil, Argentina, and Uruguay for antisubmarine-warfare training.[6] Despite
considerable United States direct pressure and indirect pressure through the
OAS, neither Mexico nor Brazil sent forces to the United Nations action in
Korea. The Mexican ambassador convincingly pleaded domestic restraints to
any contribution, and the Brazilian ambassador gave the usual promise to
consider a role, from which nothing ever eventuated.[7]

AUSTRALIA

The prospect of war in Asia, to say nothing of actual war, touched
Australian security much more directly than the security of the other three
powers. Immediately after World War II, Minister of External Affairs Evatt
was unsuccessful in negotiating continuation, under common auspices, of
the huge American-built base on Manus Island in the Admiralties (part of
Australia's earlier New Guinea mandate). He shared the desire of certain elements in the United States government that some kind of joint use be
arranged. The American terms, however, were one-sided, and the two governments' conditions diverged widely. Neither side perceived a common interest sufficient to lead it to modify its demands. United States officials were
cool, to say the least, to Evatt's insistence that the bargain include some
kind of security pact for the South Pacific open to other Commonwealth
countries. The project collapsed when appropriations for the United States
Navy were cut back drastically and its tasks contracted to an area much further north in the Pacific.[8]

The Australians' continuing concern to keep the United States committed in the Pacific was one reason for their prompt contribution to the United Nations action in Korea. Having already dispatched to Korea the Royal Australian Air Force squadron stationed in Japan and the Australian warships then in Japanese waters, they responded quickly (ahead of the British) to the United Nations request for ground forces and by their actions markedly increased goodwill toward themselves within the United States government.[9]

The Australians were so eager to have American protection in the Pacific that they interpreted their obligations under the Southeast Asia treaty to include the joining of their armed forces with those of the United States in Vietnam, beginning in 1962. Thereafter, they followed with their own forces all the stages of escalation set by the Americans until 1967, when they had eight thousand men in Vietnam. The Australian government did not begin withdrawal of its forces when the Americans began to withdraw, for as Prime Minister John Gorton put it, he shared the United States view that those nearer the danger should bear more of the burden, not less of it, as Americans reduced their own forces.[10] But gradually the withdrawals took place, until by December, 1971, all forces were out—this time ahead of Americans—leaving behind only some advisors and instructors. The remnants of participation were quickly removed after the change in the Australian government of December, 1972.

In 1963, Australia joined the United States, Britain, Canada, and New Zealand in agreeing to cooperate in development of some kinds of military equipment with a view to standardization. To some extent, standardization also has occurred because of Australian procurement of equipment in either the United States or Britain. Although the Australian government has more than once stated its intention to seek standardization, or at least compatibility, with its allies in military equipment, the progress of this kind of jointness—whether deliberately sought or a by-product of overseas procurement—has been slow. Inevitably, standardization has the drawback of producing a kind of logistical dependence for the lesser ally.[11]

Most of the numerous space-research and satellite-tracking projects which are jointly undertaken in Australia are primarily civilian in character. Two, however, are definitely labeled defense, and some Australians believe that others easily could be converted into military projects—if such functions as surveillance of potential enemy nuclear installations by satellite are not construed as such now. The secrecy surrounding them has made their critics suspicious about just how joint these facilities are in practice.[12]

CANADA

Although reluctant to join the United Nations forces fighting under United States leadership in Korea and unwilling to participate in Vietnam except as a member of the International Control Commission, Canada did engage in several important joint measures for continental defense. The Canadian-American relationship in the North American Air Defense Command is clearly asymmetric as to input of forces and benefits in security. For a relatively small contribution, the Canadians have shared the command and avoided several unpleasant alternatives, including expensive duplication and the possibility that in an emergency the United States might take unilateral action over Canadian air space.[13] Canadians believed that an attack on Canada would be like an attack on the United States and would invoke the same response; Canada could not choose noncooperation.[14]

True to their unmilitary outlook and fearful of encroachments on their sovereignty, Canadians were hardly eager, directly after World War II, to respond affirmatively to American proposals for some joint protection of the continent, the northern areas of which had begun to appear to the Americans very vulnerable.[15] Nevertheless, by 1947 Canada had joined the United States in establishing weather, communications, and winter-condition experimental stations in the far north, had conducted joint naval exercises, and had agreed to work toward a number of objectives: interchanges of defense personnel; standardization in equipment, organization, and training methods; cooperation in weapons development; and mutual availability of defense facilities. At the same time, the two countries agreed to indefinite continuation of the Permanent Joint Board on Defense. The only United States air base to exist on Canadian soil was that established during World War II at Goose Bay, Newfoundland, when it was a British dependency. After Newfoundland joined the Canadian federation in 1949, Canada agreed to honor the rights that the United States had earlier acquired.[16]

Uneasiness over lopsided bilateral defense cooperation with the United States made the prospect of a North Atlantic alliance appealing to Canadians and helps to explain their early initiative in promoting this multilateral arrangement. As Canadians have sometimes quipped, they "brought in the Old World to correct the imbalance in the New World." Since the late 1940s, there has been a constant tension between giving priority to NATO requirements or to those for continental defense, especially after Canadian civilian leaders failed in their attempt to tie the two closely together.

The capacity for the two North American countries to be useful to each other, great in World War II, increased during the cold war, especially because of technological changes in warfare. In the words of Canadian General Charles Faulkes, "There were no boundaries upstairs. . . ." [17] Canada lay directly between the two superpowers, while its centers of population lay along its boundary with the United States. The Strategic Air Command, upon which all members of the Atlantic alliance depended for nuclear deterrence, could best be guarded at some distance, which included the air space over Canadian territory, and therefore could be guarded in part by Canadian forces. Other aspects of this symbiotic relationship in which Canada could offer such advantages as expertise in military affairs and defense research, unusual geographical conditions for testing defense procedures, and ease of personal communication and understanding among defense officials might be duplicated in Australia, but the strategic location of Canada was unique.

The degree of integration in North American air defense is unparalleled in the defense relations of the United States with any other country. [18] The three electronic networks, the Mid-Canada line, the Pinetree line, and the DEW (Distant Early Warning) line, were created at different times for warning, tracking, and eventually intercepting bombers. All on Canadian territory, they were constructed partly by Americans and partly by Canadians; formulas for sharing the costs and manning the stations varied. [19] The whole system was integrated and centrally controlled at what became NORAD headquarters in Colorado Springs. Eventually the system was linked with the Ballistic Missile Early Warning System, its sites located in Alaska, Greenland, and Britain, yet part of the warning system for NORAD as well as for NATO. [20]

The electronic warning systems were constructed during the 1950s, prior to the formal establishment of NORAD in 1958 but as part of the growing integration of continental defense which culminated in the joint command. NORAD integrates those parts of the services of the two countries which together defend the continent against air attack—through surveillance, detection, and possible destruction of enemy bombers. The watch, composed of specialists of both countries, integrates information drawn from many parts of the world, as it monitors missiles, aircraft, and objects orbiting in space.

A single chief (an American) has under him all forces in North America concerned with air defense; his deputy is a Canadian, and the headquarters staff is integrated. The regions of the command cross the boundaries separating the two countries; not only may the deputy commander-in-chief on occasion command American as well as Canadian forces, but those in charge of the regions include Canadian officers with responsibilities for areas in the United States. Most of the fighter-interceptor squadrons are American. As a result of a 1975 adjustment of regional command boundaries which created a new center in Edmonton, Alberta, all operations over Canada became subject to control from centers in Canada, centers manned by Canadians.[21]

Canada contributes almost 12 percent of the total annual cost of the NORAD system. From a peak of 2,053 aircraft committed to NORAD by the two countries in 1961, of which 162 were Canadian, the total had dropped to 540 in 1972, 48 of them Canadian.[22] The commander-in-chief of NORAD is responsible both to the Joint Chiefs of Staff of the United States and to the chief of the Defense Staff of Canada, who superseded the Chiefs of Staff Committee of Canada in 1964. On occasion, training exercises for continental defense have included other parts of the Canadian and American air forces and have covered states in the American South and Southwest as well as Canadian provinces.[23]

Closely related to the development of NORAD, the practices which became the Defense Production Sharing Program grew by accretion even before the two governments announced in October, 1950, an agreement on principles of economic cooperation which included the intention to renounce barriers to exchange of defense material. Numerous "understandings," through exchanges of letters, have enabled the program to function, the most important being the agreement of December, 1958, which gave more formality and substance to the program. The program provided for greater integration of the development and production of military equipment, with the aim of promoting more rational defense procurement in both countries. One vital element of the program was the requirement that military purchasers for the United States give equal consideration to potential suppliers from Canada. The two governments have taken steps to increase the flow of information between the two countries regarding defense planning and technical matters related to defense supplies, including access to necessary classified information. They have also removed such obstacles to reciprocal procurement and flow of defense goods between Canada and the United States as export licenses, provisions of the Buy American Act, and customs duties on most defense items.

Canadian officials actively sought this program as a way to maintain a Canadian defense industry, which might otherwise have fallen prey to all the disabilities that a small market and limited technological sophistication entail. Instead, Canada has been able to sell defense equipment to the Americans and, to a lesser extent, to other countries, while maintaining access to sophisticated arms at a reasonable cost. United States military officials were so eager to have a wide production and supply base to support continental defense arrangements that the Canadians were not required to match the kinds of concessions granted by the United States. The program has a high technology content and has permitted Canadian industry to provide such items as aircraft components (about 50 percent of the Canadian sales), navigation and communication equipment, components for ammunition, ship components. Hardly any complete systems have been included, but the increasing dependence of American defense industries on Canadian components has suggested the difficulty of disentangling this integrating program even if one of the two governments so desired.[24] At the Americans' request, the principle of a rough balance in the two countries' purchases from each other was accepted in 1963, but during the Vietnam war Canada's sales grew far in excess of its purchases from the United States. Yet the Canadians were able to resist pressures exerted by United States officials in 1971 to purchase specific American-made defense commodities.

Like NORAD, in which use of territory and exercise of command are to some extent and for some purposes shared, the Defense Production Sharing Program by its nature has entailed special concessions by each country to the other. Canada did not extend tariff exemptions to American defense products until 1966, and from 1963 onwards, some of its defense companies received American aid in research and development that put them on a par with those across the border. From one point of view, for the United States to remove barriers and actively open its giant market to Canadian defense producers on equal terms with Americans would appear to be an extraordinary concession. Yet the United States profited from an enlarged secure source of supply for defense materiel, from some economies of scale, from the benefits of standardization, and from a strengthened ally more politically reliable for having received this response to its needs. For neither government did economic considerations have priority over other values. In carrying out the agreements, the governments imposed conditions which tied the defense industries closely together, regardless of optimal allocation of resources.[25] Each country has procured defense items from other countries, but not on the same scale nor so unhindered by the usual governmental barriers nor through such active promotion.

Stepping up the Defense Production Sharing Program in 1960 was one way the Americans could help out a Canadian government highly embarrassed when it finally had to abandon its disastrous Avrow Arrow project. Mounting costs, shrinking markets, development delays, and rapid technological change eventually made Canada's last effort to produce a wholly new aircraft impossible. Thus the promises of the United States government greatly to increase procurement in Canada were a welcome consolation prize, whatever the feelings of Canadian nationalists that American purchases of the Arrow would have saved the program.[26]

Aside from political difficulties, to be discussed later, the major obstacle to maintaining or even increasing the jointness of continental defense has been technological change, represented by ballistic missiles and satellites, which made the use of Canadian territory seem less vital to American defense officials. Meanwhile, in the late 1960s Canadian and American views on the military threat were diverging from the near unanimity which had developed in the late 1940s. Prime Minister Diefenbaker's delay in 1962 in approving a full alert at the time of the Cuban missile crisis had a lasting effect on those planning new developments in continental defense. The prime minister did not share the sense of urgency felt by many of his subordinates and by President Kennedy's advisers, nor did his successors become enthusiastic about the plans of the Johnson and Nixon administrations for an ABM system. When Canadian government leaders were put into the picture, they passively opposed the plans. The 1968 renewal of NORAD specifically excluded a Canadian commitment to participate actively in ballistic-missile defense.

As for the continued need for joint defense against bomber attacks, the Canadian government's agreement to renew NORAD in 1973 (for two years) and again in 1975 (for five years) indicated that though bombers might be a diminishing threat, Canadian leaders agreed with their American counterparts that they remained a contingency to be guarded against.[27] Meanwhile, the two governments were cooperating in research for over-the-horizon radar.[28]

Although Canadians and Americans have engaged in numerous joint defense projects, one which began in World War II did not survive: research on nuclear weapons. Anglo-Canadian-American cooperation ended in 1946, killed in effect by the United States Atomic Energy Act of 1946.[29] The Canadians, without ever taking a specific decision, simply passed by the opportunity to become a nuclear power. In view of the exclusivist views of American leaders, this may have been prudent. In the late 1950s, however, American officials might have welcomed cooperation with Canada on atomic weaponry more than with any other country; but Canadians, in government and out, have a strong bias against nuclear weapons. They did subsequently cooperate in research on peaceful uses of atomic energy, as well as in space research.

RECIPROCITY

Changing circumstances have altered many reciprocal arrangements made by the United States and three of the middle powers within the framework of the multilateral alliances created in the late 1940s and early 1950s: NATO, ANZUS, SEATO, and the Rio pact.

Whatever capacity Mexico might have had to be useful to the United States as an ally in this period, it chose not to regard the Rio pact as imposing any obligation for advance military planning with the United States, and Mexican officials consistently have described their government as not being militarily aligned with any bloc. For a considerable period, Brazil took a different tack—except during the brief administration of Quadros and that of his successor Goulart, overthrown by the military coup of 1964.[30]

After some foot dragging over promises about limiting trade with Communist countries and about United States access to strategic resources, Brazil was one of the seven Latin American countries which accepted the American interpretation of the Rio pact as a collective-security device; in 1953 it took advantage of the United States Mutual Security Act to sign a Mutual Defense Assistance agreement. Of the relatively small amount of military aid allocated to Latin America, Brazil received the giant's share and in return promised to maintain certain military units for hemisphere defense and to live up to the ten conditions for military assistance laid down by Congress. In the twenty-year period covering fiscal years 1950 through 1969, the grand total of expenditures for military-assistance deliveries to all countries was $33,850,100,000. Of this amount, $724,900,000 went to Latin

TABLE 6 UNITED STATES MILITARY ASSISTANCE PROGRAMS: GRANT-AID
DELIVERIES TO SELECTED COUNTRIES AND TOTAL AID, 1950–1973 (millions of
US dollars)

....

	1950–64	1965	1966	1967	1968	1969	1970	1971	1972	1973
Brazil	159.7	11.4	9.5	13.4	12.6	6.6	4.3	2.0	.9	.7
Mexico	.9	.2	.2	.2	.1	.1				
Latin America	440.9									
All countries	29,430.5									

Sources: Department of Defense, *Military Assistance and Foreign Military Sales Facts* (March,
1970); *Statistical Abstract of the United States.*

America; Brazil received $213,300,000.[31] A kind of reprise of World War
II exchanges followed the intensifying of the Korean War; Brazil traded
willingness to sell strategic resources and promises to participate in hemisphere defense for broadly construed military aid which, in fact, furthered
its economic development. Considering the unlikelihood of aggression from
abroad, the fanciful nature of collective hemisphere defense, and the probable source of internal threats to Brazil, the reciprocity of United States–
Brazil defense arrangements seemed asymmetrical to many commentators.[32]
In return for some very general commitments that seemed valuable to the
global strategists in Washington, the Brazilians for many years were able to
negotiate receipt of goods and services of great substance. Table 6 shows
trends in military aid to Brazil over a lengthy period, provides a contrast between that received by Brazil and the remainder of Latin America, and indicates the very small amount which went to Mexico.

   Less asymmetrical benefits flowed to the two countries under a very
tangible reciprocal arrangement negotiated by the United States and Brazil
in 1957–1958, concerning Fernando de Noronha. On this island far out in
the South Atlantic, which had been the site of a World War II American
military installation, Brazil permitted the United States to construct a
guided-missile tracking station. As part of the agreement, the United States
furnished materiel to Brazilian armed forces and, after prolonged further negotiations, promised, in recognition of the increased strategic significance of
the poverty-stricken Northeast, to help Brazil restructure the region's transport and communications systems and aid in its economic development.
North American technicians were to construct and operate the guided-missile

installation, aided by Brazilian specialists, who would gradually take over the jobs.[33]

It was, however, with the two Commonwealth countries that the United States made important reciprocal defense arrangements. Both the Canadian and Australian foreign ministers took initiatives in launching the respective alliances which made them military partners of the United States, the North Atlantic alliance and ANZUS. The two countries appeared attractive to the United States as allies partly because of their location and military reliability and partly because their proposals fitted into broader security interests of the United States. The Americans responded accordingly.

Canadian Secretary of State for External Affairs Louis St. Laurent made his proposals in 1948 at about the time when the Brussels pact countries were also seeking a wider defense coalition and an American commitment. Canadian membership in such an alliance would make it truly a transatlantic grouping rather than merely another form of United States support for Western Europe at a time when Soviet expansion was clearly evident in Czechslovakia and Berlin. Furthermore, Canada was then a relatively important military power willing and able to help the European countries, which were only beginning to recover from the ravages of war.[34] Canada demonstrated its usefulness through the high quality of its forces, ground and air, which were eventually sent to the forward area and which were prized by NATO military headquarters and United States defense officials as a model for the forces of members of comparable rank. Furthermore, the Canadian navy played an important part in patrolling the northwestern Atlantic to guard the sea communications of the alliance.

For the Australians, on the other hand, it was more difficult to demonstrate a usefulness that would evoke the desired response from Americans. Although Minister for External Affairs Evatt had failed in the late 1940s to get a formal United States commitment for some kind of mutual defense in the South Pacific, his successor, Sir Percy Spender, eventually won it in 1951. At that time, the Truman administration was having difficulty selling its proposals for a nonpunitive Japanese peace treaty to Australia and New Zealand.[35]

Both Australians and New Zealanders needed reassurance, if the terms of peace with Japan were to be as lenient as the Americans preferred, in the light of the new menace in the Far East, this time from the Communist powers. Eager that experiences of World War II not be replicated because of another concentration of American attention on Europe, the South Pacific states wanted a treaty like that establishing the North Atlantic alliance or some tangible link to the global security system headed by the United States, in order that their defense interests would not again be overlooked. To win this, they were even willing to join a grouping that omitted Britain, but they insisted on a solemn covenant rather than merely a presidential promise.[36]

The Southeast Asia treaty, concluded three years after the ANZUS agreement, when changing circumstances led Americans to want a broader range of Pacific-area allies, appealed to the Australians as another sign of American commitment to the Far East. Compared to the earlier engagement, SEATO's meaning for the defense of Southeast Asia, its larger membership, and the opportunity to coordinate defense planning and conduct exercises were less important.[37]

Some political opponents of the government in Australia were quick to point out how much weaker the provisions of the two Pacific treaties were than those of the North Atlantic pact. In the Southeast Asia treaty, the United States agreed only in lopsided fashion to act in cases of *Communist* aggression; in that treaty, as under the ANZUS pact, it joined the other members in committing itself to act to meet the common danger "in accordance with its constitutional processes." Although the Australians succeeded in getting the Southeast Asia pact to include phrasing that looked toward joint military planning under the council set up by the pact, neither under this treaty nor under the ANZUS agreement were any forces brought into being comparable to those assembled on the central front in Europe after NATO was organized. In fact, except for a council, even an organization was missing in the case of ANZUS. Meetings with top American foreign and defense officials, much valued by Australians as an entrée into certain aspects of United States decision making, did not take place from October, 1959, to May, 1962. Australians took comfort in the scope of ANZUS, which covered attacks on "the island territories under [Australia's] jurisdiction in the Pacific or on its armed forces, public vessels or aircraft in the Pacific" (Article V). They also were pleased to underline Secretary of State Dean Rusk's affirmation, made to the Thai prime minister, that SEATO's obligation "is individual as well as collective." [38]

It was the *collective* aspect of the Atlantic alliance that accounted for Canada's responsiveness. The North Atlantic treaty offered the Canadians a fine opportunity not only to further their security through strengthening that of Western Europe but also to solve a long-standing problem that had domestic as well as foreign implications. Through the alliance, Canada could balance its relations among the two mother countries, England and France, and its giant neighbor, the United States. Canadians also hoped to make continental defense part of a larger scheme that would dilute their close military cooperation with the Americans. Canadians believed they could play a more significant role as part of a wider coalition than as just an isolated neighbor of the United States. By a unanimous vote of its parliament, Canada was the first to ratify the North Atlantic treaty.[39]

Australia's desire for ANZUS, unlike Canada's for the North Atlantic alliance, was based on a divergence of security views from those held by Americans; Australians and Americans, however, shortly came together in their perspectives. "Without the threat of Communism, there would have been—there would be—no alliance, even though the alliance was concerned with more than the Communist threat." [40] The Australian government's fear of communism was not confined to the external threat; Communist-infiltrated labor unions had caused trouble and could be dangerous at ports in time of stress. The responsibilities of Australia in itself meeting the Asian threat rather than relying only on the United States grew in importance in Australian official thinking during the 1960s, partly in response to American pressures.[41]

Canadian perspectives on NATO moved in the opposite direction, away from very real concern with Soviet intentions and capabilities in Europe. Like Australians, Canadians had undergone unnerving experiences with Russian espionage in their midst; these had helped to destroy the early postwar feeling of need to be trusting toward the Soviet Union. Later, especially in the 1960s, the Canadians veered toward the belief that the Soviet threat was not so great as to demand the kind of sacrifices in defense budgeting and international cooperation made earlier. In any case, those closer to the danger should carry much more of the burden. For the *relative* military strength of Canada had been declining with the marked rise in European defense capabilities, and technological changes in warfare were making less and less satisfactory to Canadians the particular military roles they had earlier accepted in NATO. An effort in 1960 by the Canadians to move back their forces in Germany from the front line was successfully opposed by the supreme command. The Canadians' earlier success in making their views clearly heard on alliance policy gradually disappeared in the 1960s, although they were leaders in the successful conciliation of France when in 1966 it withdrew from formal participation in the organization.

The Kennedy administration's dumbbell concept seemed to leave no room for Canada. The Canadians were cool to the proposal for a multilateral force (MLF) that was hotly debated elsewhere in 1963, and the bigger allies seemed unreceptive to their own proposals, first made in 1964, for different nuclear arrangements to meet the needs of the nonnuclear powers. Meanwhile, other allies, large and small, were reducing their own forces in the forward area, and the Canadians particularly noted the British and American dilutions of strength. Thus in 1969 Prime Minister Trudeau's government proposed drastic reductions in Canadian forces in Europe, which were modified somewhat after allied protests. Nevertheless, the forces were cut in half by 1971 to five thousand men. The ground forces finally were moved to the rear. Only three out of what had once been eight air squadrons were retained on the central front; the two having a nuclear-strike role were modified to a conventional-attack capability. The Canadians stressed that their special contribution would be provision of a more mobile force, less important on the central front, more important on the northern flank. The Canadians had to contend with the European allies' inclination to regard them as surrogates for the Americans, and they turned a deaf ear to pleas not to make reductions which many feared would spark a much bigger and more significant withdrawal of American forces. Instead of withholding a decision which came at a difficult time for the American government, the Canadian government appeared eager to move in an independent direction before a possible change in United States policy. (The United States did not make the anticipated change.) Nevertheless, five years later the Canadian government was among the strongest supporters of NATO.[42]

Despite its obvious potentiality to be useful, Canada, like Australia if not so markedly, was limited by the size of its population and economy from making a large defense contribution to the alliance led by the United States, especially when compared to Britain, France, or Germany. Furthermore, the defense efforts of Canada and Australia, like those of most middle powers, were rigidly defined by budgetary considerations, rather than by an independent strategic evaluation of the countries' needs. One reason for Canada's reduction of the number of air squadrons stationed in Europe was the desire to modernize them in such a way that the same type of equipment could be used for forces stationed elsewhere, thus saving the expense of special equipment suitable only for the European role.[43]

Just as special concessions by the United States to Canada and vice versa were made under NORAD rather than under NATO, so reciprocal arrangements between the United States and Australia were devised under ANZUS rather than under SEATO. Thus the Australian government referred to obligations under ANZUS in granting permission to the United States Navy to install the communications station for Polaris submarines at North West Cape in 1962. The same was true for the Pine Gap installation for defense space research outside Alice Springs and that near Woomera. North West Cape is on the Indian Ocean, an area not covered specifically by ANZUS, but at the time, the two governments shared concern about increasing Soviet naval activity in that area. The facilities linked Australia to American nuclear defenses, and their establishment differed, therefore, from the agreements for reciprocal use of facilities first made in 1947, at the time when Australia purchased some destroyers from the United States and the two countries granted each other the right to use certain shore dumps and bases.[44] Yet all these concessions were linked to the global strategy of the United States rather than to its interest in the immediate region of which Australia was a part.

American global strategy also motivated the Mutual Weapons Development Assistance agreement concluded between the United States and Australia in 1960, an arrangement which clearly was not a special concession to the latter, who paid its own way. Although Australia acquired important technical capabilities for developing weapons of interest to both countries, with valued contributions to Australia's own technological progress, the terms were humiliating. They were the same terms exacted of far less developed countries and specified by congressional act, but the Australian government resented having to promise such things as "to fulfill any military obligations which it has assumed under multilateral or bilateral agreements or treaties to which the United States is a party. . . ."[45] Other frictions not conducive to closer collaboration were caused by American insensitivity to the Australians' sensitivity about their unequal power status. Thus when John Foster Dulles arrived at Manila in September, 1954, to negotiate the Southeast Asia pact, he told the conferees he had only three days to spend on the task because he had a fixed date to consult with Chiang Kai-Shek, a statement which tended to put the other conferees, including the rather resentful Australians, in their place.[46] The secrecy required by the Americans regarding the dozen or so installations, defense and otherwise, which they have been allowed to build in Australia became another source of great domestic embarrassment for the Australian government of the day. Like other allies, many Australian citizens feared that such cooperation made them a prime target for the ostensible Communist enemy. Yet, unlike the Canadians, the Australians put relatively few constraints on the use of their territory; in particular, they had no central control over the North West Cape station.[47]

Recriprocal concessions for a mutually desired objective are somewhat distinguishable from actions of two countries which move in parallel lines agreeable to both countries and toward a common objective but without special agreement on any linkage. Thus Canadian services in providing United Nations peacekeeping forces, something which the United States could not do if it wished, furthered American interests in curbing violence. Australia has long had a security interest in the area of Malaysia and Singapore, to which it has contributed forces since 1955 in collaboration with New Zealand and Britain (ANZAM). Prime Minister Menzies was satisfied with the response he received from the United States when first these forces were sent: that United States cooperation was "implicit in the Manila Pact" if ANZAM forces protecting nonself-governing Malaya needed it. After establishment of the independence of Malaysia, which did not join SEATO, Australia sought further American assurance at the time of the Indonesian-Malaysian "confrontation," in 1963–1964. Although the responses were ambiguous, the Australian government declared itself satisfied that its troops were covered by ANZUS "in the Pacific area." [48]

In the late 1960s, when Malaysia and Singapore were faced with British withdrawal from the Far East, United States officials commended the Australians for promising to help fill the vacuum.[49] Although the officials avoided giving any American guarantee to help in case of trouble, they were happy to have the Australians perform a function that the Americans were unfitted to perform.

SPECIFICITY

All four middle powers have shared one characteristic in dealing with the United States: in general, they preferred a relationship that was multilateral but, when specific issues arose, fell easily and even willingly into the tendency of the Americans to treat them on a bilateral basis. More marked in the cases of Mexico and Brazil, the characteristic was even observable in Canada's case, namely, in its acceptance of a continental defense arrangement essentially separate from NATO and in its preference for a defense-production sharing program not extended to other allies.[50]

What about specific responses to cooperative agreements? When both NORAD and (indirectly) NATO were put to the practical test at the time of the Cuban missile crisis, Prime Minister Diefenbaker dragged his feet before formally placing Canada's NORAD forces on alert. Canadian defense officials were, nevertheless, doing all they legally could to implement what they regarded as Canada's obligations.[51] Although Canada responded to the call of NATO for a buildup of its European strength at the time of the 1961 Berlin Crisis, it did so with less alacrity than that shown by countries which felt more threatened, and the same was true for the crisis prompted by the Soviet invasion of Czechoslovakia in 1968.[52]

In contrast was Australia's quick response to the United States request for dispatch of an air squadron to Thailand in 1962; shortly after this event, the Australians reaffirmed Secretary of State Rusk's statement to the Thai prime minister that the SEATO obligation was both unilateral and multilateral.[53] That same year Australia began to send military advisers to Vietnam, the start of its participation in the war. Watching an unfriendly Indonesia under Sukarno with growing concern, the Australians in the course of that same critical year were relieved to have special envoy Averell Harriman reassure them that New Guinea was indeed covered by the United States guarantee to Australia under ANZUS.[54] The Americans' ability to persuade their middle-power allies to support them substantially seemed to depend at least in part on how immediate and specific the peril looked to the allies' governments.

DISTANCE

During the tenure of the Australian Labor government in the immediate postwar years, as External Affairs Minister Evatt tried to give Australia a world role independent of the great powers, the United States government became somewhat estranged from this wartime ally. The scene changed markedly in 1949, when Menzies returned to power.[55] Despite the assertion of his foreign minister, Sir Percy Spender, that the Australians at first had some difficulty in recognizing the proper channels to use in the United States Department of State, former Secretary of State Dean Acheson recorded that his friend Menzies was a past master in knowing his way around Washington (as Minister R. G. Casey had been, early in World War II).[56] It was not that the Australians always got the access they desired; they found John Foster Dulles not particularly communicative, even when he went to Canberra ostensibly to discuss the Japanese peace treaty in February, 1951.[57]

From this meeting, the Australians eventually secured what they wanted. ANZUS gave Australia, in the words of R. G. Casey, "access to the thinking and planning of the American Administration at the highest political level . . . and . . . in turn the means of putting our own views forward at the same level in complete frankness and friendliness!" [58] From his soundings among Washington officials and members of Congress, External Affairs Minister Spender knew that although Americans were warm to his country, it was "on the international plane, rather small fry." [59] With ANZUS, Australians hoped to overcome some of their sense of remoteness from global affairs.

In somewhat the same position as the Australians, the Canadians found that the promises to "consult" which were embedded in formal agreements often turned out to be mostly a right to be informed. Nevertheless, they found comfort in being definitely more inside than outside, and indeed in defense matters they were usually more inside American decision making than were most of the other allies. For this reason, they continued to value both NORAD and NATO as ways to maintain the close association in discussions of defense matters which would affect them.[60] The Canadians firmly opposed any suggestions of a tripartite directorate for NATO, such as one composed of France, Britain, and the United States which de Gaulle had proposed and which President Eisenhower rejected. Such an exclusive leadership for setting alliance policy could jeopardize the advantages of the Canadians' closeness to the superpower.

Canadian efforts to be consulted flowed partly from the knowledge that Canadian territory would be inextricably bound up with American attempts to defend its own territory, whatever the Canadians did. They found this closeness not only "exhilarating, it was also exhausting, even, at times, alarming." [61] In the 1950's, proximity meant a continual struggle to urge caution on the seemingly impetuous Americans. In the 1960s, Canadians in principle disapproved of the antiballistic missile (ABM) system for North

America but did not try to prevent a system being inaugurated by Americans.

Australians had a very different problem, knowing that the United States could choose to disengage from the South Pacific as it never could from its immediate neighbors. Australia's friends always were far away, while it felt close to a large region of very great instability. Fortunately for Australians, their Near North began to seem somewhat less "Far" East to Americans in the early 1950s, as Asian problems drew the attention of United States officials to the Pacific. In the 1960s, as the British began to plan their withdrawal from Singapore and the Indian Ocean, it was comforting to the Australian government to have the Americans heavily involved in the Pacific. At that period, distant Australia was readier to make concessions to the United States than was nearby Canada.

As Europe receded into the distance in Canadian perspectives, the "far" north loomed much closer, as it also did to Americans, who were increasingly interested in its resources. The northern periphery of NATO Europe also began to appear closer to Canadian defense leaders: they stressed the special contribution their forces could make in supporting Norway. By inference, Canada had outworn its role on the central front in Germany.[62] Prime Minister Trudeau's discussion with Russian leaders in 1971 covered, among other matters, common (nonstrategic) interests in the north.

As the major source of defense intelligence, however, the United States remained very close to both Canadians and Australians. There could be disadvantages however. General Charles Foulkes, former chairman of Canada's Chiefs of Staff Committee, pointed out that in its dependence upon American intelligence estimates, Canada was ill equipped to correct any bias in the information so readily given; joint estimates of a threat, often a compromise between Canadians and Americans, were not always accurate.[63] At times, however, Canadians in and out of office valued access to information from the United States, classified or not, for its political uses, even if receipt implied dependence. The opposition leader, Lester Pearson, chided the Diefenbaker government in 1960 for its secrecy by stating that the Liberals secured far more information from American sources such as congressional reports than they got from their own government.[64] An Australian scholar has pointed out that the flow of intelligence coming to Australia from the United States may be a subtle kind of flattery, and once established, as it has been, "the Australian official apparatus is likely to be highly sensitive to any action which might result in having the flow limited or interrupted." [65]

Particular individuals, by their personalities, affinities, and dislikes, can reduce a sense of distance or increase it. President Johnson did not get along well with Prime Minister Pearson, who, however, had had excellent personal relations with President Kennedy. Prime Minister Diefenbaker, on the other hand, seemed almost deliberately to antagonize President Kennedy. The remarkably close associations the most important Australian leaders after Evatt had with leading American officials, attested to by both sides, have already been noted. These helped greatly to overcome other aspects of distance. The sense of closeness evaporated under President Nixon, and with the evaporation of rapport came a hardening of divergent positions.

Changing circumstances make governments come closer or recede from each other; for all four middle powers there have been such oscillations between each and the United States, especially in security matters. [66] Regardless of divergencies in security perspectives and asymmetrical influence, the Canadians nevertheless were the closest of the four countries in their ability to enter into defense debates going on in the United States. One example was a speech made by Prime Minister Pearson in Springfield, Illinois, on June 11, 1966, which was picked up by Senator William Fulbright to support his own critique of United States policy in NATO. [67]

CHANNELS OF COOPERATION

Several Canadian-American agencies to handle different kinds of defense matters have grown up, the hardy perennial being the Permanent Joint Board on Defense, whose activities have waxed and waned in response to changes in world politics and, especially, defense technology. The Canadians have put much store on the fact that its members include civilian as well as military officials; in fact, in both countries it has permitted foreign-affairs officials to get information from or put pressure on defense officials in the same government. [68] The Canadian Department of External Affairs has taken note of the availability of the board for informal discussion of ideas at a stage when they are not yet formally broached and of its usefulness in following up decisions which might otherwise get sidetracked because of the pressure of other business in the agencies supposed to be responsible for their follow-up. [69] These benefits accrued in addition to those stemming from the board's function of collecting and exchanging information between the two governments. Meeting formally at a United States or Canadian base three times a year, the board has been supplemented by a military cooperation committee which has met more frequently and which has dealt with tactical aspects of problems. It was the PJBD in which the United States discussed ABM proposals with the Canadian government at an early stage in their development; and it was the board which conducted the main discussions about renewing NORAD.

Beginning in 1949, committees and subcommittees dealing with defense production were instituted.[70] In some cases, their work was facilitated by members of Congress who have participated in the Canadian–United States interparliamentary group, a nonofficial agency of communication which has alerted legislators to the defense problems of their neighbors. Several of the committees were created in the late 1950s, constituted of officials who had regular positions in the appropriate departments and agencies of their respective governments. Among them were the senior policy committee to watch over United States–Canadian defense-production sharing, meeting from 1958 to 1965, and the Joint Ministerial Committee on Defense. The latter was intended to be a cabinet-level group when it was set up in 1958, but it has not met since 1964, allegedly because many other channels for defense discussions existed. Such committees tended to lapse when the specific problems for which they were created became less pressing than others.[71]

Among other channels for discussions with the United States, Canadians have put a high value on the North Atlantic Council. Especially since the December, 1966, meeting, when they played a role in getting it to deal seriously with East-West relations, the Canadians have viewed it as far more than a device for making defense policy for the alliance. Canada also proposed, with the support of other lesser allies, that special sessions of the Big Four should coincide with meetings of the North Atlantic Council; concurrent meetings would improve the chances of the other allies to be consulted, which might restrain the more imprudent.[72]

NORAD's specialized concern with potential enemy penetration of North American airspace has required that the procedures to be followed and the circumstances under which officers in the command can act be carefully worked out beforehand.[73] The formal agreement underpinning NORAD also commits the partners to engage in "the fullest possible consultation," an engagement which some Canadians think the United States has interpreted too narrowly.

An opportunity to get an intimate view of United States security policy was what the Australians (and New Zealanders) wanted from ANZUS, an arrangement which would resemble in trust and informative character their Commonwealth relationship with Britain. Sir Percy Spender indicated that from the start they desired a simple but effective guarantee, with uncomplicated consultative machinery.[74] A small secretariat was established in Washington, with members from the Department of State and from the embassies of the other two countries. From its inception in 1951 through 1968, only four meetings of the ANZUS council took place in either Canberra or Wellington; the others were held in Washington or Honolulu (and one ad hoc meeting was held in Geneva).[75] Eventually, the council began to meet at the time when its member officials also were attending a meeting of the council of SEATO. The Australians failed to get their original wish: a joint planning arrangement with the United States Joint Chiefs of Staff. When this desire was passed on to the Joint Chiefs by a rather sympathetic Secretary of State Acheson, the chiefs indicated that their obligations in NATO and the Inter-American Defense Board were all they could handle. The Australians had to be content with the Hawaii headquarters of the United States Pacific Fleet as the location for liaison in military planning. Acheson, knowing that the governments of the South Pacific countries felt "remote, uninformed, and worried by the unknown," arranged that at their first meeting in Hawaii, he and Admiral Arthur Radford "instead of starving the Australians and New Zealanders" would "give them indigestion," through the masses of intelligence passed on to them.[76]

Thus the Australians learned what the Canadians had often experienced, namely, that the procedures set up within formal institutions may cause a great ally to pay attention to them but that the substance of consultations might elude them. Nevertheless, such organs provided a canopy under which a multitude of informal interrelationships between defense officials concerned with technical problems rather than the negotiation of overall strategy could be built up.

The Inter-American Defense Board, a leftover from World War II, also provided a canopy, except for Mexico, which freely chose not to participate. (Even overflight privileges, which the United States had received in World War II, had to be requested of the Mexican government for each occurrence.) On the other hand, for some years Brazil acted as if it accepted the board at face value, particularly during the Korean War. This was Brazil's way of obtaining concessions in the exchange of hard-to-get items for its strategic resources, and in "mutual assistance." But the board became more and more irrelevant to most of its members' security needs.

CUMULATION AND SPILLOVER

Unlike the Inter-American Defense Board, never a genuinely multilateral agency because it was almost completely dominated by the United States, some of the other institutions for collaboration between the United States and the middle powers continued to be effective because they had very specific tasks and/or avoided spoiling a good working relationship by undertaking new ones which were divisively controversial.[77] Although the Permanent Joint Board on Defense was used by Canada and the United States from time to time after the war for the discussion of contentious new subjects, all of them were confined to the area of its competence, North American defense.

Some cooperative ventures, such as the Defense Production Sharing Program grew by accretion, with one partly successful task leading to another. Thus practice developed into a formal "program," because of the broader implications of continental defense under NORAD and because of the specific desire of Canadians to minimize the political and economic costs of constructing the Pinetree line by using, so far as possible, the products of their own defense industries. But the spillover was limited. The program did not lead to any matching of resources with forces, nor did it provide any link to a coordinated foreign policy. Some oversensitive Canadian nationalists claimed that defense-production sharing made it easier for the United States to continue the much-hated Vietnam war. The United States was not, in fact, as dependent upon the program as the nationalists alleged. Nor did the program become multilateral, although certain facets of the two countries' cooperative ventures later were introduced by each into relationships with other allies.

One of the other allies which later sought compensation for the large defense orders placed in the United States for such items as guided-missile destroyers was Australia. It had problems similar to Canada's but more pronounced: a small market for its own defense production, the need to have equipment interchangeable with that of the United States forces, and, compared to America, low research and development potentialities for high-technology products. Thus, in the late 1960s, Australia attempted to balance its overseas procurement of sophisticated items by offset arrangements, including subcontracting in Australia.[78] It also sought to persuade the United States to purchase in Australia a larger portion of the supplies for its forces in Vietnam.[79] The terms of some equipment-purchase agreements included an Australian contribution in research and development, and the Australians were assured delivery at the same time and price as in the case of American forces.[80]

Australians learned rather late that although alliance commitments such as those involved in ANZUS may spill over into a call for Australian forces to fulfill their side of the bargain, as occurred in the Vietnam war, they do not lead to special considerations in economic areas, especially trade. Nor has the intimacy in defense relations that grew out of the Vietnam undertaking spread from Asia to other areas in which the Australians have a concern. Nevertheless, some of the ways Australia implemented the alliance on its own territory meant that America's stake in Australia was growing rapidly.

An expensive lesson for the Australians was the decision to purchase twenty-four of the problem-prone F-111s when danger from Sukarno's Indonesia was acute in 1963. Thereby the Australians tied up a large part of their necessarily limited defense budget for a costly item not yet much beyond the drawing boards. A continual embarrassment to the Australian government (as it was to United States authorities), the aircraft was not delivered until ten years later.[81] High-pressure salesmanship for American weapons, itself a spillover from the increasing pressure on American defense resources caused by ever mounting technological competition, resulted in Australians' learning a lesson that American defense officials did not anticipate. The Australians were relatively willing victims of such salesmanship, to their later sorrow. "Never again" may be the response if another "sophisticated" defense system is pressed on allies somewhat unsophisticated about American military salesmanship.[82]

Unlike the great-power allies in Europe, the middle powers considered here lacked important elements of a home-grown defense industry, and their alliances with a superpower seemed naturally to spill over into defense orders placed in that country. Nevertheless, they were not completely tied to

TABLE 7   UNITED STATES DELIVERIES OF FOREIGN MILITARY SALES TO FOUR
MIDDLE POWERS, 1950–1973 (millions of US dollars)

	1950–64	1965	1966	1967	1968	1969	1970	1971	1972	1973
Australia	136.3	30.8	66.2	78.6	127.8	113.0	52.5	60.7	51.1	96.5
Brazil	17.0	3.5	13.3	6.1	15.7	17.7	11.7	1.9	13.3	25.4
Canada	588.4	45.0	37.7	30.7	17.9	28.0	49.7	30.9	52.7	39.1
Mexico	7.8	.5	.6	.5	.8	.1	.4	a	.3	.2
All countries	3345.0									

Source: Department of Defense, Military Assistance and Foreign Military Sales Facts, March, 1970; Statistical Abstract of the United States. Years are fiscal years.
a Less than $50,000.

the United States; all of them made significant arms purchases in other countries, including Italy and Switzerland. Australia resisted the F-104, purchasing the French Mirage instead. Canada (and, to a much lesser extent, Australia) sold defense items to other countries, including Brazil. The relative
importance of the four middle powers as purchasers of United States military
equipment is shown in table 7.

Especially enticing for these middle powers were the scientific and
technological projects in which they cooperated with the Americans, thereby
acquiring capabilities unobtainable on their own. For Canadians, the
spillover from purely defense matters was very important; their Defense
Research Board and defense research establishments have conducted a large
number of activities with their counterparts in the United States, some of
which activities also had British and, occasionally, Australian participants.[83]
Similar benefits to the middle powers flowed from cooperation among the
various English-speaking countries' atomic energy commissions, beginning
in the case of the Canadians with wartime collaboration.[84] Friendly working
relationships between Canadian and American specialists formed part of the
complex web of personal ties characterizing informal, unplanned connections not confined to the defense area.

In the Australian case, the major scientific ventures that spilled over
from the alliance and from defense collaboration were in space research. As
a result of a cooperation in which Australian territory was especially useful,
Australian scientists and technologists through their extensive collaboration
with the National Aeronautics and Space Administration developed an expertise otherwise hard to achieve.[85]

Spillover from alliances to military purchases takes on a different aspect south of the United States border. American military authorities, backed up by Congress, have long sought to standardize Latin American defense equipment with their own. This objective often was used as an argument to bolster mutual aid programs. But Congress grew increasingly concerned about financing arms sales to disliked governments in Latin America, and legislation has prevented defense authorities from providing Latin Americans with the more sophisticated arms systems. Among others, Brazil has turned to European suppliers for such items as supersonic jet aircraft (for which Americans could discern no function in Brazil's internal security problems). Thus Congress ineffectively tried to prevent a spillover but was caught between two objectives. Another kind of spillover occurred in the late 1960s, as Brazil's military dictatorship became more and more estranged from the United States. A projected large sale of M-16 rifles took three years to clear the multiple hurdles in the path of an export license, getting well tangled in controversy among American officials, only to end up with cancellation of the order by Brazil.[86]

Mexico, which has made only modest demands and has accepted little financial assistance in buying what it has procured from the United States, has not presented the problems created by Brazil. Mexico merely has tried to purchase in the most economical market while avoiding unwanted ties.

A notable case of a defense agreement failing to spillover into the economic sphere is the North Atlantic treaty, in which Article 2 provided, inter alia, for economic collaboration. This is sometimes known as the Canadian article, since it was the Canadians who pressed for it at the beginning and constantly tried to give it substance.[87] They did not want a mere "old-fashioned military alliance" and in the drafting of the treaty persisted in seeking inclusion of an article which called on members to cooperate in economic and social and cultural fields as well as defense concerns. The other members were bemused or indifferent, and the idea of broader collaboration seemed finally to be laid to rest when the three-man Committee on Non-Military Cooperation examined the functioning of NATO after the Suez crisis and found that objectives strictly economic in nature could better be dealt with by other international organizations. (Perhaps the Canadians will have the last word, however, if NATO's Committee on the Challenges of Modern Society, set up under American prodding in 1969, continues to attract interest and effort.) [88]

ADMINISTRATIVE TREATMENT VERSUS POLITICIZATION

The cumulative experience of partnership in World War II probably revealed itself most of all in the formation of close professional ties between military officers of the United States and those in Australia, Canada, and Brazil. Such personal relationships were more significant than formal institutions in furthering collaboration after the war, although the latter helped to foster new relationships. Professional military officers who knew each other's probable reactions tended to deal with common matters as problems to be solved rather than issues to be negotiated so as to preserve their respective country's status above all other considerations.

Some arrangements for common training or personnel interchange have been relatively formal programs. On a bilateral basis, the United States armed forces have made such exchanges with the British, Canadians, and Australians; military officers of these nationalities served in the same capacity in the United States as they did at home, while American officers performed correspondingly in Britain, Canada, and Australia. The choice often fell on officers who had attended a defense college of the host country. A small program, it has nevertheless been a genuine exchange, and the visiting officers not only have had some command duties but have been valuable sources of information about differing methods of accomplishing a function.[89]

Of the three Commonwealth countries, exchanges of serving officers with Canada are by far the most numerous. Also, more Canadian military officers study in the various defense colleges of the United States and more Americans in Canadian institutions. For example, Canadian air-force officers have regularly attended the Air University, and there has been a week's exchange of students between respective colleges for talks by the other's instructors.[90] At a lower level, admission to the United States Military Academy, which was offered to a limited number of Latin American students by congressional act during World War II, was extended in 1948 to Canadians.[91]

On a smaller scale, similar exchanges have taken place with Australians. The Royal Military College at Duntroon has conducted an annual staff exercise in which representative from the United States, as well as Britain and New Zealand, have participated.[92] The sending of Australians to England for advanced military education gradually is being supplanted by visits to the United States for such studies, in part because they are associated with major naval and aircraft purchases made in America.[93] With a prospective increase in advanced military education in Australia, interchange with the United States could become greater.[94]

Arrangements in which Latin American military officers have participated differ from those involving the Commonwealth countries. The training facilities of the United States Military Assistance Program have included courses at the Command and General Staff College (which in 1970 enrolled 103 students who were officers in the armed forces of fifty countries, both developed and less developed) and at other staff colleges of the services.[95] During fiscal years 1950–1969, out of a total of 297,087 officers trained under the Military Assistance Program (more than 202,000 of them in the United States itself, the remainder overseas), 6,296 were Brazilians and 570 Mexicans.[96]

The Inter-American Defense College at Fort McNair, Washington, which was established in 1962 after long controversy within the Inter-American Defense Board, has enrolled students from the military services of the Latin American members and a few civilians as well. In 1968 Brazil sent 25 students, the largest number of Latin Americans out of a total of 227. Mexico, which had earlier opposed the establishment of the college, preferring that Latin American countries send to each other selected military officers for advanced courses, sent 16 students during that year. Its was the fourth largest number enrolled after those of the United States (33), Brazil, and Argentina (22).

The American objective in establishing these training programs for Latin Americans was not only to improve the military capacity of friendly countries but also to supply them with officers who would tend to favor American interests because of augmented understanding—and, presumably, sympathy. How did this work out in Brazil? Although training in the United States undoubtedly contributed something, the more important socializing of Brazilian military officers toward American-sponsored ideas occurred among those participating in the Brazilian Expeditionary Force in World War II. It was they who actively responded to later American initiatives and who were happy to have American assistance in creating their Escola Superior de Guerra in 1958, which in turn developed doctrines of development and foreign policy conducive to further cooperation with the United States and to an active welcome to American investment.[97] In any case, Brazil has a very large military establishment and its officers have habitually fought bitterly among themselves, with one faction supporting the current government while another plotted to dispose of it.[98] Those who had been trained by Americans were not always on top. Some officers were extreme nationalists, and among the latter were those who became dissatisfied with the early policies of the Castelo Branco regime. Eventually, under Costa e Silva, officers who were even more nationalist and far less well disposed to the United States came to dominate.[99]

Canada and, later, Australia have incorporated into their own defense organizations many of the practices and procedures already used in the United States, facilitating communication between counterparts. But Canada has taken a course in unifying its services which is unlikely to be copied by the United States (and those Canadian officers who were unhappy found sympathy at the time among their military fellows in the United States).[100]

Close professional ties between citizens engaged in defense research (civilian as well as military) have been a feature of Canadian-American relations, and the same has been true of the almost unique personal relations existing between Canadian and American military officers. For each other, the term *foreign* does not seem applicable.[101] Large numbers of Canadian officers are scattered throughout the United States, not just at NORAD or in the Canadian joint services administration in Washington. There are countless instances where individual or agency military contacts cut across national boundaries to forward a particular interest inside their own defense system. Thus members of one service in one country could secure otherwise hard-to-get information about another service through their counterparts in the other country.[102] Of the total of 12,900 visits of Canadian officials to the United States in 1968, those by persons from the Department of National Defence numbered 8,313. A similarly large proportion of United States public servants going to Canada were defense officials.[103]

Canadian military leaders were active promoters of the integrated defense of the continent which culminated in NORAD. They have worked most harmoniously with their counterparts in this command.[104] For many years Air Marshal Roy Slemon held the post of deputy commander while Americans came and went, and the expertise and experience he acquired prompted the confidence in him by his associates which surmounted the Cuban missile crisis controversy with Diefenbaker's government. The Vietnam war, however, did eventually put some strain on the mutuality of views which earlier was so marked between American and Canadian military officers.

DOMESTIC POLITICS

Those actively engaged in cooperative projects have not always succeeded in preventing their tasks from becoming politicized, for their interests were different from those of the politicians. (Canadian military officers, knowing the limits of their budget and other resources wished close contact with Americans in order to make them go as far as possible and be most effective; Americans wanted the kind of integration this close contact made possible; thus, on both sides of the border, a shared objective within the military services was a rational means to more security.) As Jon McLin has pointed out, in Canada "almost any significant issue of defense policy . . . will involve the U.S. also" and therefore is potentially controversial because of Canadians' sensitivity regarding their country's sovereignty, which in turn stems from the disparity in Canada's and America's power.[105] Although Australia and the United States have become more and more involved in each other's politics, the United States has figured much more in Australian domestic affairs. The electoral campaign of the Liberal-Country party coalition regularly suggested that the Australian Labor party, if it came to power, would destroy Australia's fine relationship with the United States, Australia becoming less staunch an ally and thus less likely to get aid, if needed.[106] This line lost its appeal eventually, partly because of the Vietnam war, but Labor's victory did indeed result in much greater tension between the two countries.

The naval communications station at North West Cape aroused strong Labor party opposition, even though the government easily won House of Commons authorization to enter the arrangement. The facility scarcely was noticed in the United States, since it was only one among a large number of American installations around the globe. NORAD, which did not even require congressional approval in the United States, stirred up a lively controversy in Canada, partly because of the method by which it seemed to be slipped through Parliament after having already gone into effect.[107]

Because of the peculiar personal characteristics of Prime Minister Diefenbaker, this controversy and a later political conflict concerning defense cooperation with the United States, namely, the nuclear-weapons controversy, taught few lessons applicable elsewhere or at another time. Yet the nuclear-arming events were important because they show how close the United States can come to intervening in a Canadian political struggle without American officials' really meaning to do so. To put a very complicated story in a nutshell, the Diefenbaker government had accepted in principle nuclear arming of its NATO ground and air forces in Europe in December, 1957. Also, in accepting Bomarc missiles on Canadian soil as one way to get out of the embarrassment of canceling the Avro Arrow, it had implicitly accepted the nuclear warheads that armed them. Years went by while the government equivocated, failing to make the final decisions necessary to carry out these commitments. The cabinet was divided, with the secretary of state for external affairs, who was very strong for disarmament, opposing a decision, while the secretary for national defense wished to go through with the bargain. Canadian touchiness about nuclear weapons and about American influence provided the background for a first-rate duel between the governing Progressive Conservatives and the opposition Liberals, neither of which had a clear, unequivocal point of view on the issue.

Into this controversy stepped impatient American officials by means of a State Department press release issued January 30, 1963, which suggested that the Diefenbaker government was dragging its heels.[108] This followed by three weeks an interview in Ottawa in which the recently retired supreme commander of NATO, General Lauris Norstad, had noted that a bilateral agreement with the United States would be necessary if Canada was to carry out its understanding with NATO that its air division be equipped with nuclear weapons. These two events provided the prime minister with a perfect excuse to charge interference and claim his opposition was under American pressure, thereby bolstering his flagging political fortunes. But his defense minister (as well as some other cabinet members) resigned, and his government soon was ousted by losing a vote of confidence in Parliament, an event rare in Canadian politics and one which forced holding a national election to choose a new parliament. The nuclear-arms issue was only one of a great many dissatisfactions with the Diefenbaker government, but the opposition (with some courage in view of its earlier stand) fought the election campaign in part by claiming that Canada must go through with a commitment, however distasteful or mistakenly made. (Some further ammunition was supplied to the Diefenbaker forces by the release of congressional testimony given by Secretary of Defense Robert McNamara to the effect that Bomarc missiles could be vulnerable targets.) The Liberals won the election but not directly on this issue; Prime Minister Pearson, shortly after taking office, agreed to accept nuclear arms for Bomarc missiles and for the Canadian forces in NATO.[109] Eight years later, the Trudeau government announced that it would dismantle the Bomarc antiaircraft missiles as obsolete, even though United States Defense Secretary Melvin Laird urged retaining them.[110]

The insensitivity of the great ally's government to the domestic politics of a lesser ally, which is a very partial explanation of the nuclear-arms issue outlined above, showed up more glaringly in the other Commonwealth country. As in Canada, defense questions raised by the alliance with the United States have provided Australian politicians with ample electoral issues. The Australian Labor party could be counted on to look askance at defense arrangements made by the coalition government and, playing on public ignorance and government secrecy, to make these arrangements a lively campaign issue. (Until the Democratic Labor party split off in the mid-1960s, disunity within the Labor party prevented very loud objections.) Sharper divisions of opinion in Australia concerning the dangers of Communism than existed in Canada had, long before 1970, induced political arguments about defense arrangements. Australia's contribution to the forces fighting the Vietnam war had become a vigorously pressed election issue, inevitably bringing into prominence other types of defense cooperation with the United States, especially the suspect space installations about which so little was known. By 1972, these issues helped to turn out the party which had governed for twenty-three years. The new Labor government promptly adopted defense policies not only different from their predecessor's but also at variance with some United States policies. The government managed to renegotiate the North West Cape agreement to give Australia more control and to operate the base as a joint facility. It temporarily even entertained a Soviet proposal for a satellite-tracking station in Australia.[111] Although the Labor government still clung to ANZUS, it was quite content to see SEATO fade away into oblivion before its official demise in September, 1975.

Canadian restrictions on United States facilities have been much broader, reflecting a continuous government concern with popular fears regarding lack of Canadians' control over their own territory.[112] Bombers of the United States Strategic Air Command were permitted to operate in Canadian air space, but each flight had to be cleared in advance; they could refuel at air bases in Newfoundland and Labrador. Interceptor squadrons (including those with nuclear arms) apparently were not thus limited, but they could not operate from Canadian airfields except in emergencies and could not store nuclear warheads on the bases in Newfoundland and in Labrador.[113]

There has been no effective "loyal opposition" in the two Latin American countries to use defense cooperation with the United States as a political issue, but it, in fact, has been a much more salient question in both Mexico and Brazil than in the sparring contests that go on in the Commonwealth countries. Since 1952, however, there has been no open controversy in Mexico. In that year the Mexican government halted discussions about a mutual assistance agreement then being informally conducted, after sensing a groundswell of political opposition during a presidential campaign.[114] Mexico's way to avoid domestic complications was to have no active defense cooperation with the United States. After all, Mexican defense forces were intended principally for internal security, which in the Mexican view should be of no concern to the United States.

The Brazilian case is different. Aid looked more attractive to the Brazilian leaders, and they had a greater variety of uses for it, especially since Brazil was not likely to be defended almost automatically by a neighbor. Nevertheless, sentiments against defense cooperation with the United States have been easily aroused, as happened when the Brazilian Congress voted for a mutual assistance agreement in April, 1953.[115] Communists and other leftist groups have been able to play on Brazil's reputation as the "fair-haired hemispheric boy of United States military planning." [116] No genuine tie between defense cooperation with the United States and shifts in Brazilian domestic politics has ever been conclusively proved. Nevertheless there seemed to be a connection between unwillingness of the United States government to lend much aid during the Goulart regime and the apparently effusive, certainly too quickly extended, aid heaped on the Brazilian government for a time after the 1964 coup.[117] No more than in the case of the Canadians did Brazilian opponents of a particular government need the sparks from an issue relating to defense ties with Americans to light the fires under a regime already in hot water.

SUMMARY

This survey of postwar defense cooperation between the United States and its four middle-power associates indicates that there are self-generating limitations on integrative action in this field. The closer the middle power, the more its government has been sensitive to possible encroachments on its freedom of maneuver. The middle powers, while cooperating, try self-consciously to keep their collaborative ventures confined to the original channels. This effort cannot always succeed, especially when there are economic reasons for broadening programs begun for security purposes.

Not surprisingly, the more economically advanced countries proved much more capable of being mutually helpful in meeting specific defense needs that were the Latin American states, even though genuinely joint undertakings were rare. Cultural and economic closeness was more important than geographic distance, although being near or far made Canada and Australia attractive partners to the United States for different strategic reasons. At least until 1973, the Australians seemed to be the wooers in defense, while the Canadians were being wooed; then the Australians also drew back. For both these states as for the Latin countries, what were defense questions of minor political salience to the United States were high policy in the middle powers. Not only high policy in managing external affairs, these questions became domestic political issues as well. Sometimes an embarrassment to leaders, defense collaboration at other times was welcome as indirect support to governments waging internal contests, thus improving the Americans' bargaining position.

No amount of professional and personal ties could overcome differences in importance of defense issues. Nevertheless, especially when strengthened by formal institutions, such ties did permit some defense problems to be dealt with on a substantive basis and on a bureaucratic level. Thus the behavior of individual actors became easier for their counterparts in the other countries to comprehend and predict. Personal relationships among administrative officials of the United States and a middle power also blurred the image of overwhelming strength on one side.

United States defense relations with Canada and Australia were often complicated by the participation of other allies, a participation especially desired by the two Commonwealth countries but useful, too, for the Ameri-

cans, since such objectives as making equipment and practices interchangeable were thereby promoted. Changes in technology and global power configuration altered the closeness of the United States ties with all those
cooperating with it in defense, not always in the same direction. So did
domestic political shifts. The pervasive bar to close relations in the security
area, however, continued to be disparities in strength between the superpower and the middle powers; had they been comparable strength,
other factors would have prevented cooperation.

SIX

ECONOMIC RELATIONS: FOREIGN TRADE

IT IS DEFENSE QUESTIONS THAT approach most closely the core of sovereignty; yet it was on economic issues that the four countries here examined, being middle powers, seemed more sensitive to the almost overwhelming weight of the United States. Unlike defense relations, where there is a common potential foe, in the economic arena the actors were competitors.

In the number and variety of actors, also, economic relations differed from the security relationship. A large part of the economic relations between the United States and the four countries flows from the activities of nongovernmental actors: investors, traders, manufacturers, bankers, unions and the workers they represent. Yet governments hold the ring and can restrict or encourage transnational economic relations. Within a complicated set of relationships, which students of "transnationalism" have outlined, this chapter concentrates primarily on the governmental aspects.[1]

The external environment in which economic relations between the United States and the middle powers take place includes a variety of multilateral international organizations, such as United Nations Conference on Trade and Development (UNCTAD), the Organization of American States (OAS), the International Monetary Fund (IMF), the Organisation for Economic Cooperation and Development (OECD), and General Agreement on Tariffs and Trade (GATT). One organization to which neither the United States nor the other four countries belongs but which has had a strong impact upon them is the European Economic Community (EEC).

As with defense, changes during the thirty years since the end of World War II have altered economic relationships between the United States and the other four countries. The time element is especially important, since all

TABLE 8   GROWTH RATES OF POPULATION, GROSS NATIONAL PRODUCT, AND PER CAPITA GROSS NATIONAL PRODUCT FOR FOUR MIDDLE POWERS AND THE UNITED STATES, 1950–1973 (percent increase)

	Population	Gross National Product				
	1973	*1950–60*	*1960–65*	*1965–70*	*1960–70*	*1968–73*
Australia	1.9	4.3	5.0	5.1	5.0	5.4
Brazil	2.8	6.8	4.5	7.4	6.0	10.2
Canada	1.3	4.8	5.6	4.7	5.2	5.3
Mexico	3.4	5.8	7.1	6.9	7.0	6.5
USA	0.9	3.2	4.8	3.2	4.0	3.5

	Per Capita Gross National Product				
	1950–60	*1960–65*	*1965–70*	*1960–70*	*1968–73*
Australia	2.0	2.9	3.2	3.0	3.5
Brazil	3.8	2.4	3.6	3.0	2.5
Canada	2.1	3.7	3.1	3.4	4.0
Mexico	2.7	3.6	3.5	3.6	3.1
USA	1.4	3.3	2.1	2.7	2.6

Source: All figures are from Agency for International Development, *Gross National Product: Growth Rates and Trend Data by Region and Country* (May, 1974), except Brazil's increase in per capita gross national product for 1950–60, which is from ibid., May, 1973.

four countries are, compared to the United States or Western Europe, still developing. They have great resources not yet exploited which would increase their already rapidly growing gross national product, and they also are endeavoring to reduce their economies' dependence on the export of raw materials. Even with tremendous advances in industrialization, the economies of all four countries continue to be much more dependent upon outside events than is the case with the United States, which is likely to have impelled these events. Table 8 compares the rates of growth of GNP for the superpower and the four middle powers during different periods, as well as their current rates of population growth.

Immediately after World War II and as a result of it, the United States became either the most important, or one of the two or three most important, trading partners for each of these countries, even for Australia. Old triangular trading patterns had broken up, and new ones were yet to emerge. Yet wartime necessity caused each of the countries to become more self-sufficient or self-confident in meeting many of its own economic needs (compared to its prewar dependency) and gave impetus to the industrialization of each. Wartime experience had also resulted in much greater communication between each of the four countries and the United States and an increased tendency to look to it for satisfying economic requirements other than those arising from the war.

These were only the beginnings of large-scale shifts in the economic world. Among others which ensued as the years passed were the change from dollar scarcity to overabundance for most of America's major trading partners; the increasing strain on the dollar as the global currency standard led to United States efforts to correct a large deficit in its balance of payments. For many years the gap grew wider and wider between prices paid for the raw materials upon exportation of which the Latin American countries heavily depended and for industrial goods they had to import to pursue their development policies. There were frightening fluctuations in the return on their exports. Until the 1970s, the United States experienced continuing surpluses in certain agricultural products which some of the other four also exported.[2] Technological changes affected the supply of and demand for particular goods, resulting in the expansion of some industries and the decline of others, both in the United States and the other four countries, requiring politically difficult adjustments. During this period an unprecedented surge in foreign aid to the less developed countries occurred, but the waning of the cold war was followed by a marked decline in foreign aid from the United States. On the nongovernmental level, multinational corporations burgeoned, spreading into the four countries as well as elsewhere from a nucleus which was most often located in the United States. The economically advanced countries gradually but markedly reduced trade barriers, largely through international agreement (although renewed waves of protectionism often threatened the progress made). Exchange controls that had been instituted in the aftermath of the war were dropped; tariffs on manufactures in the industrialized countries were lowered or even removed over time; import quotas were largely eliminated. Thus nontariff barriers such as subsidies and discriminating customs classification are left as the chief obstacles to free trade.

All of these changes and many more in the external world had to be met by governments in which the foreign offices were by no means the sole or most important instrument for managing the relations of their countries with others. Ministries of finance, commerce and industry, and agriculture, central banks, and other agencies were actively engaged in managing these relations, management which was not always perfectly coordinated. The political process of the United States was by far the most fragmented. Both the quasi sovereignties of its executive branch and diverse congressional actors played a vital part in decisions relating to foreign economic policy, reflecting positions of many strong private interest groups.

To meet changing conditions, all of the policy makers in the United States and the four middle powers were deciding questions in the fields of trade, investment, foreign aid, monetary regulation, and in other economic areas. In bilateral relations of each of the four with the United States, issues involving trade and foreign investment loomed particularly large. Analysis in this and the following chapter will treat other kinds of foreign economic policy only as they relate to these two subjects, although the classification is necessarily somewhat arbitrary.

Only in comparison to the United States is Canada's economy small. It was, for example, the world's sixth largest trading country in 1973, had the sixth largest quota in the International Monetary Fund as of 1958, and was one of the Group of Ten, which has set monetary policy for the non-Communist world. But Canada's economy depends upon foreign trade far more than does that of its superpower neighbor. As in the case of Australia, whose population of 13 million is even smaller than Canada's, the internal market needs to be supplemented by foreign buyers, if an industrialized economy is to be maintained.

Much more than Canada, Australia has in the past depended for its trade upon Britain, for which the Commonwealth system of preferences was so important that Australia was very reluctant to abandon it, even under strong American pressure. Australia's rapid economic growth came later than Canada's, and Australia's economy has fluctuated less closely with American oscillations. Yet like Canada's, its trade relations with the United States expanded primarily at the expense of Britain. In contrast to the Canadian-American trade relationship, where the two North American countries are each other's best customers and suppliers, the United States had become Australia's third best customer by the late 1960s, topped by Britain (second) and Japan (first).[3] But for the United States, Australia was only the thirteenth most important supplier in the late 1960s and eleventh in importance as an American customer.[4] While trade between Japan and the other three middle powers has greatly increased, it is Australia which has developed a distinctively triangular trade pattern. The two members of each pair of states—Australia-Japan, Australia–United States, and Japan–United States— are major trading partners. In recent years, Australia has had a trade surplus with Japan, which has had a trade surplus with the United States, which has had a trade surplus with Australia. Although the amounts do not balance, the variations are not extreme. Australia's total trade is not in the same category as that of the stronger partners; the sum of its exchanges with its three leading trade partners was far below the total of Canadian-American exchanges.[5]

Charts A and B show the importance to Canada of trade with the United States, in the light of its total international trade position, over a number of years. Chart C shows Australia's trade with major trading partners and permits comparison of the size of United States trade with that of the others during various time intervals.

Like Canada's, Mexico's trade with the United States is a dominant factor in its economy, although the dollar value is far less, and exports represent a much smaller percentage of Mexico's GNP (about 5 percent).[6] The American share of imports into Mexico gradually declined from well over 70 percent in the early postwar years to about 67 percent by the late 1960s, and its share of Mexican exports, from more than 80 percent to about 63 percent.[7] As was true of Canada's trade until the late 1960s, Mexico has regularly run a deficit in its trade balance with the United States; but also as in Canada, it compensated for this by accepting foreign investment and, very importantly, by attracting tourists. Although Mexico has been the fifth best customer of the United States, Mexican exports to the United States have constituted a very small percentage (about 4.7 percent in 1963) of total imports into the United States.[8] Nevertheless, Mexico was the sixth largest supplier in 1970.[9]

Unlike Mexico, whose economic policy only gradually changed as one administration succeeded another in the postwar years, Brazil's tempestuous political history has been marked by sharp variations in economic policy affecting the United States. Meanwhile, the Brazilian economy moved rapidly from feast to famine to feast again, from the dizzy heights of huge foreign credits accumulated during the war, which were rapidly dissipated, to the tremendous economic boom of the late 1960s and 1970s, scarcely duplicated elsewhere, which accompanied a period of repressive dictatorship. In all these economic developments, Americans were deeply involved. Neverthe-

CHART A. TOTAL TRADE OF CANADA, 1961–1971 (in millions of dollars).

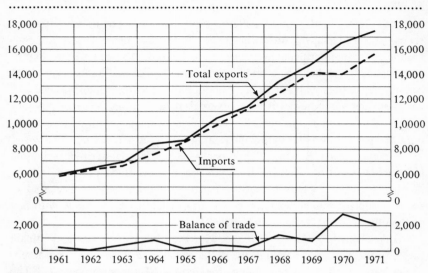

Redrawn from *Canadian Weekly Bulletin*, March 8, 1972.

CHART B. TRADE OF CANADA WITH THE UNITED STATES, 1961–1971 (in millions of dollars).

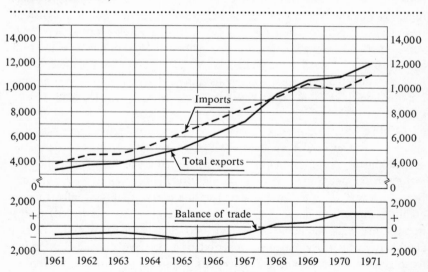

Redrawn from *Canadian Weekly Bulletin*, March 8, 1972.

CHART C. VALUE OF EXPORTS FROM AND IMPORTS TO AUSTRALIA, PROPORTIONS BY COUNTRY, 1967–1968 TO 1971–1972 (values are in Australian dollars).

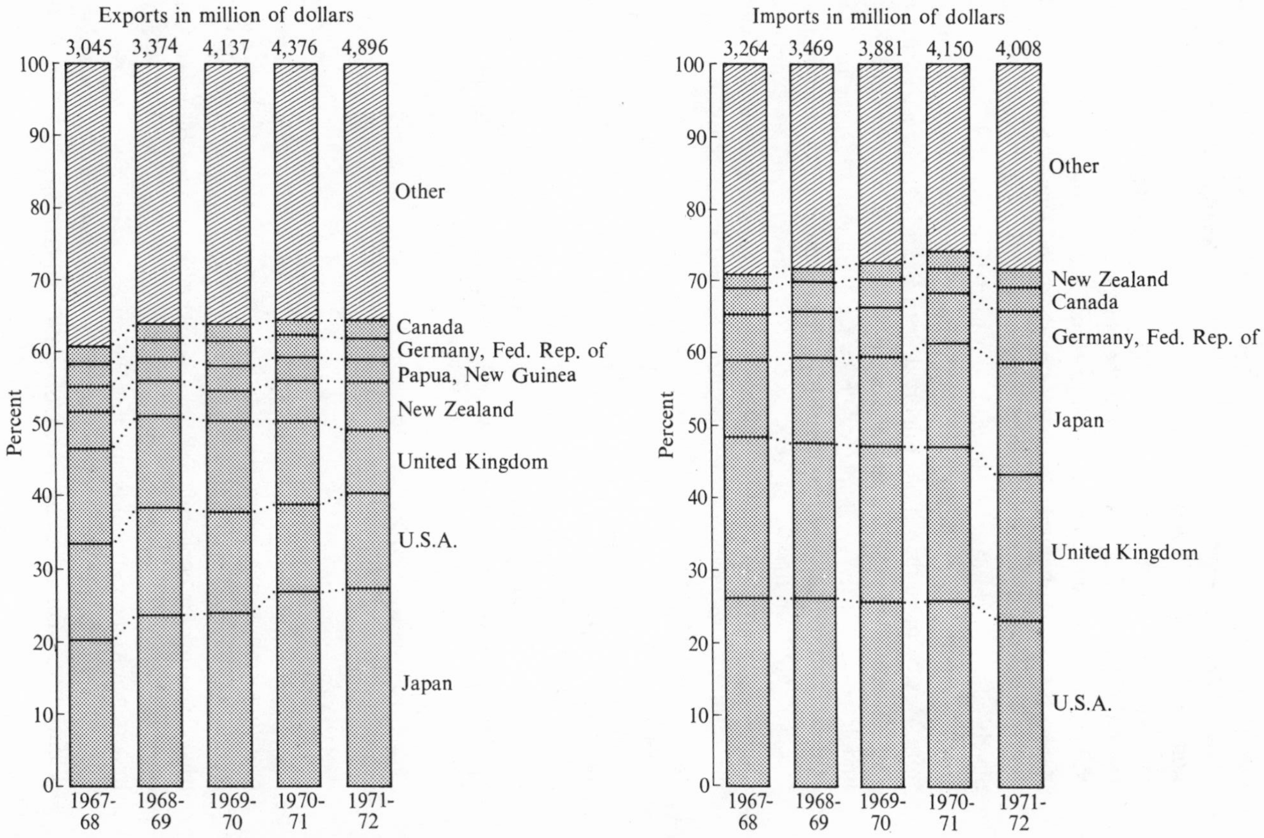

Imports in million of dollars

Exports in million of dollars

Redrawn from Australian Bureau of Labor Statistics, *Yearbook Australia*, 1973.

less, Brazil's postwar trade relations with the United States differ from those of the other three middle powers; except in 1947, until 1968 Brazil exported more to the United States than it imported from that country, even when huge United States foreign-aid expenditures were being made in Brazil.[10] The ratio between Brazil's exports to the United States and Brazil's total exports, though greater than that between Brazil and any other country, did not approach the ratio between Mexican exports to the United States and Mexico's total exports except under the unusual conditions that prevailed immediately after World War II. Instead, it varied from about 1:3 in the mid-1960s to about 1:4 in the 1970s. The United States has regularly imported from Mexico more than it has imported from Brazil's far larger economy.

Table 9 shows the amount of United States trade with each of the four middle powers at five-year intervals between 1945 and 1969; the magnitude of trade with Canada stands out sharply. For recent years the trading importance of all four middle powers, both as customers and as suppliers, is shown in comparison to total United States purchases and sales. Although the difference is not great, neighboring Mexico registers as a somewhat more important trader than the two distant states. For a recent year, 1972, Canada's trade with the United States is compared with that of other major United States trading partners, in table 10. For five-year intervals from the mid-1930s to the mid-1960s, table 11 shows the relative importance of the two neighbors as buyers from and sellers to the United States. Wartime aberrations in trade patterns can be seen, as well as trends and the much greater size of the exchanges between Canada and te United States.

JOINTNESS

CANADA

The two North American countries form a natural trading community, providing complementary markets in many ways. By 1970, trade in each direction had reached $10 billion, the largest in the world.[11] This huge, intricate network of economic relations is taken for granted by most Americans; not so by Canadians. They know that the United States is of crucial importance to their economy and that the reverse is not true.

A very large percentage by value of the trade between the two countries is duty-free, and duties on much of the remainder are very low.[12] Why

TABLE 9   UNITED STATES IMPORTS FROM AND EXPORTS TO FOUR MIDDLE
POWERS AND ALL COUNTRIES, BY VALUE AND AS PERCENTAGE OF TOTAL
UNITED STATES IMPORTS AND EXPORTS, SELECTED YEARS, 1945–1973

				Imports			
Origin	1945–49	1955–59	1965–69	1970	1971	1972	1973
			(value in millions of US dollars)				
All countries				39,952	45,563	55,563	69,121
Australia	123	140	437	611	619	807	1,062
Brazil	446	654	591	670	762	942	1,183
Canada	1,264	2,834	7,476	11,092	12,692	14,907	17,443
Mexico	240	423	812	1,219	1,262	1,632	2,287
			(percentage of total US imports)				
Australia				1.5	1.4	1.5	1.5
Brazil				1.7	1.7	1.7	1.7
Canada				27.8	27.9	26.8	25.2
Mexico				3.1	2.8	2.9	3.3

				Exports			
Destination	1945–49	1955–59	1965–69	1970	1971	1972	1973
			(value in millions of US dollars)				
All countries				43,224	44,130	49,779	71,314
Australia	177	216	815	986	1,004	842	1,439
Brazil	419	401	570	840	966	1,243	1,916
Canada	1,734	3,664	7,333	9,079	10,365	12,415	15,073
Mexico	486	819	1,265	1,704	1,620	1,982	2,937
			(percentage of total US exports)				
Australia				2.3	2.3	1.7	2.0
Brazil				1.9	2.2	2.5	2.7
Canada				21.0	23.5	24.9	21.1
Mexico				3.9	3.7	4.0	4.1

Source: Statistical Abstract of the United States. Figures for the five-year periods are arithmetic
means.

should the governments of the two countries choose to impose any tariffs
whatsoever? Or to engage in other restrictive practices, such as quotas, embargoes, licensing constraints, and protectionist classification procedures?
Aside from influential interest groups who have received protection from
competition, the main obstacle to completely free trade is the perennial fear
of Canadians that they might find their freedom of action irrevocably con-

TABLE 10   DIRECTION OF UNITED STATES TRADE, 1972

Origin or Destination	Percentage of Total Imports	Percentage of Total Exports
Canada	26.8	25.0
European OECD members	27.5	30.5
Japan	16.3	9.9
Communist countries	0.6	1.8
Rest of world	28.8	32.8

Source: Based on Department of State, Bureau of Public Affairs news release, *Trade Patterns of the West* (August, 1973), chart 3.

TABLE 11   EXPORTS TO AND IMPORTS FROM CANADA AND MEXICO AS PERCENTAGES OF TOTAL UNITED STATES EXPORTS AND IMPORTS AT FIVE-YEAR INTERVALS FROM 1934 TO 1964

	1934	1939	1944	1949	1954	1959	1964
Exports to Canada	14.5	15.7	10.2	16.2	18.4	21.2	18.1
Imports from Canada	14.3	15.1	32.5	23.5	23.2	20.2	22.6
Exports to Mexico	2.6	2.6	18.0	3.9	4.2	4.2	4.1
Imports from Mexico	2.2	2.4	5.2	3.7	3.2	2.9	3.4

Source: Statistical Abstract of the United States. Figures for Canada include Newfoundland.

stricted and their country's sovereignty swallowed up by the much more populous and more dynamic neighbor.

Piecemeal free trade has looked safer to both governments, the outstanding example being the automotive vehicle and parts agreement of 1965. Like the defense-production sharing plan (also a kind of free-trade arrangement), the automobile pact originated in Canadian efforts to narrow the increasingly large trade gap with the United States, much of it attributable to the great disparity between Canadians' output of and purchases of automobiles and parts, and to increase employment in the Canadian automotive industry. Since the Canadian government's original proposal was adoption of a tax-incentive scheme that in effect would be like a discriminatory duty on American automobile parts, the alternative of modified free trade (applying only to manufacturers, not to individual purchasers) appeared much more desirable to the Americans. The consequence of the agreement was that by the end of the 1960s, the big American-based Canadian automobile companies (which accounted for most of the Canadian output of cars) had so increased their production that an overall trade deficit with the United States turned into an unprecedented surplus. Although American exports to Canada did not spur ahead so remarkably as did Canadian exports to the United States, trade in both directions notably increased. There is no evidence that companies' profits suffered, and Canadian efficiency greatly increased as a result of the larger market.[13]

The Canadian government has long endeavored to increase the proportion of manufactured exports to total exports, thereby lessening the risks to its economy that heavy dependence on selling raw and unfinished commodities entails. To further this objective, the Canadians insisted on writing into the automotive agreement certain provisions which the Americans regarded as temporary and have since tried to have removed, as conditions changed. These provisions included guarantees that Canadian automobile production would not fall below the 1964 ratio of Canadian-produced automobiles to Canadian automobile purchases, plus clauses specifying a certain amount of Canadian components in the Canadian-assembled product. They also sought to prevent parent companies from shifting production between countries in response to market factors. The intransigence of the Canadians in the face of American pressure to eliminate those special conditions of the agreement that make concessions unequal is one reason why Americans are not likely—even if the Canadians were willing—to try a similar free-trade agreement in another industry. Since Canada's actual share of production has far exceeded the guarantees, Canadians have seemed to be more concerned about being able to control branch locations than about gaining economic advantages from a free market.[14]

In marked contrast to this joint effort to regulate automobile trade, properly thought of as, according to one commentator, "selective Canadian and American industrial integration" rather than "selective free trade," is the trade in petroleum and natural gas.[15] Following major oil discoveries in Alberta in the late 1940s, petroleum products from the Canadian West flowed freely across the border, while eastern Canada imported oil from abroad (mainly from Venezuela). This economically efficient trade pattern set by private enterprise continued until the 1973 energy crisis despite an ever more complicated system of oil import quotas imposed by the United States. These quotas, in force since the mid-1950s ostensibly for security reasons but actually to protect domestic production, were in the early years waived for imports from Canada (where much of the oil industry was owned by Americans). With the ever increasing flow of Canadian oil, the United States in 1967 replaced exemption with voluntary controls, and eventually, in 1970, imposed mandatory controls.

While the United States government without much success tried various methods of restricting the free flow of Canadian oil, the Canadian government continued to press for full access to the American market—until the global shortage of oil loomed. Then, rather suddenly in 1973, the shoe was on the other foot. The Nixon administration had in the last stages of the oil import quota program gradually raised the Canadian quota, but eventually the Canadians became concerned that their own needs might be unfilled if unrestricted amounts were exported. They imposed export licensing on oil as well as natural gas (exports of which had been limited since 1971) and later, during the Arab oil embargo, laid on an export tax which eventually was set at a high level, [16] and still later, placed quantitative restrictions on oil exports and raised the price of natural gas substantially, albeit in stages.

MEXICO

Although exemptions from United States oil import quotas were accorded Mexico for its much smaller amounts exported to the United States— accorded ostensibly because Mexican oil is also delivered overland—other trade policies of the two countries appear designed to prevent greater integration. High tariffs and an elaborate import licensing system are part of Mexico's efforts to industrialize and achieve greater economic independence. [17]

RECIPROCITY

CANADA

President Nixon's "new economic policy" of August, 1971, which unilaterally imposed a surcharge on the duties on imports, regardless of their origin, brutally broke with the custom of according special treatment to Canada. Shortsighted in many ways, the policy failed to recognize the great interdependence of trade relations between the two countries; as Canadians often argued, hurting the Canadian economy would quickly result in injury to the American economy. Since the Canadian government already had been following policies which the Nixon administration in August, 1971, was asking other governments to pursue, it particularly objected to the indiscriminate application of the new administrative orders, believing that Canada was being treated as "an involuntary hostage to bring additional pressure on a recalcitrant minority." [18]

Such indifference to common interests contrasted with earlier experiences. Canada, in 1935, had been one of the first countries to conclude a reciprocal trade agreement with the United States. By doing so, it accepted the doctrine of most-favored-nation treatment, a method which the United States insisted on as the best way to stimulate international trade. [19]

Canada worked side by side with the United States in planning the postwar array of international arrangements to foster free trade, although its contribution to the outcomes was its own, not a parroting of American positions. [20] Like the United States, Canada preferred and worked hard for rules which would be universally applied, eschewing for the most part, a regional approach. Thus reciprocity, in theory at least, was to be as multilateral as possible and, for Canada, a protection against lonely association with the United States. Yet economic circumstances drew the trade between the two countries more and more toward a relationship in which bilateral bargains were sought. In the various rounds of GATT negotiations, both countries made important concessions to each other, and in the Kennedy Round Canada secured American acceptance of an "equivalent" set of concessions for various commodities in place of making the "linear reduction" that the United States sought generally. With Britain joined in the Common Market, Canada and the United States may be driven even closer together as trading partners, despite the Canadian government's efforts to diversify its export market and despite its wooing of the EEC.

There is a huge trade between the two countries in agricultural products. The picture of reciprocity is complicated, however, because the two countries compete in selling agricultural commodities on world markets. This competition has made Canadians all the more sensitive to the unreciprocal nature of American demands for "voluntary" restrictions on the sale of some Canadian products in the American market. Each government regulates trade in ways that protect and enhance the welfare of specific regions, but doing so is much more of an imperative for the Canadian than for the United States government. The government in Ottawa is much more conscious of the need to promote national cohesion and is continually seeking to assuage regional discontent.

Led, or misled, by such considerations, Canada imposed a quota on United States beef and cattle in August, 1974, ostensibly because meat marketing and consumption in the United States was "destabilizing" the Canadian meat industry. After efforts to have the quota removed proved futile, the United States in November imposed quotas on Canadian imports, with greater political impact. This episode was uncharacteristic of the normal ways in which the two countries dealt with such problems. It was related to Americans' concern about restraints imposed by Japan and Western European countries, restraints which President Ford had warned would produce countermeasures.[21] Both governments backed off by the end of 1975.

AUSTRALIA

Unlike Canada, Australia was sufficiently reluctant to abandon its special trade ties with Britain as to impede agreement on reciprocal arrangements with the United States. Shortly after the war, Americans approached Australia regarding a treaty of "friendship, commerce and navigation," to which the Australians were then very cool. Subsequently, when they became somewhat more interested in some kind of trade agreement with the United States, the Americans pointed to GATT as the appropriate instrument for regulating their trade relations.[22] The two countries might have been readier to reciprocate were it not that Australia's major export commodities competed with the products of politically influential American groups, specifically wool, wheat, and meat. Over 75 percent of Australian exports to the United States in the late 1960s were subject to some kind of restriction.[23]

Except for a high duty on wool, the principal limitations on Australian imports to the United States were in the form of quotas. Thus the surcharges on import duties imposed in August, 1971, did not provoke so loud an outcry from Australia, since about 70 percent of its exports would not be directly affected.[24] Americans' protests had been less restrained when, at an earlier period, Australia had imposed currency restrictions to protect its own precarious balance of payments.[25]

MEXICO

Similarly effective protection secured by powerful American agricultural interests has impeded greater United States trade concessions to Mexico. Nevertheless, despite the absence of a reciprocal trade agreement and the refusal of Mexico to join GATT, from the United States it has secured most-favored-nation treatment informally and without incurring reciprocal obligations.[26]

The United States has slowly shifted away from its traditional attitude regarding "reciprocity," namely, that every trade concession must be matched by a return concession. It has begun to look with greater favor upon special treatment for certain products from underdeveloped countries, an attitude very much in line with Mexican pleas. In contrast to Canadians, who have long promoted the freeing of international trade on a global basis, Mexicans have accepted the system of quotas in general and complained only about the size of the quota allotted to them. Often, they have had a favorable quota compared to competitors, as in the case of sugar. They have based their demands for larger quotas on grounds of good neighborliness, stability, the needs of the poor, the desirability of their developing economically, and the reliability of their market. Sometimes they have had to accept reluctantly (like Canada and Australia) unilateral "voluntary" quotas on exports to the United States, the alternative being an even smaller share of the market.[27]

Disliking its asymmetrical trade relationship with the United States, the Mexican government with increasing vigor has sought to diversify its foreign trade outlets. It has achieved some success in Europe and Japan. Nevertheless, the American market remains the easiest to penetrate, and until Mexican ports are modernized, some of its trade with the rest of the world must continue to pass through the United States on its way overseas.[28] Moreover, its export potential continues to lie in agricultural or raw-material products, despite a marked rise in manufactured exports. Like Canada and Australia but far more so, Mexican manufactures cannot easily compete in price on the world market; Mexico faces the same problems of overprotection of inefficient domestic producers. Also like Canada and Australia, Mexico continues to need to import capital goods for its industrialization, thus perpetuating the asymmetrical relationship. This fact the Mexicans often have used when bargaining for trade concessions from the United States, pointing out the adverse effects on American exports of capital goods if Mexican trade is curbed.

Partly for this reason, the Mexicans protested President Nixon's new economic policy with its indiscriminate surcharge. They expected an exemption, just as in earlier balance-of-payments measures taken under the Kennedy and Johnson administrations when Mexico (like other developing countries) had been excepted from their application.[29]

In an earlier time, the United States and Mexico had each sustained the other's monetary system. The United States had assisted its underdeveloped neighbor in maintaining a stable currency. The peso eventually became sufficiently sound that it was one of the currencies used by the IMF in supporting those of other countries. As the Mexican economy grew stronger and the United States monetary situation deteriorated, there was a shift; Mexico began to support the United States, too. An earlier agreement between the two governments had given Mexico the right to draw upon the United States Treasury for $50 million to support its reserves. In December, 1965, the amount was increased to $75 million and was made reciprocal, with the United States having the same right in Mexico. The amount was increased to $100 million in June, 1967.[30] After a currency devaluation in 1954, Mexico had maintained its peso at a fixed ratio, 12.5 pesos to the United States dollar. Even during the United States monetary crisis of 1971, when the Nixon administration more or less forced a revaluation in the currencies of several European countries and Japan (as well as Australia), Mexico was able to maintain the value of its currency at the same fixed ratio to the American dollar.

BRAZIL

A nicely reciprocal trade relationship had long obtained between Brazil, the largest coffee producer in the world, and the United States, the largest coffee consumer.[31] For many years, coffee has entered the United States duty-free. The two countries were leaders in a pioneering international coffee agreement negotiated in 1940, which the Brazilians interpreted as an earnest symbol of the Good Neighbor policy.[32] By the early 1960s, African coffee was beginning to compete with Brazilian coffee; it enjoyed special preferences in the EEC. Thus Brazilians appreciated the strong push which the United States government gave to the first large-scale international coffee agreement between producers and consumers, effective in 1962, especially since it followed the Brazilian proposals rather than an alternative plan.[33]

When the time approached to negotiate a renewal in 1968, a new element had entered the picture. Brazil had begun to export soluble coffee (made in plants partly financed by Alliance for Progress aid) which competed with American products manufactured from African coffee. The American interests, claiming that Brazil's differential tax policy favored soluble coffee exports that unfairly competed with their own, managed to hold up first the negotiation of the agreement and then the legislation necessary to implement it.[34] The 1972 negotiations among the members of the international coffee agreement collapsed as a result of disagreement on prices, but by the time the coffee market had become completely free of regulation, the perennial surplus of coffee supplies had disappeared.[35] Meanwhile, Brazil's exports of coffee had declined to only about 27 percent of its total exports, which were booming in industrial products as well as new agricultural sales abroad. With strong financial reserves, a favorable trade balance, and diversified markets for its exports, the Brazilians could afford to be tough with their traditional American customers.

Brazil, along with Mexico, has sought through various international groups, including UNCTAD and inter-American agencies, to obtain a set of trade rules for underdeveloped countries different from those prescribed by the classical models accepted in the advanced countries. When little came of American promises to seek better treatment for Latin American trade in the EEC, treatment that would counteract preferences given to some African competitors by Common Market members, Brazil and Mexico joined with fifteen other countries around the world in an agreement to grant each other concessions not given to the developed countries. Although the United States was opposed to the agreement on the ground that it represented just one more attack on the principle of most-favored-nation treatment, the seventeen signatories secured GATT approval for a waiver of their GATT obligation.[36]

SPECIFICITY

Trade negotiations between the United States and each of the four middle powers have been concerned much less with general trade rules than with the removal of trade barriers on specific products. Since the most complained-about American restrictions have been specific-product quotas called for by Tariff Commission findings under congressional legislation in response to powerful American interests, the ability of any administration to respond to pleas of foreign governments has been somewhat limited. Lead and zinc quotas, burdensome to Canada, Mexico, and Australia, were in force from 1958 to 1965. No amount of complaints from any of these major producers proved effective. Disposal programs for surpluses of particular agricultural commodities also annoyed Mexico, Australia, and Canada. A congressionally imposed quota on meat imports hit Australia and Mexico particularly hard; Mexico was more inclined to plead for special treatment in the form of a larger quota than Australia's.[37] Meat had become Australia's principal export to the United States; and while that country received progressively larger quotas, not until 1972 were all quotas lifted. The change in policy was not a response to the complaints of these aggrieved producing countries but to the extraordinary rise in meat prices in the United States.[38] When beef prices began to fall, the United States, again under pressure from American cattle interests, secured late in 1974 a "voluntary" reduction of Australian exports of beef to this country.

Until the long-standing system under which sugar quotas were assigned to particular producing countries ended in 1974, annual quota allocations also evoked producing-country claims for larger amounts. However, when the former Cuban quota was allocated among other sugar exporters, Australia for the first time received a share. Furthermore, the quota for Australia was progressively increased as that country became the world's second largest exporter of cane sugar.[39] Mexico, despite having one of the largest sugar quotas, continued to plead for a still larger one. Brazil, by 1974 the world's largest sugar-cane producer, also fared very well compared to most other claimants. Table 12 illustrates how favored were Australia, Brazil, and Mexico during the last year in which the system prevailed.

As wool exports have gradually declined from their earlier first-rank importance for Australia, that country has made fewer complaints about the United States tariff on wool. Formerly, Australians continually pointed out that the United States was the only industrialized country to have a high tariff on wool. Since national boundaries do not affect favorable regional conditions for growing certain products, competitors south and north of United States boundaries frequently have pleaded for easier access to the American market for certain fruits and vegetables. Given climatic differences between separate growing regions, rationalizing the sale of these products to accord with the advancing season (as is to some extent already done) would seem economically desirable. Regardless of American response or lack of re-

TABLE 12   SUGAR QUOTAS AND PRORATIONS
ALLOCATED BY UNITED STATES TO LEADING
SUGAR SUPPLIERS, 1973

	Short Tons
Australia	209,048
Brazil	655,611
Mexico	672,239
Dominican Republic	760,127
Peru	433,020
Philippines	1,526,445
Total foreign	5,492,000
Total domestic and foreign	11,800,000

Source: Department of Agriculture, Sugar Quotas,
no. 258 (November, 1973).

sponse, Mexico and Canada were negotiating in 1973 for direct exchanges of these products.[40] With respect to duty-free tourist allowances, a strong outcry from the Mexicans met the United States reduction in 1966 of the liquor allowance for returning tourists, since liquor sales had been a lucrative source of income at the border.[41] But on the northern border of the United States, it was the small Canadian tourist allowance which caused the United States to complain in 1971. (Duty-free allowances were greatly increased for returning Canadian tourists in December, 1974.)

DISTANCE

Proximity was an important factor in making tourism very big business for Canada. More than 95 percent of its foreign tourists in 1972 were Americans, and they spent more than one billion dollars in Canada; this constituted the largest percentage of United States travel payments in foreign countries. Canadian tourists that same year represented almost 70 percent of all foreign visitors to the United States and spent more than $900 million while there.[42] Table 13 indicates the great size of the tourist traffic in both directions, as well as the large sums expended in two recent years.

Canadian agriculture, although it must compete for access to United States markets with American-grown products, has a trade advantage over

TABLE 13   NUMBERS AND EXPENDITURES OF UNITED STATES TRAVELERS IN
CANADA AND CANADIAN TRAVELERS IN THE UNITED STATES, 1970 AND 1971,
BY LENGTH OF STAY

	Americans in Canada (number)	Expenditures in Canada (thousands of Canadian dollars)	Canadians in USA (number)	Expenditures in USA (thousands of Canadian dollars)
1970				
Short-term	23,505,000	129,300	25,921,000	54,800
Long-term	13,648,000	952,600	9,735,000	833,700
Total, 1970	37,153,000	1,081,900	35,656,000	888,500
1971				
Short-term	24,112,000	132,100	24,331,000	61,000
Long-term	14,337,000	996,800	9,928,000	838,700
Total, 1971	38,449,000	1,128,900	34,259,000	899,700

Source: Canada Yearbook, 1973, pp. 770–71. Expenditures differ somewhat from those
reported in United States government data. By far the largest number of travelers traveled by
automobile.

that of other foreign countries exporting to the United States because transportation costs are lower for Canada. Excepting wheat (highly protected on
both sides of the border), the United States has taken half of Canadian agricultural exports and has supplied more than half of Canadian agricultural imports.[43] Movements of live cattle for finishing can reverse direction fairly
quickly, responding to shifts in a complex structure of prices in which considerable government intervention figures. Easy substitutability within a
product category leads the growers on one side or the other of the border to
put strong pressure on their own governments, in hard times, for protection,
as in the case of potatoes; often the government's response is to domestic
claimants for action favoring them, not to the behavior of the other side in
offering good terms. When similar products are not equally available on
both sides of the border, domestic merchant and consumer interests in an
area close to the border press for freer trade to save costs of transporting the
products from a more distant area in the same country. For products of high
bulk and low unit value, shipment north or south is usually cheaper than
east-west shipments, one example being fertilizers.[44] The importance of
transportation costs is especially marked if government action has interfered
with market determinants. Thus Canadian lumber can be more cheaply
transported to the eastern United States than can West-Coast American lum-

ber, because United States shipping laws require the latter to be carried in American bottoms, whereas Canadian lumber can seek the lowest shipping rates.[45]

The United States system of oil import quotas did not significantly counteract the natural economic advantage of Canadian oil in nearby midwestern American markets, and the oil continued to flow unabated in the 1960s and into the 1970s. When the Canadian government, faced with a possible oil shortage in the eastern provinces, began to impose its own restraints, they included a plan, regarded by many as uneconomic, to build a pipeline for carrying oil directly through Canada to that part of the country which depended on foreign imports.[46] Canadian oil nevertheless continued to move southward in record amounts throughout 1973, although Canadian officials warned that the flow would be reduced in the future. In November, 1974, the Canadian government, faced with serious depletion of the country's oil reserves, announced its intention to phase out oil exports completely. Eventually Canada would disappear from the ranks of those countries exporting oil to the United States; for many years it had been the most important. Nevertheless, the first reduction, to 800,000 barrels daily, was much higher than the amount set in the United States quota before that system was abandoned two years earlier, and only about 100,000 barrels less than the amount actually shipped in 1974. By the end of 1975, however, increasingly gloomy forecasts for Canada's future oil production impelled the government to set the following year's figure at less than 500,000 barrels and to advance the cutoff date to 1981.[47]

Although the two governments' efforts to mitigate the economic advantages of proximity suggested a wide gap in perspectives at the highest levels, at lower levels Canadian officials were closer to their American counterparts than were the officials of any other country. Any lack of information on the part of such Canadian officials has probably been no greater than that of American officials about their own government's intentions. "Misunderstandings" between Americans and Canadians have even less justification; officials on both sides know the requirements, pressures, and limitations of the other and cannot be misled about the practical limits on a response. (Of course, these observations apply not just to trade officials but across the board.) In addition, Canadian consulates in the United States as well as Canadian officials in Washington have long been active in bringing Canadian firms and trading associations together with their American counterparts and with members of Congress whose constitutents may have interests in common with the Canadians' clients.[48] If trade policies are under consideration in one government, it is customary for administrative officials to inform their friends in the other government, and if a decision goes against the preference of that other government, they are likely to try to ease the impact. In the United States ambassador's public complaint of September 25, 1974, that with respect to a variety of current Canadian trade restrictions affecting food and fuel, the United States had been "confronted . . . without opportunity for effective consultation," he took note that this behavior was contrary to customary practice.[49]

One special type of gap, discrepancies between Canadian and American official statistics on trade, was closed in 1973. As a result of reconciliation of the two government's methods of calculation, the 1972 balance between the two countries showed a Canadian surplus of $1.5 billion, as opposed to the earlier American claim that it was one billion dollars higher and the Canadian claim that it was half a billion dollars lower.[50]

AUSTRALIA

Located literally at the opposite end of the world from the United States, and lacking either the ease of informal communication that has prevailed between Canadian and American trade officials or any bilateral governmental committees, Australia has had to find other ways to overcome distance. Thus Australian government officials have made the most of international meetings and ad hoc economic negotiations to get to Washington, sometimes several times a year. Senior administrators customarily take junior officials with them for the experience gained. At international meetings Australian officials tend to associate with the Americans in their personal contacts, which is easy because of affinities between them. Yet the effort is a little one-sided, since few American administrators visit Australia and then only on brief trips.

One way to improve communications, better and cheaper air travel, has been hindered by the two governments' reluctance to grant each other's airlines more landing rights.[51] In the rather bitter quarrels of the early 1970s, the Australians appeared unwilling to make concessions that would affect their national airline even though the cost of the disagreement in income and contacts was disproportionately greater to them than to the United States. Here physical distance was accentuated by the policies of the two governments.

MEXICO

In contrast to the problems of distant Australia, Mexico's common border with the United States has induced the two governments to make exceptions in general trade rules, particularly for the communities of the two countries living next to each other. Like Canada, Mexico has received special treatment from the United States not only for oil during the period of import quotas but also for beef cattle coming across the border on the hoof, which fall under a lower tariff than that for meat. The dollars spent by American tourists in Mexico are so important a source of income that the Mexican government has exerted tremendous efforts to encourage this industry.[52] Good roads, for example, have been built to join American roads at the border. Partly because policing 1800 miles of boundary against smuggling is difficult, Mexico has established a small number of free-trade zones in population clusters near the border.[53] Unlike faraway Australia and Brazil, Mexico could offer a special lure to American tourists after the United States dollar was devalued. Americans were enticed by the fact that lower costs of getting there and a nonrevalued local currency meant that their vacation dollars would go further in Mexico than elsewhere.

BRAZIL

Without the magnet of a huge country next door, Brazil like Australia has successfully cultivated other markets as distant as those in the United States. Even less than any of the other three powers has Brazil paid attention in its trade policies to East-West ideological considerations. Regardless of the regime in power, it scarcely responded in any way to American views on commerce with Communist countries during the cold war. For example, in the summer of 1966, Brazil accepted a large credit from the Soviet Union to be used mostly to purchase industrial equipment, especially for the petroleum industry, on terms comparable with those available from Western European suppliers.[54]

CUMULATION AND SPILLOVER

CANADA

The United States and Canada have been close in another way: they both have favored freer international trade in general. This has facilitated a gradual but marked liberalization of trade between the two countries over the past forty years, liberalization not only with regard to tariffs but of valuation practices as well. Canada was rather easily weaned away from most imperial preference arrangements as the United States market loomed more important, and with the easing of barriers, trade between the two countries grew rapidly. (Heavy American direct investment in Canada, to be discussed in chapter 7, was another important factor.)

The very closeness of trading relations has produced its own problems. When, under domestic pressure, one of the two governments has on occasion acted in such a way as adversely to affect the other's trade and the other has reacted unfavorably, the governments have often compromised their differences. Each country developed ways to bring indirect influence upon the other's government, in addition to formal communications. These methods, however, did not include package deals, especially since Canadians have avoided such bargaining devices. They have shunned them for several reasons, including fear of weakening a strong position on a particular issue and divergent interests of different parts of the country. Administrators in both countries normally sought to prevent controversy from spreading from one issue area to another.

Meanwhile, the Canadian government has learned how, especially through fiscal measures, to insulate their economy to some extent. By moderating the impact of American influences, Canadians could prevent their economy from inevitably moving with the ebb and flow of the economy next door. For example, after the United States imposed the surcharge on import duties in August, 1971, the Canadian government prepared to embark on an employment- support program to help reimburse exporters who might be injured by the American action. The Canadian minister of finance took care to explain to the United States Department of the Treasury that such measures did not constitute the kind of action for which GATT rules would permit the United States to retaliate by antidumping moves.[55]

Such efforts move in the opposite direction from collaboration. Where an integrative step was taken, as in the case of the automobile industry, a limited spillover did occur. By 1970, wage rates for auto workers in Canada had risen to conform with those in the United States (a move which has raised fears among some Canadians who are worried about wage parity). There were also economic effects on industries related to automobile production, such as the machine-tool industry. But there was no more to initiate similar agreements in other areas, contrary to the expectations of some economists.

Despite great interdependence in trade, the two countries usually conducted their monetary affairs relatively independently of each other. On some occasions, they supported each other's currency in various ways, as when the United States made a special stabilizing loan to the Canadian government to aid it in its 1962 monetary crisis.[56] On other occasions they acted unilaterally even when they had multilateral obligations. The United States has repeatedly framed its monetary policies with a global perspective, only belatedly recognizing, after taking an initiative, that the two economies were too interlinked for Canada not to be dealt with on a separate basis. Canada, on its part, has been a monetary maverick at times, floating its dollar from 1950 to 1962 and again (despite American and other IMF members' objections) in 1970. When the United States government changed its view on parities and pressed in August, 1971, for the revaluation of certain countries' currencies, including Canada's, the Canadian government went its own way. However, the Canadian dollar, while continuing to float, has remained fairly close in value to the American dollar; at the time of the 1971 crisis, Canadians refused to follow Secretary of the Treasury John Connally's pressure to revalue it higher than it actually rose.[57]

AUSTRALIA

During the earlier postwar years, Australia experienced great swings in the terms of its foreign trade and, consequently, a succession of exchange crises. Lacking the easy access to foreign capital available to Canadians for export-oriented industries, Australians were less able to avoid balance-of-payments problems.[58] They were disappointed to discover that being a good ally to the United States did not help them to get favorable trade treatment.[59] As Harry Gelber wrote, Australia was "too small to compel such concessions and too rich to plead for them." [60] Nor did cooperation in defense matters protect Australia from disposal of surplus American wheat; like the Canadians, the Australians found that this practice could hurt allies, too.

Most-favored-nation treatment in GATT negotiations, of course, provided some spillover into better access to the United States market when Australia negotiated numerous trade advantages with Britain. But the Australians quickly learned in GATT bargaining sessions that they could not trade an industrial concession for an agricultural one; they had relatively few industrial products to use as leverage.

The only one of the four middle powers to belong to the sterling bloc, Australia had reason several times after World War II to leave the bloc but resisted the temptation. The informal sense of obligation and of mutual advantage keeping Australia tied to the pound was weakened when Britain in 1966 put restrictions on the outward flow of investment capital. The next year the Australian government took a "historic decision" showing that Australia had "come of age" (Minister of the Treasury Harold Holt's words), when it did not follow Britain's devaluation of the British pound with devaluation of the Australian dollar. A booming economy in the late 1960s protected Australia from the great instabilities in its balance of payments that had previously caused the Australians to be generally cautious about monetary policies. By the 1970s, Australia had greatly increased its United States dollar holdings but continued to retain the Australian dollar's parity with the pound sterling even after the announcement in August, 1971, of President Nixon's new economic policy. Not until the Smithsonian agreement of December, 1971, did Australia finally decide to fix the market rate for the Australian dollar in terms of the American dollar rather than continuing to base it on sterling, a decision which appreciated the Australian dollar by 6.32 percent above its earlier value but, overall, depreciated it in relation to parities of Australia's trading partners by 1.75 percent.[61]

When the Australian Labor party returned to office, however, the government revalued the Australian dollar twice, in December, 1972, and in September, 1973. Since at the time of the devaluation of the United States dollar in February, 1973, Australia retained its earlier gold-parity rate, the differential between Australian and United States dollars increased in three stages to 25 percent. Then, in September, 1974, the Australian government devalued its dollar by 12 percent and discontinued the link with the American dollar, fixing each exchange rate by means of a complicated formula weighted according to the importance of each country's trading significance to Australia. The Labor government had been endeavoring to reduce the unprecedentedly large international reserves which reflected a surplus in its current account in 1972 through these and other measures, including a unilateral reduction of 25 percent in all protective tariffs.[62] These fluctuations in fiscal and monetary policy reflected internal changes that resulted from the new government's political designs for redistribution of wealth, as well as instability in the international monetary system. So far as the fluctuations represented responses to United States policies, they were efforts to reduce the impact of American trade and monetary measures on the Australian economy.

MEXICO

After several years of bilateral and multilateral negotiations with the Latin American countries regarding trade issues, the United States government began to shed some of its opposition to their ideas concerning international trade. Ever since the Chapultepec Conference early in 1945, Mexico had been a leader in promoting doctrines at variance with American preferences for liberalizing world trade through the encouragement of international specialization, which to the Mexicans meant continued dependence on the sale of raw materials in the unreliable world market. Mexico became a strong supporter of the Latin American Free Trade Association, an organization which the United States only belatedly welcomed.[63] Mexico, as the third largest exporter of coffee to the United States, was pleased when the United States, dropping its earlier objections to international commodity agreements, helped bring about the 1962 international coffee agreement.[64] The Americans, however, continued to oppose a further erosion of the most-favored-nation principle embodied in GATT by refusing to accept the proposals of Mexicans and other Latin Americans for special trade preferences for Western Hemisphere countries. The American response was to press the case of the Latin Americans in GATT and the OECD in order to work out some global arrangement for special treatment of manufactures of underdeveloped countries. Not until late 1974 did Congress pass a law which authorized a generalized system of tariff preferences for such countries.[65] Mexicans often claimed that adoption by the United States of trade policies more favorable to their interests would greatly reduce their need for foreign aid. They strongly preferred to achieve economic development through exports rather than through a kind of assistance that might threaten their independence.

BRAZIL

Brazilians, whatever regime was in power, shared Mexican views on how the advanced countries, especially the United States, should stimulate development of their country through certain trade measures. They also built on the well-known American concern that they be a thriving, dependable partner in Latin America. The small sugar quota received by Brazil from the United States in 1960, when the Cuban quota was parceled out, steadily increased. The Brazilian government coupled expansion of Brazil's American market with rehabilitation of the poverty-stricken Northeast, where it began gradually to modernize the sugar industry. American interest in improving the appalling condition of this region could then be counted on when the annual United States allocations of sugar quotas were being made.[66] While the effect of the American sugar quota was to increase Brazilian sugar production to the point that Brazil became the world's largest sugar-cane producer, Brazil used another trade arrangement, the International Coffee Agreement of 1968, to reduce its dependence upon coffee production. This agreement set up a fund which could be drawn upon by producers to diversify into other activities, an idea which the Brazilians had been pressing in international negotiations for many years.[67] One effect of diversification would be lessened dependence on the American market.

CHANNELS OF COMMUNICATION

CANADA

As trade questions became increasingly interrelated with other economic policy, expanded channels of communication could be expected. Probably more bilateral governmental and private organizations exist between the United States and Canada than between any other two countries; certainly more people are involved in such groupings.[68] Many deal with trade questions, and their very existence is evidence of a response to problems arising between the two countries. Important among these organizations was the ministerial Joint Committee on Trade and Economic Affairs, established in 1953 and convened thirteen times up to 1970. About once a year the secretaries of state and cabinet-rank officials dealing with trade, finance, economic policy, agriculture (and, recently, natural resources) met to exchange information and views. Meanwhile, very active joint working groups of the committee dealt with particular issues, such as surplus-wheat disposal, energy resources, and competition between lumber industries. The committee's activities included coordination of existing programs, finding compromises for conflicting policies, and laying the basis for future joint programs.[69]

The IMF and, especially, the Group of Ten have served to keep Canadians and Americans collaborating in monetary matters despite some unilateral actions. During the 1960s, members of the Canadian Department of Finance and the Bank of Canada regularly and frequently were in close personal touch with their American counterparts to discuss matters such as capital-flow guidelines, usually without diplomatic intervention from the Department of State and the Department of External Affairs.[70] To improve communication on monetary questions, the two governments established a Balance of Payments Committee, composed of the appropriate officials from the two countries. Joint committees of this kind supplemented and reinforced less formal discussions carried on by high financial officials. None of these agencies appeared effective at the time of President Nixon's new economic policy of August, 1971.[71] The Committee on Trade and Economic Affairs last met in November, 1970, and the marked increase in controversy about trade issues since then raises a question: did this sharpened conflict prevent further meetings or would the reconvening of this committee have helped to reduce the acerbity associated with discussion of the issues?

In the private sector, the influential Canadian-American Committee, sponsored by the Planning Association of Canada (now combined with the C. D. Howe Research Foundation) and the National Planning Association of the United States, is composed of more than seventy members from business, agriculture, labor, and the professions. This committee institutes technical studies of economic issues affecting the two countries and on the basis of them takes joint positions on policy recommendations.[72] Among the groups established to ease tensions which had built up between the two countries in the late 1950s was the Canada–United States Interparliamentary Group. It meets roughly once a year to discuss economic issues of interest to those in the countries' national legislatures, as well as defense and foreign policy questions.[73]

Since the inauguration of GATT, the two governments' trade negotiations with each other have usually taken place in the course of its various general rounds of negotiations. Prior to the regular conferences, the responsible Canadian and American officials have exchanged ideas concerning the problems on GATT's agenda.[74] The Canadians prefer this larger multinational organization to any regional arrangement and have a good record of implementation. In the GATT context, whatever bargaining takes place in securing concessions is confined to trade matters and does not embrace other considerations. GATT rules (which had to be stretched far to accommodate

the automobile pact) do not favor partial steps toward a free-trade area between members (which would discriminate, in effect, against others); neither
country appears ready to test the rules' further flexibility.

AUSTRALIA

The formal institutions through which Australia and the United States
have dealt with each other in trade matters have been multilateral. Although
these have been useful channels for communication, they also have presented opportunities for confrontation between the United States and Australia, far more so than in the case of Canada. The most important, GATT, has
been one in which Australia always has been a lukewarm participant. Its
reluctance was related to policy differences with the United States and to
Australia's less-than-fervent support for the basic idea of most-favored-
nation treatment. Thus at the 1947 Geneva negotiations among twenty-two
countries which established the General Agreement on Tariffs and Trade,
Australia almost broke off talks because of United States congressional action raising further the tariff on wool; the crisis was ended only by a presidential veto.[75] GATT did not end existing preferences, but it did serve to
prevent granting of new ones.[76]

A continuing obstacle to Australian-American cooperation through
GATT has been a difference over the treatment of agricultural exports.
Australia has been mainly interested in gaining better markets for its agricultural exports, while the United States, which from the beginning successfully insisted on special treatment for this sector, sought waivers for particular farm products, most of them competitive with Australian exports.
Australia and other contracting parties brought an action against the United
States in 1957 to nullify its complete ban (for "defense purposes") on the
import of butter and other dairy products; although the right to institute retaliatory actions was recognized in GATT, such actions did not satisfy Australian needs.[77] Gradually, Australia articulated the doctrine that it occupied a
midway position between the developed industrial countries and the underdeveloped raw-material exporting countries and therefore should be accorded the right to different treatment from the former.[78]

Australia came close to withdrawing from GATT at the 1955 negotiating round; eventually it received concessions sufficient to lead it to remain a
participant. These included some guidelines on American practices of dispos-
ing of agricultural surpluses, a matter on which other members also sought

United States agreement.[79] This issue was liquidated during the Kennedy Round in the 1960s when members adopted an international grains arrangement to aid underdeveloped countries.[80] However, during the same round, Australia, like Canada, secured exemption from the across-the-board tariff cuts sought by the United States as a general objective. This across-the-board method would have worked inequitably for Australia, in that government's view, because of Australia's special tariff structure attuned to the stage of its economic development, that is, because it was less industrialized than many of the other countries and had unusually high tariffs on some manufactures to stimulate its own production of them.[81]

The Australians' perception of their country as midway in development (though admittedly one of the rich countries) brought them into conflict with the United States (as well as some other developed countries) during the 1960s in UNCTAD as well as in GATT. Special treatment for the manufactures of underdeveloped countries seemed reasonable to Australia and New Zealand. Both governments had accepted the legitimacy of the underdeveloped countries' desire for an organization like UNCTAD and took the lead in helping to establish it while other, even more developed countries dragged their feet. Australia later rejected the GATT formula for aiding industrialization of the underdeveloped countries, namely, through gradual elimination of tariffs imposed on their manufactures, a method favoring the more industrialized members' interests. Australia then inaugurated its own program of selected preferences to aid less developed countries, in line with what it viewed as its special position. Against American opposition, Australia eventually obtained GATT approval of the waiver necessary to make this program legitimate.[82] Because the Australians viewed themselves as still industrializing, they stayed out of the OECD long after it was organized, joining only in 1971.[83] To them this group had looked like a caucus of the completely industrialized countries, whose interests differed from Australia's.[84]

MEXICO

As a spokesman in inter-American agencies or in UNCTAD, Mexico had occasionally found the United States more attentive to its claims for special consideration in trade matters because a politically significant group of states was involved. Yet Mexicans were never happy with the OAS as a forum for promoting their interests, not only because they believed it too asymmetrical an organization, given its one giant non-Latin member, but also because the United States had long been reluctant to accept Mexican and other Latin American demands for giving the OAS a stronger economic focus.[85] They welcomed other international organizations, especially United Nations–affiliated groups such as UNCTAD, as means for amplifying their voice when expressing grievances to the United States.

An important exception was GATT. For Mexicans, it was a club of industrialized and wealthy countries dominated by the United States.[86] They disregarded American hints that their absence from the Kennedy Round would deny them an opportunity to uphold their special economic interests and that the informal most-favored-nation treatment accorded by the United States was not a general one equivalent in assurance to that GATT members enjoyed. Yet they were quite ready to participate in international commodity agreements which included consumer as well as producer states.

Mexican leaders never spurned opportunities for bilateral contacts with United States officials, formal and informal. Much was made of meetings between the two presidents, and the Mexican chief executive on numerous occasions was able to address a well-attended joint session of the United States Congress and in frank fashion criticize American policies. Mexicans continually stressed the need for prior consultation when the United States was about to make a move affecting their trade, and they took full advantage of various propitiatory actions by the United States government, as in an intergovernmental consultative committee on cotton.

The members of the Mexican congress took seriously their interparliamentary group with members of the United States Congress, publishing the discussions in full and using these meetings to put forth every conceivable trade demand. As in other organizations in which the United States was represented, they shied away from discussions of a political nature, especially global questions, and went right to the point of their economic grievances. Measured by the responses of the American members of the interparliamentary group, this forum was remarkably effective in reaching those in the United States government who would make decisions affecting the Mexican economy. Genuine personal friendships were formed which stood Mexico in good stead. Another important instrument for exchanging views on commercial matters and for suggesting ways to facilitate trade has been the Joint Mexican-American Trade Relations Committee, established in October, 1965. In addition, there have been formal and informal conferences participated in by businessmen from the two countries and by high trade officials.[87]

BRAZIL

Despite a preference for the more specific bilateral arrangement when it favors them, the Brazilians have turned increasingly to international agencies, especially those where the addition of other voices may increase the impact of their own voice.[88] This was true with respect to cotton exports, in which they have competed directly with the United States. In the International Coffee Council, which by 1970 had forty-one producer members and twenty-one consumer members, Brazil was a leader of the former, the United States of the latter. Unlike Mexico, Brazil early joined GATT. But, unhappy with the way in which they thought it served mainly the developed countries, the Brazilians turned to UNCTAD. Like the Mexicans, the Brazilians had endeavored unsuccessfully to give the charter of the OAS a more economic emphasis. They later worked with the Economic Commission for Latin America to elaborate trade doctrines more suited to the interests of others in the hemisphere than the United States. Although originally enthusiastic about the Latin American Free Trade Association, the Brazilian government's ardor cooled after the change in regime in 1964. As Brazil's huge economic potentialities gradually began to materialize, the traditional Brazilian reluctance to be lumped together with Spanish-speaking countries in a Latin American framework again became manifest.

ADMINISTRATIVE TREATMENT VERSUS POLITICIZATION

CANADA

Whether the United States and Canada are discussing trade matters with each other in a multilateral organization or working more informally through officials responsible for some specific question, their responses to each other's needs are sometimes more informed if the departments of state or external affairs become involved. This is one reason why members of these departments seek, often vainly, to monitor the multitude of informal contacts between opposite-number experts in the two governments. The diplomatists believe that thereby they can anticipate and thus forestall political crises; this monitoring function is especially important when only one government (usually the United States) is acting in an area of interest to the other. The involvement of informed officials in the foreign ministries actually may prevent problems from becoming serious political issues that then must be dealt with on the highest levels of the two states' governments.

The more agencies within either government that are involved, the greater is the likelihood that a trade question will have policy implications and that some agencies will be less concerned with Canadian-American trade relations and the substance of the problem and more concerned with their own bureaucratic positions, with their country's trading relations with third countries, or with some domestic political advantage.[89] Because of the huge size of the United States government, these other concerns are more likely to develop on the American side, to the detriment of Canadian trade interests. On the other hand, a particular trade question is more likely to rise to the attention of top levels of decision making in the Canadian government than in the United States government, because of the greater importance of foreign trade to Canada.

Canada is not invariably the loser when a trade question becomes a matter of high policy in the United States. Under the aggressive leadership of Secretary of the Treasury John Connally, who was neither internationally minded nor Canadian-oriented, the new economic policy of President Nixon not only made no exceptions for Canada but also prompted bilateral trade talks with Canada to secure certain concessions.[90] Differences on some matters which had earlier been only trade controversies had become politicized. The Canadians resisted any package deal and so firmly stood their ground that unlike others with whom the United States government was negotiating, they avoided yielding to the American demands. Meanwhile, they successfully pressed the Americans, including President Nixon himself, to declare that fruitful trade between the two countries did not require that the Canadians always be in deficit.[91] Although this politicized trade controversy was created at the level of the highest authorities in the United States, it did not have to remain at that level but could be defused by them after negotiation and then settle back to more routine treatment.

AUSTRALIA

Lacking the frequent and informal contacts between lower-echelon bureaucrats characteristic of Canadian-American relations, the Australians have of necessity depended heavily upon personal visits by high cabinet officials, especially those dealing with trade and finance, and by the prime minister to discuss with their counterparts in Washington trade matters of particular concern. This practice accentuated the tendency to politicize trade disagreements, because controversies could not easily be solved at the lower levels of trade specialists. Since for a lengthy period during the long Menzies regime the ministers of trade and of treasury were political competitors, trade became mixed with other concerns, and minor trade questions could rise to the highest levels within the Australian government itself. Nevertheless, once the cabinet had accepted a line of action, this clearly became the government position. But when high officials went to Washington to negotiate, as on questions of meat imports or surplus-commodity disposal, they encountered the well-known complexity and discordant actions typical of the United States government. Not only must they deal with officials in large numbers of agencies that had other interests besides Australian trade, but also, once a bargain had been struck, it could be overruled in Congress, where other concerns were paramount. Such was the case with meat quotas. Since much of Australia's trade interests traditionally centered on agricultural exports, Australian officials' dealings were often with the Department of Agriculture, which the Department of State has found hard to coordinate with United States international trade policy. Thus on the American side of the Australians' trade negotiations, political matters regularly intruded, too. Added to these problems was the complicating factor that in both countries the products most likely to be involved were the object of extensive government regulation or of some kind of subsidy, inevitably politicizing trade negotiations.

MEXICO

Trade issues with the United States from the start were likely to be highly charged with political implications for Mexicans, so vital were they to Mexican national objectives, especially since theirs was a much more managed economy. However, the keys to the levers which the Mexican government employed to promote its industrialization and economic independence were often hidden from outsiders. Thus, although tariffs were applied to specified classes of imports, licenses and other qualitative controls were administered on ad hoc and not easily visible bases.[92] Tariffs themselves have constituted about one-quarter of the state's revenues, making them an important element in the budget. Thus their reduction through trade concessions might involve substantial shifts in fiscal burdens, in turn drawing in other political interests, those which would have to provide new revenues.

United States leaders of both parties have on occasion made promises to Mexico and other Latin American countries which would have favored their trade, but which failed to be implemented, at least in the short run. Such failures to carry through often were due to bureaucratic controversies within the executive branch, where the proposed trade policy ran into conflicting interests in some agency whose consent was necessary. Special treatment for manufactures from developing countries was approved in principle by the administration in the mid-1960s. Not until 1973 was legislation which would make good on this promise proposed in Congress.

BRAZIL

The coffee trade has always been tied in with paramount political concerns in Brazil, and it became similarly politicized in the United States in the early 1960s because of its link to Alliance for Progress objectives. There had been a period when the two countries had had reciprocal interests in this commodity, as in other tropical crops. In contrast, shipping questions only in recent years have become highly controversial because of a marked change in Brazilian maritime policy. Intent on fostering its own merchant marine and borrowing some American practices, Brazil has been firm in preserving this interest against United States pressure, making a matter of high policy the issues of shipping conferences and cargo reservation.[93] Like Mexico, Brazil's developing status inevitably assures that trade dealings with the United States will not be routine but will concern the highest authorities.

DOMESTIC POLITICS

CANADA

Issues which become highly politicized and concern authorities at the top level in foreign relations are often rooted in some domestic political conflict. The intransigence of both the Canadian and American sides in the bilateral trade discussions which petered out in 1972 were related to the forthcoming elections facing Prime Minister Trudeau and President Nixon. On neither side could negotiators make concessions without running the risk of adverse effects on the governing party, faced with demands to aid its ailing economy. Not just national elections but relations between the chief executive and legislature or the federal government's relations with province

ECONOMIC RELATIONS: FOREIGN TRADE   143

or state have at times politicized Canadian-American trade questions. Canadians fear the power of Congress to circumscribe the president's authority in foreign trade, and with good reason. Especially because of the structure of Congress, provisions may be enacted into law protecting and favoring special interests as though the provisions involved only domestic questions and could override overall foreign trade policy; Canada (like the other middle powers of this study) has suffered in consequence.[94]

On both sides of the border, trade in agricultural products quickly becomes highly politicized, with special sectional interests wielding strong political influence. Agricultural competitors on the American side often had the edge because Congress is so structured—and the Senate so powerful—as to be particularly responsive to pleas for protective legislation for members' regions. Although wheat accounts for half of the total Canadian agricultural exports and its sale is managed by the official Canadian Wheat Board, the United States exports even larger quantities of this politically sensitive commodity. Unlike Canadian oil producers, Canadian farmers have no American lobbyists to aid them, although at times there have been Canadian spokesmen testifying before congressional groups studying agricultural trade problems. That great irritant to Canadian-American relations during the 1950s, the United States program for disposal of agricultural surpluses, appeared to take away traditional markets upon which a very important part of the Canadian economy (and polity) depended. When he announced changes in the program in July, 1958, Secretary of State Dulles alluded to Canadian pressure. John Diefenbaker, whose success in leading his party to victory in the Canadian election of 1957 was to make him prime minister, had campaigned on the promise to try to divert to Britain about 15 percent of Canadian trade with the United States.

Canadian exporters have not been completely at the mercy of Congress. Because of the separation of powers, there have been occasions when the president could do the prime minister a political favor. Thus in 1963, President Johnson vetoed a congressional act favoring lumber interests in the Northwest which would have been detrimental to Prime Minister Pearson's lumber constituency.[95] Ten years later, the Canadians were not so favored in the Michelin tire case. In its program to aid poorer regions' economic development, the Canadian government helped Nova Scotia obtain a branch of the French company, exports of which to the United States ran into a United States Tariff Commission determination that a countervailing duty be put upon them. This was a response to an American tire company's complaint that the Michelin tires were subsidized, but to the Canadians the United States action was inconsistent with the United States policy to provide special export aid to certain American companies under the 1971 Domestic International Sales Corporations (DISC) law.[96]

AUSTRALIA

For some of the same reasons as in Canada's case, Australians have regarded Congress as a greater hindrance than the executive branch to better access to American markets. The United States Senate, especially, is so organized that special interests which compete with Australian interests can secure legislative approval of the quotas which form so large a part of Australian complaints about trade restrictions. On occasion, though not necessarily in direct response to Australians' representations, a president has successfully opposed legislation detrimental to their interests. President Truman scuttled a high wool tariff bill during the GATT negotiations in 1947, and Lyndon Johnson did the same thing during the Kennedy Round.[97] Australian meat imports to the United States have been adversely affected by the strong American meat lobby, operating in Congress to establish quotas. When a meat scarcity and soaring prices developed in 1972, however, the administration found it politically desirable to take the opposite line. At least for a time, it was Australia's turn to call the tune and set the price when United States officials pleaded for larger quantities. The market could not be completely ignored; when it shifted, and United States producers were experiencing price declines resulting from new surpluses, Australian meat exports again suffered—and even more than in the past.[98]

Some of the Australian complaints about American treatment of their major exports have stemmed from the ability of the Country party to make or break a Liberal government. Agricultural interests were especially strongly represented in this small swing party, and its long-time leader, John McEwen, was minister of trade during a lengthy period of the coalition government. Although Australia no longer "rides on the back of the sheep," its beef was temporarily in great demand in the United States in the early 1970s. Agricultural trade issues might change but not their importance in the domestic politics of the two governments. Domestic repercussions in Australia from the United States government's manipulation of the market in beef from 1972 to 1975, resulting in undersupply and then oversupply in Australia, put intense political pressures on the new Labor government. This government's trade policies differed markedly from those of the Liberal-Country party coalition; all the disruptions in previous Australian-American trade patterns were not due to initiatives taken by the United States. Like the Canadian provinces, the states in Australia have vigorously sought trade outlets abroad, occasionally embarrassing the national government as well as getting in each other's way. Their power in Australian governments and in politics permits them to act quite autonomously in this field.

MEXICO

In the Mexican case, too, it is the United States Congress which is faulted when, through inertia or opposition, it fails to do its part in carrying out an administration's promise or when it sets quotas on imports of cotton, lead, zinc, or beef that frustrate Mexico's ability to compete in the American market. Anticipating that they would fare better under quotas than under free trade, however, the Mexicans tried to get the best deal possible rather than fight the system.

Mexico's own political structure has affected its foreign-trade policy. With an essentially one-party system and the aggregation of interests taking place within the executive branch, Mexican presidents have needed to be very sensitive to the demands of many divergent groups.[99] Opposition to Mexico's joining GATT when it was first organized came from an influential business group, Camera Nacional de la Industria de Transformacion (CNIT). Later, when the advantages of membership in GATT could be perceived by the government, both rightist-nationalist business groups and leftists promised to make sufficient trouble that the domestic political costs seemed to outweigh the benefits to be derived from membership. Absence of a "loyal opposition" increased the dangers from such interest groups.

BRAZIL

While American instant-coffee processors, even when organized into the National Coffee Association, hardly seem important enough to dictate public policy, the way in which Congress is organized did permit them to have a large voice in a matter of great importance to Brazil.[100] On the Brazilian side, the coffee elite had traditionally been so powerful in that country's government that they had been continuously appeased. For many years, national policies encouraged producers to increase rather than reduce coffee production, as Brazil asked the outside world to make adjustments to supplies far in excess of amounts demanded at the current price. Only in 1966, a few months after the military dictatorship took over, did the Brazilian government "courageously" impose a policy of radical reduction in coffee growing, such areas to be planted with other crops.[101] At the same time, it began to liberalize its import rules to make its protected industries more competitive.[102] Apparently, if one is to judge from Brazil's previous history, a less dictatorial regime would have been unable to take steps so unpopular with important economic groups.

SUMMARY

Only with Canada does the United States carry on a fairly extensive trade free of customs duties. Even in the Canadian case, what might be a single market continues to be impeded by various kinds of government action on both sides of the border. On the other hand, the automobile pact represents a noteworthy step taken by the governments themselves in the direction of greater trade integration. Geographical proximity has made for closeness in trade matters. Like Canada, Mexico from time to time enjoyed some mutually beneficial special trade arrangements with the United States, for example, in the relatively free movement of cattle and oil north across the border. Yet trade issues were the ones on which the Mexican government most often confronted the United States government, for its economic-development plans depended heavily upon increased exports. The Australians were not only the farthest away geographically, but also in their relations with the United States they had the hardest time catching the ear of its government. Also, a more responsive relationship was impeded because Australia's traditional exports competed with the output of American producers who commanded a strong political influence. Furthermore, institutional ties were lacking. Brazil, though also far away, could claim United States attention because its exports of tropical commodities, especially coffee (but, significantly, not soluble coffee) complemented American trade interests and because, for numerous economic and foreign policy reasons, its chronic foreign-exchange crises had involved Americans. By the 1970s, however, Australia and the United States were coming closer to each other on some trade matters; the opposite trend could be seen in Brazil's case. In both cases, part of the explanation was the growing importance of their trade relations with Japan as their own economies developed.

Bargaining power in trade matters depended on having alternative markets to those in the United States, something more readily available to the distant countries than to Mexico and Canada, for whom the huge market next door was irrestible. Bargaining power also depended on the importance to the United States of the middle power's trade. Only in the case of Canada were imports into the United States at all sizable compared to total United States imports (about 25 percent). Even in Canada's case, this figure was relatively low compared to the ratio of its imports from the United States to its total imports (about 70 percent). Bargaining power also varied with the scarcity and desirability of the commodity to be traded, which, as in the case of oil, might change over time. The United States economy was so immense that the imports from none of the four middle powers, not even Canada, were a sizable percentage of total American production, and the political impact of their trade interests was puny compared to that of competing domestic interests in the United States.

The four middle powers have been at least as responsible for barriers to trade with the giant power as was the United States. Such obstacles, however, usually have been imposed to protect industrializing efforts in the middle powers, while a major block to greater trade liberalization in the United States has been the influential agricultural interests which compete with those in the less developed countries. American agricultural producers were able to summon special support in Congress because of its manner of organization. Specific import quotas imposed by Congress for certain commodities—not confined to agricultural products—were especially resented by the middle powers. Congress is ill designed to respond directly to friendly foreign governments' trade interests and cannot do so on an individual-country basis.

Prewar American leadership in pressing for reciprocal trade concessions was after the war channeled through multilateral organizations which would secure such liberalization on a global basis, an objective only genuinely shared with the United States by the Canadians. The other three middle powers continued to favor more limited kinds of preferential systems, secured through particular international organizations. In all four of the middle powers, as well as in the United States, trade policy was determined by a great variety of domestic political considerations, some of them rooted in the constitutional system. The result was that trade policies were unlikely to be determined primarily on the merits of the exchanges in question but rather were more often mixed with political considerations. In bilateral negotiations, however, bargains usually were confined to economic matters and did not spill over into other issue areas. Higher levels of authority often were involved, sometimes creating, at other times smoothing over, trade controversies. Sometimes the diplomats were needed to handle crises which technical experts could not manage; higher state interests might call for some kind of compromise—if only an agreement to postpone further discussion. Yet for the two neighbors of the United States, other kinds of trade contacts, official or nongovernmental, were sufficiently extensive that proximity facilitated trade just as it offered advantages in easier transportation.

Trade questions inevitably involved monetary issues. Although the United States and its two neighbors each conducted independent monetary policies, coordinated mainly through multilateral channels, the United States authorities during much of this period tended to support the Canadian dollar and Mexican peso when either of these was in trouble. Both neighbors reciprocated in various ways, thereby contributing to the soundness of the three currencies. The import-duty surcharge of the Nixon new economic policy shocked each neighbor by its lack of customary discrimination for its special case, especially since the trade of each with the United States had normally helped that country's balance of payments.

Trade and monetary issues also were closely tied to foreign-investment questions in the relations of Canada and Mexico with the United States. During this period, in all three interrelated aspects of foreign economic policy, the bonds between the United States and Australia increased, especially in comparison with the formerly predominant British ties to Australia. In a fourth aspect, United States foreign aid, Brazil was also linked to the United States, since Brazil's export and import capacity, balance-of-payments problems, and capital expansion were a common concern of their two governments. Foreign investment and foreign aid are the subjects of the following chapter.

SEVEN

ECONOMIC RELATIONS: FOREIGN DIRECT INVESTMENT

IN ALL FOUR MIDDLE POWERS, the multinational corporation and, particularly, foreign direct investment by American enterprises have become a sensitive issue. At an earlier period, protective tariffs in the host countries that were costly to leap over and, later, expanding possibilities for profit making in rapidly developing markets and pressures from competitors already established abroad have led to extensive United States investment in these countries. From Table 14 a comparison can be made of United States direct investment in each of the four middle powers and between that investment and total United States direct investment abroad, for seven recent years. A further comparison can be made among main categories of industry, which shows that much more has been invested in manufacturing than in extractive industries.

Not only the size and number of American enterprises but also their purported behavior irritate many groups in the host countries. Complaints against the foreign companies include inadequate attention to export opportunities, too few nationals in high managerial and technical positions, failure to purchase needed equipment in host-country markets when available, little research and development done locally, too little interest in community affairs and local social customs, indifference to host-country interests in plant location, squeezing out of smaller domestic enterprises, and in general, the exhibiting of a "branch plant mentality." For the most sophisticated critics, the vital issue is that the main corporate decisions are made in the home office of the multinational corporation, usually in the United States, in ways which often seem insensitive to the host country's concerns. In addition, resentment is aroused when the United States government attempts to exert extraterritorial power by applying its export, capital-flow, and antitrust rules to American subsidiaries abroad.

TABLE 14   UNITED STATES DIRECT INVESTMENT IN FOUR MIDDLE POWERS
AND ALL AREAS, 1968–1972 (millions of US dollars)

Year	All Areas	Australia	Brazil	Canada	Mexico
1968					
All industries	64,983	2,652	1,484	19,535	1,466
Mining/smelting	5,435	365	81	2,638	112
Petroleum	18,887	b	83	4,094	44
Manufacturing	26,414	1,412	1,022	8,568	1,003
Other industries	14,247	875	299	4,235	308
1969					
All industries	71,016	2,947	1,636	21,127	1,640
Mining/smelting	5,658	396	99	2,769	136
Petroleum	19,882	b	100	4,361	35
Manufacturing	29,527	1,573	1,115	9,406	1,109
Other industries	15,948	978	322	4,591	360
1970					
All industries	78,178	3,304	1,847	22,790	1,786
Mining/smelting	6,186	478	131	2,989	153
Petroleum	21,714	b	118	4,807	33
Manufacturing	32,261	1,715	1,247	10,059	1,199
Other industries	18,035	1,111	351	4,935	401
1971					
All industries	86,198	3,730	2,066	24,105	1,838
Mining/smelting	6,685	600	119	3,246	127
Petroleum	24,152	b	145	5,149	30
Manufacturing	35,632	1,859	1,419	10,590	1,268
Other industries	19,728	1,271	382	5,121	413
1972					
All industries	94,337	4,123 a	2,505	25,771	2,025
Mining/smelting	7,110	703	149	3,455	124
Petroleum	26,263	b	164	5,301	32
Manufacturing	39,716	1,983	839	11,639	1,409
Other industries	21,249	1,428	564	5,378	461

Source: Department of Commerce, *Survey of Current Business,* October, 1967, October, 1970, October, 1971, October, 1972, September, 1973, August, 1974. Investment is measured by book value at year end. The department's revised figures are used in table. Industry categories for 1968 differ somewhat from those for later years.

a Incomplete figures.
b Put in "other industries" category to avoid disclosure.

Canada is notorious for having the most extensive American direct investment; it represented over 30 percent of all American direct investment abroad in the 1960s.[1] In some Canadian industries, it is uniquely large in proportion to the total investment—as much as 90 percent—and it increased at a startling rate during the 1950s and 1960s.[2] With a few exceptions, there has been an almost completely free market for the flow of capital between the two countries, and in most cases investors could respond easily to economic stimuli, almost unfettered by government interference. The inevitable nationalist reaction to so large a United States economic presence in Canada became evident in the 1960s and intensified in the 1970s. Table 15 shows for the year 1967 the kinds of Canadian enterprise in which over half of the voting stock was in American hands, the proportion so held, and the size of these investments. Table 16 indicates the predominance of United States direct investment in 1970 compared to that of other major investing countries.

Both the flow of American capital and the concern about it came later to Australia, which also had been very open to foreign direct investment. Like Canada in an earlier period, the almost chronic deficit in Australia's current account made foreign capital to cover the balance very welcome. Exciting discoveries in iron ore and petroleum produced a tremendous boom in foreign investment in the 1960s, reminiscent of Canadian experience. Unlike those in postwar Canada, however, the major foreign investors in Australia continued to be British. In the late 1960s they were overtaken by the Americans, who invested especially heavily in manufacturing, extractive activities and agri-business; the British and the Americans between them accounted for 90 percent of all foreign investment. Japanese investors, however, were beginning to assume major importance by the end of the 1960s.[3] Nevertheless, between 85 percent and 95 percent of Australia's capital investment has come from local sources.[4] Australians have tended much less than Canadians to invest abroad, and then mostly in Papua–New Guinea.[5] Table 17 shows for a decade of rapid increase in foreign investment in Australia the annual amounts coming from the major investing countries and how they were distributed between direct and portfolio investments.

Far less open to foreign direct investment than the two Commonwealth countries, Mexico's revolutionary doctrine based on unhappy experiences in the Porfirian period have dictated a preference for portfolio investment by

TABLE 15 CANADIAN INDUSTRIES HAVING MORE THAN 50 PERCENT
OF VOTING STOCK IN UNITED STATES HANDS, 1967

Industry	Assets (millions of Canadian dollars)	Percentage of Voting Stock Held by Americans
Iron mine industry	1,441.6	85.8
Oil and gas well industries	4,505.7	65.0
Nonmetal mining industry	916.7	65.0
Fruit and vegetable canners	343.4	62.3
Rubber products	503.1	82.9
Synthetic textiles	613.1	71.5
Paper products industries	239.9	53.3
Boiler and plate industries	95.9	68.9
Metal stamping industry	626.4	60.3
Commercial refrigeration	37.2	59.4
Machinery industries	1,225.6	73.8
Motor vehicles and parts	1,990.1	95.6
Truck bodies	100.2	55.8
Small electrical appliances	71.0	81.8
Major appliances	132.6	58.5
Industrial electrical equipment	624.6	89.6
Battery manufacturers	29.5	73.6
Nonmetallic mineral products	242.1	61.4
Petroleum refineries	4,059.0	72.0
Pharmaceuticals	256.8	68.6
Paint and varnish industries	165.4	67.1
Soap and cleaning compounds	153.7	62.1
Toilet preparations	94.8	66.4
Industrial chemicals	997.5	58.9
Scientific and professional equipment	257.7	62.0
Sporting goods and toys	109.3	51.3

Source: Based on table prepared for House of Commons Standing Committee
on External Affairs and National Defence, Minutes of Proceedings and Evidence,
July 13–27, 1970 (including the eleventh report to the House by Chairman Ian
Wahn), p. 40.

TABLE 16   FOREIGN DIRECT INVESTMENT IN
CANADA BY LEADING COUNTRIES AND TOTAL,
1970 (Canadian dollars)
....

Total	26,500,000,000
United States	21,500,000,000
Britain	2,500,000,000
Japan	103,000,000

Source: International Canada, October, 1973, p. 275.
Japanese investment had increased 47 percent from previous
total in 1969.

TABLE 17   ANNUAL INFLOW OF FOREIGN PRIVATE INVESTMENT INTO
AUSTRALIAN COMPANIES, 1966–1974 (millions of Australian dollars)
....

	1966–67	*1967–68*	*1968–69*	*1969–70*	*1970–71*	*1971–72*	*1972–73*	*1973–74*
				Direct Investment				
Undistributed income								
Total	115	228	249	221	247	231	310	413
Britain	60	116	140	147	139	106	154	173
USA	47	88	94	63	91	114	146	219
Japan	n.a.	2	3	−2	−3	−1	6	4
Other direct								
Total	248	333	349	512	658	652	40	147
Britain	33	−8	78	94	156	155	58	76
USA	157	249	189	296	238	250	−28	37
Japan	7	13	15	21	65	60	−20	31
			Portfolio Investment and Institutional Loans					
Total	153	402	405	274	655	600	104	−106
Britain	27	269	263	111	255	158	−108	−150
USA	78	51	38	−3	141	194	−37	−76
Japan	n.a.	n.a.	n.a.	n.a.	n.a.	n.a.	51	59

Source: Based on table in Australian Bureau of Statistics, *Overseas Investment, 1973–74* (1975),
p. 14.

foreigners and for credits and loans from international agencies. The Nacional Financiera, the government agency for fostering development, was created in the early 1940s in part to limit dependence upon private direct investment and to reduce the role of foreigners in Mexican enterprise. It borrows abroad and relends on favorable terms to Mexican entrepreneurs. Foreign enterprises have been "encouraged" to invest their profits in Mexico rather than to take them out. By carefully husbanding its reserves and moving forward in economic development in such a way that reserves were not threatened and development projects were not thwarted by foreign-exchange bottlenecks, Mexico managed to accomplish what few underdeveloped countries have found possible. It achieved a markedly rapid growth rate with very little inflation until the 1970s (when the worldwide inflation finally hit Mexico, too). The Mexicans did all this with a freely convertible currency and no restrictions on the export of interest and dividends on foreign investment.

The amount of United States private investment in Brazil was about the same as in Mexico until the 1970s, when it surpassed that of Mexico; the gap is increasing. However, American direct investment in Brazil is considerably smaller than in Australia and very much smaller than in Canada. By the 1970s, it had reached about two billion dollars. Foreign investment from certain other countries forms a larger part of the picture than in Mexico, although American investment constitutes about half the total coming from abroad.[6] Despite its immense potential for profitable foreign investment, Brazil until the late 1960s was less attractive than Mexico. It lacked Mexico's political stability; it imposed various restraints on profit remittances, and especially in the early 1960s, its inflation was rampant, far worse than in any other Latin American country.[7] Unlike the fairly steady Mexican policy toward foreign investment, Brazilian investment policy varied greatly as successive regimes in Brazil behaved very differently toward foreign investors. Even within a particular administration, the Brazilian president might start out, as did Juscelino Kubitschek, by encouraging foreign investment, and end by discouraging it, even if not directly intending to do so.[8] A major factor in the Brazilian "economic miracle" of the late 1960s was foreign investment, for which the military regime furnished very hospitable conditions.

JOINTNESS

CANADA

Large numbers of joint Canadian-American private enterprises have been formed, most of them to undertake activities on the Canadian side of the border. For example, several American and Canadian companies have been jointly engaged in developing a large iron-ore mining and marketing complex on the Quebec-Labrador border.[9] The tariff structure, however, often prevents a genuine economic integration of an industry, as in the case of chemicals. In that industry, because of tariffs, duplicated processes in the two countries have caused uneconomic fragmentation on the Canadian side, with too many firms and products and too short production runs for efficient organization. (Some of these conditions have been associated with the existence of branch plants of American corporations.)

Among measures proposed or undertaken in recent years by the Canadian government to limit foreign (chiefly American) influence are some which would make multinational enterprises more joint. These include inducements to fill a certain percentage of seats on boards of directors with Canadians and the provision of opportunities for Canadians to purchase stock in American corporations operating in Canada.[10] Other government measures would move away from jointness or even exclude American enterprise. Rules place certain sensitive types of enterprise, such as banking, insurance and communications, off-limits to foreign investment.[11] The Canadian Development Corporation, a crown corporation, was created in 1971 to encourage establishment of Canadian-owned, managed, and operated enterprises, thereby reducing the need for American participation in future developments.[12]

On the American side, a series of measures taken in the 1960s to meet the balance-of-payments problem through decreasing the flow of capital abroad also had the effect of slightly restricting the integrated capital market which currently existed between the two countries. The United States first instituted an "interest-equalization" tax on short-term capital outflows in 1963, then laid down "voluntary" guidelines for American direct investments abroad in 1965, and finally established stringent mandatory guidelines for such investments in 1968. The first step began with President Kennedy's sudden proposal to Congress in July, 1963, which caught Canadians by surprise. Over the following weekend huge sums of Canadian currency held by American subsidiaries were converted into American dollars at a rate which soon would have wiped out the Canadian reserves. The situation was righted only on the succeeding Monday morning when high Canadian officials flew to Washington to seek an exemption for Canada. They were able to persuade American officials to exempt new Canadian securities by showing that otherwise there would be an adverse effect on Canadian imports from the United States, worsening the United States trade balance and hence overall balance of payments.

In applying the guidelines of February, 1965, United States authorities also exempted Canada from restrictions on capital outflow; when these rules were further tightened late that year, Canada sought and eventually secured an ambiguous kind of exemption when American subsidiaries in Canada were told, in effect, that the rules governing repatriation of profits did not really apply to them. Even though the 1968 mandatory guidelines made Canada a special case, a Canadian monetary crisis was necessary to prompt the United States authorities to exempt Canada totally. In return for these various instances of special treatment, the Canadian government had to make a number of promises about the level and content of its foreign-exchange reserves, about the exercising of surveillance over capital leaving the country (to prevent "pass-throughs" of American funds), about agreement to purchase United States government securities, and about other measures of like nature.[13] Meanwhile, in 1966 the Canadian government issued twelve "principles" of its own to guide subsidiaries in Canada, including retaining enough earnings for growth after paying a fair return to owners. Gradually, the very tight connection between Canadian demand for and American supply of capital began to loosen as other sources of funds for Canadian development opened up.[14]

AUSTRALIA

Restrictions similar to Canadian rules have excluded foreigners from Australian banking, aviation, television, and radio. Otherwise, the Australian government until 1973 actively encouraged the flow of capital from abroad, and so did the state governments, especially through tax lures.[15] The Australian government's Visiting Expert Agreement program, for example, attracted American technicians and other specialists who had skills not readily available in Australia to live there for up to four years while enjoying special income-tax concessions.[16] Devoting a remarkably small proportion of their GNP to research and development, the Australians have been especially eager to secure the technological and managerial knowledge which foreign enterprise offers. Like Canadians, Australians have wanted more of the processing of their valuable natural resources to take place in Australia, rather than having their country become the "quarry of the world."

Many joint ventures and licensing arrangements have been made by Australians and Americans operating on a private basis. However, large numbers of the bigger American companies have preferred that their Australian subsidiaries be wholly owned by the parent company.[17] One reason given was the companies' desire to reinvest their profits in Australia rather than declare larger dividends, a choice which, they said, might be more difficult if they had large numbers of Australian shareholders.

MEXICO

Unlike the governments of Canada and Australia, the Mexican government has constantly and closely regulated foreign investment. Since the settlement of the oil-expropriation controversy, not the United States government but only the government of Mexico has been involved with private American entrepreneurs operating in that country. Partly because of its ambivalence about foreign direct investment (wanting the technological contributions and managerial skills but not the other foreign influences that might accompany these), the Mexican government has been highly pragmatic in dealing with foreign enterprise. Regardless of the techniques for controlling it, however, the Mexicans have since the 1950s almost continuously pressed for greater and greater Mexican sharing in the equity arrangements. Not satisfied with a formal 51 percent majority ownership, they have sought higher percentages and eventually have maneuvered to eliminate jointness entirely by buying up the whole or almost the whole of some enterprises. These they do not necessarily operate as government corporations; instead they may sell shares to private Mexican investors. For only certain kinds of enterprises, those which would eventually result in greater *Mexican* development (not just "growth") has the government actively solicited foreign capital. It has sought enterprises which would merely complement Mexican endeavors rather than take their place. But a need to balance the outflow of funds resulting from interest payments on increased borrowing abroad in the 1960s impelled the Mexicans to continue to encourage foreign investment of a kind that would actively promote Mexican exports.[18] Despite the prolonged period in which foreigners shared in Mexican enterprises, by far the largest source of funds for the Mexican development "miracle" came from Mexican investors themselves.[19]

Besides requiring majority Mexican ownership—which has not meant necessarily control and is sometimes waived—the government has required the use, so far as possible, of Mexican labor and Mexican materials, as well as Mexican technicians and managers. In the Mexican calculations, joint ventures are perceived as a temporary evil.

BRAZIL

Like the Mexican government, the Brazilian government continually has intervened in matters of foreign investment. It too at an earlier period joined with the United States government in bilateral governmental committees to study and make recommendations for Brazilian economic development. Both the national and state governments in Brazil on occasion have joined with a private foreign company in operating enterprises to further the objective of development. During the military dictatorship, for example, a mining venture has involved the United States Steel Corporation, and Philips Petroleum has joined the Brazilian government in establishing a huge fertilizer company. Such ventures are in addition to the many privately owned joint enterprises between Brazilian and foreign companies, which are often truly multinational in the sense that they join foreign companies from several countries, not only the United States. Nevertheless, Americans have been predominant among foreign investors in Brazil, and other governments have tended to follow American patterns in seeking protection for their nationals' investments. For example, a model was set for Germany when the United States obtained a guarantee from the Brazilian government in 1965 that protected American investment from certain risks, including expropriation, inconvertibility, war, and revolution.[20]

One effect of the economic boom which Brazil began to experience in the late 1960s was a marked improvement in its current-account balance. Until that time, the country was continually faced with a dilemma. The constraints imposed by its foreign indebtedness meant that to continue the country's growth its monetary and fiscal policies had to be adjusted to the demands of its creditors. This indebtedness was so large and involved so many governments as well as private groups that, in fact, the creditors and Brazil had a common interest in the periodic "rescalings." From time to time, these adjustments in Brazil's immediate financial liabilities were negotiated between Brazil and its American and European creditors, "the Club of Hague." Without these joint arrangements, the Brazilians would have continued to have difficulty getting further foreign exchange. Except for right after World War II, when Brazilian foreign credits were quickly squandered, the foreign-exchange bottleneck existed for decades, and it was a major impediment to the economic development which both Brazilians and the foreign creditor countries desired.

RECIPROCITY

CANADA

Very different were the problems caused by the asymmetry between Canada and the United States in the investment field. Nevertheless, trade-offs at the government level are difficult because the physical assets at stake mostly are located in Canada. However, since the United States government has taken numerous actions which impinge on American investment in Canada and the Canadian government has increasingly concerned itself with this subject, some bargaining opportunities concerning American capital there are conceivable. Since the United States government has not been indifferent to the interests of American investors in Canada, a pattern not of joint treatment of each other's investors but of action-reaction to American investment in Canada can be seen.[21] Compromises and/or acquiescence characterize this pattern, as may be seen when the United States imposed guidelines on American corporations having subsidiaries abroad.

Canadians invest more per capita in the United States than Americans do in Canada, and there are several big Canadian corporations which have subsidiaries in the United States. In fact, next to Britain, Canada is the largest source of foreign direct investment in the United States, and the amount has been greater than American direct investment in the 1970s in either Mexico or Brazil. Nevertheless, a large part of the Canadians' money in the United States is in portfolio investments, which have been more attractive to the cautious Canadian than were new business ventures at home. A decade of Canadian direct investment in the United States is shown in table 18, with amounts and the major types of enterprise into which it was put. Chart D

TABLE 18   CANADIAN DIRECT INVESTMENT IN UNITED STATES BUSINESS
ENTERPRISES HAVING A CANADIAN INTEREST OR OWNERSHIP OF AT LEAST 25
PERCENT, 1963–1972 (millions of US dollars)

	1963	1964	1965	1966	1967	1968	1969	1970	1971	1972
Total	2,180	2,284	2,388	2,439	2,575	2,659	2,834	3,117	3,339	3,612
Petroleum	213	205	208	98	99	100	132	190	207	268
Manufacturing	1,063	1,129	1,219	1,342	1,397	1,413	1,644	1,836	2,025	2,194
Finance and										
Insurance	337	382	370	386	354	376	325	324	305	310

Source: Statistical Abstract of the United States.

CHART D.   DISTRIBUTION OF FOREIGN DIRECT INVESTMENT IN THE UNITED
STATES, 1962 AND 1971.

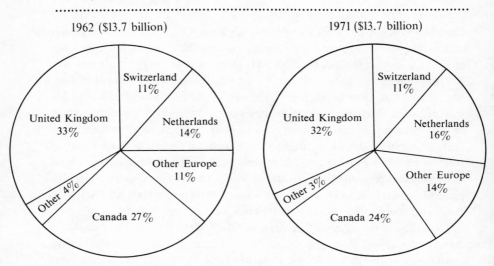

Redrawn from *Survey of Current Business,* February, 1973.

shows the importance of Canada among foreign countries with direct investments in the United States in 1962 and almost a decade later.

Changing economic and social factors may reinforce unilateral action
by the Canadian government to alter investment trends, including efforts to
diversify sources of funds for direct investment in Canada. The well-

publicized attempt by the Canadian Development Corporation to buy a controlling share of Texas Gulf, Inc. suggests some lack of reciprocity in the pattern of take-overs. American companies—to be sure, not government corporations—had been doing the same thing in Canada for years. In this reverse case, the American company, which derives the major part of its income from Canada, resisted the effort in two court actions in the United States. The Canadians eventually settled for a somewhat smaller percentage of shares than originally sought, and four members of the Canadian Development Corporation were added to the board of directors.[22]

AUSTRALIA

Reciprocal arrangements between the United States and Australian governments have been limited to the double-taxation agreement of 1953, which included provisions for one government, in some cases, collecting taxes on behalf of the other. The Australians anticipated that concessions, especially those which limited to 15 percent the tax imposed by the country of origin on dividends paid to residents of the other country, would result in encouraging American investment in Australia.[23]

In return for great hospitality to overseas capital invested in new ventures during the Liberal–Country party coalition, Australia obtained marked economic improvements, especially through technological advances.[24] Industries have grown up partly through American development, where little existed before, as in cotton growing and petroleum refining.[25] Others, such as air transport, were molded by American techniques, capital, and equipment.[26] Most American investment has been in new, large-scale industries that affected the whole Australian economy, directly and indirectly through their influence on their local suppliers.[27] Some Australian commentators have declared that Australian enterprise has become more competitive, less restrictive, and that standards of quality and efficiency have been markedly raised under the influence of foreign investment.[28] Despite these reciprocal advantages, the costs looked sufficiently great to the Australian Labor party that the earlier hospitality for foreign investment declined noticeably under its aegis—and so did the amount of new investment.

MEXICO

Regardless of numerous and complicated regulations and restrictions, apparently applied arbitrarily in some instances, American investment has continued to pour into Mexico. Until the mid-1960s, American capital constituted about 80 percent of total foreign investment, although this proportion has since declined. American investment tends to be concentrated in manufacturing, where in the mid-1960s it constituted about one-fifth of all capital in that sector.[29] American investors have big stakes in the largest businesses, and the prominence of their products makes them easy targets for nationalist complaints, especially when as in the 1960s American investors were buying up existing Mexican companies.[30] The green revolution, which is Mexico's most remarkable miracle, came about in part through Mexican collaboration with American producers, United States Department of Agriculture advisers, American state agricultural schools, and the Rockefeller Foundation.[31] In cotton, which became one of Mexico's most important exports in the 1950s, big American companies have been the middlemen between growers and purchasers abroad.[32]

Both in agriculture and in manufacturing, Mexico's advantages to the American investor were, inter alia, good and steady financial returns from getting inside a highly protected and booming market, absence of competitive Mexican products, low labor costs, and favorable tax policies.[33] In return, the Mexicans acquired not just access to needed capital but, more important in the long run, modern techniques and commercial knowledge. Meanwhile, their economy grew at an increasingly rapid rate.[34] The conditions under which foreign-owned enterprises operated were more or less negotiable, and foreign investors have not been completely at the mercy of Mexican officials so long as the foreign companies controlled techniques desired in their host country.[35] Only when financial returns markedly declined have government restrictions led companies like some big American-owned mining companies to sell a majority or all of their shares to the Mexican government. This was the case when Mexico bought out Azufrera Panamerica and thereby gained control of 90 percent of the sulfur industry.[36]

Impelled by the unemployment resulting from the ending of the *bracero* program, the Mexican government took advantage of certain United States tariff regulations to institute a border industrialization program. Under it, Mexico has permitted duty-free importation of semifinished materials to be worked on by Mexicans in American industries established in Mexico along the border; the further-processed materials are then exported to the United States, the only American duty levied being on the value added in Mexico.

This system has combined Mexican labor with American enterprise to supply semifinished products for markets in the United States. Often two complementing factories are established very close to each other on each side of the border. These synthesize production, and there may be only one director and managerial staff for both. By 1970, there were already more than two hundred companies of greatly varying size, most of them in about a dozen cities near the border, and they produced a great variety of goods, such as electronic equipment, musical instruments, and textiles.

For the American companies, one incentive was low-cost but reliable labor willing and able to perform routine duties well. Furthermore, the companies, confronted by high-cost labor in the United States, could continue profitable operations in the face of competition from other countries, particularly in the Far East. The American communities involved prospered with the increased production and wealth generated, while the system has helped greatly to meet serious unemployment problems in Mexico. In 1971, products worth about half a billion dollars were the result of a doubling of production during the previous two years. But with recession and inflation in both countries, the ten-year partnership faltered. A number of American companies moved away to areas of even cheaper labor, because of a rise in operating costs resulting from government-mandated wage increases in Mexico. The labor force employed diminished to about 50,000 workers, with the closing of large and small plants and drastic reductions in operations of those remaining. Meanwhile, American labor unions were stepping up their opposition to the border-plant program.[37]

BRAZIL

Labor controversies had little to do with the issues arising from American investment in Brazil. And, as an editorial in the *Jornal do Brasil* once put it, although United States investment in Brazil could not compare to that in Canada, even in the absence of the cultural and economic factors underlying the symbiotic relationship of the two North American countries, the United States government had a genuine interest in Brazil's developing a strong economy.[38] In addition to wider political interests related to the whole hemisphere, the United States government was continuously concerned about how private investors were treated. From time to time the Brazil government was under pressure to respond when the treatment was unfavorable. Thus two months after the extreme leftist governor of Rio Grande do Sul, Leonel

Brizola, expropriated the local telephone-company subsidiary of International Telephone and Telegraph in February, 1962, his brother-in-law, President João Goulart, had to discuss with President Kennedy an overall policy of purchasing foreign utilities. A formula was adopted which would compensate International Telephone and Telegraph for the expropriation, under which payments would be made and then be invested in other, less sensitive Brazilian enterprises.[39] However, when the formula was to be applied to the American and Foreign Power Company, the largest utility in Brazil, a dispute over the value of the property continued into the Castelo Branco regime, when it was finally settled.[40]

As for private foreign investors themselves, Finance Minister Delfim Netto claimed in 1968 that Brazil offered profits, security, and freedom of movement to private foreign investors; but this had not always been the case in earlier periods. Because of balance-of-payments difficulties and inflation (galloping at times), the Brazilian government many times after World War II imposed some kind of restriction on the convertibility of the cruzeiro. Then it would grant special exemptions, so that foreign exchange would be available to outsiders whose business it wished to cultivate. The Brazilian government was sufficiently eager to obtain capital and technology that it provided a variety of inducements. Among them, at one time or another it excused foreign firms associated with Brazilian enterprises from providing foreign-exchange cover when importing machinery, guaranteed protection against inflation for the working capital which the firms brought in from abroad, and manipulated in the firms' favor restraints which had been imposed on remittance of profits abroad. The effect of some of these inducements sometimes favored foreign investment over domestic, a fact which did not go unnoticed by Brazilian interests.[41]

The industrial boom during the military dictatorship (much of the rapid growth followed on steps taken by earlier regimes) appeared to some observers as one occurring to an economy in which Brazil, with its plentiful, low-wage labor force, had become a giant factory for large foreign enterprises. Meanwhile, however, Brazil gradually was building up its basic industries to the point at which it could determine future economic moves more independently of foreign private investors. The Brazilian government might then determine reciprocal benefits on its own, without fear of an unfavorable response from those with foreign capital.

Before this point had arrived, and while in the 1960s the United States was still spending immense sums in foreign aid to Brazil for a variety of programs, American business groups benefited. Export-Import Bank loans, for example, aided American exporters by furnishing Brazil with credits to secure their commodities. Much aid was "tied"; thus a great deal of the money ended up in private American enterprise.[42] In the periodic "bail-outs," United States loans to help Brazil surmount its balance-of-payments crises, the aid funds often merely passed from the United States government to private American organizations (the banks and others who had extended credits to Brazil earlier.) Thus in the early days of the Alliance for Progress, a significant portion of the aid funds did not end up actually being spent on new projects inside Brazil. Some of these funds went directly to the Export-Import Bank.[43]

SPECIFICITY

CANADA

Very unreciprocal were the various manifestations of "extraterritoriality," that is, the ways in which the United States government sought to extend its authority over subsidiaries of American corporations located abroad.[44] The United States has made some specific exemptions on an ad hoc basis with respect to American subsidiaries operating in Canada, when particular cases arose. This has not satisfied those Canadians who were sufficiently concerned about the potential threat to their country's sovereignty to urge the government to lay down a general policy on foreign investment that would obviate the rather humiliating need to seek concessions from a foreign government in specific cases. Merely protesting the rules and then accepting exemptions seemed to the protesters to be a procedure which suggested acquiescence in the general principle of extraterritoriality.[45]

When the Canadian government in June, 1965, adopted restrictions and differential taxes to protect Canadian publications' advertising revenues against powerful American competitors circulating in Canada, it exempted the Canadian editions of *Time* and *Reader's Digest*. Its reasons for exemption were never fully divulged but many Canadians suspected that the exemption was in response to strong pressure from highly placed American officials. For several years, the exemption continued to irritate Canadians. Finally, in January, 1975, the Canadian government announced its intention to abolish the tax concession.

Canadians have been most sensitive to foreign direct investment when it involves take-overs of existing domestic enterprises; such action appears to the general public not to add to, but to subtract from, Canadian enterprise. By the 1970s, the Canadian government and the Ontario government had become sufficiently concerned that they were reacting to specific cases of such take-overs. Thus the federal government prevented execution of a plan by Denison Mines, Ltd. to sell a large share of its uranium-mining enterprise to an American-controlled company, a plan which had attracted great public attention. Much Canadian publicity also attended the unsuccessful planned take-over by American book companies of two of the last few remaining Canadian publishing houses.[46]

AUSTRALIA

In this area, Australians were also slow in becoming concerned, but by the late 1960s their government had taken a few specific steps to discourage take-overs. In the lurid glow of the ITT scandals in San Diego and Chile in 1972, the Australian government stood in the way of ITT's buying up an Australian frozen-foods company. It also began to formulate general rules restricting such foreign take-overs.[47]

American investment has tended to concentrate and become dominant in a few specific industries.[48] One of the most important is motor vehicles. Like those of Canada, Mexico, and Brazil, the Australian government in 1971 singled out this industry for special attention. It imposed a requirement that 85 percent of the components of cars assembled in Australia be of Australian manufacture.[49]

It was not just foreign take-overs but also specific practices engaged in by foreign companies which produced negative reactions from the time of Prime Minister Gorton onward. These practices included restrictive licenses which seemed to cut down prospective exports, inadequate opportunities for Australians to hold shares or participate in management, and competition with Australian borrowers in Australian financial markets.[50] Concern with this last practice led the Australian government in 1967 to support establishment of the Australian Resources Development Bank, which facilitates movement of local capital to desired areas of investment and, later, to establish the Industrial Development Corporation, for the same purpose.

MEXICO

The Mexican government began to restrict take-overs rather late (1972) in its history of regulating foreign investment. As in the other four countries, this action followed upon some rather unsettling individual cases. In general, the intricate system of controlling foreign investment that prevailed throughout the postwar period could be summed up, as the United States Department of Commerce suggested, in the term "selective." [51] Since 1944, when the major law governing foreign investment was enacted, foreigners or Mexican companies with foreign partners have been required to get specific permission from the minister of foreign relations to own or control enterprises in any of several specified industries, including forestry and cattle-raising, as well as manufacturing. [52] Administrative flexibility typified Mexico's treatment; general rules did not change so much as did application of the rules.

There were countless ways in which foreign companies were dependent upon discretionary action by Mexican officials. The companies needed specific approval to import materials, to employ foreign personnel, and to secure production quotas, as well as to obtain tax concessions, public facilities, or credits. Even constitutional prohibitions might be bent on occasion, as in the case of foreigners acquiring property within 100 kilometers of the frontier or within 50 kilometers of the shore. Numerous exceptions have been made to the requirement for 51 percent Mexican ownership. A large number of ministries and agencies have a share in the regulation of foreign investment. To the novice, complete administrative chaos has seemed to prevail, but to the knowledgeable or those with well-placed Mexican friends, the same situation has offered many opportunities for negotiation. [53] New laws and decress put into effect in 1972 followed familiar patterns. Again singling out the automotive industry, the government increased requirements for Mexican ownership of auto-parts manufacturers, further limited importation of foreign-made components, and imposed new restrictions on the variety of models to be produced. [54] Accustomed to such government regulation, American companies took these measures in stride.

BRAZIL

Like the other three countries, Brazil has reserved certain industries— or parts thereof—for domestic investment. The most important of those has been oil producing; after a stormy legislative passage of the authority, President Vargas created a monopoly, Petrobrás, in October, 1953. After that date, no new drilling could be undertaken and no new refineries could be built privately, although existing refineries and private distribution networks were permitted to continue operations.[55] This move was intended to ''emancipate'' Brazil from certain forms of foreign domination. The mining of ore, particularly iron ore, had traditionally been closed to foreigners; this taboo had grown up from the days when taking gold away had made Brazilians fearful that all that would be left to them of their invaluable mineral resources would be the holes in the ground. In the late 1960s and early 1970s, as it became evident that government enterprise was failing to produce the mineral products necessary for Brazil's own industry, despite Brazil's immense natural resources, some restrictions gradually were removed. Specific concessions were the objects of intense public scrutiny, especially when the foreign company given concessions had a poor image.[56]

During the early years of the military dictatorship, the Brazilian government under Castelo Branco tended to respond with specific measures to the requirements of foreign investment and American officials' ideas on how to stimulate it. For example, when foreign capital did not pour in at once following the ousting of the regime that had frightened investors, Brazilian authorities quickly relaxed the previously imposed rules which had restricted some profits from leaving the country.[57]

DISTANCE

CANADA

Even the self-confident Canadians have exhibited some fears of alienating foreign investors, but geographical and cultural proximity to the source of what they have continued to desire under conditions determined by themselves has given them the advantage of leeway. However, as in other fields, the distance between the two countries appears greater to the Canadian than to the American. Thus sociological as well as economic integration flowing from United States investment has aroused political reactions on the Canadian side, especially when American businessmen have failed to note that they were operating in a foreign country. On the other hand, American associates in multinational corporations probably are better informed and more attentive to Canadian interests than are other Americans.[58] The interchange of personnel at all levels from training through management to boards of directors widens the social as well as the economic ties between the two countries. This process is unpleasing to Canadian nationalists who instead emphasize the asymmetries presented by preponderant American interests in Canada and put pressure on the government to be less hospitable.

AUSTRALIA

Americans who came to Australia to serve in high management positions usually did not remain long before being replaced by Australians who had been prepared to take over their work.[59] It is less common for Australians than for Canadians to move to high executive positions in the parent companies. As for tightness of the parent company's control of its Australian subsidiary, an intensive study conducted in 1961–1962 indicated that manufacturing subsidiaries often had considerable local autonomy. Nevertheless, for decisions on major capital outlays or product innovation, the faraway head offices normally had the last word, although much initative might come from the Australian branch.[60] The same could be said for subsidiaries in Canada, but in both countries the degree of decentralization varies greatly among United States companies.[61]

MEXICO

American investors are likely to know or think they know more about conditions in Mexico than about those in other Latin American countries, because it is close. For many of their enterprises, also, proximity has meant easier communications and transport. The agricultural revolution in Mexico has taken place in areas adjacent to the United States, so that in some ways the new methods and increased productivity are simply an extension southward of similar kinds of large-scale irrigated agriculture in Arizona and California.[62] Obviously, the whole border industrialization program depends upon proximity to the American market. And there is the psychological impact on Mexican entrepreneurs of a dynamic modern economy close at hand.[63] Nevertheless, the Mexican government has sought to escape from the eager embrace of American investors by going farther afield and seeking to interest other foreign investors. Thus it arranged for a German firm to develop a new type of steel making at Altos Hornos.[64]

BRAZIL

Continued and growing private American investment in Brazil rests partly on the expectation that someday a "huge internal market" will develop; faith in the distant large country's asserted future potential is a substitute for detailed knowledge about current realities, such as is available for nearby Mexico. Although there has been sharp competition from investors from other countries, not much further away than is the United States, the way of American investors has been eased by efforts of the United States government to promote economic development in Brazil through foreign aid and private foreign investment.[65] Especially during some regimes, however, American and Brazilian doctrines were far apart on certain issues, most notably on the proper scope of state enterprise.

During the Goulart regime, some American officials felt that Brazilians with whom they had previously associated deliberately stayed aloof. With the coming of the Castelo Branco regime, earlier close associations were resumed for a while. Many of them, however, did not last through the Costa e Silva presidency, for the military officers who had been friendly to the Americans were not those now in the ascendant.[66] In general, Americans have been less likely to settle in Brazil than the nationals of some other countries having important direct investments there (e.g., Germany, Italy, and Japan). Furthermore, when Americans have been stationed there, they have tended to insulate themselves from the community.[67] Thus personal associations even on the spot did not lessen social distance.

CUMULATION AND SPILLOVER

CANADA

For Canadians, their very personal closeness with Americans presented many psychological dangers to their autonomy. For them, the most galling aspect of American direct investment in Canada, however, has been the spillover from the presence of private American enterprise into American government policy (or vice versa). United States practices of extraterritoriality have been most prominent in Canada because of proximity and size of investment, although they have aroused anger and resistance in Europe, too. The United States government has on occasion tried to implement foreign or domestic policy by applying it to American subsidiaries abroad through the Trading with the Enemy Act, the antitrust laws, regulation of the sale of securities, and monetary regulation through "guidelines." The United States tried to prevent affiliates of American enterprises from evading the law and gaining unfair competitive advantage, which the companies might do by establishing different policies for their subsidiaries in Canada. Some of these United States government efforts, such as requirements of the Securities and Exchange Commission for publicity on securities traded on American stock exchanges, could serve certain Canadian interests as well.[68] Other policies, notably those which prevented "combines" of firms to export more efficiently or to trade with certain Communist countries, ran counter to Canadian policy. But whatever the coincidence or lack of it between Canadian and American policy, the real rub was the implications for Canadian sovereignty. For Canadians it was the worst kind of integration.

The number of foreign-assets cases involving "trading with the enemy" has been small, and with Canadian objections they were resolved in Canada's favor. However, the threat of punitive action against the parent company or American corporation officers if the law was not observed by Canadian affiliates has assertedly prevented more Canadian exports to Cuba, Communist China, and North Korea; such an effect has been suspected but is impossible to prove.[69] In any case, this kind of spillover, in which American foreign policy is pursued through American private enterprise operating in Canada, would seem likely to diminish rapidly with changes in United States policy regarding "trading with the enemy." [70] Yet even in 1974, there was a flare-up in Canada over some American opposition to the sale of Canadian-made locomotives to Cuba by a company which was partly owned by Americans, a controversy not settled until an American director resigned and much ill will in Canada had been generated.[71]

Antitrust cases have been far more numerous than trading-with-the-enemy cases. Since the problem of combinations in restraint of trade is shared by the United States and Canada with other members of the OEDC, many commentators on both sides of the border have recommended multilateral action to harmonize regulatory measures, which are more restrictive in the American system.[72] When the United States Department of Justice attempted in the 1950s to secure data on operations of American firms in Canada, the Ontario legislature passed a law preventing such transfers of documents, and other provinces followed suit.[73] Pressure on the Canadian national government to forbid foreign-owned enterprises operating in Canada to adhere to extraterritorially imposed rules has led to legislative proposals to control such practices.[74]

AUSTRALIA

Extraterritoriality, by which the United States government tried to extend its jurisdiction abroad to American-owned companies, has been a much greater irritant in Canada than in faraway Australia, where both practice and sensitivity to it were less evident. However, there has been a cumulative economic effect from American direct investment. Once American companies have secured a foothold in Australia, they have tended to plough back their profits to expand their enterprises there, sometimes branching out into other types of industry. In the past, this has not been unwelcome. Concerned that United States government restrictions on capital outflow imposed in the 1960s would limit Australian economic growth, which had greatly depended on foreign investment, the Australian government asked its reserve bank to take steps that would prevent American enterprises from compensating for such restrictions by borrowing heavily inside Australia. To do so would divert local funds from Australian-owned enterprises, the government reasoned.[75]

Less generously than for Canada, the United States nevertheless softened the impact on Australia when implementing balance-of-payments measures adopted prior to 1971. It did so under considerable pressure from the Australian government. Australia usually was classed with the next most favored developed countries. In applying guidelines for the outflow of American capital, United States officials also gave some informal favors to Australia, such as favorable treatment with respect to loans from the Export-Import Bank.[76] Unlike most major traders with the United States, Australia could not add to the balance-of-payments problem, since its manufactured exports to the United States were small, and American exports to Australia were comparatively large. The greater the American investment in Australia, the larger would be the imports of American products into that country.[77]

Some Australians believed that having such a large American stake in the Australian economy would improve the chances that the great ally would continue to be interested in Australian security. However, as Australians grew more economically assured and felt less desire for foreign investment regardless of cost, the two policy questions of security and access to overseas capital have apparently become more independent of each other, as well as of United States policy.

MEXICO

For the Mexicans, these two concerns were entirely separate, although their relative military safety permitted greater attention to other matters. Mexico's security position was such—with its great neighbor to the north and its small neighbors to the south—that very little needed to be spent on national defense. The resulting savings were one factor that enabled the government to invest heavily in economic development and to be selective about the foreign aid it accepted. Within the economic field, many Mexican regulations on foreign investment were due precisely to fears that such capital would bring with it control over Mexican industry by outsiders, a spillover the Mexicans had learned to dread from the Porfirian period. Other rules were designed to encourage the accumulation by Mexicans of technological and commercial expertise. A new class of managers has indeed developed among Mexicans. This in turn manifests itself in increased Mexican self-confidence in managing the economy. American respect for Mexican capacity has risen accordingly.

BRAZIL

Unlike their circumspect behavior towards the Mexican government during the last thirty years, United States officials did not hesitate to express their views on Brazil's treatment of foreign investment. Unilateral aid on a very large scale gave them opportunities to offer advice that were lacking in the case of Mexico. Thus questions about foreign investment frequently expanded into monetary matters and foreign-aid issues. After somewhat strained relations between the two governments because of Kubitschek's financial management, American authorities welcomed the brave beginnings of the Quadros administration's exchange reforms early in 1961. Not only was Brazil able to secure a stretching out of its indebtedness to American and European creditors, but it also secured new credits from United States agencies. The new Kennedy administration was eager to see the Brazilian government fare well, for the sake of hemispheric stability and the continuation of free government in Latin America.[78] The picture quickly changed, and even more rapidly under Goulart. Following on Governor Brizola's expropriation of the International Telephone and Telegraph subsidiary in Rio Grande do Sul came the Hickenlooper amendment to the 1962 foreign-aid bill in the United States Senate. Under it, United States aid to any country was to be suspended where arrangements for compensation had not been made within six months following expropriation of an American company.[79] During the same troubled period, the Brazilian Congress legislated a restraint on the remittance of profits abroad that was much opposed by interested Americans.[80] This move contributed to frightening away further foreign investment and added to the coolness developing between the Brazilian government and United States officials. Nevertheless Goulart's finance minister, San Tiago Dantas, secured some American concessions when he went to Washington in 1963 to take the preliminary steps which were to lay the foundation for another renegotiation of Brazil's indebtedness. The Kennedy administration promised him $398.5 million in aid, but most of it was not to be payable until Brazil carried out some specific measures of financial reform and stabilization.[81]

The final rescaling of the debt did not occur until after the military took over, when Brazil's foreign creditors agreed to ease greatly the terms of interest payments.[82] Relieved that the new government had brought an end to the earlier chaotic manipulation of Brazilian monetary rules and that "sound" monetary policies which also dealt boldly with inflation were being instituted, the United States provided Brazil a giant share of American foreign-aid funds.[83] The largesse continued for several years, despite growing dissatisfaction with other aspects of the military regime.[84]

CHANNELS OF COMMUNICATION

CANADA

Canadian sensitivity about United States use of American-owned subsidiaries in Canada to implement its foreign and economic policies called for means in addition to the usual diplomatic channels by which the two governments could discuss their concerns. Besides the ministerial Joint Committee on Trade and Economic Affairs, which served such a purpose for many years, more informal avenues for responding to problems of the legal "outreach" of the United States government followed conversations in Ottawa in 1958 between Prime Minister Diefenbaker and President Eisenhower. One was the agreement in 1959 between the heads of the respective departments of justice, William Rogers and Davie Fulton, regarding antitrust actions.[85] The agreement to consult in order to avoid intrusions into each other's jurisdiction in antitrust cases was reconfirmed by later administrations. On occasion, Congress has unwittingly affected Canadian interests when legislating for some unrelated question. For example, the 1964 Securities and Exchange Act had the effect of threatening penalties to Canadian officials of companies the securities of which might be traded across the counter in the United States without their knowledge.[86] Such kinds of unintended consequences have been somewhat reduced by the communication occurring within the Canada–United States Interparliamentary Group. Inside the executive branch, formal and informal contacts with Canadians alerted interested United States officials to the preparation of two Canadian government studies of foreign investment made in the late 1960s and early 1970s and prepared them for their contents.

AUSTRALIA

Such communication was out of the question for the Australians; it took the very top Australian leaders to get the Australian case before the United States government when the latter laid down restrictions on the export of capital. Prime Minister Menzies wrote President Johnson in detail regarding the proposed 1965 guidelines, mentioning that Australia had refrained from asking for exemption, since it had not wished to embarrass the United States in negotiations with certain other countries.[87] After pointing out Australia's special role in United States trade, he sought assurances that there not be a substantial reduction in the flow of private capital to Australia. President Johnson in reply referred to the special role of the United States dollar in the international monetary system and expressed the belief that his program was unlikely to have serious adverse effects on Australia. He promised, however, that in any specific case he would ask the secretary of the treasury and secretary of commerce to "give a careful hearing to Australia's view." [88] Somewhat more responsively in respect to the 1968 guidelines, the undersecretary of state for political affairs was sent to Canberra to discuss their impact with the Australian cabinet, Australia by then being an active ally in the Vietnam war.[89]

Exhibiting a very different attitude towards the IMF and the World Bank than that entertained for ideological reasons by the earlier Australian Labor party government in the 1940s, the Menzies government made Australia an active member in these agencies.[90] Their meetings were occasions for regular visits to Washington by Australian financial officials. Not being among the Group of Ten, however, Australia was less well placed than Canada to express its view when President Nixon embarked on his new economic policy. On the unofficial level, important ties have developed between Americans with business in Australia and their local associates. The same holds true for the other three countries, but for the distant ones— Australia and Brazil—such ties may be less taken for granted.

MEXICO

Unlike the Australians, who for a long period had seemed somewhat insensitive to the dangers of foreign direct investment, the Mexicans have sought to counter the risks while enjoying the fruits by working through several multilateral agencies. In order that they would not lose out in the competition because of their stringent rules, they have pushed for a uniform code of investment through the Latin American Free Trade Association as well as through UNCTAD.[91] Another multilateral agency through which Mexican government officials are in contact with Americans on investment matters is the Inter-American Development Bank, where from a legal point of view all member countries are on a par. The president of the bank, Antonio Ortiz Mena, an internationally respected former Mexican finance minister, was the candidate favored by the United States for the post in 1970; he was opposed earlier by a group of South American governments that were reported to fear some special relationship between the United States and Mexico which could affect them adversely.[92]

The Mexicans sought to stress the multilateral character of the Alliance for Progress, from which they secured help in expanding their structural base for development. They were able to get an especially large share of Alliance for Progress funds because they had fitted their proposed projects into a general plan formulated in 1962. This was in line with the decisions of the Punta del Este conference, which organized the Alliance for Progress and set up a review agency, the Inter-American Committee on the Alliance for Progress, usually known by its Spanish acronym, CIAP.[93] Under the auspices of the alliance, Mexicans also worked with Americans in carrying out various training projects for other recipients, combining Mexican facilities with American money.[94] In addition, they have obtained soft loans from the World Bank and the Inter-American Development Bank in their search for capital on terms that were advantageous but that avoided outright dependence upon the United States. "Multilateral" could sometimes mean some-

TABLE 19   UNITED STATES GOVERNMENT FOREIGN GRANTS AND CREDITS TO
BRAZIL AND MEXICO, 1965–1972 (millions of US dollars)

	1965	1966	1967	1968	1969	1970	1971	1972
Brazil	153	235	141	199	99	93	98	53
Mexico	38	54	50	53	16	−1	−18	−10

Source: Statistical Abstract of the United States. Negative figures appear because total of grant
returns, principal repayments (and/or foreign currencies disbursed by the government) exceeds new
grants and new credits used.

thing different from the usual North American usage; Mexico, like Brazil
and other Latin American states, tried to get the United States to accept a
legal obligation to render foreign aid to needy members, when the OAS
charter was being reformed in 1966.

BRAZIL

More than the Mexicans, the Brazilians liked to deal directly with
United States officials, relying on American views of their special position
among South American states, although they did not pass up opportunities to
bolster their views through multilateral means. President Kubitschek had
been looking for a way to economic development that would reduce dependence when he proposed in 1958 his Operation Panamerica. His proposal
would have involved all the Latin American countries, along with the United
States, in furthering their development through cooperation and long-term
planning.[95] The United States government scarcely took note of the Brazilian pressures for such a program until the Kennedy administration came in
and Cuba became Communist. Although the subsequently American-sponsored Alliance for Progress was supposed to further social reforms as well as
economic growth, the projects aided by the United States in Brazil in fact
concentrated on the latter.[96] Table 19 compares the large amount of American foreign aid going to Brazil from 1965 through 1972 with the small
amount which went to Mexico.

President Kubitschek, like the Mexicans, had been disappointed that
the multilateral character of the Alliance for Progress disintegrated; the Brazilians then settled for United States unilateral aid under the program. In the
1960s, very large loans and grants came Brazil's way from the United
States, bringing with them great numbers of aid officials, who worked on

many technical levels and prominently in the big agricultural development projects of the poverty-stricken Northeast. Eventually, the close association of American officials with Brazilian officials in the aided projects produced unfavorable political repercussions in Brazil. Americans tended to stand at the side of Brazilians in the more naturally disliked agencies, such as those dealing with taxes or wage-and-price policy, thereby complicating the task of gaining acceptance for austerity measures.[97] When Ambassador John W. Tuthill assumed his duties in Brazil in the late 1960s, he made a herculean effort to reduce the United States official presence in Brazil, swollen by administrative officials for the giant aid programs, as well as by the military mission, representatives of the United States Information Service, CIA, and others.[98] In carrying out this reduction, for which he had received United States cabinet backing, he encountered strong bureaucratic opposition in other parts of the American government.[99]

Because of its periodic need for outside assistance with monetary difficulties, Brazil had often been involved with the IMF and had had its own ministers on the board.[100] On more than one occasion, however, it came into conflict with officials in that agency, who differed sharply with Brazilian plans to stabilize the currency. In these disputes, Americans were involved, not only through the IMF but also in negotiations which required the imprimatur of that organization. Although the Americans were said to be less rigidly orthodox and doctrinaire in dealing with Brazil's problems, their conditions for good monetary management in return for help were either evaded or violated, until the military regime accepted the measures. However, by 1968 Brazil's position was sufficiently strong economically as well as politically that it could, against American advice, ease credit and wage restrictions.[101]

More and more Brazil, like Mexico, sought through UNCTAD to be heard as an advocate for third-world economic-development concerns. In such a role, these Latin American middle powers inevitably cast themselves as political adversaries of the United States.

ADMINISTRATIVE TREATMENT VERSUS POLITICIZATION

CANADA

With a myriad of official and private contacts with Americans, the Canadian government for many years was satisfied to deal case by case and at the bureaucratic level with problems caused by American direct investment. However, this ad hocery, as they called it, often was decried by Canadian nationalists. A certain amount of it was inevitable as a response to United States policies that often were framed in a global perspective, with an after-the-fact willingness to adapt them to Canadian requirements.

The opposite development occurred on the Canadian side when an American investment became a *cause célèbre* and resulted in new legislation. When the First National City Bank of New York bought the small, Dutch-owned Mercantile Bank of Canada in 1963 and prepared greatly to expand it, the Canadian government responded with a restrictive amendment to its banking law. This limited foreign ownership of a bank to 25 percent of its shares whenever assets had increased to twenty times its authorized capital, and the amendment applied retroactively. The United States Department of State protested the action not only for its retroactivity but because it was "discretionary." Some hints also were dropped in Congress that Canadian banking agencies operating in the United States might be less favorably treated in the future. The Canadian government, however, was not deterred from proceeding. Nevertheless, it imposed the new requirements at a less drastic rate and on more generous terms, giving the bank five years after 1967 to adjust to the requirements.[102] What seemed like a simple economic question to the Americans became a political matter to the Canadians.

For most cases which became politicized and involved the highest authorities, the major costs were temporary indisposition of agency officials on either side to treat the others' current requirements as expeditiously and accommodatingly as had been the normal practice; the cost was not the imposition of some restrictive general policy. However, an overview of accumulated irritations by a high-level group, such as appeared in the bilateral Merchant-Heeney report of 1965, has sometimes cleared the air of animus and permitted the return to more responsive practices at lower bureaucratic levels. This may be especially necessary on the American side because of its notoriously uncoordinated government; asymmetrical systems of decision making have resulted in asymmetrical responsiveness.

Numerous Canadian students of the problems raised by foreign investment have advised their government that there are other ways of preventing a more populous and dynamic country from filling vacuums than adoption of unpleasant and risky restrictive policies.[103] These other ways include upgrading of Canadian rules on combines, stricter protection of holders of securities, inducements to more vigorous Canadian entrepreneurship, and attracting foreign investment from more diversified sources, all of which methods the Canadian government was pursuing by the early 1970s. The United States government could not possibly make an antagonistic response to such general policies.

AUSTRALIA

Measures to counter the ill effects of foreign direct investment did not concern the Australian government until the late 1960s, although the problem had already become politicized. The Country party leader, John Mc-Ewen, who was minister of trade and industry, had been opposing the more liberal views of the head of the Department of the Treasury, William McMahon. In December, 1968, Prime Minister Gorton pressed the Australian stock exchanges to alter their rules in favor of more voting power for Australian stockholders of those companies listed with them. He also spoke out against export-franchise restrictions.[104] Yet no serious policy changes occurred until the Australian Labor party took over in December, 1972. Meanwhile, during the 1960s foreign capital was pouring in. The restraints adopted later were administered in a flexible, pragmatic fashion to the point where their implementation aroused uncertainty about what was the Labor government's policy.

MEXICO

There was little doubt about the Mexican government's intentions. No matter how patternless or ad hoc individual Mexican official decisions regarding foreign investors might have seemed, the general movement was relentlessly toward Mexicanization, not so much toward state enterprise as toward private firms which were state directed and manipulated.[105] Comparisons between nationalization of the oil industry in the late 1930s and the closing out of foreign investors from railroads, electric-power production, sulfur mining, and the telephone system at later stages reveal the pragmatic process of the postwar years. The case of electric-power production in 1960 was especially illuminating, since nationalization was done with practically no fuss and to the apparent satisfaction of the companies involved.[106] Whether or not a calculated response, Mexico's acquisition of Azufrera Panamerican came just twelve days after the United States Tariff Commission had determined that Mexico was dumping sulfur in the United States.[107]

Some industries have been acquired gradually by the government until they became government monopolies, affording no further opportunity for foreign investment. Besides oil, electric power, and railroads, they included some fertilizers, basic petrochemicals, and telegraph and radio communications.[108] In 1962, the government determined that the Mexican automobile industry would move from merely assembly to production of components. With hints that smaller foreign automobile companies were interested in entering Mexico, the government eventually persuaded the two largest American companies to cooperate. Yet by administrative discretion, some parts of the automobiles continue to be imported.[109] From time to time, the government has issued lengthy lists of industries it wants established and for which many favors and exemptions are available to the fortunate applicant.

Embedded in the Mexican constitution is a "Calvo clause" requirement to which foreign investors must agree before establishing enterprises, namely, to renounce the right to have recourse to their own governments for diplomatic protection in case of conflict with a Mexican ruling. Nevertheless, Mexican administrative authorities regularly have been mindful of the potential costs of treating American investors in ways which the latter would regard as unacceptably discriminatory or confiscatory.[110] So far, the administrators have succeeded in maintaining that balance between lures and sanctions which has been basic Mexican policy.

BRAZIL

For the most part, the Brazilians highlighted the lures in their policy declarations, but practical implementation was another matter. After Vargas's presidency, succeeding governments sought to encourage foreign investment by enunciating policies of reassurance to outside capital. Respected *técnicos* high in the administration took steps to counter the ills of the Brazilian economy which were hindering increased investment. Yet the pull of intricately related political interests often impeded the carrying out of these policies. The *técnicos* were a type of administrative official with whom American authorities could easily discuss substantive problems. But their very aloofness from political styles of thought caused their replacement from time to time, especially in the more populist regimes.[111] They returned in the early days of the military dictatorship, and this time the kind of monetary and fiscal measures popular with United States officials succeeded. The military leaders gave them a relatively free hand.

There was another obstacle to effective cooperation. As more than one

American observer could say, "The Brazilian secret weapon is inertia."
This weapon could cut both ways: unfavorable laws, such as limits on the
amount of local capital a foreign company could borrow, could remain on
the books, unimplemented. Interstices in the rules against foreign ownership
of television facilities could be filled in by powerful mass media partly controlled from abroad.[112] On the other hand, promises of the Brazilian government to reform some objectionable practice often went unfulfilled. Yet the
climate created by a particular administration seemed to be more compelling
to foreign investors than the actual implementation of its policies.

DOMESTIC POLITICS

CANADA

Concern that administrative action should faithfully reflect policy
helped to create domestic political problems for Canadian leaders. General
policies on direct investment by foreigners have been very difficult for Canadian governments to formulate, although since the mid-1950s the governments have been under constant pressure from their members and the opposition to lay down some general rules. The foreign-owned firm is always a
lively domestic political issue; take-overs, even though they constitute a
small percentage of the foreign investment problem, are a particularly
touchy aspect. Aside from the inherent difficulties of drawing up rules which
would control but not frighten away desired capital nor alienate Canadians
linked with foreign enterprises, the government has had to deal with groups
expressing many conflicting attitudes.

Among those who have kept the issue lively are leaders of the New
Democratic party, upon whose support the Trudeau government was dependent between the 1972 election and that in July, 1974, which gave the Liberals a safe majority. To complicate matters, most of the provincial governments have actively sought American investors. Since the provinces have
constitutional jurisdiction over such enterprises as mining, it would have
been difficult for the federal government to take strong measures in many
fields where foreign investment was prevalent.

After many years of study and several reports, the Trudeau government
in May, 1972, brought forth proposals to screen certain kinds of new investment—those involving take-overs—to ensure that they would be "of signifi-

cant benefit to Canada.'' So modest were the proposals that the government was moved to strengthen them in revising the bill which was finally passed in December, 1973. The Foreign Investment Review Act included the screening not only of take-overs but also of the establishment of new businesses by foreigners or the opening of new enterprises by existing foreign-controlled firms operating in an unrelated activity. It also provided for consultation with the provincial governments.[113] Although general rules were formulated to carry out the new law, there were no immediate signs that the government had abandoned its pragmatic style of dealing with each case on an ad hoc basis. Nor were there signs that certain types of American capital were not still desired: the Canadian government's acceptance of the United States bid to the energy conference of February, 1974, included an invitation for United States investment in the development of the Athabasca oil sands in Alberta.[114]

United States officials had become aware by 1970 of how direct investment by foreigners in Canada, especially by Americans, was agitating Canadian politics; they usually have been cautious to avoid statements appearing to interfere in what they always pointed out was a domestic question for Canadians to decide. By contrast in the 1950s, when the issue first became prominent, even President Eisenhower's speech to Parliament in 1958 stressed the importance to Canada of American capital.[115]

AUSTRALIA

By 1972, when the Australian Labor party returned to power under Prime Minister Gough Whitlam, the issue of foreign investment, particularly by Americans, had churned up lively domestic political controversy in Australia, too. The Liberals had continued to play down public concern about increases in foreign investment and Prime Minister Gorton several times had pointed out how difficult it would be to frame rules which would control but not stop the flow of the desired capital.[116] The Australian states, like Canadian provinces, were especially eager to entice foreign investors. The new Labor government, however, did adopt a more restrictive policy. Among several moves to raise the proportion of Australian ownership and control, it imposed a careful screening procedure for proposed take-overs of Australian enterprises by foreign investors and required that 30 percent of borrowed foreign capital be deposited interest-free in the Reserve Bank of Australia. And the Labor government chose to make these moves with great fanfare.[117]

With changed circumstances, intraparty differences, and domestic discontent, some of the rules were subsequently relaxed. Meanwhile, the government purchased shares in some enterprises and itself entered the mining industry. Further relaxation of restraints was likely under the Liberal government which succeeded Whitlam's in December, 1975.

MEXICO

No issue in Mexican politics is more sensitive than that of foreign investment. No matter what government officials may declare regarding the desirability of particular kinds, there will always be critical voices in the Mexican Congress. There have been differences among Mexican business interest groups on how to deal with the problem. As in the other three countries, those associated with foreign enterprise in some direct or indirect way have taken a more benign view than those operating purely indigenous enterprises. In recent years, however, the various confederations of business interests have been converging, as the Mexican economy grew stronger; foreign investors have begun to appear more like competitors than associates. Traditionally, the most vocal opponent and the one pressing hardest for strong government curbs has been the Camara Nacional de la Industria de Transformacion (usually referred to as CNIT). This is a group of smaller Mexican business interests which sprang up during World War II and which has been more nationalistic than the other three business associations, which have worked closely with American and other foreign investors.[118] As in other countries, many Mexican intellectuals are ideologically opposed to foreign investment. So politically delicate is the subject that detailed statistics on the extent of foreign investment are much more readily obtained from United States government sources than from sources in Mexico.[119] Government measures to deal with foreign investment also have had to avoid too great an appearance of building up government monopolies or promoting state enterprise, since Mexican capital necessary for continued economic development could be very flighty if the owners suspected too leftward a movement in general policy.[120]

BRAZIL

As in Mexico, the regulation of foreign direct investment has long been a lively political question in Brazil, offering great demagogic appeal, which a government's opposition can exploit in attacking the authorities for ostensibly favoring foreign investors. Prior to the military dictatorship, government policies regarding foreign investment had often got caught in the cross fire between those controlling the federal government and the state governors or other political competitors such as Leonel Brizola and Carlos Lacerda. Particularly volatile issues have been the degree to which the petroleum industry should be nationalized, the remittance of profits overseas, and "denationalization" (foreign take-overs). Some Brazilian opponents of foreign direct investment did not distinguish between the United States government and private foreign investors in complaining that their economy was being controlled from abroad. (Nor did they distinguish between Canadian and American ownership of utilities.) With the coming of the military dictatorship, its frustrated opponents used the foreign-investment issue as a main instrument in attacking the government, which they accused of being too friendly to non-Brazilian enterprise. Their complaints were not stilled by replies from those in the government that the foreign investor was often used as a scapegoat for the deficiencies of Brazilians.[121] The military themselves were divided on the issue; the nationalists among them began to dominate toward the end of the Costa e Silva presidency.[122] The sharp splits among different political factions over issues of foreign investment were elements in the overthrow of at least two regimes. Note the final cries of Vargas and Goulart. Vargas's suicide note charged that "a subterranean campaign of international groups joined with national groups" had sought, inter alia, to prevent imposition of limits on excess profits and that "profits of foreign enterprises reached 500 percent yearly."[123] In Goulart's address to the sergeants on March 30, 1964, a speech which immediately preceded the military coup, he claimed that the campaign aganst him had been funded in part by "enormous international petroleum interests" who were opposed to his making Petrobrás a government oil-refining monopoly and by "the large foreign medical firms."[124]

Although these allegations were exaggerated or without much foundation, there was a connection between American investment in Brazil, United States foreign aid, and United States foreign policy, as a result of which Americans did become involved in Brazilian politics. It was, in fact, the unarticulated but very real security function of the Alliance for Progress which produced such large amounts of United States foreign aid to Brazil. When the military dictatorship overthrew the unstable and unfriendly Goulart, the temporarily reduced flow increased very substantially. But the penetration of United States foreign aid into Brazilian domestic politics was not very skillfully masked. United States assistance had been markedly curbed toward the end of Goulart's regime, as a sign of irritation with his apparently "leftist" or "pro-Communist" behavior; instead it was proffered to some of the state governments, whose leaders happened to be competitors of Goulart.[125] Yet even after United States officials became troubled by the drastic dictatorial measures taken by the Costa e Silva government in December, 1968, they feared that they might risk nationalist reactions if they cut the aid program abruptly; "reviewing" it was their only option.[126] By the 1970s, Brazil had so profited from United States aid that its government no longer needed to heed American actions or criticisms.

In Brazil as in Mexico, the issue of foreign investment became intertwined with domestic political controversy regarding the maldistribution of income, since foreign enterprises were associated with the wealthy elite. Governments in both countries (with temporary exceptions in Brazil) had been concentrating on increasing the size of the pie, leaving for the 1970s the task of helping the least advantaged obtain a slightly more equitable share. Thus government opponents in these two developing countries of Latin America could easily proclaim some form of the *dependencia* theory, that is, that foreigners (Americans chiefly) were through their investments allying themselves with reactionary elites bent on preventing fundamental social and economic reforms. Those of socialist bent in Canada and Australia sometimes used similar if much milder arguments in pressing their respective governments to take a more nationalist stand on foreign investment.

SUMMARY

For political opponents in the middle powers, direct foreign investment was often synonymous with American multinational corporations, which were sometimes regarded as having United States government backing. The asymmetrical relationship between the United States and the four countries showed up strongly in the field of foreign investment, since none but the Canadians had any significant investment of their own in the United States (or in other countries). Pressures which the critics exerted in the host countries were directed against their own governments. These governments usually first responded to the challenge of foreign investment by seeking to make foreign-controlled enterprises as joint as possible. One way to do so was to require that nationals of the host country own a certain percentage of a foreign company's subsidiary. However, the ultimate aim, more clearly articulated in the Latin countries, was to loosen the connections between such enterprises and their foreign management. The shift away from jointness was to be gradual in most cases, but in both Mexico and Brazil occasionally outright expropriation occurred. Meanwhile, the host governments could lighten restrictions on certain foreign operations and offer lures to desired investment in return for the advantages such enterprises offered: technical and managerial skills, access to foreign markets, easier acquisition of capital equipment.

Only in the case of Brazil did the United States government express directly a strong interest in the kind of treatment American investors received. United States officials were concerned not just about the interests of these investors but also, for foreign policy reasons, wanted Brazil to prosper and develop along American-approved lines. Monetary stability and cessation of balance-of-payments crises, so greatly desired by Americans and Brazilians alike, came only after the military regime took hold. Meanwhile, with the huge foreign-aid programs in Brazil in the 1960s came hundreds of American officials. Their presence inevitably led to United States involvement in domestic politics, until the independent strength of an increasingly repressive military dictatorship cooled relations between Brazil and the United States.

Like the Brazilians, the Australians remained eager for all capital obtainable until the 1970s; they began seriously to attach conditions only when the Australian Labor party came to power. In both Australia and Canada, the federal government and the member units (provincial or state governments) appeared to be pulling in opposite directions. In contrast to Canada's and Australia's policy of almost completely free inflows of direct investment, Mexico very stringently regulated foreign investment, although placing no restraints on the outflow of interest and dividends and keeping the peso freely convertible. Mexican rules did not frighten away potential investors nor incur pressure from the United States government, partly because they were discriminatingly imposed.

The mix of lure and restraint varied not only by country but also by successive governments within each country and by type of industry. The host-country governments treated specific kinds of foreign-owned enterprises differently. Foreign take-overs of domestic enterprise were especially likely to be the object of regulation, since they seemed to add little to the host country's economic development and aroused domestic resentment. Administrative discretion where the rules were not immediatly obvious to the outsider appeared to characterize Mexican treatment of foreign investment; yet there was a pattern which led inexorably toward eventual Mexicanization. Until domestic pressure built up, the Canadian government was inclined to deal separately with each case where foreign investment had raised some problem; that is, it followed an ad hoc approach without much reference to settled public policy. For these two neighbors of the United States, proximity enhanced their attractiveness to American investors. Thus American capital and enterprise were exceptionally prominent in their countries. This predominance called for the host governments to respond to the problems and opportunities thus presented. However, their very closeness to the Americans caused the Canadians to come to feel that they were no longer master in their own house, especially since American enterprises operating there did not always act as if Canada were a separate and independent state. The much sharper economic and cultural contrasts beyond the southern border of the United States were the foundation for the Mexican success in fostering the border industrialization program, a plan which deliberately attracted certain kinds of American enterprise for limited purposes. Geographical distance from the United States had a cultural counterpart in Brazil: the frequently large gap between policy and administrative implementation. This gap sometimes made the issue of foreign investment even more politically sensitive.

Heated as the question of foreign direct investment has been in all four countries, it was made the hotter in Canada by the American government's practice of extraterritoriality—seeking to extend its jurisdiction to American-owned enterprises in Canada for carrying out certain foreign or domestic policies. Despite need for the United States government to be more responsive to Canadian complaints, the ultimate remedy has lain at the Canadian government's door, as Canadian officials have increasingly recognized. The growing concern of important segments of the Canadian public over the pervasiveness of American enterprise in their country has politicized foreign-investment questions. This development has not necessarily killed off chances for eventual solutions, made on the merits of the case, for particular foreign investment problems. When intergovernmental discussions of such

issues have engaged those at high levels of political authority and, especially, when the diplomats most knowledgeable about the other country have
been engaged, settlements responsive to the desires of the Canadian government have eventually ensued.

Fortunately for Canadian-American good feeling there has been an
elaborate network of formal and informal, public and private, bilateral agencies for discussing issues requiring a response from those in one of the two
countries. The Mexican government, which has much the most stringent
rules for foreign investment, has sought to get some kind of multilateral discussion and agreement on rules for foreign investment; such a code would
protect it from being discriminated against because of its stricter regulations.

The Brazilians, on their home grounds, had plenty of contact with
United States officials. Their economic problems and the fact that their government was much more often the recipient of American advice were results
not necessarily of their physical distance but rather of the special characteristics of their politics and economic management. Yet their country had an
advantage Australia lacked: Brazil could stand, like Mexico, for a whole
group of states in a very sensitive region. Australia, with New Zealand, was
at the end of the world. Having learned that a military alliance did not bring
special consideration for their trade interests, the Australians had to depend
upon the increasingly large American direct investment in their country to
attract the attention they desired from officials in faraway Washington. But
the immense increase in foreign direct investment produced a marked shift
in Australian government policy when the Australian Labor party took office, even though its electoral success was not directly related to this issue.

Whereas on issues of foreign trade many of the obstacles to freer
exchange were erected on the American side and the United States government was not consistently sensitive to each country's individual trade needs,
in investment matters the initial government actions were usually taken by
the host country, concerned about the expansion of United States economic
power through private enterprise. Yet the growth of American investment in
these countries stemmed in part from trade barriers that they themselves imposed in the interest of eventually achieving greater freedom of economic
action and less dependence upon sympathetic American responsiveness. Significantly, the foreign investment which ensued apparently has played a role
in creating the foundation for a practical independence much greater than did
the trade barriers, which tended to protect uneconomic local enterprises.

Nevertheless, the success of the host countries in seeking greater freedom from American decisions on trade and investment depended greatly on the kinds of governmental intervention. To succeed, the host countries needed to make nice distinctions between when to respond to the desires of the Americans and when to proceed regardless of American preferences.

EIGHT

GLOBAL ISSUES OF FOREIGN POLICY

ON THE GREAT ISSUES OF world politics that transcend specific problems in their bilateral relations with the United States, the four middle powers have consistently put autonomy above a united front. Both independence and the appearance of independence have been important to them. When common action with the United States seemed indicated, they have sought to be treated as full partners and allies on the inside when critical decisions were being made. Each of the four has struggled against the American habit of overlooking or resisting these efforts to have a larger and earlier share in international decisions for a collaborative effort. Whatever the case for a great-power directorate in allied decision making in worldwide war, all four countries found it irritating when peace settlements were being arranged and more and more irksome in subsequent years. Each continued the effort to be heard on global issues, that is, those directly affecting the general configuration of power on the world scene.

In this chapter, as elsewhere, observations must take account of time, especially as modified behavior reflected realignments in world politics, changes in power position, and shifts in domestic governments. Except for those associated with the Middle East, issues did not continue to be "burning." And experience has altered the expectations, identifications, and demands of all the countries here considered. As members of the United Nations, all four countries and the United States had to take some kind of stand from time to time on pressing global issues, even though that stand sometimes could take the form of abstention, as Mexico's frequently did. But the intensity of their interest varied greatly. What they cooperated in or differed about also varied; some issues concerned mainly how to use an organization in which they were members or ways to pursue a common venture, while others concerned their general posture toward third countries, especially the Communist states.

This chapter does not include matters dealing with NATO (which are applicable only to Canada), even though these might have important foreign-policy as well as security aspects. It includes issues arising in two regions that also involved important collaboration in defense, those relating to war in Korea and Indochina; controversy over each of these areas agitated world politics for long periods. Disagreement regarding how to deal with China and Cuba remained on the foreign-policy plane.

Canada, Australia, Mexico, and Brazil have been middle powers in more than one sense; on occasion, the government of each has envisaged itself as a useful intermediary between the United States and some friendly or antagonistic country. All four governments had to contend in varying degrees with the American leadership's sense of mission and their continual pressure for uniform behavior. Meanwhile, all of them have been more concerned with the economic aspects of foreign policy than with world political alignments, ideology, and superpower rivalry. For both Canada and Australia, an additional prime concern during a long period was the maintenance of harmony between the United States and Britain. For Mexico and Brazil, the highest foreign-policy principle was nonintervention, and their main foreign-policy interests were North-South issues. East-West issues affected them only slightly, although both explicitly renounced any interest in joining some third bloc of nonaligned states.

Yet each of the four countries had distinctive foreign-policy orientations. Brazil's perennial aspirations to be some kind of world power contrasted with Mexico's usually more restricted outlook. Some Mexicans even called their country's earlier postwar demeanor "hermetic." A more outward-looking tendency, beginning with President Adolfo López Mateos, also particularly characterized President Luis Echeverria's conduct. Styles differed also; the Brazilians usually behaved with tactical flexibility and conciliatory gestures, while the Mexicans were more rigidly principled and readier for confrontation. Australia faced the world in a way different from Canada's orientation, because of its vulnerability to outside anticolonialist opinion with respect to Papua–New Guinea and its (gradually eroding) White Australia policy. Unlike the other three, whose main foreign-policy concerns were in regions culturally similar to their own, Australia lay in a region consisting of countries of very different culture (except for New Zealand), thus accentuating the Australian sense of isolation.

Whatever the underlying harmony of interest, each of the four states' relations with the United States on matters of world politics may seem to highlight opposition more often than common enterprise, because of the nature of the questions involved. Responsiveness still is the key, rather than agreement.

JOINTNESS

Since foreign policy on global issues determines the stance of the state with respect to other states, a political question involving states and major choices rather than a technical problem to be solved by experts in agreement on political values, it is by definition high politics. Necessarily, such a policy requires the attention of the highest authorities. That they should combine with those of another state to determine a unified policy is hard to imagine, since the jointness of such a policy would undermine the autonomy of each state. Nevertheless, in formulating a policy, a government is likely to consider the views of others, which thus become elements in the decision. Such was the case for all four middle powers when they withheld recognition of the Communist government in China for many years. Successive Canadian governments were, in fact, often accused by some Canadians of giving undue weight to United States preferences. When Canada eventually broke the international logjam to establish diplomatic relations with the People's Republic, its leaders had very much in mind possible American reactions—including eventual American recognition. While joint policy making may be absent, there can be a common orientation or parallel policies, sometimes adopted by one of the middle powers for reasons quite different from those prompting the Americans. During a long period, Australia, Brazil, and Mexico, for domestic reasons or because of experience with Soviet espionage in their countries, pursued the kind of cold-war policies adopted by the United States. Brazil at one point went even further and broke off relations with the Soviet Union. As Lester Pearson explained to his countrymen, a proper regard for national interests did not require or permit disagreement for its own sake, just to give an appearance of independence. Yet even the Canadians, who in the early postwar years stressed the general conformity of their foreign-policy views with those of the Americans, began to change. By the 1960s, they occasionally found it desirable to move first, before the less maneuverable American government could do so.

On some issues in certain periods Canada and Australia were closer to a joint policy with Britain than with the United States. At the 1954 Geneva conference on Indochina, where the two middle powers were not official participants but present because the conference ran concurrently with one on Korea, they bolstered British efforts to hold the Americans back from intervening when the French were about to pull out. In the 1967 Arab-Israeli war, Mexico and Brazil joined other Latin American members at the United Nations to produce a response distinct from that of either the Soviet Union or the United States.[1]

Not infrequently one or more of the four middle powers took considerable pains to stress lack of jointness with the United States. Both Canada and Australia did so when the United States appeared to be taking so militant a stand on the issue of Quemoy and Matsu that they, too, were threatened with involvement. Both governments tried to influence the United States government to be more cautious in backing the Taiwan government on this issue. This was the first time that the Canadian government had taken a public stand in opposition to the United States in the area, although it had strongly differed privately with the Americans on several occasions during Korean crises.[2] Australia was eager to dissociate its obligations under ANZUS from the Quemoy-Matsu controversy. This was the era in which John Foster Dulles was active, and his intense pressures on others to conform often produced equally strong counterpressures. (The style was different, but the unwillingness to share policy making was no greater than with his predecessor, Dean Acheson.)

On other occasions, all four middle powers were ready to give positive support to a United States policy or course, although the degree of joint implementation varied greatly, as in the Korean War. For it, Australia readily offered forces from all three services. Canada's participation was more circumspect, and after MacArthur crossed the 38th parallel, the Canadians tried to influence American policy to be more conciliatory. Mexico and Brazil gave verbal support through the United Nations and sent food and medicine, but each declined to offer any armed forces to what was in any case a rather lopsided form of joint enterprise.[3]

In some other cases the middle power would merely go along, not resisting but not fulfilling American desires. Such was the case when trading with Communist China was frowned upon by the United States. Whenever sales to China were of genuine economic help to themselves, the middle powers seized the opportunity, and the Americans acquiesced.[4] Although Australia maintained a different standard for trading with China from its standard for trading with the Soviet Union, in line with American preferences, it sold the Chinese important nonstrategic items, including wheat, as did the Canadians. The trading policies of these two middle powers were much freer than the total embargo of the United States. Mexico also sold agricultural products, its trade being limited by what could be profitably offered and taken. Trade with Castro's Cuba was even less closely coordinated with American policy and more dependent on market advantage. Both Mexico and Canada traded at will, except that for a time Canada carefully monitored its trade to prevent pass-throughs of American goods. Despite a total disbelief in the effectiveness of economic boycotts, the Canadians were a little more cautious with respect to trade with the People's Republic of China; in that case, the political stakes were much higher.[5] Brazil, even after accepting willingly the OAS rule of no trade with Cuba, sold corn shipped in Soviet vessels, ostensibly because of the humanitarian appeal made to it.[6]

Overlapping these cases, in still other instances, the middle power mildly opposed American policy or dragged its feet sufficiently that the United States government gave up, or an accommodation was reached. Neither Mexico nor Brazil usually was prepared to give greater political authority to the OAS than the OAS possessed as a result of a strict reading of the Act of Bogotá or to stretch the provisions of the Rio pact. For different reasons, the two countries objected to the authorizing of joint inter-American peacekeeping actions in which they might be subjected to pressures either by the dominant North American member or by rival local states. Just as a discrepancy between the actions of these countries and those of the United States flowed from the Latin American guiding principle of nonintervention, so certain convictions of Canadian leaders pulled Canada apart from the United States, as in Canadian preferences for universal membership for the United Nations, belief in the uselessness of trade embargoes, and distrust of absolutes as guides to foreign policy.

On one set of issues, arms control, each middle power took its own special direction, which coincided only very generally with American preferences, although never in outright opposition. Australia, for example, so strongly feared the effects of atmospheric testing of hydrogen bombs in the Pacific that it was the first to sign the test-ban treaty.[7] It was far less enthusiastic about the nonproliferation treaty and, concentrating only on how the treaty might restrain Australia, was slow to sign, until various reservations about provisions were satisfied or their claims abandoned.[8]

Alarmed by the Cuban missile crisis, Brazil led a move to create a Latin American nonnuclear zone, which was quickly picked up and pressed by Mexico. Meanwhile, Brazil's ardor waned, and its hopes for developing its own peaceful atomic devices grew.[9] Brazilian action and inaction on the spread of nuclear devices diverged more and more from American preferences on the issue. Canada, always a vigorous promoter of nuclear arms control, never diverged as far from the American position as certain "neutral" countries who occasionally pressed for unverifiable methods of control. Like the Mexicans, however, the Canadians tried to persuade the United States (and the Soviet Union) to go much further in some directions, such as banning all underground testing, regardless of the size of the device, and enlarging the scope of international supervision over fissile material. Whether or not pressures from these middle powers contributed to the modification of United States policy, it did move in the late 1960s and early 1970s in directions preferred by these countries.[10]

Votes in the United Nations General Assembly offer tempting if probably misleading "objective" evidence that the United States and one or more of the middle powers had a common policy on some issues. As Francisco Cuevas Cancino, a long-time Mexican delegate, pointed out, such votes conceal as much as they reveal. An abstention (a favorite Mexican position) may be more significant than a favorable vote; the reasons for a particular vote are numerous and include arm twisting by a great power or logrolling or indifference to the issue.[11] The intensity of opposition signified by a vote of no is hard to measure. Remembering all these and other objections to particular interpretations of such voting, one still can note that Mexico's voting record on many issues diverged most among the votes of the four countries from that of the United States and that Australia's came closest over a long period (the main divergencies being those associated with the Suez crisis).[12]

An examination of the votes on admitting the People's Republic of China to the United Nations, although complicated by whether it was an "important question" requiring a two-thirds vote and by the two-Chinas issue, does reveal Canada's gradual divergence from the United States position. First, it abstained in 1966 on a resolution which would have seated the People's Republic while expelling Nationalist China; the other three powers voted against the resolution along with the United States.[13] When the People's Republic finally was admitted and Nationalist China expelled, Canada voted for this action along with all the other NATO countries except the United States.[14] With the changes in numbers and character of the membership and the kinds of issues raised at the UN, American concern to line up votes has diminished (and United States and Soviet positions are less frequently diametrically opposed). Perhaps the vote on China was the last important gesture of jointness sought by the Americans on a cold-war issue.

Voting in the United Nations following the invasion of Egypt at the time of the Suez crisis put Australia in conspicuous opposition to the United States. This behavior was only the tip of the iceberg in the principal foreign policy controversy with the Americans arising during the Liberal party's long sway. Prime Minister Menzies's sympathies were so completely with the British and his concern for the Suez Canal so great that despite misgivings among other members of his government, he took the lead in opposing efforts by the United States and others conciliatory to Egypt. His behavior was in marked contrast to that of the foreign minister of a sister Commonwealth country, which was more concerned about Anglo-American harmony and less dependent on the canal. Lester Pearson won international renown for his efforts to smooth over and start healing the sharp division between the United States and its European great allies, Britain and France. After some preliminary hesitation the United States government welcomed his proposal to establish the peacekeeping United Nations Emergency Force.

In more frequent opposition to United States foreign policy, Brazil and Mexico tried to block the Americans' cold-war use of the Organization of American States to oppose potential Communist advances in the Western Hemisphere. These efforts began in 1954 at Caracas, when Mexico merely abstained from a watered-down resolution on the United States proposal to call a meeting of consultation in case "the international Communist movement" threatened to dominate the political institutions of an American state. They reached a high point at the Punta del Este meeting in 1961, the very calling of which Mexico opposed. At this conference Mexico joined Brazil and four other Latin American states to make hollow the American victory of fourteen votes to oust Castro's Cuba from the operations of the OAS. The harder the Americans pressed, the more determined were the Mexicans to uphold their view that it was illegal to use the OAS to punish countries which altered their domestic political systems in a "socialist" direction. By mid-1964, Mexico was the only Latin American country that had not severed relations with Cuba.[15]

Like Mexico, the non-OAS member Canada also maintained diplomatic relations with Cuba. Just as the United States government eventually adjusted to Mexico's recalcitrance, so it acquiesced in Canada's refusal to cease trading with Castro's Cuba. Earlier, in the 1955 package deal to admit new members to the United Nations, the United States also eventually adapted to Canada's position, despite Secretary Dulles's sharp criticism of the Canadian delegation led by the foreign minister, Paul Martin, for the way it took the lead in this step.[16]

Sometimes opposition to the pressure for a common policy, when that pressure involved the penetration of one country by groups in another, could be very strong, even though the penetration was not official. When McCarthyism was sweeping the United States and the demands to combat internal "Communist subversion" were heavy, Canadians felt the impact, too, and strongly resisted the Americans. Lester Pearson testified that the only time he really felt any personal pressure from Americans in public office to alter his behavior was when some members of Congress (the McCarran committee on internal security) tried to get testimony from the Soviet defector, Igor Gouzenko, who was living in Canada.[17]

Without parallel in the relations of the United States to the other three countries, the United States government publicly noted its concern about a domestic condition in Brazil. Rumors of torture being used against political opponents produced early in May, 1970, discreet expressions of concern over the allegations.[18] Brazil was not so distant from Americans that the character of its government was lost to sight; the visit of President Emilio Garrastazú Médici to President Nixon in December, 1971, produced a demonstration near the White House against the Brazilian dictatorship.

Despite the absence of joint foreign-policy decisions, there have been instances of joint participation in military ventures having strong foreign-policy overtones. The Brazilian dictatorship eagerly accepted a major responsibility for the OAS peacekeeping force which was stationed in the Dominican Republic after the American intervention in 1965. The commander of the one-horse-one-rabbit (actually three rabbits) enterprise was a Brazilian, with an American as his so-called deputy.

Far more momentous was the Australian partnership with the United States in the Vietnam war. The Australian government responded readily to

American suggestions and even went further at some points. Thus Australian leaders upbraided America's allies in Europe for not supporting the Americans; Prime Minister Gorton lauded the American bombing of North Vietnam and expressed disdain for "the things called peace talks" being held in Paris in June, 1968.[19] The Vietnam experience of "jointness" with the Americans—in which the Australians were scarcely consulted about American moves while being expected to confer with their great ally about their own and where they had no part in the negotiations for ending the war—was an important ingredient in the overturn of the long-standing coalition government of the Liberal and Country parties.

RECIPROCITY

The lesser ally that chose to be associated with the superpower inevitably looked as if it were a satellite, despite the voluntary nature of the relationship, because its voice in the joint enterprise was small, if it had any at all.[20] From long experience, the Canadians and Mexicans were more sensitive to this danger of an unequally reciprocal relationship in any association with their great neighbor. Thus on global issues, they preferred to work through multilateral organizations which magnified their voice, brought others into the bargaining situations, and offered more ways to trade off concessions.

Their very proximity made a genuinely reciprocal relationship with the superpower hard to develop on global issues, if only because consciousness of disparities was greater than if they had been distant. So an "independent" foreign policy was especially and continuously prized by the next-door neighbors of the United States. But the two middle powers differed in the ways in which they demonstrated their independence.

Canadians often jogged the American policy makers' elbows to suggest more conciliatory action or less reliance on military force, partly because they feared that precipitate behavior would involve them involuntarily. They were especially sharp critics of what they perceived (correctly, no doubt) as provocative steps taken by the United States during the Korean War and brinkmanship during the Quemoy and Matsu crises; their interest in the Far East derived almost exclusively from the United States presence there. Until the 1970s, the Mexicans restricted most of their diplomatic efforts to regional affairs of immediate impact on Mexico and to arms-control endeavors, where, being like the Canadians so close to one of the nuclear powers, they felt a special concern. To be heard, if not necessarily responded to, they had to offer something. Many Australians have contended that the Canadians were in a more advantageous bargaining position than was an ally far away, since the United States could not separate its own security from that of its neighbors and thus had to take account of their behavior. As Australia's minister for external affairs rather wistfully put the point in 1964, "friends" implies the duty to consider the effect on allies of proposed policies.[21] Whether or not distant countries might possess bargaining advantages unavailable to those close by, some reciprocal interests could be discerned.

Most of the bargains were implicit rather than explicit; too much publicity would have destroyed their usefulness. Mexican leadership in promoting a nonnuclear zone in Latin America was appreciated by American leaders, who understood that the treaty, once generally accepted, was more likely to restrain the Soviet Union than the United States and was in line with American efforts to stem the proliferation of nuclear weapons.

Paradoxically, the more independent Canada seemed to others, the more useful it could be to the United States, as when it was chosen for the International Control Commission in Indochina in 1954 (and later to serve on the truce observation team, the International Commission of Control and Supervision, following the cease-fire agreement in Vietnam in 1973). Although chosen as a representative of the West, Canada would not have been acceptable to the adversaries of the United States if it had been expected to follow American policy slavishly.

Although their international role protected the Canadians from American importunities to participate in the Vietnam war, the independence of those Canadians serving on the ICC had been harshly tried by the resolute uncooperativeness of the Communists. This led to Canada's reluctance to become a member of the ICCS in 1973, although the Canadian government felt an obligation to serve, after its persistent pressure on the United States to withdraw from the war. The Canadians were especially loathe to participate in the ICCS because they had not agreed to the terms negotiated by the United States which were supposed to end the war. The costs of following an impartial line during the war often were fairly high, but they were exacted mostly by America's adversaries. They became so onerous subsequent to the United States settlement that Canada finally withdrew from its domestically unpopular international role, despite heavy American pressure to continue participating in the ICCS.[22]

The cost in good relations with the United States of habitually trying to brake rash or militant United States actions seemed minimal to Canadians, and the cost of dragging their feet in the OAS and opposing United States policy towards Cuba seemed similarly low to Mexicans. Such actions did occasionally produce some private and personal annoyance among American leaders.[23] Although Mexico resolutely refused to cut itself off from Cuba and gradually expanded its ties during the 1970s, it quietly kept track of the comings and goings of Cuban Communists via Mexico, to its own advantage as well as that of concerned American officials.[24]

Whether or not the United States government would have been so tolerant of Australia's or Brazil's deviations from "loyal" behavior, governments of these countries did not test the limits during most of the postwar years. During the Quadros-Goulart period, numerous gestures of independence on global issues, mostly without substantive changes in positions, seemed to cool relations with the United States government. Yet the most likely causes for disaffection were more tangible: unfavorable treatment of American investment, deliberate cold shouldering of American officials in Brazil, and failure to carry out promised fiscal reforms. But inconceivable from Canadian or Mexican lips were such expressions as Australian Prime Minister Holt's assurance on a Washington visit in June, 1966, "All the way with LBJ!" and Brazilian Foreign Minister Juracy Magalhaes's "What is good for the United States is good for Brazil." [25]

These distant countries had political objectives which would have been irrelevant to the close neighbors. For a long time, the Australian government was willing to go very far to ensure a continued United States commitment in the Pacific. Australians explained later that their ready response to American pleas for burden sharing in Vietnam was due to intense concern with the aggressive tendencies of Sukarno's Indonesia, as well as to fear of Communist China. Brazil always had cherished an unspoken but not unrecognized desire for a close relationship with the United States that would maintain the power balance in South America. Otherwise, the Brazilians feared being outweighed by Spanish-American states and were continually conscious of the power of their archrival, Argentina. Changes in the global configuration of power and in the domestic politics of the two distant middle powers were followed by their diminished need for reciprocity. Australia under Prime Minister Whitlam cut away from close association with the United States in the Far East, in some instances proclaiming policies contrary to positions taken by the superpower ally. Brazil expanded its influence in South America in what its neighbors regarded as a form of imperialism.

SPECIFICITY

Although both Australia and Brazil did succeed in achieving their balance-of-power objectives, the United States government's record of responsiveness to specific diplomatic interests was poor. Australia failed to secure American backing in its effort to save West Irian from Indonesia's grasp; the Americans had different interests in Indonesia, which caused them to be halfhearted and vague in reassuring the Australians engaged militarily in the confrontation with Indonesia at the time of the Malaysia crisis.[26] Later, a Brazilian government's demand for reciprocal nuclear disarmament by the greater powers in return for Brazil's renunciation of nuclear ambitions went unanswered.

Reciprocal favors seldom could take the form of clear quid pro quos, especially since a principal desire of the United States was for loyal support and of the others an equally vague desire for ''good relations'' or diplomatic credit on which to draw when needed.[27] These were the kinds of considerations entering into decisions on voting in the United Nations. Because of diplomatic usage, documentation of threats and promises used by those who engaged in arm-twisting pressures is difficult, but a general reference to ''good relations'' usually was sufficient.[28]

At the birth of the United Nations, however, the middle powers did have something special to offer—and several specific claims to make—of great concern to the United States. Creation of a general international organization and approval of a modified version of the Dumbarton Oaks draft, on which the major powers had already agreed, required a wider consensus, for which the middle powers' support was indispensible. This opportunity to put on the table their own preferences as to how the United Nations should be organized and what its powers should be was actively pursued by all of the four middle powers. The final version of various clauses could be traced to their influence. Foreign Minister Evatt claimed to be spokesman for the lesser powers, but some of his most significant contributions were particularly appropriate for Australia, including provisions safeguarding "domestic jurisdiction." [29] Mexican and Brazilian inputs were more generally harmonized with those of other Latin American countries in the conference at Chapultepec preceding that in San Franciso.[30] The strong Canadian delegation at the United Nations Conference on International Organization won respect generally but especially with the Americans, who had very close personal contacts with them.[31]

There were other specific international tasks of advantage to the United States, among others, that these middle powers, whether close or far away, could perform. Canada's outstanding contribution to United Nations peacekeeping activities did not depend on association with the United States, although the government of that country benefited from Canada's filling a role impossible for a superpower. Brazil also has taken part in several United Nations peacekeeping enterprises, in addition to the OAS-sponsored operation in the Dominican Republic. Neither the Australians nor others in the United Nations have been much interested in Australia's providing such forces. The Mexicans have eschewed a peacekeeping role for particular reasons, among them unwillingness to provide their military officers with the kind of service which might conceivably bring them back into political life.[32]

On some occasions, one of these countries has served as a liaison with an adversary or aided the United States by bringing other friendly states around to the American view. The Brazilians helped to modify some Latin American demands on the United States when the constitution of the OAS was rewritten in 1966. Aiding the unwieldy and inflexible United States government to move away from a policy stance to which it seemed frozen appeared to be a speciality of the Brazilians, as well as the Canadians. At least some American officials appreciated Canadian leadership bringing Communist China into the international community.

Specific kinds of diplomatic moves, especially retaliatory measures, were out of bounds for the middle powers, regardless of proximity, or for the United States either, and for various reasons. The United States could not afford such threats in the case of Mexico and Brazil because of the impact on its relations with the rest of Latin America. In the cases of Canada and Australia, attempts to intimidate would have had unfavorable effect on relations with Britain and other associated friendly powers. But for Canada and Mexico such actions would have been even more difficult in view of the complexity of their relations. The capacity for depriving the neighbor of something valued was not one-sided.

DISTANCE

Some global issues had particular local implications for the superpower's neighbors. In the Cuban missile crisis, which marked the turning point in the cold war, the United States had a special need for its nearest neighbors to understand its action. This concern was demonstrated by the sending of special high-level envoys to Ottawa and Mexico City to explain the situation, Mexico being the only country not in NATO so treated.[33] The crises raised in acute form the meaning of "consultation" and of "prior notification"; Prime Minister Diefenbaker excused his grudging response by noting that the consultation promised in the NORAD agreement did not precede the United States efforts to activate Canada's obligations under it. However, informally acquired information had in fact alerted the Canadian government.[34] On being shown by the special envoy the address that President Kennedy was about to give, Prime Minister Diefenbaker objected to one paragraph, which was then altered just before the president went on the air.

Although Australian leaders were much more frequently surprised by American actions, they often contended that the substance of these actions, especially during the Vietnam war, was made known to them earlier. (The Canadians could not be caught off base when President Nixon suddenly sprang his intention to visit Peking in 1970, since they already had made their own rapprochement with the People's Republic of China.) Under the Whitlam government, Australia ostentatiously went its own way regardless of previous sentiments about consultation.

The Cuban missile crisis corresponded in time with a period in which the Brazilian government under Goulart was deliberately alienating itself from United States officials, but at other periods, when Brazilian-American relations were friendlier, American leaders took care to touch base with Brazilians when Latin American policy was involved. They clearly believed that Brazil was not very distant, in this context, and they often had discussions with Brazilians prior to inter-American meetings. This consultation was all the more necessary because of the cultural distance between the United

States and Brazil—and Mexico, as well. Both Latin American governments stressed a juridicial approach to relations, which meant pressure on the United States to bind itself legally to courses American officials might claim to prefer but with which United States actions were sometimes at variance. Some of the distance was also measurable in language; the gap between American views and theirs on OAS matters was often narrowed after careful attention to editing proposals. The somewhat superior knowledge possessed by Mexicans of the behavior of the quasi sovereignties in Washington also helped diminish distance by the injection of realism into their expectations.

Just as different Brazilian regimes in the 1960s purposefully moved their country away from and back into the so-called Western camp, so there could be other ways of creating distance from the United States. In 1967, President Gustavo Diaz Ordaz of Mexico, for example, canceled the trip he was to make to Ottawa following one to Washington and instead made one directly from Mexico; he did not wish to have his visits to the two North American capitals so closely linked.[35]

The faraway Australian leaders, on the other hand, regularly stopped in Washington on their way to or from Commonwealth conferences, thus helping to bind together discussions with the British and American allies. The Australians had to struggle hard to develop the personal contacts and sources of information so much desired by those far away from the center and to create the kind of personal trust enjoyed by numerous Canadian officials. Prime Minister Menzies's behavior at the time of the Suez crisis was said to have dealt a serious blow to the confidence-creating work of his foreign minister, R. G. Casey, in Washington; perhaps Menzies intended his mediatory attempts at the 1960 United Nations General Assembly to compensate for his earlier actions.[36]

To get the kind of information which diminishes distance, some has to be given. The Canadians cultivated their access to other countries, and from the trail-blazing trip made by Lester Pearson to Moscow in 1955 onward, they particularly tried to keep open channels to the Soviet Union. Even Prime Minister Trudeau capitalized on his much vaunted trip to Moscow in 1970 by reporting to President Nixon on his impressions. Such communication channels could be opened up by nonneighbors of the United States, as well; the United States has a mutual agreement with Australia and Britain in addition to Canada to monitor communications throughout the world.[37] However, the Canadians have had another advantage over those farther away. Their leaders have had many opportunities to address important parts of the American public and used them to lay out their views, whether in a university lecture series, a press club, a chamber of commerce, or whatever forum lay handy. The other side of this coin, however, was one well recognized in Mexico as well as Canada. The American press could often express views about their policies which they regard as inimical to their interests and these were quickly picked up by the local media. United States officials then had to defend themselves by making clear that such views were not those held by the United States government. Such transnational relations were much more unusual for Australia; and the boycott and counterboycott carried on by Australian and American unions against shipments from each other's country as a result of President Nixon's Christmastime bombing of Hanoi in 1972 were almost unprecedented.

Revulsion against the Vietnam bombing was common throughout the world of America's friends. It was the special relationship of Canada that made its parliament's unanimous condemnation attention getting. On less critical occasions, however, the greater likelihood that Canadians would be heard could mean that by agreeing to listen American officials might avoid the need to comply. And regardless of the Canadians' superior knowledge of whom to talk to and where and when, this advantage could not cover up the fact that with Canada as with the other middle powers, the distance one way was greater than the other way.[38]

CUMULATION AND SPILLOVER

Despite the apprehensions or claims of some people in the four middle powers, no connection between closeness of economic ties with the United States and inability to follow an independent line on global issues can be convincingly demonstrated. On the contrary, the two countries whose foreign policy in world politics most varied from the American line, Canada and Mexico, were the two most closely linked economically to the United States. Unlike Mexico or Canada, each a country in which a particular position on a foreign policy issue usually is carefully coordinated within the government so that it speaks with a single voice, in the United States the government is notorious for fragmented policy making. Policy on global issues can be kept separate from foreign economic policy. American efforts to isolate its cold-war opponents through collective trade restraints were an exception to the rule.

Even on the question of trading with Communist China, the Canadians were less cautious than the Australians and usually were successful in their resistance to direct United States efforts to curb American subsidiaries in Canada from participating in such deals. The Australians were readier to listen to American advice on the ill effects of giving any kind of aid to the Communists and less likely to resist on principle the extension of United States law to Australia's foreign trade.[39] Yet like the Canadians, they did not follow the American example of isolating themselves entirely from the People's Republic of China. In the absence of diplomatic relations between the governments, Australian tourists and athletes went to China, just as Canadians, notably journalists, traveled there for other than trade purposes. The Chinese Communists did link some trade questions with recognition policy, which the Australians discovered when their sales of wheat and wool dropped, while Canadian sales to China soared as Canada began its rapprochement with the government in Peking.[40] Australia's recognition of the People's Republic and other signs of a growing gap between United States and Australian foreign policy proceeded apace with closer economic links between the two allies.

Regardless of the connection or lack of it between economic ties and foreign policy, the two Latin American countries strove continually to gain some economic advantage from foreign-policy issues which arose between them and the United States. They insisted that American proposals for promoting inter-American security required as a basis the spread of economic prosperity and "justice." They claimed that funds saved by arms-control measures which reduced military expenditures should be made available for economic development of the less developed countries. The Mexicans and the Brazilians had their eyes on industrialization, not only for welfare reasons but also because they expected to feel less vulnerable to outside pressure of any kind as a result. As this process proceeded in their countries—as well as in Australia—they did in fact behave in a more independent fashion on global issues, coming a little closer to the mode long adopted by the more economically advanced Canadians. Within the global foreign-policy area, behavior on some issues clearly spilled over into other questions. The Cuban missile crisis gave impetus to Brazil's initiative in promoting a Latin American denuclearized zone. When a later Brazilian regime resisted the broad obligations under either the treaty creating a nonnuclear zone in Latin America or the universal nonproliferation treaty, they did so in terms which suggested that adherence might reduce their chances to play a larger role in world politics. Thus they voiced their objection to "widening the nuclear gap" between the nuclear powers and the others and referred to "nuclear dependency."

CHANNELS OF COMMUNICATION

These foreign-policy declarations of independence were public poses. Until the 1970s, Canadian and Australian leaders (except for the somewhat atypically abrasive Diefenbaker in Canada and Evatt in Australia) preferred to make their views on global issues known to Americans through "quiet diplomacy." That much maligned phrase represented their belief that to keep the channels of communication open they should endeavor not to embarrass the United States government publicly when they had divergent advice. But the preference of the Australian foreign minister, R. G. Casey, for "constant and rapid exchange of confidential telegrams between capitals" was no substitute for the ubiquitous personal communication links built up over decades by the Canadians.[41] Such dependence upon personal friendship, however, could open the Canadians to a risk not run by the Australians, a risk, in the words of one of the latter, of "deeply wounding their colleagues" in case of opposition by one of their governments. There were disadvantages to quiet diplomacy, as Sir Alan Watt has pointed out. As practiced by Australian leaders, it left the Australian public ignorant of why the leaders took particular steps, made Australia look like an American stooge in others' eyes, gave the leaders no leverage with Americans who shared their views and needed support against official policy, and prevented wholesome domestic restraints on the leaders' misjudgment.[42] Public reaction against this style contributed to the sharp reversal of policy when the Australian Labor party came to power.

For dealing with European questions, Canada looked to the North Atlantic Council. That body was useful for unpublicized pressure on the United States to act cautiously, for securing information, for ameliorating Franco-American conflicts, and for promoting détente with the East. There were always some allies who would join the Canadians in these efforts.[43]

On other questions, however, the Canadians constantly urged the United States to act under the auspices of the United Nations and did so even at the time of the Cuban missile crisis.

The Rio pact, like the North Atlantic treaty, grew out of dissatisfaction with the way in which the United Nations was able to handle vital security matters. Yet the Mexicans, who prior to the San Francisco conference had been of like mind with other Latin American governments in claiming a special place for regional organizations in the United Nations Charter, later changed their attitude. They feared that the provisions of the Rio treaty were being dangerously stretched by the United States to fight the cold war, to turn the inter-American system into a military alliance against outsiders, and to legitimize joint antisubversion actions that were undermining the principle of nonintervention. Although this distrust came to a head with the rise of Castro in Cuba, Mexico began its resistance to these American uses of the OAS earlier in the 1950s. In response to the Bay of Pigs affair, Mexico went to the extreme of sponsoring a "renegade Latin American" resolution at the United Nations, which in effect condemned the United States action. (It was joined by Brazil and the Communist countries, among others.) [44]

For Mexico, the primacy of the United Nations was asserted in legal terms; OAS sanctions against Cuba in 1961 were an enforcement action, which required the approval of the Security Council of the United Nations. The Brazilians were more flexible and less inclined to insist that the United Nations had primacy over the OAS as the appropriate forum to deal with alleged threats to the hemisphere. Yet they, too, opposed the United States in 1954 when it successfully prevented Guatemala from having its case considered at the United Nations. The rather blatant ways in which the United States used the OAS for its own purposes, not always widely or genuinely shared with other members, stiffened the Mexicans' distrust. Some Mexicans, while recognizing that even the OAS was preferable to being all alone with their giant neighbor, would have preferred a Latin American organization which excluded the United States. [45]

Despite its defects, the Mexicans appreciated the OAS as a means by which the foreign ministers of Latin America could meet regularly for an exchange of views. For both Mexico and Brazil, membership in this large regional group enhanced their influence at the United Nations, making them more desirable as members of committees dealing with global issues. Regardless of other countries' views of Latin American solidarity and regardless of early American expectations of having a trustworthy block of Latin American votes in the United Nations, cohesion among the Latin American members has not been outstanding. Nevertheless, the Latin American members have regularly caucused together prior to taking critical actions, and the United States is not a party to these caucuses.[46] Unsubstantial as "Latin America" is as a community, whether economic or political, it is more a reality than any artificial "community" on foreign-policy issues with the Colossus of the North.

Even more artificial a community would be an OAS containing Canada. The famous empty chair at the Pan-American Union earlier was vacant through American preference, later by Canadian choice. Latin Americans, including Brazilians, have from time to time made clear that Canada would be welcome, and Mexico has pressed Canada to join. President Kennedy made a rare blunder in expressing the American desire for Canadian membership when speaking in Ottawa in 1961. At this point Canada had seemed ready to join; so great was Canadian sensitivity to American pressure that membership in such circumstances became out of the question.[47] From that time onward, joining OAS looked more and more like asking for trouble, in view of the various crises in the Caribbean. No matter how Canada might have acted in the OAS, it would have been labeled either an American stooge or disloyal to its greatest friend.[48] Canadians were glad that they did not have to take a stand when the United States intervened in the Dominican Republic in 1965. In typically cautious and incremental fashion, Canada joined a number of inter-American agencies and commissions and eventually became an official observer in the organization itself, which by then included some of the Caribbean Commonwealth countries.

Nonmembership in the OAS avoided the kind of self-imposed restraint that Canadians on occasion exercised in bodies where the United States also participated. Their public behavior in the United Nations during the Korean War belied their strong opposition to American conduct respecting China; for the sake of the larger community, Canada did not press to the limits its opposition to United States policy. Why make matters even worse, asked Lester Pearson. A similar self-restraint, here in the name of the larger Latin American community, can be discerned in Mexico's actions in the OAS.[49]

Canada, Mexico, and Brazil are members of the Eighteen Nation Disarmament Committee (now twenty-four), where they have taken positions independent of American preferences. Mexico and Brazil have participated in this committee as nonaligned representatives, Canada as part of the West. Both the Soviet Union and the United States are obliged to hear and respond to their views, and Canada has availed itself of this chance to promote its desires even more vigorously than have the two Latin American members.[50]

Following Foreign Minister Evatt's flamboyant career in the United Nations, a distinct decline in enthusiasm for the world organization within the Australian government set in. His successors showed signs of real distrust of an organization where Australia's friends were not numerous. They preferred a smaller organization in which their special cultural and security ties with the Americans and British would permit them to have a larger voice. Until the 1960s, Australia's policies regarding dependent territories, apartheid, and the claims of underdeveloped countries were out of tune with those of most of the United Nations membership, even including the United States.[51] The Australians' fears of the United Nations were not alleviated by their unhappy experience at Security Council and General Assembly meetings during the Suez crisis. Physical distance aggravated their problems of maneuverability and embarrassed their delegates, who lacked the quick means of communication exploited by Canada's Pearson.[52] Better the double standards in SEATO, concluded the Australians, than this unwieldy group, especially for genuine communication.[53]

The Canada–United States and Mexico–United States interparliamentary groups have dealt with global issues as well as economic questions, thereby adding channels of communication outside the executive branch. However, the delegates have been well briefed by their respective foreign ministries, which results in more or less amplifying official positions with their opposite legislative numbers.[54] In any case, American members have had little success in interesting either the Canadian or the Mexican delegations in global questions, compared to economic issues, which come closer to home.[55]

DOMESTIC POLITICS

No matter how well developed or numerous the channels of communication, United States perspectives on particular global issues might easily differ from those of each of the middle powers for reasons other than those imposed by the external world.[56] Not uncommonly, for example, either Mexican leaders or American officials have commented that they "understood" the reasons for opposing policies; they did not press more vigorously for changes in attitude because they were aware of a delicate domestic political situation faced by the hesitant government. The likelihood that some internal political restraint might be operative often curbed even the making of a request.

Constitutional restraints on the American government and, especially, the independent role of Congress have been given and accepted as explanations for the failure of the United States government to respond favorably to the desires of a middle power. Thus in negotiating the South East Asia treaty, Secretary Dulles insisted that the guarantee of military support by each member in case of attack on another member be qualified by the phrase, "in accordance with its constitutional processes"; the Australians recognized this to be in deference to the United States Senate.

One case in which the separation of powers in the United States government was not accepted as a legitimate excuse for nonaction was that concerning the Canadian ambassador to Egypt, Herbert Norman. The Canadian government in 1957 made an official protest about the release by the Senate Subcommittee on Internal Security of testimony repeating an old and unsubstantiated charge that Norman had Communist sympathies and might be linked to a Soviet spy ring. In a heated exchange of notes, the State Department disavowed any responsibility for a senatorial action. It did request, unsuccessfully, the subcommittee to refrain from further publicity of this kind. Shortly after the second episode of such publicity, Ambassador Norman committed suicide in Cairo. The Canadian government threatened to provide no more security information, as it regularly had done, unless it received particular assurances that such material would not be turned over to agencies that the executive branch could not control. Four months later such safeguards were promised. President Eisenhower himself had made a noncommittal response to the Canadian protests. The whole affair meanwhile reverberated in Canadian domestic politics, as government opponents in the current electoral campaign seized upon it as an issue.[57]

Some aspect of the East-West competition usually showed up in foreign-policy shifts that flowed from changes on the domestic front, such shifts being common in all the four middle powers as one government succeeded another. Independence from United States foreign-policy leadership inevitably was part of the issue. The most marked variations occurred in Brazil. Following President Kubitschek's modest efforts to play a distinctive role on the world scene, his successors, Quadros and Goulart, deliberately took stands out of line with American preferences on certain global issues. The Brazilian policy in the OAS deliberations concerning Castro's Cuba, which was in accord with Mexican policy, marked a very definite alienation from earlier cooperation with the United States. Was it independent of domestic pressures, too? Brazilian leaders regularly asserted that their country was invulnerable to subversion from outside Communist influences, but there were important political groups which did not believe this and were anxious about Brazil's stance with respect to Cuba in particular.[58] Almost with the suddenness of the coup of 1964, Brazil's foreign policy again shifted as a result of internal politics, politics scarcely related to the outside environment. Almost at once the government broke off relations with Cuba. In the following year, it readily participated in the Dominican Republic peacekeeping action and in other OAS matters reversed the course set by Goulart's foreign minister, San Tiago Dantas. In doing so, the Brazilians diverged from Mexico's position and followed the American course. In addition, however, the military regime significantly changed its arms-control policy, diverging from that of Mexico but moving in some defiance of the United States, too. When Castelo Branco was succeeded by Costa e Silva and especially after Garrastazú Médici came to office, the whole tone of Brazil's voice on global issues took on a much more nationalistic, less pro-American quality.

Foreign-policy changes following presidential elections were much less marked in Mexico once Lopez Mateos had set his government on a course characterized by wider concerns and more active, more positive positions on global issues.[59] Like Brazil, Mexico's main interests were along North-South lines rather than East-West demarcations. In another and related alignment, that organized by the Arabs against Israel, Mexico was, besides Brazil, the only Latin American state to vote in the 1975 General Assembly of the United Nations for the resolution equating Zionism with racism. It quickly felt a backlash from domestic groups in the United States and Canada, who withheld their tourist patronage.

East-West issues could not completely be ignored, not only because they were of concern to the United States, but also for domestic reasons. Lopez Mateos proved a master in manipulating Mexico's stance on Castro's Cuba. The Cuban revolution was initially quite popular among many groups in Mexico, but not all, and one of his problems in a period of economic recession and possible flights of capital was to satisfy various business interests while at the same time following a policy towards Cuba desired by more leftist elements. The strong resistance his government put up to American moves to isolate Castro was partly attributable to Lopez Mateos's attention to balancing his domestic political pressures.[60] Yet the Mexican government's policy with respect to Communist states did not correspond to its treatment of possible Communist elements within the country. Furthermore, even though Soviet officials could be and were expelled from Mexico for allegedly giving aid to potential disrupters of the system, shortly thereafter high Soviet leaders could be and were welcomed on legitimate missions. Though less blatantly than the Brazilians, the Mexican government could repress undesired opposition in a manner which had an effect on Communist or leftist groups similar to the effects of the more frightening measures of the Brazilian government under the generals.[61] Concentrating on the effects, United States officials ignored the means and were content that although the Mexican and Brazilian governments might not accept collective inter-American measures to curb subversion, they were capable of handling this problem nationally.

In style, although not necessarily in substance, successive Canadian governments differed from each other in their treatment of global issues and coordination with United States policy thereon. Prime Minister Diefenbaker's government was a particularly stormy one in this respect. Quiet diplomacy was not his way of doing things, and he took ample advantage of the many opportunities to gain popularity by pulling the eagle's feathers (a political temptation which has been ever present in the middle powers). Even before coming into office, Diefenbaker led the Conservative outcry in Canada against Lester Pearson's "traitorous" failure to uphold the British in the Suez crisis. This was one of a large number of dissatisfactions that led to the downfall of the Liberal party in 1957. But Diefenbaker's complaints were not about Communist influence.

Several times a Canadian government came close to recognizing the People's Republic of China, but it hesitated because at that point the Chinese were behaving in a manner considered outrageous or because it feared unfavorable repercussions in the United States. Just as significant, the government also drew back because of divisions of opinion domestically.[62] Eventually, when Prime Minister Trudeau came into office, this question was ready-made for his new look at Canadian foreign policy. The domestic political advantages reaped from his change of policy were not unrelated to the fact that it appeared to be taken independently of the United States.[63] This did not mean that his government would not align itself with the United States when desirable. Thus Canada welcomed Secretary of State Henry Kissinger's summons to frame a new Atlantic Charter in April, 1973, while pointing out somewhat later that Canada's relations with Europe differed from United States relations with Europe.[64]

Much wider shifts occurred in Australia as a result of electoral changes. With the noteworthy exception of the Suez crisis, the Liberal-Country party coalition, especially after Menzies had left office, followed American policy on global issues fairly closely. Strong anti-Communist sentiment in Australia, including some among elements of the opposition, itself greatly divided on the China issue, provided underlying support for the government. But Menzies and his Liberal party successors followed the rule of letting the public know as little as possible about their foreign-policy thinking. Their electoral downfall in 1972 could be explained in part as a public revulsion against Vietnam policies only gradually understood. (That they did not fall sooner has usually been attributed to divisions within their opposition.)

Having campaigned on proposals carrying a strong flavor of independence from the United States, Australian Labor party leader Gough Whitlam, on coming to power, quickly and with much flourish struck out on a foreign-policy line very different from that of his predecessors. His behavior was slightly reminiscent of Australian Labor leader Herbert Evatt's many years before. One of Prime Minister Whitlam's earliest acts was to recognize the people's Republic of China. His castigation of the Christmas bombing of North Vietnam made President Nixon so angry that Whitlam almost had to invite himself to a talk with the American president on his way through Washington to a Commonwealth conference in Ottawa, a sanction more severe than was visited on Canadians for their own outcries.[65] Australia also soon established diplomatic relations with North Vietnam, severed them with Taiwan, and recognized East Germany. Whitlam's government called upon both the Soviet Union and the United States to exercise restraint in the Indian Ocean, after expressing disapproval of American plans to expand the naval facilities on the island of Diego Garcia.[66] Respecting the American position in the Indian Ocean as on other issues, the new Liberal government which overturned Labor late in 1975 shifted to a friendlier orientation towards the United States, without reversing some of Whitlam's diplomatic acts.

SUMMARY

The pull in all four middle powers toward demonstrating independence of the United States on global foreign-policy issues shows the difficulty of diplomatic collaboration between such states and one so asymmetrically powerful as the United States. The inequality in impact on world politics has not precluded selective responsiveness. However, it was usually the middle powers which listened—when the Americans gave them the opportunity of hearing United States intentions. Less frequently the Americans paid attention to them, although in Canada's case, it was not for lack of the Canadians trying and sometimes succeeding. The four were thus in a somewhat less advantageous position than the great powers allied with the United States— Britain, France, and Germany—or the great adversaries—the Soviet Union and Communist China; this was the nature of the game.

The absence of genuine and reciprocally balanced consultation meant that the four lesser powers were freer to follow their own foreign policies. Yet even though American diplomats might at the time interpret a particular manifestation of independence as an obstacle, thwarting United States objectives, the divergences were within limits which over the long run could not be proved adverse to United States interests. Furthermore, there was usually a strain towards accommodation on both the American side and that of the middle power. To amplify their voices, all four, but especially Canada and Mexico, strove to get like-minded states singing in the same key; in this way the harmonization might be closer to their tastes.

Regardless of consultation or of multilateral support, the neighbors, Canada globally and Mexico regionally, have been throughout the period the most independent in their foreign-policy stances. Except where the United States stipulated that security issues were involved (much of this period was one of cold war), there was little connection between any other issue area and the position of the middle powers in facing third parties. Divergences within the pairs, Latin American and Commonwealth, were more easily traceable to domestic political considerations.

When taking their stand on global issues, the two middle powers closest physically to the United States seemed most motivated to appear autonomous; in this respect, neighborhood had a negative influence on community, at least as interpreted by the Americans. However, the Canadians, by far the most intimately acquainted with the main streets and alleys of

Washington, best understood how far they could go and still be effective when disagreeing with the superpower's government.

In an era of rapprochement, the loosening of certain kinds of ties formed around global issues of another day may make proximity less relevant. Yet mounting concern with economic issues on a world scale may mean that neighborhood will retain significance in the policymakers' calculations. And the kind of role played by these middle powers at San Francisco may again come to the fore.

NINE

NEIGHBORHOOD ISSUES

UNLIKE DISTANT Australia and Brazil, Canada and Mexico each share with the United States certain kinds of concerns which arise from their being next door to one another. These concerns include, among many, development of the great river systems which flow from one country to the other and often form part of the border; the preservation and improvement of the environment, including very specific pollution problems; the availability of scarce energy resources; the policing of the borders for drug traffic and illegal passage of persons; pest control; fire fighting; transport and communications; health and safety regulations; sharing of fisheries resources; and cultural and scientific exchanges. (Some of these matters concern more distant countries, too, but proximity makes them more pressing problems.)

In contrast to the global issues discussed in the previous chapter, the fence-line types of questions treated here are not only generalized concerns but also affect particular groups on each side of the border. Interest in them is intensely focused, pressure groups play an important role in controversies about them, and they are deeply imbedded in domestic politics. Many different agencies on the national level participate in decisions about them, legislative bodies are very important actors, and other levels of government are actively engaged in solving them. Handling these bilateral neighborhood issues differs from coping with purely domestic questions because the number of different jurisdictions is doubled, and so are the constituencies concerned. In addition, on both the northern and southern borders of the United States, special bilateral agencies have been established to deal with many of these types of issues, and transnational combinations of interests are not uncommon.

For both Canada and Mexico, time has been an important element, since the United States has developed economically beyond the points reached by these neighbors, although in directions they expect to follow. The Americans felt sooner the need for collaboration or for taking unilateral action, which would be to the disadvantage of the less developed countries at a later stage. In some areas, this meant that if the United States acted first, vested interests could be built up which would be very difficult to restrict when the neighbor was ready to act. The time aspect has been especially noteworthy in the case of river development.

RIVER DEVELOPMENT

Four great river systems, two on the northern and two on the southern borders of the United States, have long involved it in controversy and cooperation with its respective neighbors. On the Mexican border, the uncertain course of the Rio Grande raised boundary-line issues for over a hundred years, with partial settlements in 1906 and 1933, the abortive arbitration of the Chamizal dispute in 1911, which was eventually settled in 1963, and a presumably final settlement of all boundary-line questions in 1970.[1] Equal, if not greater, controversy arose over managing the uses of the Rio Grande waters for domestic purposes, flood control, and irrigation. In the huge arid region crossed by the other great southwestern river, the Colorado, the questions of who got how much of the river's scarce water—and what would be the quality of that water—were the issues, partly settled in 1944 by the Treaty on Utilization of Waters of the Colorado and Tijuana Rivers and of the Rio Grande, although some of the questions have continued to the present. Problems on the smaller boundary river, the Tijuana, have been treated similarly to the problems of the great rivers.[2]

Of more recent origin was the issue to the north of how to manage the waters of the Columbia River, which the United States primarily wanted for hydroelectric power, not yet needed by Canada, and which the United States wished to control against floods. The twenty-year discussions between the United States and Canada on the development of the Columbia River ended in the signing in 1964 of a protocol to a 1960 treaty, which was not ratified by the Canadian parliament until the later date.[3] Much more lengthy negotiations over the creation of the St. Lawrence Seaway, with accompanying development of hydroelectric power, culminated in authorization to proceed in 1954. The first accord in the perils-of-Pauline struggle to achieve the St.

Lawrence seaway was the treaty signed in 1932, which the United States
Senate rejected in 1934.[4]

JOINTNESS

Except for the basic and implementing agreements to proceed jointly in
the development of the four great river systems, no joint action in the sense
of a single operating agency for any of the systems has been set up. With respect to the Mexican-American undertakings, supervision and control are
exercised by the International Boundary and Water Commission, but each
national section is separately responsible for its country's share in construction of such joint projects as the great dams on the lower Rio Grande (Falcón and Amistad), as well as for the 1933 rectification projects on that river
which straightened and stabilized its course. Joint control with separate responsibilities prevails also for the new channel and the new international
bridges constructed under the Chamizal Agreement of 1963. Maintenance is
similarly shared in this way. Financial costs are divided more or less
equally.

On the Canadian border, four different Canadian-American agencies
supervised, coordinated, and controlled various aspects of the St. Lawrence
Seaway and power projects, but the construction and operation were done by
separate national, state, and provincial agencies.[5] As for the Columbia River
development, although the International Joint Commission played an important role in preliminary studies, it was given authority in the treaty only to
act as a kind of arbitral body in disputes arising under the agreement.[6] For
both rivers, projects could have been undertaken separately by the two countries to accomplish most of their objectives. The threat to go it alone, made
by Canada in the late 1940s when the seaway proposal was dragging its
weary course through labyrinthine American governmental proceedings,
eventually produced the agreement.[7] In the West, Canada's well-known
General Andrew J. L. McNaughton, who strongly opposed the terms of the
Columbia River treaty, had an alternative plan, under which the projects affecting Canada would have been entirely a Canadian undertaking.[8]

There were two guiding principles for sharing the potentialities inherent
in the joint scheme that were laid down by the International Joint Commission in its preliminary work on the Columbia River development. They were
that the development be so undertaken as to secure maximum economies and
that both countries be net beneficiaries, with the benefits equitably distrib-

uted. These were by no means fully followed in the eventual agreement. As a result of various political pressures and rigidities and some noneconomic objectives, the two countries failed to obtain significant economies which could have been achieved from pooling the technical possibilities of developing the Columbia River system.[9]

RECIPROCITY

The Columbia River bargain involved exchanging different kinds of benefits. Under the treaty of 1960, Canada was to construct storage facilities for 15.5 million acre-feet of water; the water would be used largely for power and flood control downstream in the United States. In return, Canada was to receive half the increase in power which was generated in American plants benefiting from Canadian stream regulation, as well as a sum of money equal to half the value of the reduction in flood damage in the United States made possible by the reservoirs. The developments included a transboundary storage project with reservoir headwaters going 42 miles up into British Columbia but with the dam constructed on the American side. Each country was to bear the cost of building the facility on its side in exchange for benefits it would receive within its own reaches of the river. British Columbia Premier W. A. C. Bennett had other objectives, which he achieved in the 1964 protocol that altered the provisions of the 1960 treaty. According to the revised terms, Canada's rights in the power generated downstream for 30 years were to be sold for a lump sum (which Bennett wanted to use for development of his own Peace River program), and the flood control benefit payments were increased.[10] By the revision, Bennett put another hole in the long-standing Canadian policy of not selling to the United States large blocks of hydroelectric power for a long period, a principle which began to change in 1959.[11] Since 1964 Canadians have continued to argue among themselves about whether their negotiators made a good bargain, at least for the future day when Canada would be readier to make use of the potential hydroelectric power of the Columbia.[12] They often overlooked the fact that Canada obtained a precedent-breaking concession from the United States, namely acceptance of the principle that compensation was due one riparian owner because his activities on his portion of the river benefited the downstream neighbor.[13]

Canadians also complained later about the bargains struck for developing the St. Lawrence Seaway, with its intricate meshing of responsibilities for canals, locks, dams, dredging, and power works. Here much more complicated interests had to be balanced. For long periods, conflicting interests represented by port cities, railroads, shipping companies, unions, farmers, electric-power concerns, iron and steel companies—to say nothing of provincial and state authorities—failed to sort themselves out into coalitions which finally would bring about a bargain. Pressures on one side of the border were constantly out of phase with those on the other. Further complicating the process was the effort to combine increased hydroelectric-power generation with improved navigation. Occasionally, the impatience of Ontario and New York authorities to get on with the power projects led to threats to ignore the seaway possibilities, threats which stimulated negotiations on the latter. Although in general the rule that each country pay for the construction necessary on its side was observed, a report made in 1971 to the Canadian Ministry of Transport declared that Canada actually was paying for about two-thirds of the total public investment in canals, locks, and channels (although in the waterways above Lake Erie, where American use was much greater, the United States met most of the cost). In annual expenditures, Canada was paying about five-sixths of the investment costs and shouldering about six-sevenths of the deficits.[14] The Canadians wanted to ease their financial burden by increasing the tolls, but the United States authorities opposed increases. Much of this controversy stemmed from the earlier determination to make the seaway pay for itself, a decision which had been necessary to secure acceptance of the seaway by many who otherwise would have strongly opposed it. Meanwhile, the United States had forgiven part of the debt incurred for the construction of facilities on its side, thus reducing the pressure for increased tolls.

Agreements with Mexico did not stay settled either, despite the wide scope of the 1944 rivers treaty. Some new issues reflected changes which were brought about by the more dynamic, richer partner, an asymmetry which no formal agreement could eliminate. As in the Canadian cases, the national impact of the river developments on Mexico was much greater than on the United States, although the local impact on those American states immediately involved was at least as large as the impact on the less affluent partner.[15]

For more than twelve hundred miles, the Rio Grande forms the boundary between the United States and Mexico, and important cities lie on both sides. Thus although Mexico was downstream with respect to both the

Colorado and the Rio Grande and thus presumably in a weaker position, its bargaining position on the Rio Grande was considerably better. What it did or did not do on its side of this river could affect important interests on the American side. Partly for this reason, when negotiating the 1944 agreement, Mexico sought to combine the arrangements for the two river systems. The American states most immediately affected by actions on the Colorado unsuccessfully endeavored to keep them separate. For the scarce water of the Colorado, Mexico had to compete with several powerful and thirsty states of the American Southwest, states with rapidly growing needs for more water; a somewhat different set of states—including Texas—were concerned about the Rio Grande. With some diplomatic aid from the United States Department of State during the intricate bargaining between the American states themselves on the final terms of the 1944 treaty, Mexico overcame the vigorous objections of some of the states, particularly California, and secured more water than they had wanted to relinquish, although less than Mexico had sought.

The implementation of the treaty's provisions for the Rio Grande has proceeded fairly smoothly, including the construction of the Falcón and Amistad dams. But the terms of the treaty regarding the Colorado's waters did not specify the quality of the flow to be delivered to Mexico. Both above and below the border, agricultural development was proceeding rapidly, making the river ever more valuable. An unanticipated consequence of an irrigation project in Arizona (the Wellton-Mohawk) brought about the most prickly issue assailing Mexican-American relations in the 1960s, namely, the salinity of the Colorado as it reached Mexico. Disastrous effects on irrigated Mexican farms produced Mexican outcries of treaty violation. Although the United States denied a legal obligation, in 1965 an amicable solution appeared to have been found. The United States agreed to change the pumping arrangements seasonally on the American side and to construct a bypass canal extension from the Wellton-Mohawk to drain off to the Gulf of California the saltiest water below the principal Mexican diversion point when irrigation requirements in the Mexicali Valley were at the lowest point.[16] Unfortunately, this mainly technical solution did not eliminate the problem for Mexican farmers; American authorities believed the farmers should use better water conservation methods and gave technical aid toward improving them. Continued pressures from Mexico for further steps produced an agreement in August, 1973, under which the United States was to build a huge desalting plant with a drainage system into the Gulf of California, meanwhile supplying clean water by diluting the normal flow with fresh storage water. The United States also agreed to support a Mexican program to rehabilitate the damaged land.[17] Salinity on the lower Rio Grande, which affects both sides, has been attacked through a diversion canal to the Gulf of Mexico, constructed by Mexico but with half the cost borne by the United States.[18]

The Chamizal convention of 1963, transferring disputed territory to Mexico and fixing the channel of the Rio Grande at the point between El Paso and Ciudad Juarez to prevent future shifts in its course, gave effect to the arbitral award of 1911, which the United States had earlier repudiated. But neither side insisted on the other's giving up the juridical position it had formulated after the 1911 fiasco. The agreement included some smaller transfers of territory to the United States and, in addition, construction of a new, unbreachable channel for the river, new bridges, and other facilities. The costs for these works would be shared equally.[19]

SPECIFICITY

It was in the nature of these agreements that they be highly specific as to acre-feet of water, kilowatt hours of power, financial costs of construction, responsibility for maintenance. Not all aspects could be specified, however, such as the exact tolls to be charged on portions of the St. Lawrence Seaway; such questions remained for further controversy and subsequent agreement. That the 1944 treaty on water utilization of the Rio Grande and Colorado did not state specifically that the water Mexico was to receive should be of usable quality was a matter only faintly troubling to the Mexicans at the time, who did not visualize future developments which would make their entitlement unusable, but the Americans could not, in practice, stand on the letter of the treaty.[20] The kind of good faith shown eventually in the Colorado case was observed more quickly in the fairly flexible and more loosely defined ways in which the United States and Canada dealt with the smaller rivers traversing their borders, which required some accord in managing.[21]

CUMULATION AND SPILLOVER

That a harmonious solution to river problems with Mexico had advantages beyond the immediate economic ones was much in the minds of American negotiators in 1944. World War II issues, the hopes of the United States for good results at the San Francisco conference on the United Nations charter, the Good Neighbor policy—all of them factors making good relations with Mexico desirable—played a part in the terms that the United States accepted.[22]

Elaborate ceremonies always accompanied the dedication of projects implementing the treaties, at which the heads of state referred to other foreign-policy objectives said to be furthered by these cooperative endeavors. The Chamizal settlement wiped clean a slate of legal guilt which had resulted from the United States rejection of the arbitral award in 1911 and replaced this sorry record with a picture of good will and constructive cooperation. It got a tumultuous reception in Mexico.

Although the St. Lawrence Seaway and the Columbia River negotiations overlapped in time by ten years, that they affected very different geographical interests seems to have prevented the negotiations themselves from running together. Different sections of the country and separate regional concerns were involved. Within its own area, however, the St. Lawrence Seaway brought about the formation of an International Association of Great Lakes Ports, which became active in the 1970s in seeking increased European use of the Seaway.[23]

CHANNELS OF COMMUNICATION

The interparliamentary groups, both Canadian-American and Mexican-American, have helped to promote congressional understanding of some of the river projects, which was desirable, because they required congressional action for implementation.[24] Far more important, however, have been the International Boundary and Water Commission (IBWC) and the International Joint Commission (IJC), which function in somewhat similar fashion on the Mexican and Canadian boundaries, dating from 1889 and 1909, respectively.[25] The scope of the International Boundary and Water Commission was increased in 1944 from the original charge to resolve territorial problems caused by changes in the river course to cover also the control and utilization of the waters of the Colorado and Rio Grande (and Tijuana). The commission has tried to detect problems early, and this has been made possible by constant surveillance of potential problem areas along the boundary and by continuous communication between the American and Mexican sections and their subordinate bodies. Although political entities—their respective governments—must authorize agreements made between the two commissioners who head the national sections, their studies, investigations, and planning are primarily on a technical engineering level. In proposing solutions, however, they have tried to keep in mind the political, economic, and social factors involved.

Like the Mexican-American organization, the International Joint Commission, on the northern border of the United States, requires some kind of authorization by the individual member governments for its various activities and depends upon the governments for the implementing of its recommendations. Its functional scope is wider, however, and its supervisory activities cover a much greater geographical territory.[26] Like the IBWC, it can hear individuals and institutions directly, but in addition private interests desiring to take certain steps affecting the rights of those on the other side of the border must receive its permission after hearings held in the locality.[27] The six commissioners (three from each country) tend to act not as delegates but as a single body whose members are uninstructed by their respective governments. This holds also for its subordinate boards.[28] Like its counterpart on the Mexican side, the work of the IJC is a continuous informational, investigatory, supervisory, and coordinating type of activity, not confined to specific settlements of differences.

ADMINISTRATIVE TREATMENT VERSUS POLITICIZATION

Despite continous communication between each of the two bilateral commissions and other interested officials, formally and more commonly informally, issues as large and multifaceted as the four river developments inevitably became high policy matters. In fact, they called for formal bilateral international agreements, usually treaties, to register some of the major accords they had reached. The rather frequent meetings of the United States president with his counterpart in Canada or Mexico have been important in stimulating the necessary negotiations for individual settlements as well as for approving the culmination of negotiations. Top-level desire for the agreements was of course crucial; presidents since the 1920s had wanted a settlement of the Chamizal controversy, but it was not finally solved until John F. Kennedy pushed it through after his meeting with López Mateos, who had pressed the need upon him in 1962.

Studies and recommendations preparing the way for these formal settlements did come from both bilateral commissions. However, the St. Lawrence Seaway was far too complicated a political problem and the Columbia River project too controversial for the IJC to handle. The latter provided one occasion on which the IJC split nationally, led by the very determined General McNaughton on the Canadian side.[29] So difficult had it been to balance all the interests in the Columbia River agreement that there was no disposition among either Canadian or American federal officials to reopen the negotiations (except for one or two provisions) when the British Columbia premier refused to give his necessary concurrence.

DOMESTIC POLITICS

The Canadian provinces' constitutional powers and the determination of the provincial premiers to exercise their prerogatives to prevent or modify the international agreements could be seen not only in the Columbia River case, but also in the St. Lawrence Seaway. Premier Mitchell Hepburn of Ontario exerted his utmost powers in the late 1930s to restrain Prime Minister King; Hepburn sometimes acted in concert with Quebec Premier Maurice Duplessis, who continued his opposition into the 1950s.[30] Although the American states were less powerful legally, one reason even so persuasive a president as Franklin Roosevelt was unable to carry through his objective for the St. Lawrence waterway was that it involved several states, crucially New York, as well as a multitude of other competing domestic interests.

With respect to the Colorado, an interstate compact for dividing rights to the water was involved, as well as contracts between some of the states and the federal government for financing certain canals and dams. Thus the contest between the states was waged partly in Congress among some very influential and powerfully placed Senators.[31] All of the river developments required some congressional action, and the diverse economic interests were well represented among opponents and proponents of various plans for these bilateral projects. In addition, there were some party differences, although these were less important in the United States than in Canada, where the Cooperative Commonwealth Federation (CCF) and its successor, the New Democratic Party, opposed the Columbia River provisions. But even within the executive branch of the United States government, disagreement on terms, especially with respect to the Mexican developments, divided the three affected departments, Interior, Commerce, and State, each of which had different constituencies; only the State Department was concerned with the foreign-relations aspects. Part of the difficulty in negotiating the Columbia River agreement flowed from the three changes in the Canadian government that occurred during five years of bargaining. There was a shift in the United States administration as well.[32] The American change, however, worked to the advantage of getting an agreement, since the Republicans, who were displaced, had been hostile to federal development of hydroelectric power. One of the inflexible objectives on the American side was to get Canadian clearance for constructing the Libby Dam in Montana, the building of which had been so strongly supported in the Senate that ratification of a treaty would depend in part upon its inclusion, whether or not justified from an economic and engineering point of view.[33] As for Mexican domestic pressures, one of the reasons the Mexican government pressed so hard for a solution to the Colorado salinity problem was the threat to the national government from leftist opposition groups and students in Baja California, who were causing civic disruption in protesting the effects of the saline water on irrigated farms in that area.

Considering the immensely complicated national counter pressures, the important role of Congress in realizing the agreements, and the multifunctional aspects of the river developments, their achievement not only registered responsiveness on the part of the governments concerned but also explained the persistence of controversy about them throughout many years.

ENVIRONMENTAL QUESTIONS

JOINTNESS

The disposal of sewage and related sanitation problems antedates more recent kinds of environmental concerns. It is the main type of environmental problem that has engaged Mexico and the United States as neighbors. This may be partly because Mexico is less developed and less anxious about other environmental dangers. Only in the 1970s did Mexico begin to take action on air pollution.[34]

Along the border there are fourteen pairs of twin cities, and the International Boundary and Water Commission has dealt with sanitation problems of several of these municipalities. In some instances, it has had the responsibility not only of investigating and recommending solutions but also of being the instrument through which international sewage treatment plants were constructed and operated.[35] To handle part of the sewage-disposal problem of Tijuana, the commission was instrumental in the construction of an international pipeline about one mile long which connects the domestic works in the two countries. In case of an emergency in the Tijuana system, this pipe can be used to discharge its sewage into the American disposal system, which is connected with that of San Diego.[36]

RECIPROCITY

Although antipollution measures in boundary waters must be joint to be effective, the precedent-setting efforts of the United States and Canada, especially on the Great Lakes, have depended on reciprocal action in the form of national projects which were jointly coordinated, formally and informally. The IJC first studied the pollution of some of the boundary waters in 1912. It efforts culminated in a draft treaty submitted in 1920, which was never acted upon by the two governments.[37] Shortly after World War II the governments tackled the question again, but it was not until the 1960s that serious efforts were made to solve the pollution problems of the Great Lakes. Investigation by the IJC and continuous interchanges among Canadian and American officials resulted in the Great Lakes Water Quality Agreement signed by President Nixon in Ottawa in April, 1972. Each country committed itself to carry out a comprehensive program to combat pollution in Lake Erie, Lake Ontario, and the international section of the St. Lawrence River, accepting the water-quality objectives recommended by the IJC. The governments agreed to impose uniform standards and to embark on concerted programs on their respective sides, to control the waste disposal of their cities and industries, with special attention to phosphates (the main cause of the pollution). They also agreed to make provision for preventing and controlling oil spills and for strengthening regulations to control discharges from vessels plying those waters. (In addition, they asked the IJC to extend its water-quality investigations to the relatively unpolluted Lake Huron and Lake Superior as well as to study pollution from land drainage, agriculture, and forestry.)

Five state, one provincial, and many municipal governments also were involved in the carrying out of this agreement. The complicated network of responsible authorities made progress toward the final agreement slow, requiring many years of study and negotiation. In both countries, new environmental authority and new agencies were prerequisites, but growing public concern about the environment was a stimulus. The Canadians continually prodded the negotiations, believing that their cities and industries were responsible for only a minor proportion of the pollution. Investigations confirmed that 30 percent of the pollution in Lake Ontario and 20 percent in Lake Erie came from Canada. The Canadians also felt that they suffered proportionately more damage from the pollution, since much of their industrialized area and population was located in this region. Under the agreement, Canada was planning to spend $250 million beyond current appropriations for pollution control; the United States government, while not promising further funds than those already appropriated for water quality, did intend spending about $2.7 billion over a five-year period. The federal government was to put up about half the cost of waste-disposal programs, the cities and industry doing the rest. Not lack of money but an "administrative morass" partly attributable to Environmental Protection Agency procedures was said to be the main reason that implementation on the American side was slower than earlier contemplated. In their impatience, the Canadians overcame their customary reluctance to grant administrative authority to the IJC and agreed to giving it unprecedented powers of surveillance and monitoring to see that the programs were carried out.[38]

SPECIFICITY

A source of potential pollution which was decidedly unilateral and even more precisely located than those on the Great Lakes was the underground testing of nuclear warheads in the Aleutian Islands carried on by the United States in October, 1969 and November, 1971. Massive outcries from the Canadian public, very heavy parliamentary pressures on the Canadian government, and almost unprecedented diplomatic notes of protest to the United States government preceded the blast on Amchitka in November, 1971, feared for its massive power and location in an area of potential earthquakes. Just prior to that, one hundred members of Parliament had signed a telegram to President Nixon pleading with him to cancel the test. With only one dissenting vote, Parliament had passed a resolution introduced by Secretary of State for External Affairs Mitchell Sharp, calling on all nuclear nations to cease such tests but addressed particularly to the United States government.[39] That government, while replying that the Canadian view "would be taken into account," in fact paid no more heed to Canadian objections than to those in Alaska or among environmentalists in the United States. The reason given was that national security took priority over the small chance of some environmental damage.[40]

DISTANCE

On the map, Amchitka is far away from most of Canada, but the Canadians did not conceive it to be so and were the more alarmed because of their dread of the nuclear arms race. The effects of pollution are usually greater the closer the source, but some environmental concerns are global. Canadian and American views have coincided or supported each other on the general objectives of positive international action to save the high seas far from their borders from further despoliation.[41] However, they have differed quite markedly on methods, partly because of their different maritime interests.[42]

Canada has one of the longest coastlines of any country in the world, but a small merchant marine, while the United States is a major maritime country and the world's leading naval power. For the Americans, the tradition of freedom of the seas weighs more heavily than for Canadians, sensitive to what happens anywhere near their shores. Thus in April, 1970, the Trudeau government declared that disputes arising out of Canadian claims to conserve and manage the living resources of the sea or out of the prevention or control of pollution threatening its coasts were not subject to the World Court's jurisdiction. The Canadian government viewed itself as a pioneer on the frontiers of an undeveloped international law regarding uses of the seas. At the same time, Canada parted company with the United States and joined many others by declaring its territorial seas to extend out to twelve miles; eventually, even the United States was prepared to accept this broader limit. The two countries were in tune at the 1970 NATO colloquium on oil spills, which recommended that under auspices of the Intergovernmental Maritime Consultative Organization deliberate oil discharges at sea be eliminated by 1975. And they were similarly in harmony at the 1972 Stockholm conference on the environment in supporting the principle that one state should consult others if a contemplated development might have injurious effects on them and should be held responsible for reimbursement if there were damages. Nevertheless, in the early 1970s the gap between Canadian and American policies on many aspects of the law of the sea widened.[43]

CUMULATION AND SPILLOVER

Canadians have become particularly aware of their vulnerability to oil pollution, due to several unhappy experiences with tanker accidents off their coasts; these represented literally the most unwelcome kind of spillover and cumulative anxiety. Their concern grew with the sharply increasing American demand for oil and came to a head with the United States plans to construct the Alaska oil pipeline. Their opposition focused on the transfer of oil from the terminal of Valdez in Alaska to a Puget Sound refinery; the opposition was made more bitter by an actual oil spill at Cherry Point just south of the Canadian border in June, 1972, which damaged Canadian territory. Strong pressure from representatives of all parties and from the British Columbia government produced unanimous resolutions in the House of Commons on two occasions. The second one proposed referring to the IJC the whole question of oil movements through the Straits of Juan de Fuca, Georgia Strait, and Puget Sound. After some temporizing to await domestic developments in the United States, the Canadian government did suggest such a reference, but the United States rejected it. Instead, following an American suggestion, a committee on transborder environmental problems was organized, which drafted recommendations for preventive action and contingency plans to meet oil spills in various regions. The Canadian officials refused to regard this activity as a sign that they accepted the Alaska oil tanker route to Puget Sound.[44]

Meanwhile, American opponents of the Alaska pipeline had managed, through administrative hearings, congressional hearings, and the federal courts, to force postponement of decisive action. In some of these processes Canadians, both members of Parliament and private citizens, participated. The question of alternatives centered increasingly on the Mackenzie Valley, already the site for a projected gas pipeline. The Canadian government did not push this alternative route very hard, owing to potent domestic opposition to it. However, it appealed to many, both Canadians and Americans, since it would not go through earthquake-prone country, as did the Alaska route, and it would link up with pipelines in the American Middle West, where the need for additional supplies of oil was greatest. But despite some backing from members of Congress for this alternative route, Secretary of the Interior Rogers Morton turned it down. He claimed it would be much longer, cost more, and require several years of study, arranging for financing, and negotiation before it could be built. (The Canadians half-heartedly tried some other unsuccessful ploys.) One last court hurdle in the path of the Alaska pipeline, concerning the width of the right of way, was overcome by congressional action in August, 1973. Strong urging from President

Nixon and hysteria over the energy crisis ended the fight. American opponents and the Canadians had lost. The Canadians had to settle for discussions between appropriate officials of the two countries on technical problems arising from oil-tanker traffic.[45]

CHANNELS OF COMMUNICATION

Despite the reluctance of the United States to use the IJC to deal with politically inflamed issues, the commission proved itself over many years to be a handy instrument where mostly local interests were immediately involved, as in the precedent-setting Trail Smelter controversy of the early 1930s, the first to deal with atmospheric pollution.[46] A second air-pollution controversy was referred to the IJC in 1966 following strong representations from residents of Windsor concerning Detroit industry.[47] Very detailed and extensive studies of both the Detroit-Windsor and Port Huron–Sarnia areas preceded the commission's report in 1972. Its action dampened a smoldering political conflict, as the commission could show definitely that about 90 percent of the particulates and 94 percent of the sulfur oxides in the Detroit-Windsor area originated on the Michigan side; while in the Port Huron–Sarnia area, Canada was the source of about 52 percent of the particulates and 27 percent of the sulfur oxides. As with the Great Lakes water quality recommendations, the IJC submitted a comprehensive plan for correction, involving specific air-quality objectives, schedules for implementation, coordinated procedures to respond quickly to adverse atmospheric conditions, more air quality research, and a new role for the commission, that of surveillance and monitoring, which would include a permanent international advisory board and citizens advisory groups.[48]

Even without such authority, the IJC has an important task in attacking water pollution in the St. John River basin. Here its investigatory body includes officials from both federal governments and from Quebec, New Brunswick, and Maine. They are charged with not only investigating but also exchanging information, consulting, coordinating, and recommending action. Furthermore, this enterprise forms a pilot project on control of inland water pollution for which Canada is responsible under the NATO Committee on the Challenges of Modern Society.[49] The problem remains that the IJC has to depend primarily upon publicity, persuasion, and informal negotiation to get its recommendations implemented. Its strength lies in the composition of its technical bodies, which include operating officials from federal, state or provincial, and local governments on both sides of the border, who work together to seek solutions.[50] Local hearings are also useful, and some of its studies have provided the evidence for citizens' law suits, as in the case of the pollution from Detroit industries.[51]

For bilateral understandings with weight, the diplomats eventually have become involved, sometimes leading to executive agreements.[52] The ministerial committee meetings on environment which were instituted in 1972 could play an important role, as the trade and finance committees did in the past. Not to be forgotten is the Canada–United States interparliamentary group, which gave important place to environmental problems in its meetings in the 1970s, thereby sensitizing the members from each legislature to the problems faced in the country of their opposite numbers.

ADMINISTRATIVE TREATMENT VERSUS POLITICIZATION

Lake Michigan lies outside the jurisdiction of the IJC, but its water level can affect the lower lakes in the Great Lakes System and the St. Lawrence. Thus a domestic sanitation question eventually involved the highest political authorities of Canada and the United States when Chicago diverted water to dispose of its wastes downstream. Long an interstate controversy, the issue was temporarily settled by a United States Supreme Court decision of 1930, under which Chicago was required gradually to reduce its diversion to about one-seventh of the amount it had drawn regularly since early in the century. When congressional legislation was sought to overturn this decision and permit much larger quantities, Canadians were among the opponents of the move. In the tortuous course of this eventually abortive attempt to increase the approved amount of water diversion, an effort which went on throughout the 1950s, the Canadian government entered the legislative process on many different occasions and at many different access points. For some time, the battle seemed to favor the proponents of a larger diversion of water. However, President Eisenhower's two vetoes, the advocacy of Canada's rights by the Department of State, the influence of Senator George Aiken, a leader in the Canada–United States interparliamentary group, and the effective intervention of Canada's Ambassador Arnold Heeney with Majority Leader Lyndon Johnson helped to bury the proposal. The final blow was a ruling that this type of bill had to be referred to the Senate Committee on Foreign Relations jointly with the Committee on Public Works, since it involved more than domestic interests.[53]

DOMESTIC POLITICS

The foregoing issues (and others not included) seemed to fall into a pattern in which a great industrial neighbor produced unwanted environmental effects upon a lesser one, while not being as responsive as the latter wished in curbing ecological damage. Canadians, especially in Parliament, were generating very heated emotions about their vulnerability to others' pollution; when the second voyage of the *Manhattan* through the Northwest Passage to the areas of Arctic oil exploration was in the offing early in 1970, their opposition exploded. The first voyage, in the summer of 1969, had been welcomed by the Canadian government. Officials saw possibilities of mutual advantage if this route to the East Coast and Europe for new oil supplies could be safely developed, and the government cooperated in several ways in carrying out the voyage.[54] But it was under heavy pressure from all parties, including its own back-benchers, to assert its sovereignty over waters never clearly accepted as being either territorial or international (the islands were not an issue). Conservation, nationalism, fear of American encroachment, the Arctic mystique which affects many Canadians, and electoral advantages all pointed in the direction of some action. After months of internal debate, the government came out in April, 1970, with two declarations, one dealing with fisheries (to be discussed below), the other unilaterally claiming the right to control the uses of these northern waters for about one hundred miles from the Canadian coastline to prevent pollution. (The government was careful not to make any sovereignty claims.)

The United States government, which had been discussing quietly with Canadian officials the undesirability of the action, reacted at once and sharply in rejecting the claim. This response exactly suited the needs of the Trudeau government, which obtained even more domestic acclaim for its declaration. The United States objected to unilateral declarations that set unwelcome precedents in other parts of the world where much larger claims to what was formerly regarded as the high seas were being made. Canada reacted negatively to the vague and procrastinating United States suggestion for an international conference to take multilateral action. The Canadians declared that they could not wait until the damage was done; instead, they would help to forge new law. They reminded the United States that it also from time to time had made unilateral declarations about controlling the use of international waters, as when it was conducting nuclear tests. These points won domestic political applause; nevertheless, legal scholars found some of the Canadian claims somewhat dubious. Some Canadians, who found the confrontation tactics objectionable, suggested that Canada's objectives could have been secured at least as effectively through the normal negotiating processes. But this would not have answered the domestic political needs of the Trudeau government.[55]

FISHERIES

JOINTNESS

In the 1970s, environmental concerns and conservation interests have aggravated controversies over fishing rights, traditionally a troublesome issue between Canada and the United States. Fish respect no national boundaries, but fishermen are supposed to do so. In former times, the high seas meant joint fishing rights. In 1964, Canada began to follow the lead of some less developed countries for whom fishing is an important industry by reaching out to claim jurisdiction over fishing rights in what the United States had traditionally regarded as common fishing grounds. While some other countries, especially in South America, have made claims of sovereignty, Canada has stressed that the 1970 closing lines were only to apply to fishing, not to freedom of transit, a distinction it had proposed at the 1960 United Nations Conference on the Law of the Sea and which had been accepted later by the United States among others.[56]

RECIPROCITY

When in December, 1970, the Canadian government declared new closing lines for fisheries covering much larger areas than earlier, United States fishermen were exempted. An agreement on reciprocal fishing privileges already had been concluded with the Americans, who had their own exclusive fishing areas. It was further extended in 1973.[57] Nevertheless, the United States officially protested this unilateral extension of Canada's jurisdiction, especially in view of the forthcoming United Nations conference that was to deal with questions of coastal states' fishing jurisdiction.[58] Mexico and the United States had earlier concluded an agreement on reciprocal fishing privileges for the area in the Gulf of Mexico nine to twelve nautical miles off each other's coast.[59]

SPECIFICITY

These agreements were very specific as to the rights accorded. Provisions excluded certain kinds of fish and specified the fishing methods that would be accepted, as well as the precise areas in which the privileges were extended.

DISTANCE

Controversies over fishing rights are by no means confined to neighbors; the United States, several European countries, Japan, and Russia have been involved in sharper conflicts far from their borders where reciprocity did not operate. However, when Brazil followed four other South American states in claiming exclusive fishing rights in an area 200 miles out to sea, it was willing to negotiate bilateral agreements. That with the United States, in which the latter tacitly ignored the general claim, included an unprecedented provision. The United States Department of Commerce was to license a specified number of shrimp boats to fish off the Brazilian coast during 1973, in what the Department of State called a "voluntary conservation" move. The United States would make an annual payment to Brazil to enforce the accord and would grant Brazilian naval authorities boarding and searching rights for American fishing vessels in the zone.[60]

CUMULATION AND SPILLOVER

Despite traditional concern for the freedom of the seas and for the strategic consequences if its naval and merchant vessels were deprived of free transit, the United States has recognized that fish supplies have indeed been endangered by overfishing and pollution. Under pressure from Canada and a large number of other states as well as some domestic fishing interests, the United States has moved closer to accepting a wider zone for territorial seas, provided unimpeded transit through and over international straits was guaranteed. In their preparations for the 1974 United Nations Conference on the Law of the Sea, Canada and the United States were in agreement that measures should be taken to ensure conservation of the living resources of the sea. Meanwhile, however, the Canadians greatly expanded their fishing claims. At the Caracas conference, they, like the Mexicans, were asserting that coastal states should have special rights at least two hundred miles offshore.[61] The United States accepted the concept of an economic zone in which the coastal state would have broad control over coastal and anadromous types of fish. A tentative consensus on a 200-mile economic zone developed at the Geneva session of the Law of the Sea Conference in the spring of 1975.

CHANNELS OF COMMUNICATION

More immediately applicable to conservation of fish than the 1974 United Nations Conference on the Law of the Sea are the numerous international commissions to which the United States and Canada belong, most of them multilateral, such as the fifteen-nation International Commission for the Northwest Atlantic Fisheries, where each member is responsible for enforcing the regulations on its own nationals.[62] With so large a membership, however, conservation standards are difficult to raise, and the 1973 efforts of some members, including the United States, failed to do so even in the face of threatened extinction of some kinds of catch. However, under Canada's prodding, the ICNAF did accept in September, 1975, more easily enforced conservation measures, which would substantially reduce the catch of ground fish by regulating the number of ships and fishing days permitted off Canada's eastern coast (the Grand Banks). [63] A number of commissions on the western coast of Canada and the United States are organized to conserve particular kinds of fish; the commissions include bilateral agencies for halibut and salmon. In 1955, a Great Lakes Fisheries Commission was set up, which has instituted an effective program for control of the destructive sea lamprey.[64]

ADMINISTRATIVE TREATMENT VERSUS POLITICIZATION

Once organized, bilateral commissions in the past tended to deal with fisheries problems on a relatively routine level. The Pacific Salmon Commission, for example, has acted like an international game warden. Even while the two governments were at odds over the legal aspects of Canada's fisheries closing lines, they were cooperating in other ways. One was a project to rear salmon which at maturity would stay close to the North American coast rather than move to Greenland waters, where commercial fisheries of other countries were decimating their numbers.[65] Details of the reciprocal fishing agreement of February, 1970, between Canada and the United States were worked out by fisheries experts from private industry, state, provincial, and national governments under general supervision of professional diplomats. As the Canadians became more assertive, renewal of reciprocal fishing privileges encountered difficulties in 1973, and extension for only a year resulted. Problems arose particularly with respect to Pacific salmon, and the Canadian attitude was reflected in Minister of Conservation and Fisheries Jack Davis's comments which suggested that the goal was for United States fishermen to get more of "their own fish" and Canadians to get "more of our own." [66] The United States has accepted the idea that those fish which spawn in fresh waters of a particular country are—despite their later wanderings—in some way especially the fish of the country that provides the environment in which they can flourish.

DOMESTIC POLITICS

When the Canadian government declared extensive fisheries zones on the eastern and western coasts closed to others, the announcement did not arouse the same national fervor as the simultaneous declaration about the Arctic.[67] It was, however, a response to the demands of the fishing interests, resentful of many foreign countries' fishing practices, not just the Americans'. The governments of both Canada and the United States, under pressure from some parts of their countries' fishing industries, had to move cautiously, since they not only had a common interest in conservation, but also their nationals were accustomed to fishing near each other's coast. Furthermore, the United States was the market for a large percentage of the Canadian catch. In both countries but especially in the United States, those engaged in fishing for highly migratory species far away from the national shores are opposed to the claim of fisheries interests pressing for state control of wide coastal zones.

The course of international negotiations on fisheries has been marked by Canadian aggressiveness in the 1960s and 1970s.[68] Canada made the claims; it was the United States which had to respond. Yet the gaps between their respective national positions, although sometimes pronounced, did not prevent a general tendency to accommodation after hard bargaining.

NATURAL RESOURCES: WATER, HYDROELECTRIC POWER,
NATURAL GAS, AND OIL

Of the two neighbors of the United States, it was Canada that possessed in more alluring plentitude the kind of natural resources becoming scarce in the United States; "continental" meant North American when Americans made energy proposals. (Mexico's oil, in a different category, will be touched on below.) In contrast to environmental questions, on issues relating to national resources, it was Americans who were the initiators and the Canadians the reactors. The kind of response forthcoming reflected some degree of clash between environmental concerns and the demand for access to scarce resources.

JOINTNESS

The rising tide of Canadian nationalism in the late 1960s seemed to make obsolete the common desire expressed by Prime Minister Pearson and President Kennedy in 1963 for cooperation "in a rational use of the continent's resources." [69] As American proponents of a "continental energy policy" grew more impatient of national boundaries which seemed to impede a rational exploitation of resources they could not control, Canadians became more suspicious that their "birthright" might thus disappear in asymetrically joint undertakings before they were ready to use it themselves. One energy fuel, hydroelectric power, has escaped this divergence of interest. With technological changes and the opening up of a huge hydroelectric potential in their territory, Canadians have come to accept long-term sales as well as short-term exchanges of power so long as they were controlled; an extensive electric-power grid crosses the border. [70] Nor did the Canadians fear to enter such joint arrangements with American groups, public or private, to inventory fuel possibilities as the study of Arctic natural gas resources or the hydroelectric potential of the upper Yukon watershed. Technical collaboration between the two countries' geological-survey groups raised no political problems. [71] Under the spur of the 1973 fuel crisis, the two governments informally supported the application of a group of more than twenty American and Canadian corporations which sought in March, 1974, permission from the appropriate United States and Canadian authorities to build a pipeline from the Arctic to carry Alaskan and Canadian natural gas 2,625 miles along the Mackenzie River valley for delivery to southern Canada and the United States. [72] Nevertheless, the political aspects are so complicated that ultimate approval is uncertain. Meanwhile, an American firm was putting up very strong competition in seeking official approval for an all-American route along the Alaska oil pipeline (the gas to be liquified later); among its arguments was the alleged unreliability of the Canadian route because it could not be controlled by the United States.

RECIPROCITY

One reason why the Canadians back away from "continental" policies is that reciprocal arrangements usually involve the sale to Americans of Canadian resources, many of them nonrenewable; the resources move in a southward direction, not in a genuine or balanced interchange.[73] One exception was an arrangement made at the time of the 1967 Middle East war, when oil supplies seemed threatened. The two governments agreed that in a future emergency American oil would be sent to eastern Canada (which depended on currently cheaper foreign oil supplies), the American oil to be balanced by Canadian oil moving to the western United States.[74] Until 1973 the fact that most oil moved southward did not trouble the Canadian government, which continually sought an American market unimpeded by quotas.[75] In March of that year the Canadian government shifted to a policy of restraint on the export of oil, just as it already had done with gas.[76] This apparently abrupt change, with its everincreasing restrictions, was a response to anticipated scarcity made more alarming by greatly increased American consumption. Yet the nature of the shift seemed reminiscent of unilateral changes in American policy regarding Canadian oil imports, which were dictated by such considerations as alleged national security and the likelihood of political cutoffs of other foreign supplies or by the pressures of large American oil interests.

SPECIFICITY

Prior to the Canadian shift on oil and even after its declaration, the Nixon administration sought to get the Canadians to consider a continental energy policy.[77] This very general concept, highly foreign to the way the United States government usually operates, boiled down to one or two specific desires. The Americans wanted Canada to recognize the vulnerability of its East Coast, dependent upon foreign oil, since they did not want to be obliged to meet a sudden scarcity by sending American oil north. This vulnerability could be lessened by building a pipeline eastward to Montreal. The Americans had earlier opposed such a pipeline when the production-consumption balance was quite different, and they were concerned about the pipeline's effect on the political situation in Venezuela, the major source of Canadian East Coast oil.[78] The Americans were also interested in buying more natural gas in return for easing the quota of March, 1970, on Canadian oil, a relaxation which the Nixon administration felt forced to make later anyway.[79]

DISTANCE

Canadian natural gas and oil were particularly attractive to the Americans since the sources were secure, reliable, and easy to reach; furthermore, the supplies were being produced predominantly by American-owned subsidiaries. Some interprovincial pipelines even traversed American territory, and an American extension eventually was built south to Chicago. Physical proximity, however, did not always correspond to similarity of perspectives, especially in the face of looming scarcities. Earlier, Canadians' concern for the security of their East Coast supplies lagged behind that of the supplier-of-last-resort Americans. Being so close, Americans sometimes talked or acted as though they could open or close the Canadian gas and oil cocks at will, and the earlier Canadian eagerness to sell did not help to disabuse them of the notion. It took time for some Americans in administration and in Congress to learn that "continental" tends to be a pejorative term to Canadian nationalists.[80]

American leaders learned more quickly how far American attitudes diverged from Mexican views on oil. In 1948, a time of acute international insecurity, Mexican as well as Brazilian oil appeared to some United States officials to be a useful source in a period of short supplies, if exploitable with American aid. Soundings were fruitless, as Mexican officials would respond only in terms of exclusive control, which was quite unacceptable to Americans. That Americans would try such a method of meeting an anticipated scarcity only a decade after Mexico's oil expropriation indicates surprising distance in attitudes.[81] At a later stage, when national security again partially dictated United States oil policy, quotas on foreign oil were lifted for Mexico, but the amount which moved northward was comparatively small.[82]

Still later, at the height of the 1973 oil crisis, major American oil companies continued to furnish limited supplies to their traditional markets in Canada and Mexico for further processing.[83] However, even more than Canada, Mexico was able to supply its own needs. It was also reentering the export market in 1974 after being absent for many years. A spectacular discovery of new oil reserves in the autumn of 1974 put Mexico in a strong bargaining position vis-à-vis the United States, which was much interested in access but was offered no favors in the highly competitive scramble for supplies.[84] The Americans at least could find comfort in the typical Mexican response to a new situation. The government quietly decided for the time being to seek only observer status in OPEC while selling its oil at the high prices set by that organization. In May, 1976, however, it announced its intention to join.

CUMULATION AND SPILLOVER

Oil and natural gas, which are often found in conjunction with each other, appeared to be naturally linked for bargaining purposes. But Canadians, with one exception, were wary of licensing sales of scarce gas in order to get United States approval of heavier exports of oil.[85] Energy, Mines, and Resources Minister Joseph Greene encountered so much disapproval when he agreed in October, 1970, to the sale of large quantities of gas that the next applications were rejected.[86] Meanwhile, the thirst for more water in the American Southwest, which spawned some ambitious private proposals for moving Canadian water southward, so alarmed Canadian nationalists that they did not need ex-Prime Minister Pearson's warning not to permit negotiations for water and for oil to get mixed up together.[87] Package deals were carefully to be avoided. The contemplated gas pipeline through the Mackenzie Valley spilled over into an additional argument for the use of that route for the oil pipeline from the Alaskan fields, but there was an undertow. Such undertakings would be very difficult to finance without further large American investment funds, and such investment was strongly opposed by Canadian nationalists, especially those in the New Democratic Party.[88]

CHANNELS OF COMMUNICATION

Canadian sensitivity to sharing decisions about the use of their resources with the United States renders the likelihood of joint agencies to plan in these fields very small. Discussions, formal and informal, continually take place among those occupying similar administrative offices in the two governments such as in the Department of the Interior and the Ministry of Energy, Mines, and Resources.[89] On the Canadian side, a National Energy Board was established in the late 1950s at about the time that the United States had lifted a quota on the import of Canadian oil, a quota that had been in effect for two years. Members of this board have been in contact with the Federal Power Commission, which has similar licensing powers, especially since both agencies may be involved in some transactions like pipelines. In the 1973–1974 energy crisis, there were almost daily exchanges between appropriate officials, especially after Energy Policy Administrator John Love took a team to Ottawa to sound out Canadian views. The series of decisions to curtail the flow of gas and oil to the United States have regularly been preceded by discussions with American officials who would be concerned with their effects.[90]

ADMINISTRATIVE TREATMENT VERSUS POLITICIZATION

An energy counsellor, attached to the Canadian embassy in Washington, has maintained regular contacts with a great variety of United States officials in the executive as well as legislative branches.[91] Yet oil and gas have become so charged with nationalist sentiments on the Canadian side and with security and oil-industry sensitivity on the American side that routine discussions between counterparts and energy specialists could not substitute for high-level negotiations, although they could prepare for them.[92]

For reasons often only secondarily related to the other country, both the United States and Canada have formally adopted policies which restricted the free flow of gas and oil between them. More directly shaping United States policy than Canadian pressure for access to markets were estimates of the security of overseas sources, diplomatic or political pressures on or by foreign countries which were important suppliers, and the balance of political influence in Washington between domestic oil companies and the big international corporations. (At least until 1973, consumer and environmental influences were minimal.)[93] Canada eventually followed the lead of its neighbor in imposing its own restraints, but on exports rather than imports.[94] As in Mexico, it became Canadian policy to replace some crude-oil exports with exports of refined petroleum products.

Just as the instituting of American oil import quotas in the 1950s was followed by establishment of a Canadian Royal Commission on Energy, so did the sharp increase in the American appetite for gas and oil spark a Canadian energy study in the early 1970s which was to lay the basis for a new national policy in that field.[95] Although Canada had been the major exporter of petroleum to the United States for many years, more was being pumped out than was being discovered, and Prime Minister Trudeau began planning late in 1973 to make Canada self-sufficient by the early 1980s. This was close to the target date used by President Nixon in declaring his own self-sufficiency objective. A rational exchange of oil, that is, one that would take advantage of location, which had been partially realized earlier, seemed to have succumbed to nationalism on both sides.[96]

DOMESTIC POLITICS

Considering that fresh water is a renewable resource, unlike fossil fuels, the rising Canadian nationalism which implacably demands a ban on exportation of water southward appears to many observers an irrational reaction to the "continental pull." [97] Considering that Canada may have one-seventh of all fresh surface water in the world and that interbasin transfers are not uncommon on either side of the border, the extreme sensitivity of the Canadian government to continuous pressures to keep it all in Canada seems to be more directly related to the domestic political-party balance than to objective calculations of Canada's economic interests.[98] Environmental concerns have intensified the opposition in Canada to grand diversionary schemes, as such concerns do also in the United States.

In any case, water, like natural gas and oil, is primarily under provincial control. Elaborate negotiations between levels of government would be necessary either to impose or to lift some restraints on the flow of these resources southward. During the energy crisis of 1973–1974, there was a clash of interests among the provinces and between oil-rich Alberta and the federal government. Controversy arose concerning price control for oil and at what level of prices, if imposed, concerning division of windfall profits from sales to the United States, and concerning the federal export tax and its proceeds. Complicated bargains were struck at the formal conference convened to settle these issues, in many of which American consumers as well as American oil companies were involved but not participating.[99]

Twice, in 1956 and again in 1966, proposals for delivering Canadian natural gas from the west to Ontario via pipeline aroused political reactions. On the first occasion, even though the proposal rejected a transfer system which would cross the border instead of the longer, more expensive all-Canadian transmission eastward, the plan became so heavily entangled in Conservative-Liberal party politics in the ensuing conflict in Parliament that it furnished a leading issue on which the already weakening Liberal government lost power.[100] On the second occasion the Canadian federal government forced Trans-Canada Pipe Lines to keep its planned main pipeline north of the border, although a portion, approved by both the Canadian National Energy Board and the United States Federal Power Commission, was built south of it, supplying American markets, too. Against the geographical rationale were ranged Canadian and American business interests, fear of increased American influence through investors and regulatory agencies, public versus private ownership issues, and Canadian political-party concerns.[101]

OTHER NEIGHBORHOOD ISSUES

There are many other issues which can arise only between countries with a common land frontier. In Canadian-American and Mexican-American relations they provide opportunities for both cooperation and controversy, as the following discussion, based on a somewhat random selection of issues, amply illustrates.

JOINTNESS

Between the several Canadian provinces and neighboring American states there are joint forest-fire arrangements, some informal, others as formal as that between Quebec and New Brunswick and seven American states. In this instance, the Canadian federal government gave its approval to the two provinces to enter into the Northeastern Forest Fire Protection Compact.[102] In a buffer zone ten miles wide on either side of the border between the Yukon and Alaska, fire fighters from one side can attack a fire on the other at once without application to enter.[103] From 1947 until 1971, when the arrangement was terminated through American initiative, joint weather stations were maintained in the Canadian Arctic.[104] Beginning in 1968, a few officials from the national park services of the two countries have exchanged positions.[105]

Personnel exchanges involving the Smithsonian Institute and the Library of Congress, among others, with their counterpart institutions in Canada have also taken place. Two weather stations have been jointly maintained by the United States and Mexico, manned primarily by Mexicans.[106]

RECIPROCITY

Health and safety, which generally call forth much international cooperation, have been natural areas for many reciprocal arrangements between the United States and neighbors north and south. Canada and the United States have cooperated in the use of radio-telephone communication for distress calls and for safety and navigation on the Great Lakes, with special attention to providing compatibility between regulations and equipment.[107] Following the disastrous consequences of hurricane Beulah the previous autumn, in May, 1968 the United States and Mexico established a joint committee for mutual assistance in disasters such as hurricanes, floods, fires, and earthquakes.[108]

SPECIFICITY

Not just diplomatic declarations of scientific-exchange intentions, but a number of specific scientific projects have been formally agreed upon between the United States and Canada. These are in addition to the informal contacts and collaboration among individual agencies, officials, and university scientists that take place on a scale rare between any two other countries. Sometimes the habit of informal interchange grows out of specific collaborative efforts, as in atomic energy work at Los Alamos. Of the nearly thirty bilateral scientific and technological agreements concluded by Canada up to 1969, about one-half were with the United States, and many were in some way related to defense research.[109] With the indispensable cooperation of NASA and American launchers, Canada has put into orbit several satellites for scientific studies, as well as one for its own telecommunications system.[110] As part of the World-Wide Geodetic Satellite Program, Canada and the United States have prepared an unprecedentedly precise geodetic grid by means of a joint satellite triangulation survey.[111]

The tracking stations which the United States has established in agreement with some other countries, such as that at Guaymas in Mexico for joint civilian space research and on the Brazilian island of Fernando de Noronha for missile tracking, were chosen for locational reasons other than proximity.[112] Satellite-tracking stations in Australia were desirable not only because of their very distance from the United States but also because of the technological capacities of the Australians who would be working at them. Of the twelve jointly maintained stations there, NASA had six that were operated by the Australian Department of Supply in 1969.[113] Next to Canada and Britain, Australia has had the most scientific exchange agreements with the United States.[114]

DISTANCE

Cross-border movements of people usually are easiest between neighbors, whether the individuals involved are (1) immigrants, (2) migrant workers, (3) draft evaders, (4) criminals, or (5) tourists, to name five significant categories. Transit across the northern and southern boundaries of the United States is among the most intense in the world.

1. United States immigration laws were drastically altered in 1965, abolishing national-origin quotas; part of the legislative bargain worked out for this major reform was hard on the neighbors. It imposed for the first time a quota on immigrants from the Western Hemisphere.[115] Thereafter, numbers of legal immigrants from Canada dropped drastically from the largest of any country to tenth place, while immigrants from Mexico, formerly the second most numerous became the most numerous (counting only legal immigrants). (Some of the earlier immigrants from Canada actually had only passed through there from another country less favorably located.) Meanwhile, the intricacies of the law produced a huge backlog of applicants, extending into future years' quotas. The State Department, cognizant of the diplomatic reaction, wanted to put Canada and Mexico on separate, large quotas but failed in a 1973 attempt.[116] The law had no effect on Australians, very few of whom had ever migrated to the United States, nor on Brazilians, who had been very low on the list of immigrants.

Table 20 compares numbers of immigrants to the United States who last resided in the four middle powers during the year prior to the reform and for three years thereafter. Table 21 shows native-born Canadian and Mexican immigrants for 1968 through 1973, indicating opposing trends for the two countries. Table 22 shows that far more Americans have migrated to Australia than Australians to the United States. (The proportion of Americans in the total immigration there is nevertheless small.)

The composition of the Canadian migration has changed, with more professional and highly trained persons and fewer manual workers coming in.[117] Meanwhile, the resentment felt by many Canadians about the brain drain south began to lose its foundation as the tide turned. From being the third largest source of immigrants into Canada prior to 1968, Americans in 1972 topped the list of those migrating to it, having surpassed the British and Italians.[118] Unlike the United States system, Canada's immigration rules apply the same point system to all countries.[119]

2. Migrant labor from Mexico has been an issue since World War II. Varying interests in the United States and Mexico have prevailed to produce either some kind of concerted official program regulating the flow, as was the case during the war and from roughly 1950 to 1965, or unilateral efforts

TABLE 20   IMMIGRANTS TO THE UNITED STATES, BY MIDDLE-POWER COUNTRY
OF LAST PERMANENT RESIDENCE, 1965–1968

	1965	1966	1967	1968
Australia and New Zealand	1,803	1,890	2,128	2,374
Brazil	3,677	3,054	2,544	3,503
Canada	50,035	37,273	34,768	41,716
Mexico	40,686	47,217	43,034	44,716

Source: Statistical Abstract of the United States.

TABLE 21   CANADIAN-BORN, MEXICAN-BORN, AND TOTAL IMMIGRANTS TO
THE UNITED STATES, 1968–1973

	1968	1969	1970	1971	1972	1973
Canadians	27,662	18,582	13,804	13,128	10,776	9,000
Mexicans	43,563	44,623	44,469	n.a.	64,040	70,100
All countries		358,579	373,326	370,478	384,685	400,063

Source: Canada Yearbook, 1973; Statistical Abstract of the United States. Of total immigration
into the United States, 1961–70, Canada's percentage of 12.4 and Mexico's of 13.7 were by far the
highest.

TABLE 22   AUSTRALIAN IMMIGRANTS TO THE UNITED STATES AND AMERICAN
IMMIGRANTS TO AUSTRALIA, 1971 AND 1972

	1971	1972
Australian residents intending long-term stay in the United States, including former settlers [a]	2,126	2,917
Long-term or permanent movements to Australia of Americans	12,600	10,500

Source: Official Yearbook of the Commonwealth of Australia, 1973, p. 154; *Australia
Handbook, 1974,* p. 38.

[a] Former settlers (persons who had emigrated to Australia from elsewhere) constituted by far the
largest number.

to stem it. Both governments were ambivalent about the programs, and the
pressures changed with economic changes, especially the increasing mech-
anization of agriculture in the United States. Following a joint arrangement set up for wartime conditions, temporary farmworkers were admitted
by mutual executive agreement under specified circumstances. After a few

years of such ad hoc arrangements, admittance was specifically authorized by Congress in an addition to the Agricultural Act of 1949. American and Mexican officials examined potential migrants at recruiting stations in Mexico, after which they were taken to an American reception station to sign a standardized contract legally supported by the United States government. Ambiguities in the administrative agreements gave rise to almost continuous negotiations on their fulfillment. A hiatus occurred in 1954, but another compromise was then reached, which included new conditions sought by Mexico.

Reciprocal benefits flowed from the agreement, on the American side chiefly to certain agricultural interests in the Southwest. Especially during World War II and the Korean War, the Mexican migrants also contributed scarce labor to American agricultral production. For Mexico there was a substantial flow of dollars sent back by the workers, and even more important was the training and social education they brought home with them. Furthermore, the movement of migrants was a political safety valve, reducing the extreme restlessness of unemployed labor, always a worry to the Mexican government. Given all the difficulties of policing more than two thousand miles of border, the two governments benefited from a legalization of the flow.

Further guarantees of specific improvements in working conditions for the braceros continually were insisted upon by the Mexican government, which also sought United States action to enforce the rules. Congress has been willing to legislate only penalties for breaking whatever rules were laid down, not penalties for employing illegal migrants. On the American side, the Department of Labor and Department of Agriculture were responsible for the bracero program, not the State Department; this meant considerable bureaucratic tension between the two responsible departments. The Department of Justice and Department of Health, Education, and Welfare also eventually became involved. The main political tension, however, came in Congress where agricultural interests seeking cheap labor at first held the upper hand. Eventually opponents, who regarded the whole system as either immoral because it was a kind of legalized exploitation or as a danger to American labor standards, became dominant.

Although the program came to an abrupt end in 1965, the problem of desperate Mexican workers seeking to enter the United States legally or illegally has continued and is likely to do so as long as there is a great disparity in living standards between countries which border each other. Significantly, predominantly Mexican-American labor groups, such as Cesar Chavez's farmworkers union, are hostile to the entrance of Mexican laborers who will undercut their bargaining position. A relationship which was once legally controlled by agreement between the two governments has disappeared, ending the quarrels about its details, but subsequent unilateral measures have raised other problems. The Mexican government's proposal to renew a seasonal migrant-workers agreement was turned down by the United States government in August, 1974.[120]

The 1965 United States revision of immigration laws proved particularly unworkable in regulating immigrants coming primarily for a job rather than to settle. The Immigration Service has been unable to cope with the large numbers of illegal entries, sometimes estimated in the millions, a very large proportion of which appeared to be Mexican and spread all over the country, although many Canadians were also said to be illegal workers on the northern border.[121] Of those actually caught, by far the majority were Mexicans, many of whom had been caught before. Even an electronic fence, introduced in the Chula area in 1970 and three years later extended along much of the border, could not stop the flood, and the method was questioned by the Mexican government as well as by some members of Congress. Since illegal migrants already were a point of friction between the United States government and Mexico, matters were not improved by revelations that corrupt immigration personnel of both countries had operated a system of blackmail under which those caught were shipped at their own expense to points in Mexico far distant from the border unless they paid off the (private) carriers who would otherwise transport them.[122] A special arrangement for workers from Canada and Mexico who crossed the border only for the day, returning home after work, was also the object of criticism by some American senators usually regarded as liberal.[123] For various years from 1960 to 1973, Table 23 gives numbers of Canadian and Mexican laborers specially permitted to come into the United States to work.

Illegal blue-collar workers were attracted by the opportunity to earn higher wages in the United States, but the 1965 law presented a special problem to businessmen and highly trained Canadians that was partially remedied by a 1969 amendment. This was brought about in part by the representations of the Canadian delegates to their American colleagues in the Canada–United States interparliamentary group.[124] For such persons, there

TABLE 23   CANADIAN AND MEXICAN LABORERS ADMITTED UNDER WORK
PERMITS TO THE UNITED STATES, 1960, 1965, 1968–1973
....

	1960	1965	1968	1969	1970	1971	1972	1973
Agricultural workers								
Mexican [a]	427,240	103,563	6,127	0	0	0	0	0
Canadian	7,804	8,149	4,687	3,366	3,156	6,156	1,895	1,458
Woodsmen								
Canadian	n.a.	13,281	9,522	6,374	8,238	7,178	7,373	8,310

Source: Statistical Abstract of the United States, 1974, p. 101. The other major source of
temporary workers was the West Indies.

[a] After 1964, Mexican agricultural workers came under the same law as others, legally entering
only when like workers were unavailable in the United States.

has been a genuine continental market of opportunity, only slightly ham-
pered by Canadian restrictions and somewhat more by anomalies in the
American system.[125]

3. For Americans seeking to escape military service, Canada achieved
notoriety as a haven during the Vietnam war. Canada was the preferred destination, because it was easy to cross the border and to fade into the Canadian scene, illustrating again that the northern neighbor serves as a safety
valve for dissatisfied Americans. The Canadian government, well supported
by its public, put no obstacles in their way and only slightly differentiated
for a time between draft evaders and deserters. Significantly, the United
States government made no effort to persuade the Canadians to do otherwise.[126]

4. Violators of United States law have always found the long borders
north and south conveniently accessible. (Apparently organized crime
operates on a continental basis, at least in the East.[127]) However, law enforcement officers, state and provincial as well as federal, formally and,
much more significant, informally cooperate with each other.[128]

Exchange of intelligence between the Royal Canadian Mounted Police
and the Federal Bureau of Investigation has been frequent enough to cause
resentment by those suspicious of their motives. Sometimes cooperation on
the southern border is not universally appreciated either, as when the Arizona highway patrol informally (and extralegally) provided the Sonora police with tear-gas grenades and other weapons to help subdue a student up-

TABLE 24   TRAVEL TO THE UNITED STATES FROM FOUR MIDDLE POWERS AND ALL COUNTRIES AND FROM THE UNITED STATES TO THREE MIDDLE POWERS, 1968, 1969, 1972

Country of Tourist	Number of Tourists Coming to USA		
	1968	1969	1972
Australia	44,208	49,109	89,626
Brazil	36,838	34,983	54,755
Canada	8,597,000	9,400,000	8,646,000
Mexico	506,094	1,028,718	1,377,143
All countries	10,785,802	12,347,269	12,884,801

Country Visited	Number of US Tourists Visiting		
	1968	1969	1972
Australia	102,635 [a]	135,559 [a]	77,827
Brazil	33,399	35,558	62,524
Canada	10,264,532 [b]	12,697,759 [b]	36,245,990

Source: United Nations Statistical Yearbook, 1970, 1974. Discrepancies make figures not strictly comparable. Most of them coming from the United States, 1,664,500 persons visited Mexico in 1968; 1,817,800 in 1969.

[a] Includes American servicemen on rest-and-recreation leaves, 63,192 in 1968; 85,477 in 1969.

[b] Omits visitors staying less than 24 hours.

rising during the state's gubernatorial elections in 1967.[129] On the formal side, the United States and Canada signed the world's first treaty to declare airplane hijacking a nonpolitical and therefore extraditable crime, a principle that also was applied to attacks on foreign diplomats.[130]

5. On both sides of both borders of the United States, the tourist trade carried on by Americans and Canadians or Mexicans is greater than for any other set of countries related to any of them. Table 24 compares travellers to the United States from each of the four countries examined in this book and from the United States to each, in selected recent years. That cross-border tourism is big business for the United States and its two neighbors can be seen from Table 25, showing expenditures by Americans in Canada and Mexico and of Canadians and Mexicans in the United States for selected years from 1960. Almost as many Canadians visit the United States as Americans visit Canada, in absolute terms, and in both directions by far the most important mode of travel is the automobile.[131] In 1970, 37 million Americans went to Canada, and close to 36 million Canadians came to the

TABLE 25   EXPENDITURES OF UNITED STATES TRAVELERS IN CANADA AND
MEXICO AND CANADIAN AND MEXICAN TRAVELERS IN THE UNITED STATES,
SELECTED YEARS, 1960, 1965, 1970–1973 (millions of US dollars)

	1960	*1965*	*1970*	*1971*	*1972*	*1973*
In Canada	380	600	1,045	1,111	1,036	1,122
In Mexico	383	540	740	832	950	1,152
By Canadians	469	490	896	934	922	1,046
By Mexicans	226	390	545	565	615	694

Source: Statistical Abstract of the United States, 1973, p. 213, *1974,* p. 215.

TABLE 26   OVERSEAS VISITORS TO AUSTRALIA, FROM
LEADING COUNTRIES OF ORIGIN AND ALL COUNTRIES, 1969

	Short-term	*Long-term*
United States	50,082	3,761
Britain and Ireland	34,684	3,303
Canada	7,516	1,068
New Zealand	82,595	9,799
Papua–New Guinea	25,368	448
All countries	361,277	26,867

Source: Official Yearbook of the Commonwealth of Australia, 1970.
Short-term visit is less than twelve months.

United States, a large portion staying only one day.[132] In contrast, the attractiveness of Australia and Brazil for Americans tourists is seriously dulled by the expense of getting to these distant places. Nevertheless, the United States supplied a sizable proportion of tourists to Australia, as may be seen in Table 26, which compares America with other important sources of visitors in 1969; the short-term figure is swollen by American servicemen from Vietnam.

Tourism is one kind of movement of persons which none of the governments tries to restrict but in fact strongly encourages.[133] An exception to the very marked Mexican efforts to attract American tourists was President Diaz Ordaz's legislation to put an end to the notorious Juarez divorce mill which had provided so many Americans with easy divorces; he called it a discredit to Mexico abroad.[134]

CUMULATION AND SPILLOVER

Cultural spillover, where the movement across borders involves ideas, skills, attitudes, and modes of behavior, produces in the United States and its neighbors different responses depending upon what is being exchanged and in which direction. With some important exceptions, the government of neither of the neighboring countries has seriously tried to restrain the very asymmetrical impact of the Americans on its country, despite the strong fear of being engulfed found among both Canadians and Mexicans and some strong nationalist pressures to counteract the impact.[135] For English-speaking Canadians, the fear flows from the fact that their culture is deceptively similar, for Mexicans (and also for French Canadians), because they are different. The exceptions are mainly radio and television regulations and Canada's tax policies, which fall more heavily on foreign periodicals. These cases indicate the difficulty of clearly separating out protectionism for cultural reasons from that which is basically due to economic motivations of particular groups.

The similarities and differences in American, Canadian, and Mexican cultural perspectives help to account for the almost completely unrestrained movements of students and scholars; Canadians and Americans study, research, and teach in each others' country because they are alike and Mexican and Americans because they are different.[136] Canadian students in the United States in the late 1960s constituted the largest number of foreign students, Mexicans the fifteenth largest.[137] In the 1960s, Canada was the leading host country for American students, Mexico the fifth.[138] With the very rapid expansion of Canadian higher education in the late 1960s, which outran the supply of Canadian instructors, large numbers of Americans went north to teach in Canadian universities.[139] An unofficial backlash ensued, with some vocal members of Canadian academia, teachers and students, calling for the "Canadianizing" of their schools. On the other hand, Canadian scholars and professors in the United States (some of them hindered by a quirk in the United States immigration rules) were less numerous than those from some European countries and, in the early 1970s, were about on a par with Australians.[140]

Table 27 compares United States students in the four countries under study and the total number abroad in institutions of higher learning during a recent seven-year period, indicating the relative importance of the neighbor-

TABLE 27   AMERICAN STUDENTS IN INSTITUTIONS OF HIGHER LEARNING IN
FOUR MIDDLE POWERS AND TOTAL ABROAD, 1966–1972

Host Country	1966–67	1967–68	1968–69	1969–70	1970–71	1971–72
Australia	134		168	230	202	159
Brazil	28		23	28	13	17
Canada	3,444	4,324	4,912	5,447	5,265	6,517
Mexico	1,735	2,407	2,975	4,402	4,109	4,373
Total abroad	21,600	25,359	25,117	32,148	32,209	34,218

Source: Institute of International Education, *Open Doors,* annual issues.

TABLE 28   FOREIGN STUDENTS FROM FOUR MIDDLE POWERS AND ALL
COUNTRIES IN UNITED STATES INSTITUTIONS OF HIGHER LEARNING, 1966–1972

Home Country	1966–67	1967–68	1968–69	1969–70	1970–71	1971–72
Australia	864	919	1,042	1,077	1,045	891
Brazil	885	1,101	1,169	1,349	1,473	1,502
Canada	12,117	12,144	12,852	13,318	12,595	10,396
Mexico	1,855	2,009	2,031	2,501	2,689	2,501
Total in USA	100,262	110,315	121,362	134,959	144,708	140,126

Source: Institute of International Education, *Open Doors,* annual issues; *New York Times,*
October 23, 1972.

ing countries as host. Table 28 shows a similar importance for foreign
students coming to the United States. A somewhat different picture is por-
trayed in table 29 comparing host and home countries of faculty and mature
scholars. Exotic character rather than ease and familiarity attracts scholars
who want to study a foreign culture. This puts Canada lowest in importance
among the four countries and favors the two Latin American countries. But
Canada supplies the most foreign scholars to the United States, followed by
Australia, the other culturally similar middle power under study.

Cooperative undertakings between Canadian and American educational
institutions are common. On the Mexican side they are less so, although still
frequent. The Technical Institute of Monterrey (founded in 1942 and privately endowed) became affiliated with the Southwest Research Institute of
San Antonio, Texas, in 1951.[141] Unprecedented was the establishment of a
branch of the Autonomous National University of Mexico in San Antonio,

TABLE 29   AMERICAN SCHOLARS ABROAD AND FOREIGN SCHOLARS IN THE
UNITED STATES FOR FOUR MIDDLE POWERS AND ALL COUNTRIES, 1968–1972

Host Country	American Scholars Abroad			
	1968–69	1969–70	1970–71	1971–72
Australia	89	76	84	92
Brazil	138	100	90	105
Canada	69	70	95	79
Mexico	155	126	134	154
Total abroad	5,639	5,310	6,291	6,305

Home Country	Foreign Scholars in USA			
	1968–69	1969–70	1970–71	1971–72
Australia	401	457	428	354
Brazil	105	129	136	94
Canada	584	677	652	579
Mexico		93	101	68
Total in USA	12,100	12,659	12,047	10,313

Source: Institute of International Education, Open Doors, annual issues.

sponsored by the Mexican government and business and city officials of San
Antonio.[142] Unlike Canadians, some Mexican student exchanges are subsidized by the United States government; on occasion, Mexican officials
have expressed the wish that teachers should go to Mexico, not students to
the United States, an apparent fear of cultural adulteration.[143] Several Canadian universities are members of the American Association of Universities
and Colleges.

　　Evidence abounds that at least in English-speaking Canada and the
United States a cultural community exists among those active in education,
science, the arts, and religion. There are joint or affiliated professional associations, whose annual meetings not infrequently take place in Canada.[144]
Honors, prizes, and scholarships coming from private sources are awarded
somewhat indiscriminately to Canadians and Americans. Canadian educational materials find a ready market in the United States.[145] Many Canadian
professional schools are accredited by the appropriate American association
for certifying standards.

　　Standards for particular products or practices prevailing in the United
States sometimes have served as models in Canada. Changes in American

criteria have usually been followed quickly in Canada, including those established by the United States Food and Drug Administration.[146] Canadian and Mexican models are less frequently noted by Americans. Those Canadian or Mexican examples which are followed or observed in the United States are usually of an unofficial nature, making them the more noteworthy as cases of spontaneous cultural diffusion. (The Shakespeare Theater at Stratford, Ontario, is a Canadian example; humanitarian practices in the state penitentiary at Toluca in Mexico have attracted the attention of American penologists.) [147] Some American practices have served as horrible examples which the neighbors strive to avoid, since they are fortunate enough to have the opportunity to take another course. Canadian city planners have learned lessons from American mistakes.

Both Canadian and Mexican governmental authorities have exercised some kind of influence over the media of informal cultural penetration of the general public, especially radio, television, and even the press. They have done so to protect their peoples from being blanketed by strong American cultural influences. English-speaking Canadians are particularly susceptible; for example, about three-quarters of them live within listening range of American radio.[148]

Early in 1970, the Canadian Radio and Television Commission tried to curb this influence by mandating that material on Canadian radio and television contain a specific percentage of "Canadian content." [149] It also forbade the extension of microwave cable to northern communities outside the range of American broadcasts, but later rescinded the ban under domestic protest.[150] Conflict became heated in 1975 as Canadian authorities sought to curb by various measures their viewers' exposure to American television advertising and stimulate Canadian commercials. In all their efforts to shield Canadians from American television, Canadian officials were bucking their countrymen's preferences for the American program over the far less opulently financed local output.[151]

After 1965, the Canadian government was under heavy pressure no longer to except the Canadian editions of *Time* and *Reader's Digest* from those non-Canadian magazines ineligible for the tax deduction for advertising costs granted to domestic periodicals. Very strong counter pressures, especially from the American side, delayed action until 1972.[152] Canadian book-publishing companies feel squeezed between British and American companies, which dominate the market. When one of the last Canadian prestige book publishers, Ryerson Press, was sold to an American firm, there was a loud outcry, including protests from moderate nationalists, who felt that Canadian writers would also be squeezed out, too, as a result.[153]

American press sources for Canadian newspapers are very prominent, and Mexican newspapers also are likely to carry large amounts of material emanating from the United States. Except on the business pages, news about Canada and Mexico is scarce in American papers, with a few notable exceptions. Unofficial penetration of America's neighbors through the press, television, and radio irritates nationalists, especially since the means to counteract it are few. Nevertheless, to offset some of the imbalance, the Canadian government has instituted an office of cultural affairs in its Washington embassy.[154]

The southern neighbor of the United States has expressed particular concern about illegal removal of pre-Columbian artifacts. Here the problem was that something was taken away rather than forced upon the smaller country. Sensitive to this concern, United States officials secured the return to Mexico of some artifacts illegally removed. President Johnson accepted an agreement proposed by President Diaz Ordaz, which was implemented through a bill sponsored by the State Department; it barred the importation of unlicensed archeological and architectural treasures from Mexico, Central America, South America, and the Caribbean. A United States–Mexican treaty, signed in 1970, in effect permitted Mexico to sue in United States courts for the recovery of illegally removed objects.[155]

CHANNELS OF COMMUNICATION

In the southwest of the United States, once part of Mexico, all the border states have formed semiofficial committees and associations with those on the Mexican side for cultural cooperation. These states include Texas, New Mexico, Arizona, and California.[156] Across the Canadian as well as Mexican borders of the United States, direct cooperation between technical experts of American state governments and their counterparts, without federal intervention, is common. Yet on the national level a similar kind of practical interchange has taken place among officials concerned with such matters as plant and animal diseases, agricultural improvements, conservation measures, forestry, and tourism. Often both national and state officials may be involved, and sometimes the associations are trinational, experts meeting each other from all three countries. Private American

TABLE 30   VISITS OF CANADIAN AND AMERICAN CABINET OFFICERS,
HEADS OF AGENCIES, AND OTHER FEDERAL OFFICIALS TO EACH OTHERS'
COUNTRIES, 1968

Agency (Canadian) [a]	Canadians to American Agencies			Americans to Canadian Agencies		
	Washington	Elsewhere	Total	Ottawa	Elsewhere	Total
Agriculture	36	368	404	28	168	196
Communications	65	67	132	120	17	137
Energy, Mines and Resources	105	688	793	85	81	166
Fisheries and Forestry	27	376	403	32	175	207
Indian Affairs and Northern Development	21	117	138	18	59	77
Industry, Trade and Commerce	120	348	468	67	12	79
National Defence	2,032	6,281	8,313		3,251	3,251
National Health and Welfare	29	94	123	25	23	48
Supply and Services	84	213	297	70	30	100
Transport	102	289	391	72	145	217
Dominion Bureau of Statistics	89	124	213	11	4	15
National Film Board	22	141	163	8	40	48
National Research Council	113	498	611	307	9	316
Total, all agencies	3,034	9,866	12,900	943	4,151	5,094

Source: House of Commons Standing Committee on External Affairs and National Defence, Minutes of Proceedings and Evidence, November 20, 1969.

[a] Only individual agencies the personnel of which made more than 100 visits are listed; the total, however, includes visits from all thirty-six Canadian federal agencies.

foundations have actively sponsored research in these neighboring countries, the most prominent example being the Rockefeller Foundation's assistance in Mexico in producing new grain varieties, which gave rise to the green revolution in other less developed countries.[157] Some sense of the frequent personal contacts between Canadian and American officials on the federal level may be derived from Table 30, which shows for the year 1968 how many officers of different national agencies crossed the border in each direction to the others' capital or elsewhere.

ADMINISTRATIVE TREATMENT VERSUS POLITICIZATION

Transportation questions, an obvious matter of common concern between neighboring states, normally have been handled on a relatively low bureaucratic level, whether national or state and provincial. Usually outside the range of high policy-making officials are the promotion of automobile safety, trucking regulations, air-traffic control, and highway matters.[158] However, in June, 1973, the six New England state governors and the premiers of the maritime provinces and Quebec met on Prince Edward Island to discuss cross-border cooperation in transport and trade, the first of an annual series of conferences of this transnational group.

The first consolidation of passenger train service under AMTRAK eliminated the runs between New York and Montreal; soon it was found desirable to restore this service, although not on the same route.[159] The Montreal–New York air-passenger traffic grew heavy enough in the early 1970s to justify an extension of Eastern Airline's shuttle system.[160] The new service set off a reaction which ran counter to this practical response to a transnational interest. Air Canada, subject to this extra competition and seeking United States permission for routes to other American cities than the few it enjoyed, pressed the Canadian government to end the customary preflight United States customs clearance enjoyed by air travelers to the United States from several major Canadian cities. On both sides of the border, conflicting commercial interests greatly complicated the four-year negotiation of the first major air agreement since 1966. At the heart of the controversy were expansions of approved routes, and the convenience of pre-clearance for customs became a pawn in the struggle.[161] The government of Canada threatened to eliminate this privilege entirely (it had been abandoned by Air Canada early in 1973), but by the autumn of 1973 a new agreement was reached, which included not only new routes but also reciprocal pre-clearance privileges for those traveling from the United States to Canada.[162]

DOMESTIC POLITICS

More frequently it has been American efforts to protect some United States domestic interest that have caused controversy across a border. Shortly after the war, United States measures to help the Mexicans to eliminate foot-and-mouth disease in cattle, which had prevented Mexican cattle from being exported into the United States were so drastic—involving killing infected animals—that the Mexican government was faced with strong opposition from cattle raisers. Opposition prompted joint development and administration of an effective vaccine, which eventually solved the problem in a more politically acceptable manner.[163]

Several years later, an uproar arose from the Nixon administration's efforts to solve the American drug problem by cracking down on one of the common routes by which large quantities of drugs entered the United States, namely, various ports of entry along the Mexican border. As far back as during World War II, the United States government had exerted pressure on Mexico to cooperate in stopping the smuggling, and the Mexicans had been relatively responsive, although they sometimes questioned whether this was not a global problem rather than one which was especially appropriate for them to solve for the Americans. Suddenly in September of 1969, Attorney General John Mitchell ordered Operation Intercept, a thoroughgoing search of every vehicle and person crossing the Mexican border into the United States that caused cars to be backed up for hours in the hot sun. Not only did intense inconvenience to both Mexicans and Americans result and outcries come from merchants in all of the thirty twin cities, but also the Mexican government was furious at this blow to its dignity. The methods had to be abandoned within two weeks and new ways of binational "cooperation" negotiated, which were called "Operation Cooperation." Very little in the way of drugs was seized, but this action did coerce the Mexicans into greater activity. Meanwhile, the United States provided airplanes, technical aid, and funds for an intensified Mexican drive against the cultivation of and traffic in drugs.[164] Under constant United States prodding, impressive actions have been taken by Mexican authorities, and exchange of information has risen. Yet the flow continues from the poor to the rich country over a long border presenting almost insuperable obstacles to effective surveillance. The ill-conceived Operation Intercept appears to have been an effort of the Nixon administration to gain a domestic political advantage without serious concern for the side effects.[165]

SUMMARY

Because neighborhood issues involved interests on both sides of the border and because the interests could reciprocate to increase the common welfare, a certain degree of integration is more noticeable here than elsewhere. This was especially true of river development and of less politically sensitive matters of mutual interest such as forest-fire fighting, pest control, health, and safety. The material advantages of cooperation are easy to see, specifically affecting local interests and involving private individuals and groups who were related to each other in intricate webs that crossed the borders. In environmental questions a convergence of views has been discernible, even though pollution threats appear to come much more from the giant neighbor.

From some perspectives, Mexico seemed more distant than Canada, as there were more ways that Canadians and Americans could help each other. At least, Americans far from either border could see Canada as a neighbor more readily than Mexico, in conducting scientific research, for example. Officials could act together more readily when, as in the Canadian case, there were easily identifiable counterparts in administrative systems that had almost interchangeable parts. Similarly, as private individuals Canadians and Americans were less easily distinguishable, in their educational systems, for example.

The very similarity of Canadians and Americans set up in Canada a countertrend to nourish Canadian differences, a nationalistic tendency sustained also by the difference in size of population and degree of economic development. Where resources desired by Americans were scarce or threatened to become so, neighborliness gave way to intense competition. Here Canada had the edge on Mexico because of the richness of its natural endowment, so useful in helping to even up the balance of capabilities between the otherwise disparate neighbors. On both sides of the United States border, water resources became a highly political issue as they became more and more valuable to Americans. Depletion of fisheries also sharpened potential conflicts, helped along by newly stimulated nationalism. What softened the confrontation was the implicit though unexpressed capacity to retaliate, greater between neighbors than with those far away. For this as well as other reasons, Canadians were careful to prevent negotiations about one issue from being combined with those on another. In this endeavor they were often aided by the American officials involved, who also feared such packaging.

The very remarkable International Joint Commission of the United States and Canada and the International Boundary and Water Commission established by the United States and Mexico have functioned in nonspectacular but highly successful ways. Although these commissions were limited in scope, by their very achievements they have broadened out their activities to take on new tasks. Because neighborhood issues loom large to particular delegates of the two interparliamentary groups and their solution often depends upon some congressional action, these groups have played a role in alerting members of the United States Congress to their concerns.

Day-to-day official interactions between the giant and its two neighbors normally involve only experts and administrators close to the problem, and this is true also for state, provincial, and local officials. Yet the very difficulty of reconciling the myriad of local interests and the complicated network of governmental authorities sometimes forced issues upward to higher political levels, occasionally requiring discussion among heads of state and formal executive agreements or even treaties to help solve them. The Great Lakes water-quality problem was one such issue. (Following the conclusion of such contracts between high-level authorities, those in lower bureaucratic levels then carry on.) Matters which might have only secondary political interest among the immensity of problems facing the huge United States government could become major political questions to the neighbor. Such were modifications in United States immigration rules for Mexico. Yet when the United States government, as under President Nixon, deliberately chose for political or security reasons to embark on an action potentially harmful to a neighboring country, protests of its citizens carried little weight compared to domestic American pressures. The anti-drug drive on the Mexican border, Operation Intercept, and the deafness to Canadian pleas regarding the trans-Alaska oil pipeline illustrate the seamy side of neighborliness. Like the more diffuse threats of being blanketed by American culture and life style, these insensitive policies could have longer-run ill effects on the neighboring countries' responsiveness to American interests. Ignoring the legitimate interests of the neighbors might put them more nearly in the position of far-away countries like Brazil and Australia, while they retained the special capacities to thwart American purposes which only neighbors possess.

TEN

CONCLUSIONS: ATTRACTION AND RESPONSE

EXCEPT AS IT IS MEASURED ON maps, the distance between the United States and each of the four middle powers—Canada, Mexico, Australia, and Brazil—has shrunk in the three decades of this study. There have been deviations from a standard of good neighborliness, but the trend has been toward ever greater awareness by the United States of each of the others and by each of them of the United States. This is most clearly apparent in Canadian-American relations and in Mexican-American relations, and more clearly apparent in the perceptions of the United States by Canadians, Mexicans, Australians, and Brazilians than in Americans' perception of the four countries. The United States seemed closer to the four middle powers than any of them seemed to the United States.[1] Yet, depending on the time, circumstances, and issue area involved, the superpower was not always the actor that had the greater influence in their mutual attraction.

If the trend toward all-around greater awareness and the central fact of asymmetrical attraction are clear, the pattern is otherwise complex and difficult to grasp. This study has covered more than thirty-five years of rapid change in each of the five countries and in the political environment of the world. It has covered a wide variety of issues, each with its own lines of cleavage and potentials for consensus. Each phase in the relations between the United States and one of the four middle powers has shaped the perceptions and the realities of subsequent phases. Changes in key personnel and intermittently overriding domestic political calculations obscure underlying patterns. Yet there are patterns of responsiveness and cooperation. They may be described in terms of common and conflicting interests, avoidable and unavoidable responses, sensitivity and insensitivity to opportunities for joint benefits from cooperation, and consequences for the political systems formed by the relations between the United States and each of the four middle powers. Once delineated, these patterns tell us something about the conditions in which influence is exercised when the United States and a middle power are attracted to each other in meeting particular kinds of problems. And they suggest how responsiveness could be reconciled with the unequal power of the two partners, to the advantage of both. The patterns appear in greater detail in the case of Canadian-American relations, which nevertheless are in some aspects less special than they are illustrations of the kinds of relations which are conceivable between the United States and other middle powers drawn to each other.

COMMUNITY OF INTEREST AND EQUAL CONCERN

Patterns of responsiveness between each of the four middle powers and the United States were more likely to develop when there was a genuine community of interest felt strongly on each side. The extreme peril sensed by the Canadian and Australian governments at the outset of World War II made them more eager than at any subsequent time to enter joint military undertakings with the United States. Their countries lacked the great war potential of the United States, but these lesser powers had significant contributions to make to the general effort of the Allies. A sense of common danger and complementary needs made some real reciprocity possible. As the threat of enemy action shifted away from the North American continent, Canada's usefulness to the United States as a kind of defensive glacis diminished. Meanwhile, faraway Australia offered an indispensable staging base in the Pacific, gaining in return protection from invasion.

The two Latin American countries were less touched by World War II militarily, and the Mexican government saw to it that its primary objective, a final solution to the oil-expropriation issue, was achieved before military concessions were made. The Latin Americans were ready with general expressions of support, but specific contributions to the war effort were much harder for the Americans to secure, and when secured were usually in return for objectives dearer to the Mexican and Brazilian leaders, aid in their economic development. Nevertheless, in the end both countries did something without precedent; they sent military forces abroad (small in Mexico's case), and both accepted what was harder for the Commonwealth countries to acquiesce in, Allied command, which really meant American direction. Partly because of historically bred fears of American intervention, the Mexicans were especially cautious in providing concessions involving use of their territory. With shifting fortunes of war, the American military lost interest, in any case; but they did not give up so easily with the Brazilians, with whose circuitous responses and friendly procrastination they were less familiar.[2]

There was no real counterpart in the Mexican and Brazilian cases to the highly responsive Canadian-American Permanent Joint Board for Defense, although institutions formally similar were created. Neither war nor time could wipe out the cultural distance between North American and Latin American officials, and the geopolitical imperatives were less pressing than those which compelled an intimate Canadian-American military collaboration. Yet neither culture, which bound the Americans close to the Australians and Canadians, nor ease of communications, which the latter enjoyed with the Americans up to the highest political levels, could bring the Australian and Canadian leaders into the highest councils of war. The British undertook to speak for them, if not always in what they regarded as their own interests. However, the war-induced cooperation between the United States and the two Commonwealth countries eventually loosened the military ties of the latter with Britain, especially at the practical level of standardized equipment and practices. The necessities of war not only stimulated the industrial development of each of the four middle powers but also realigned their economies; these economies, especially those of the two neighbors, became more and more tied to that of the United States.

In the global realignment of power that followed World War II and the widespread attendant feeling of intense insecurity, neither Latin American country felt greatly threatened. Thus the Mexicans and Brazilians did not feel compelled to respond very specifically to a series of American overtures for collaboration in meeting the asserted cold-war menace. The Mexicans remained as aloof as possible, while the Brazilians repeated the pattern of World War II responses so as to get more United States aid for their economic development. American efforts to link the Latin American subsystem with the global defense lineup were notably unsuccessful.

The Canadians and Australians, on the other hand, did feel imperiled. Both had enjoyed rewarding wartime experiences with Americans. Through military collaboration in war they had learned that in cooperating the benefits were great and the risks slight. Thus each was ready to respond and even to take initiatives to which the Americans responded, leading toward multi-lateral security arrangements against expansion of the Communist world. Remoteness from the power center of the non-Communist world made the Australians especially eager, particularly as they were dubious about what they considered to be soft peace terms offered to Japan. Probably overes-timating the danger to their security, they were somewhat envious of the Canadians. Canada, they thought, would be protected regardless of what the Canadians did. Distance fortified their ignorance of how little they needed to reciprocate in order to assure United States military actions in the Pacific once a Communist threat appeared real to the Americans.

For both of the Commonwealth countries (as for Brazil, too), the trans-national professional-military ties of World War II days made it easy to con-tinue cooperation in defense activities. Because Canada was situated be-tween the United States and the Soviet Union, its defense became even more closely integrated with that of the United States than it had been in World War II. The Permanent Joint Board on Defense continued to function for continental defense, although its importance was dwarfed by the large and complicated operation represented by NORAD and the three electronic air-warning systems linked to it. The defense-production sharing program that began in the late 1950s in some ways went further than World War II exchanges of war materiel, and numerous joint defense research projects were undertaken. The Australians also were partners in some American-directed research projects. Along with the Canadians and the British, they were part of a military intelligence network and participated in military per-sonnel exchanges and in standardization efforts; thus geographic distance did not seem to inhibit defense cooperation of this nature. But Canadians and Americans as immediate neighbors responded to each other's perception of common defense needs in much more extensive and variegated ways than did the others. Partly because of this close bilateral relationship, Canadians in the 1950s especially prized the multilateral setting that NATO provided, where they could have the protection of company in dealing with the Ameri-can superpower on defense matters. Furthermore, NATO offered them, as to a lesser extent ANZUS offered the Australians, the kind of access to mili-tary planning denied them during World War II by the great-power bellig-erents.

As cold-war pressures which NATO was designed to counteract less-ened, so did the earlier strong domestic support in Canada for collaborating with the United States in defense matters. Meanwhile, military technology, which earlier had made access to Canadian territory so attractive to American military planners, changed in ways that decreased the Canadians' need to respond to United States defense overtures and the Americans' need to make these overtures to Canada. Reacting to shifting domestic pressures, Prime Minister Trudeau chose to cut sharply Canadian contributions to NATO while reasserting the importance of continental-defense arrangements under NORAD. However, the advent of ABM systems opened up another rift in the close defense cooperation of Canada and the United States, in the same way that the immediate postwar nuclear-bomb developments had brought to an end close wartime Canadian-American cooperation in atomic bomb research. In both cases, Americans chose the unilateral path. Responsiveness works both ways, and Canadian-American relations have promptly reflected downward as well as upward changes in the estimates of useful collaboration. Changes in military technology had already made distant Australia attractive to American defense planners as a collaborator in space undertakings, and Australians were less demanding than Canadians in negotiations to establish such enterprises.

Peril from the international environment had until the 1970s stimulated an unprecedented degree of defense collaboration between the United States and both Canada and Australia under American leadership, collaboration far greater than in other areas. Some of the organizations formed as a response to common needs during this period have continued to function, albeit with changing tasks, but there has been little or no spillover into other functional areas. These cases are thus consistent with a body of theory which posits a discontinuity between welfare issues and those involving high politics.[3] Whereas in earlier times all politically influential groups in the middle powers thought worthwhile the kind of sacrifices necessary for defense collaboration, some of them later began to value much more highly other kinds of government activity. They resented junior-partner status, whether or not their country was getting a bargain in national security. As perceptions of immediate danger decline, there appear to be self-generating limits to combining a defense effort. When one partner is far more powerful than the others and the burden of responding affirmatively is on the lesser power, military cooperation may be the victim of its own success.

UNEQUAL OR CONFLICTING INTERESTS AND AVOIDABLE
INSENSITIVITY

That the middle powers were readier to respond positively in defense matters, which touch the core of national independence most closely, than in
economic affairs is not strange; the fear of losing something greatly valued
often induces greater sacrifices than the possibility of enlarging a coprosper-
ity sphere. When the fear is removed, however, so is the basis for response.
In more recent years, willingness of the middle powers and the United States
to respond favorably to each other's defense proposals has been declining; in
any case, the United States expected more of Canada and Australia than either of the middle powers asked of the Americans. Meanwhile, responsiveness has been increasing in some economic-issue areas, but only where
both countries had a relatively equal interest in accommodation and were
sensitive to each other's needs. The postwar period saw a gradual shift
toward comparative affluence for all four middle powers (although Canada
started from a relatively strong position). At the same time, the overpower-
ing economic strength of the United States began to decline and its economy
exhibited serious weaknesses. Meanwhile, Japan and the Common Market
emerged in the 1960s as major economic actors rivaling the United States.
So far as trade was concerned, the drawing power of the huge American
market had earlier put the onus on the United States for responding to the
need to expand the area of fair exchange. Although all of the four middle
powers maintained high tariffs on numerous commodities, the major source
of controversy was not their barriers but those imposed by their somewhat
insensitive great trading partner.

The Canadians, whose trade with the United States was far greater than
that of any other country, shared the American doctrinal preference for
regulating and coordinating international trade practices on a global basis
through such organizations as GATT and the OECD rather than through
exclusive market arrangements or special regional considerations. Nevertheless, Canada received special treatment from the United States on trade in
certain commodities, reflecting not only ease of transportation across common boundaries but also the importance of private American interests in
Canada. Mexico was in a similar situation. Whatever the government roles
in restricting or stimulating exchanges, the private trade relationships between Canada and the United States have been the most integrated in the

world, and for both Canada and Mexico the United States is much the most important importer of their goods. Many commodities have crossed the border duty-free, some under special governmental arrangements or sanctions, such as the automotive pact between the United States and Canada and the border industrialization program of Mexico.

Distant Brazil's important tropical products have also entered free, and unlike the other three middle powers, Brazil has usually enjoyed a favorable trade balance with the United States. In any case, it has been somewhat less dependent upon exports to the United States. The complementarity of Brazilian-American trade was lacking for Australia; its major exports have been highly competitive with American commodities. Thus the growing Japanese market, useful to the other countries which also were trying to multilateralize their trade, was especially valuable to Australia, which otherwise had been odd man out and especially vulnerable to trade restrictions imposed by the United States.

The United States has been only moderately receptive to the pleas of Mexico and Brazil, speaking for Latin America or underdeveloped countries generally, that special trade favors be extended to their manufactures. However, it did respond, in the case of coffee, to their desires, for international commodity agreements that would maintain the prices of raw materials. The huge American sugar market, which until 1974 Congress parceled out by quotas, had been a bone of contention for Mexico and Brazil especially. Their arguments did not focus on the quota system but on their desires for a larger share—and they have been especially favored.

Other congressionally imposed quotas have been a source of great irritation to all of the middle powers, especially because Congress has been particularly unreceptive to removing them. Administrations have also imposed quotas, implausibly justified in terms of national security, which restricted trading opportunities of the four less developed countries. In both cases, United States officials have usually been more attentive to private American economic interests than to those of friendly governments. The conflict, therefore, was not so much intergovernmental as transnational, with private interests competing across national boundaries. In large part, this was also true of the United States programs for disposal of surplus commodities of the 1950s. As the 1973 embargoes on some agricultural products showed, the United States is likely to turn the spigot off or on regardless of effects on other friendly countries when a trade question arises in the context of urgent domestic claims and becomes a matter of high politics. The four middle powers follow the same practice, but with less weighty consequences for the United States.

Reciprocity is at the heart of trade, and all the middle powers have had exports of interest to American importers which have tended to even the balance on particular trade questions. Inherently restrained by their overall weaker positions, the middle powers have usually been reluctant to permit bargains in this area to become part of larger package deals that include settlements of other issues, where their position might be less strong. Australians learned the hard way that Americans also kept trade issues separate from their defense commitments. Spillover into political areas was resisted by all four middle powers when the United States tried to get them to channel their trade to suit the East-West conflict in which it was the Western leader. Only grudgingly and to an extent conforming to their own trade interests did they respond. Meanwhile, they suffered no observable retaliation by the United States for their efforts to expand their trade with Communist countries.

Closely intertwined with trade, foreign investment, if left alone by governments, also would tend to respond to private interests in profit making and to flow relatively freely. This has occurred between the United States and Canada, despite a few Canadian restrictions on foreign investment in particular kinds of enterprise and some United States restraints on capital outflow imposed in the 1960s. A distinctly negative Canadian response met efforts of American officials to apply certain United States laws to American companies' Canadian subsidiaries. This practice of extraterritoriality may have exerted subtle restraints on such subsidiaries, but in the instances where the effort was public, the Americans gave way in the face of Canadian opposition.

American direct investment in Canada is far greater than in any other country, so overwhelmingly great that the Canadian government began in 1973 to formulate rules for guiding the inflow of foreign capital. In what is still a relatively free transnational capital market, Canadian investment in the United States has been substantial also, although much of it has been in portfolio rather than equity investment. The responsiveness of private interests to a hospitable economic climate could also be seen in the late 1960s in Australia, where (after earlier Australian conversion restrictions had been removed) American direct investment was greater than in either Mexico or

Brazil. Its rapid increase induced the Australian Labor party government to lay down restrictions after coming to power. Both Latin American governments have imposed numerous kinds of restraints on foreign investment, as well as offering inducements. However, the proximity of Mexico to the United States and its appearance of much greater stability during most of this period helped to account for the fact that American investment there was about the same as in the much larger South American country and has represented about four-fifths of all foreign investment in Mexico.[4] Distance is not the only factor, but conditions in neighboring countries are likely to be better known to investors, increasing their confidence if there are favorable signs.

Foreign investment has long been a matter of high policy for the Latin American governments. The same has become true in Canada, as the tremendous growth of American investment has required the federal government to react at the highest levels; it eventually became so in Australia, especially after the Australian Labor party took over the government in 1972. These governments have been responding, not to the United States government, but to behavior of Americans in private enterprise. These American investments have created transnational interest groups, however, since private citizens in the host countries were also profiting from foreign investment. Furthermore, the provincial or state governments of Canada and Australia have often worked at cross purposes to those groups in their own countries who saw a dependent situation emerging and who were seeking a government response for nationalist reasons. The United States was familiar with a similar situation in Mexico; controlling foreign investment was one aspect of the Mexican revolution, in part a reaction against a kind of economic imperialism. That country's expropriation of oil-producing properties in 1938 marked a turning point. Since that time, it has been more and more feasible for governments concerned about American investment in their countries to take what measures they will to satisfy their discontented citizens. Governments' responding to domestic pressures through such local political remedies runs counter to the tendency towards greater interdependence which capital flows might otherwise have strengthened.

For the most part, so far as the four middle powers were concerned, United States officials usually have confined themselves to the role of interested bystanders. They have recognized that regulations for foreign investment were matters for local determination, and they were well aware that interference could be counterproductive to American interests. The opposite anticipation, however, guided their behavior in Brazil, where in the early 1960s they responded to the expropriation of some American interests in the state of Rio Grande do Sul by taking sides in domestic politics. Thus the foreign-investment issue spilled over into another area but was eventually confined. The adversaries of the Brazilian military officers who seized the government in 1964 happened to be the same groups that American officials had been opposing. However, the new leaders gradually shook off the need to depend upon favorable responses from the United States government to advance their economic objectives.

All of these four middle powers have been confronting not just an American phenomenon, but a growing transnational category of unofficial actors, that of the multinational corporations. These companies operate within their boundaries for the most part unconstrained by United States government action. That most of the capital has flowed in one direction has obscured the nature of the problem. To avoid the unwanted consequence of stringent national control over foreign direct investment, especially if such control might chase it away, a more worldwide response by both host and home-country governments would seem necessary and possible. It is not sufficient for the governments of the host country and the United States simply to coordinate their policies in some kind of bilateral agreements. To be effective, a wider multilateral approach seems called for than the original proposal of Mexico's President Echeverria when he asked Canada and Latin American countries to agree to a common code of treatment for foreign direct investment. He later sought American support for a "Charter of Economic Rights and Duties." The United Nations General Assembly approved it in 1974, but the United States voted against the charter because the articles were too one-sided. Studies in the OECD and in the United Nations of the multinational corporation point in the direction of global response to the problem of enjoying the benefits from this means of economic development at the least cost to other values, but formidable obstacles stand in the way of a political solution satisfactory to all.

Private trade and investment have produced some of the monetary issues arising between the United States and the middle powers. Measures to deal with these problems are inherently intergovernmental. The fairly relaxed and sometimes positively helpful United States government response to monetary policies adopted by the middle powers earlier in the postwar period began to tighten up and become more immediately self-serving when the United States itself encountered balance-of-payments difficulties in the 1960s. Not just a change in America's relative position economically but also a change in administration helped to account for this trend away from neighborliness. Responsiveness to Canadian and Mexican problems had earlier helped not only the neighbors but also numerous private American interests with connections in those countries. President Nixon's new economic policy of August, 1971, was shocking to these two as it was also to other friendly powers which had not contributed to America's difficulties. It was an abrupt shift away from the mutual responsiveness to each other's monetary problems that had been experienced earlier by both Canada and Mexico in their relations with the United States. Their pleas to receive the special exemptions usually accorded in the past were ignored. In return, the Canadian government successfully resisted American proposals for a package deal to handle the monetary crisis that would have included trade issues also. The two governments eventually agreed to disagree. Many important trading countries besides Canada and Mexico reacted strongly to President Nixon's monetary policies and helped bring about a retraction by December, 1971, of the most objectionable unilateral steps in his international monetary policy.

The American monetary crisis had global impact, calling for some move by the IMF. The Group of Ten, which dealt with the crisis, included Canada, but this was only one of the channels through which Canadian and American monetary officials had customarily dealt with what was a common problem. Routine, frequent, and informal contacts in addition to meetings of the more formal joint ministerial committee on economic affairs had earlier ensured mutual responsiveness on a bureaucratic level for monetary as for trade and investment issues. Such channels improved the chances that these issues would be considered primarily on their merits. That they failed so to function in 1971 illustrated the importance of personalities. The monetary crisis was handled by Secretary of the Treasury John Connally, whose interest in and knowledge of Canada were minimal and whose undiplomatic approach to policy quickly became apparent. After this monetary problem became a matter of high policy, the carefully discriminating treatment of those involved could no longer be expected. The innocent suffered along with the others, especially when those in the United States government best acquainted with them were not at the top level. For Canada and Mexico, one special channel of protest continued to operate, their respective inter-parliamentary groups with members from the United States Congress.

Most supplementary protest channels have been lacking in the monetary relations of the United States with Australia, which normally has received less responsive treatment from the Americans. Distance, membership in the sterling bloc, less participation in international organizations dealing with monetary questions, and a less significant position in the world's economy have all been factors explaining this difference in treatment.

The other distant country, Brazil, until the late 1960s had been in al-most chronic monetary difficulties. As Australia had done in an earlier period, Brazil from time to time responded to its own problems by restric-tions on the convertibility of its currency. During various Brazilian monetary crises the United States felt compelled to render aid which the Americans always accompanied by advice and conditions to strengthen Brazil's usually ineffective efforts to stabilize its currency. Inevitably, this process spilled over into Brazilian domestic politics, accentuating Brazil's image of depen-dency. Officials in the United States government were clearly relieved when the Brazilian government was taken over by those who would enforce strict economic policies regardless of their popularity, a practice which eventually brought to an end the client relationship that had required them to respond to American direction in monetary matters (though not always to follow it).

Other forms of foreign aid also occasioned controversy between each of the two less developed countries and the United States government during the period when United States aid programs were stimulated by the East-West conflict. Relations between giver and recipient are never easy, espe-cially when they are close to one another. Such was the experience here, even though the role of Americans as the givers was somewhat deceptive, since important private American interests were also being served through the various tied programs. The Mexicans, ever touchy under even the slight-est American pressure on their diplomatic orientation, responded to the dilemma posed by the desire for aid in the early postwar years by seeking assistance in the form of repayable loans and by stressing their requirements for expanded trade rather than for aid to meet their industrialization goals. On the other hand, they responded with alacrity to the Alliance for Progress concepts, partly because aid under its auspices appeared in a multilateral guise. Furthermore, they were proud to join in Alliance projects to which they made a contribution through technical aid to other countries. Private

American assistance, very important for Mexico's technical development, was welcomed. The Mexicans knew that issues of government aid, by its very nature, cannot be decided on their merit.

Faraway Brazil was another story.[5] The Americans often envisaged relations with it as a means for exerting indirect influence in South America. Such a political spillover role corresponded to Brazilians' aims to raise their own status on that continent. The foreign aid wants of Brazil were immense, and the United States responded by providing it with a giant share of what was available, along with a huge foreign-aid establishment. Through foreign aid, the American presence was palpable in Brazil, and the dominance of the United States showed even when the Kennedy administration reshaped President Kubitschek's proposal for Operation Pan America into the Alliance for Progress. Political manipulation by Americans seemed inevitable. Its likelihood was all the greater because differences within the United States government about the size, nature, and objectives of its aid programs operating in Brazil spilled over into domestic politics with some of the contending Americans allied with local groups. It may have been that, as Thomas Hughes once said, "The United States Government is always meeting the United States Government . . . coming back." [6] Brazilians and Americans on the spot may have learned to predict each other's behavior. Yet mutual awareness did not lead to closer coordination of policy, since the Brazilian goal was independence from United States government influence.

With Canada and Australia, less separated from the United States by level of economic development, the principal foreign-aid questions related to coordinating policy. In practice, this has primarily meant exchanges of information, and there has been relatively little harmonizing of their respective aid policies except through multilateral agencies such as the Development Assistance Committee of the OECD and the Colombo Plan. Distant Australia was a latecomer to the former and an initiator of the latter, in which the American role is far less important.

Neither faraway Australia nor Brazil has had labor problems with the United States; for the southern neighbor of the United States, migrant labor throughout the postwar period has been a major issue because much better work opportunities lie just across the border of Mexico in the United States. Organized American labor has viewed this migrant labor as penetration in the wrong direction, the United States, although it was not so seen by American employers of the Mexican workers. For many years the United States government was more responsive to the latter's interest. During the period of legally regulated migration under the bracero program, the United States responded also to the increasing demands of the Mexican government to impose particular employment standards. Despite its economic advantages, the proud Mexicans were for a long time somewhat ambivalent about extending the program; meanwhile "liberal" and labor interests were growing stronger in Congress vis-à-vis those agricultural employers still interested in hiring Mexican labor. So the program died. The numbers of illegal Mexican migrants subsequently mushroomed, but Congress has not responded to pressures to make their employment (as opposed to their entrance) illegal. Nor did the administration agree to a renewed program sought by Mexico in 1974. In a feedback from the demise of the bracero program, the Mexican government instituted its border industrialization program, which the United States facilitated. Despite this and other Mexican measures and vigorous American policing efforts, the illegal-migrant movement thus remained a major social and political problem spoiling relations between unequally wealthy neighbors.

The primary labor issue between Canada and the United States has involved not governments but the "international" trade unions, whose domination by American leadership has become more and more repellent to Canadians. Once only, when the United States refused to extradite an American union leader wanted in Canada for a crime connected with illegal union activities was there a serious controversy about labor matters between the governments. At that time, United States officials clearly were responding to pressures from domestic interests, regardless of the merits of the issue.

In general, however, the United States government was more likely to be sensitive to the economic concerns of the middle powers in relatively prosperous periods, when the disparity in economic strength between the superpower and the others was more visible. (There were exceptions, as when certain allegedly suffering American domestic interests were pleading for some special discriminatory aid from the national government.) Conversely, when the middle powers began to feel their economic strength increasing, they tended to break away from cooperative policies based on common interests which they no longer felt to be common. But neither of these tendencies was irreversible.[7]

AVOIDABLE AND UNAVOIDABLE RESPONSES:
ISSUES AND ACTORS

Global foreign-policy questions tend to be less specific than economic issues and to make up an area which is inherently a concern to those on the highest political levels and where they negotiate for the state as an entity in world politics. Even more than in other issue areas, the need of the four countries to respond and the kind of response they made varied with changes in the world configuration of power, to which these issues were closely related. All four were middle powers of distinctive significance in world affairs. Like other weaker states, all four were also at one time or another under very strong internal domestic political pressure to appear independent of the United States in their foreign-policy orientations. Thus not joint policy but only the readiness to consider each other's views was the optimum friendly response to be expected in the relations of each of these countries with the United States. Until the late 1960s American domestic politics was less closely connected with the foreign-policy of the superpower. One exception was the period of McCarthyism, when excesses, especially in Congress, spilled over into Canadian and Mexican relations, souring both.

During the height of the cold war, the United States, as the leader of the non-Communist world, was especially demanding of conformity from its allies. Living next door and close under an umbrella of military security provided almost involuntarily by the United States, Canada and Mexico diverged more often and more widely from a particular stand desired by the leader than did the more remote countries. Mexico was the outstanding opponent of American efforts to use the OAS in the diplomatic contest with the Communist countries. During one phase in the gyrating Brazilian domestic political struggles, Mexico was joined by Brazil, only to be deserted after a change in Brazil's regime. The Canadians, often fearful of rash American ventures, sometimes merely dragged their feet, as in some phases of the Korean War, but they took their own initiatives at other times. They were joined by the Australians in the crises over the islands of Matsu and Quemoy. At least once, during the Suez crisis, the United States responded favorably to a Canadian initiative. For the most part, however, diplomats from the four countries learned that the political reward for responding to American preferences was principally early information on United States perceptions of what the proper course should be and of its likely action. No penalty beyond some temporary coolness appeared to follow the failure to respond, while unwanted responsibilities could be avoided. Experience in getting the United States to respond to a policy initiative that a middle power desired was usually frustrating. The Canadians learned that while quiet diplomacy might occasionally find a responsive audience among their manifold contacts in the United States, open verbal confrontation was far less effective than simply proceeding on an independent course. Eventually, as in the case of recognizing Communist China, the United States followed suit after others had done so. The Canadians also learned, as did the others, that on global issues they were more likely to catch the eye of the Americans for some desired policy shift if they were part of a multilateral organization.

Since global foreign-policy issues pit state against state in world politics and engage the highest policy levels, there was little reason to expect the United States to be very amenable to the efforts of a lesser power to modify the giant's course. Yet the willingness to listen depended very much upon the personalities of those currently leading the United States in foreign affairs. Dean Acheson heard more than John Foster Dulles; the Kennedy administration was rated highest on this score by the others. Yet even it had troubles with the recalcitrant Canadian prime minister, John Diefenbaker, even as he did with his own adversary, Lester Pearson, friend of the Kennedy government. The Vietnam war excesses of the increasingly deaf Nixon administration alienated all the others, notably the Trudeau government. In the early 1970s, the weaknesses of the United States had become apparent, and its allies were responding to détente rather than to American advice. As a consequence, neighbor Canada's friendship began to seem somewhat more valuable; its voice became a little more audible. Thus President Nixon publicly praised "a lively diversity of views" to the Canadians. But after his bombing of Hanoi during the 1972 Christmas season, he turned a cold shoulder to the new leader of distant Australia, Gough Whitlam, for Whitlam's breaking Australian precedent and making clear that Australia also entertained views at variance with those of the United States. In a longer time perspective, American leaders would have perceived the complementary roles which all four of these countries could play in promoting those foreign-policy interests which they held in common with the United States. There are functions such as mediation or moderating conflicts or providing valuable information which they could be expected to perform in return for an attentive hearing of their own views on foreign-policy alternatives. However, even short-term pique among American leaders has not spilled over into serious consequences for the solution of issues in other functional areas.

Least affected by failures to respond in unrelated matters are those issues such as river development and environmental quality which arise from two neighbors having a common border. These quite specific questions which occur because of contiguity attest to the existence of very concrete regional interests shared by Americans with Canadians and/or Mexicans, and they have arisen in areas where the influence bases were more balanced than elsewhere. They constitute important exceptions to observations that distance no longer has much international significance. As in other issue areas, not just geography but changing circumstances also made the neighbors more or less responsive to common problems. Here, however, it was not primarily changes in the world configuration of power but economic and technological changes which altered the conditions for responsiveness during the period under review. A list of issues compiled in the late 1960s when Canada and the United States had ''essentially identical interests'' included some which by 1973 had already become divisive.[8] For example, the alarming depletion of fisheries resources was providing the occasion for the Canadian government to take a more and more nationalistic view of who should fish where under whose authority and to turn away from further joint conservation measures.

Timing played an important part in the readiness of two neighbors to seek mutual benefit from cooperative development of rivers they shared. Both Canada and Mexico faced a dilemma: responding affirmatively to a giant partner who usually moved faster and with greater resources, physical and technical, than they were prepared to move, or running the risk of losing potential benefits if they waited until they were ready. However, the benefits were sufficiently great for both the greater and lesser neighbor and the potential harm from failing to respond was sufficiently alarming to both that very substantial joint programs were undertaken.

When Canadians and Americans became acutely aware of common pollution problems in the 1960s, the ability of each to respond was complicated, as in the case of river development, by the multitude of jurisdictions and private interests involved. Some scholars have contended that if a functional problem becomes politicized and a broader number of groups develop a concern in it, the states involved may be more likely to integrate their efforts. The Canadian-American response to environmental problems through joint measures taken by new or expanded bilateral organizations seems to confirm their view.[9] Furthermore, in responding to pollution questions and river development, the neighbors agreed on how to share the costs, actions which confirmed that the undertakings were joint. However, where politicization of environmental questions went so far as to touch on national security and became a matter of high politics, as in the case of American nuclear tests on Amchitka and Canadian claims to protect vast regions of Arctic waters, responsiveness fell almost to zero. As for the politicization of the trans-Alaska pipeline question, although remarkable transnational interest groups were formed to oppose it for environmental reasons, they were insufficient to move the United States government from its intention to proceed. The signals from the Canadian government for some preferred practical alternative were, in any case, consistently weak.

That the stronger of two potential partners may view merely as a problem to be solved in pursuing a common objective a question which appears to the weaker to constitute a political issue to be negotiated is amply illustrated by the treatment of North American natural resources.[10] The Americans usually looked upon Canada's natural gas, oil, and water for electric power as increasingly desirable resources to be exploited and shared on an economic basis; the Canadians saw them as extremely useful and limited possessions not to be exchanged merely for American money here and now. The greater their scarcity value for the giant neighbor, the greater the need for the Canadians to make some response to appeals for a continental energy policy, but not necessarily in the direction desired by the Americans. Energy resources could be bargained over, but not Canada's own water, what the nationalists often called its birthright. There were very articulate Canadian voices objecting to selling the abundant fresh water of the northern country to a thirsty neighbor, even when none had been sought and even though water, unlike oil, is a recurring resource. In any case, the Canadians were adamant about avoiding any package deals; trading a concession in one area for an American concession in another might weaken their very strong bargaining position.

On less politicized issues, or those which had become muted through earlier agreement, the International Joint Commission responded effectively on the administrative level to a very large number of border, principally water, problems. On the southern border of the United States, an equally remarkable bilateral institution, the International Boundary and Water Commission quietly handled questions which could have been very explosive between the two neighbors, partly by trying to anticipate emerging problems. Both these organizations had highly specific tasks in performing which the great difference in overall power between the two member states was relatively unimportant. The pragmatic quality of the commissions' operations, which helped explain their effectiveness, would have been threatened had they been charged with negotiating issues about which the two state members had become politically sensitive.[11] Less specifically designed for particular neighborhood issues but closer to some important political centers, both Canadian-American and Mexican-American interparliamentary groups provided channels through which interests of one country on border questions could be communicated to those with power to respond in the others; the members from the less powerful partner in each group were readier to use it for such purposes than for more generalized exchanges of views on global issues. But much of the day-to-day responsiveness to each other's needs which characterized the multifarious interactions of Canada and the United States on neighborhood problems has been due to close and informal contacts among bureaucrats charged with a task to perform.[12] Sometimes it has been easier for them to cooperate with counterparts on the other side of the border than with their own official colleagues, with whom they are often competing for some internal administrative reason unconnected with the job at hand.

Faced with common welfare problems in the fields of public health, safety, parks, forest fires, crime control, and scientific research, the United States and its neighbors have dealt with them through relatively unorganized, bureaucratic contacts across the border. In earlier years, drug traffic would have been added to that list. However, responding to a serious internal problem, the Nixon administration sought domestic political rewards by employing the full power of its law-enforcement machinery on the Mexican frontier. In the brief period of its exercise, this action thoroughly alienated Mexicans and innocent American border crossers alike. The United States government showed more sensitivity to Canadian feelings in refraining from asking for any action against the American draft evaders and deserters who fled north during the Vietnam war. This was a good illustration of the anticipated reaction preventing the making of a claim.

Although globally an improvement, in its 1965 immigration reform the United States took a step away from neighborly liberality by imposing a

Western Hemisphere quota which limited Canadian and Mexican immigration. That year also saw the termination of the joint Mexico-United States bracero program controlling the movement of migrant workers.

Other movements of persons and ideas across the northern and southern boundaries of the United States in both directions have gone relatively unhindered by government action during most of the postwar period. So permeable are the borders that the Canadians and Mexicans, but particularly the Canadians, have increasingly felt the penetration of American practices to be a threat to their own cultures. However, there is little that the United States government could have done to respond to this apprehension. Meanwhile, with much encouragement and scarcely any formality, huge numbers of tourists move back and forth over the continent as though it were one great common patrimony. These tourists form a private complement to the person-to-person official interchanges, so easy between the United States and Canada and the United States and Mexico, so difficult in the case of faraway Australia and Brazil.

We have seen how changing circumstances have altered the perception of common interest and increased or decreased the need for pressures on the governments to respond to each other in different issue areas. How did the differential nature of the issues themselves help to explain variations in readiness to cooperate? Within each issue area, what other factors conditioned the response of the United States and each of the middle powers to each other's requirements?

CONDITIONS FOR AFFIRMATIVE RESPONSE

If United States relations with each of the other countries in different issue areas are compared as to frequency or intensity of **joint** bilateral activity, only Canada, and then primarily in the continental context, engaged in genuinely common security enterprises, whether in World War II or later; Australian-American defense efforts were somewhat intermixed in both periods but to a far lesser extent. Only between Canada and the United States was there a significant sector of absolutely free economic interchanges; though private activities, they took place under a regime established by the governments. Foreign direct investment is in one sense inherently joint, although again primarily private actors are involved, but jointness in expanded forms was increasingly being either required or, on the other hand, pinched off by the host-country governments. Again, the most extensive American direct investment was to be found in Canada, although a very significant proportion of the foreign investment in the other three countries was also American. Only Canadians, in turn, had noteworthy direct investments in the United States. But Canada was a middle power like the others; with a different role in global foreign-policy matters, none of these states was as likely to be acting jointly with the United States in such matters as in other issue areas, or as some of the greater powers did. While the least degree of jointness was observable in global foreign-policy issues, the greatest was to be seen in neighborhood issues. Not surprisingly, the number of different kinds of bilateral problems and opportunities arising from neighborhood issues (which were jointly tackled by the United States with Canada and with Mexico) was noteworthy both in extent and, despite inevitable frictions, in the satisfaction of both sides.

Far more numerous than joint enterprises were examples in all issue areas of **reciprocity** in the relations of the United States with the four lesser powers, although the asymmetry in capability was reflected in readiness to respond and in American pressure on the others to do so. During World War II, their extreme sense of insecurity to some extent overcame the middle powers' reluctance to involve themselves in reciprocal security measures; mutuality of benefit went along with the greater capacity of Canada and Australia to cooperate with the United States in defense measures than was the case with less developed countries. Significantly, very little defense collaboration occurred on American soil. Cold-war insecurities were felt primarily by Canadians and Australians among the four middle powers, and these culturally and economically similar countries offered greater advantages to the United States for meaningful alliances. In contrast, trade issues affected all four middle powers very intensely; there were genuine examples of reciprocity in exchanges between the United States and Mexico as well as Brazil, the more tropical and less competitive with the United States of the two developing countries. The period covered by this examination was one in which the huge American market was much sought after and sometimes arbitrarily controlled to restrict certain imports from the four countries, but the fact that reciprocal advantages from trade were not even more thoroughly exploited was often the fault of the barriers set up by the middle powers. In the related matter of investment, reciprocal advantages were markedly different between home and host country, despite a common economic interest. The ever present and growing fears among groups in the host countries that foreign direct investment meant foreign (read American) control over vital aspects of their economies made this a very sensitive issue. Yet on global foreign-policy issues, the kind of reciprocal advantage from diplomatic cooperation was such that the four middle powers exhibited their greatest freedom of maneuver in this field of activity. Nevertheless, they seldom diverged dramatically but only in degree from lines pursued by the United States on East-West issues. In the inter-American subsystem, in which they were leaders, Mexico and Brazil deviated more sharply from the United States. Neighborhood issues almost inevitably required reciprocal treatment, because Canada and Mexico each shared border problems and opportunities with the United States. However, differences in power and in the timing of mutual benefits caused the lesser neighbors to be suspicious and made them less ready to respond. Especially with respect to natural resources, the concept of continentalism was to be shunned. Not so on environmental issues, since the giant neighbor was the big source of pollution.

Even during World War II, the exact extent of cooperative activities in defense was usually made **specific** in carefully negotiated arrangements between the United States and each of the middle powers; the Latin American countries were usually readier to respond on a general level than to make specific concessions. Postwar security relations were formally specified in multilateral treaties between the United States and Canada and Australia respectively; these agreements were the reference points for subsequent specific cooperative activities in defense. Specific concessions on import items were necessary to implement formal (and with Mexico somewhat informal) trade agreements between the United States and each of the others. On direct investment issues, the United States government played a very small role, but when Americans were investing in the other countries their treatment was often handled specifically, case by case, by governments of the host country to the extent that they did regulate foreign direct investment. In contrast to global foreign-policy issues, where agreement was usually on a very general or abstract level, neighborhood issues necessarily had to be dealt with very specifically and required bargaining about details. The advantages of cooperation or the injuries from failure to cooperate were very tangible here; furthermore the causes of friction and of competition were most specific in neighborhood relations.

During World War II, the more geographically **distant** the country the easier it was for that middle power to enter into defense collaboration with the United States; the neighbors were wary. In the postwar years, the kind of distance which facilitated cooperation in security matters was cultural; Canada and Australia were closer in capacity and outlook. Because closeness in perspective was combined with a location far away, it was the Australians who until the 1970s most sought collaboration in defense. In trade matters, however, they were at the greatest disadvantage, while the neighbors of the United States were most likely to obtain the kind of concessions they desired, access to the American market. American direct investment was greatest in the neighboring countries, arousing greater fear of undesired consequences there than in the more distant countries; the Australians only began to exercise control over foreign investment in the 1970s. Somewhat similarly, on global foreign-policy issues, the more distant countries tended to follow a United States line more closely than did the neighbors; proximity had a negative influence on foreign-policy coordination, as Canada and Mexico strove to look independent or struggled to differentiate themselves from American measures they disliked. Neighborhood issues depended upon proximity to be meaningful. In the varieties of cooperation on welfare matters Canada seemed closer than Mexico because of the cultural affinity occasionally deplored by Canadian nationalists.

Cooperation in defense, even in World War II, did not **spill over** into other issue areas, except that the Latin American countries profited economically from some defense agreements. However, cumulated experience made postwar collaboration easier. Because of the awe-inspiring power of the United States, collaboration was carefully channeled by the smaller powers to preserve their freedom of action in other matters. Bargaining in trade matters was also confined to that issue area except in Brazil's case. There, until the late 1960s, trade questions, monetary issues, and foreign-aid matters tended to coalesce, in part a result of chronic balance-of-payments problems. The most distasteful form of spillover attributable to foreign investment was the practice of the United States of exercising extraterritoriality with respect to American investment in Canada. However, in Canada as in the other less developed middle powers, with increasing economic prosperity flowing in part from foreign investment, economic questions could be kept even more separate from other issues as time went on. This separation was always true for foreign-policy orientation, where economic considerations had little influence. The principal example of spillover from foreign-policy coordination was Australia's involvement in the Vietnam catastrophe. On neighborhood issues, both Canada and Mexico made sure that there was no spillover from any specific question into other issue areas. Within a specified area, however, experience with neighborly cooperation often led to greater readiness to deepen and widen programs, especially on environmental problems.

During World War II, the most notably effective **channel for communication** on defense issues was the Canadian-American Permanent Joint Board on Defense, which carried over into the postwar period. For some time after the war, professional ties formed between members of the United States military forces with counterparts in all four middle powers also continued; these tended to help overcome differences in power. On trade matters, the most important channels were multilateral, although Mexico stayed out of GATT, depending instead upon its special relationship as a neighbor to the United States. Later, like Brazil, Mexico took a leading part in UNC-TAD, which the developing countries hoped would form a counterweight to the developed countries' domination of the world's trading system. Among the four middle powers, a special relationship in trade with the United States was most important for Canada. In this field as in investment matters, frequent, often informal, transnational contacts between Canadian officials and their American counterparts have been very effective channels for communication on a personal basis. For all four middle powers the principal agency for coordination or orientation in foreign-policy matters in the early postwar years was the United Nations. Its importance for this purpose diminished with changes in that organization. Thus diplomatic, state-to-state channels remained the primary channel for negotiations on global foreign-policy issues; for Canada the North Atlantic Council also served as a link in this process. Quite a different story was sketched out on neighborhood matters: the long established Canada–United States International Joint Commission and Mexico–United States International Boundary and Water Commission grew increasingly useful as agencies for cooperation. For handling neighborhood issues, additional important channels were formed by private transnational associations, personal contacts between responsible federal officials, and contacts between states and provinces on the northern border of the United States and between states of the United States and of Mexico on the southern border.

Security issues during World War II inevitably involved the **highest levels of government,** and President Franklin D. Roosevelt played a prominent role here as elsewhere. Even the absence of his attention affected the outcome, as was the case with many issues of concern to the Australians. In the postwar period, once the United States had formally entered into collective defense agreements with Canada and Australia respectively, specific questions could more readily be dealt with at lower levels of administration, often on a multilateral basis. Trade matters could normally be handled by specialists on a bureaucratic level, but since they often constituted problems deeply affecting the whole economy of the less wealthy countries, issues might rise to the highest levels of policy making in periods of crisis. The consequence was usually the smoothing over of the controversy sufficiently for such an issue to be manageable by the appropriate bureaucratic authorities who were more knowledgeable about particular countries. A noteworthy exception to the conciliatory effect of attention by the highest authorities was President Nixon's bombshell, the new economic policy of August, 1971. Its spokesman, John Connally, was no diplomat. All global foreign-policy issues were matters for the highest levels of policy making in all the governments, again in marked contrast to neighborhood issues. The latter usually arose at a local level or on low levels of the bureaucracy, although great projects such as the St. Lawrence Seaway or the management of the waters of the Colorado River and the Rio Grande required formal negotiation and embodiment of some of the agreements in treaties. Yet the day-to-day handling of problems common to the United States and one or the other of its neighbors routinely took place on lower levels, including states and provinces, and involved specialists on particular matters rather than diplomatic negotiators.

Domestic politics did not significantly affect defense cooperation during World War II. For some time after the war, internal politics had little influence on the readiness of the middle powers to work with the United States on security matters. The exception was Mexico, where domestic considerations prevented any real defense collaboration with the United States. Political conditions inside Australia strongly supported defense cooperation for a long period, then abruptly shifted in 1972 with the coming to power of the opposing party. Backing in Canada for defense cooperation with the United States gradually diminished, as noteworthy internal divisions developed on this subject, mostly between parties or wings of parties. In all five countries, economic sectors rather than political parties played significant domestic political roles in determining how freely trade moved between the four middle powers and the United States. The agricultural sector was particularly influential. In addition, the United States Congress was an important actor in this field, and so were the Canadian provinces. On issues of foreign investment, the Canadian provincial role and that of the Australian states were marked, especially when the regional governments competed with the national government. Yet for all of the four middle countries, foreign direct investment was a major issue internally and an increasingly controversial question. As for host-country treatment of American investors, only in Brazil did the United States government become involved in domestic politics in promoting the interests of this group. With party changes came changes in the readiness of three of the smaller powers to coordinate foreign-policy orientation with the United States, while in Mexico where the PRI remained the only operative party, its "institutionalized revolution" prevented foreign-policy coordination with the United States. The period in which the Watergate scandals preoccupied the United States government coincided with that in which the Trudeau government was based on a shaky coalition, and under these circumstances, negotiations over many Canadian-American issues became stalemated. Neighborhood issues again presented a very different picture. Such issues usually involved not political parties but very vocal domestic interest groups on the two sides of the border, some working together with those on the other side, while others were in competition.

Summarizing various aspects of United States collaboration with each of the four middle powers indicates that the kind of response to an initiative varied with the kind of issue, that the issues were likely to be kept separate, and that mutuality of advantage was not ruled out by asymmetry in power rank. Also, proximity was only one factor in promoting one government's awareness of the other's needs, and a highly variegated and intensive network of communication, which might follow from recognizing common interests, might also promote further cooperative response. Thus an elaborate system of interrelationships has grown up between the United States and each of the middle powers, revealing a high degree of attraction. Interdependent relationships were most intricately developed in the case of Canada, which in a sense sets standards of emulation—or avoidance—for other middle powers, depending on their own preferences.

NATIONAL INTEGRITY AND FUNCTIONAL COLLABORATION

What are the political consequences flowing from those interrelationships formed in the various issue areas? It is infrequent for anyone on either side of the United States–Canada border to express a desire for as much as a free-trade area, and Canadians have grown increasingly eager to stay as clearly separate and distinct from Americans as they can stay without threatening the advantages of association. The Canadians have a distaste for formal governmental organizations and agreements linking them with Americans; this reflects not only their customary pragmatic approach but also their increasingly felt need to avoid organized commitments which might bind them in the future.[13] The Mexicans are even more distrustful of formal bilateral ties to the United States. The distant middle powers, less conscious of the pull towards the United States in any case, came later to the stage of vigorously affirming their autonomy. Yet all four middle powers still face the problem of catching the attention of the United States government when they wish to do so. Formal institutions may be created to respond to felt needs, but their operation will not ensure future responsiveness, only the likelihood that some will hear.[14]

Despite these limitations on formal ties between the two North American countries and despite the constant domestic pressure on the Canadian government to behave "independently," in many issue areas Canada and the United States have clearly developed an informal "concordance" or "reconciliation" system, where issues are dealt with more or less on their merits.[15] And in others there is a strain toward what in another political context has been called a community characteristic, harmonized or compatible policies.[16] The Canadians and Americans do not have to spend their energies arguing about the scope, methods, and goals of nonexistent formal organizations, as do those in the European Community.[17] Meanwhile, the *effects* of some kinds of community integration which are deliberately aimed for in Europe have already taken place through "partial incorporation" of the practices of one North American country in the other. Such a process has occurred through parallel action, unplanned by a central authority, as in the case of safety regulations and merchandizing standards.[18] As Harold Lasswell observed about world revolutionary movements, this kind of incorporation can also restrict the pressures for greater integration. Other cooperative objectives can better be achieved multilaterally.

Continuity with the global system appears even clearer when the Australian-American relationship is considered; a major reason for American interest in Australia has been other systems. The social, political, and economic structure of Australia is sufficiently similar to that of Canada and in essence to that in the United States that most of the conditions for a close cooperative relationship exist save one, ease of physical communication. No matter how rapidly persons and words can pass back and forth between Australia and the United States, the process is still costly compared to that for countries closer together. Spontaneity of response is hindered by the fact that it is night in one place when it is day in the other. Despite these practical problems, the postwar period saw many instances of close or parallel action taken by Americans and Australians and considerable cooperation based on complementary capabilities combined with mutual confidence. That other opportunities have so far been missed by the two countries was due not only to distance but to the kinds of leadership in both.

Despite geographical contiguity, cultural and economic distance plus historical tradition prevent Mexico from forming relationships with the United States similar to Canada's. Nevertheless, except in the military field, the striking economic development in Mexico has been accompanied by some remarkable cooperative enterprises, especially along the border. However, Mexicans are looking southward as they develop industrially and have been taking initiatives in the direction of community with other Latin American countries closer to them culturally and less advanced.[19] As for Brazil, in addition to its even more marked drive for greater regional influence, cultural differences combine with physical distance to prevent Brazilians and Americans from having the kind of neighborly relations existing in North America, whether cooperative or competitive.

However elusive the character and confusing the direction of the association between the United States and the four middle powers, some collective needs have clearly been met. Each bilateral system has demonstrated that it is capable of coping with some shared problems. And this was accomplished without the lesser powers losing their dignity. Why not more? The explanation for missed opportunities lies partly in the nature of the systems formed by their relationships to each other, partly within their own political systems. Again, the two North American countries illustrate the limits of integration when the United States is one party.

THE EXERCISE OF INFLUENCE IN THE POLITICS OF
ATTRACTION

Regardless of type of issue, disparity in influence coupled with Canadian caution and the provinces' powers often raised a particular issue to one of high politics in the less influential country; meanwhile, the same question continued to be a bureaucratic problem to be solved on its technical merits so far as the Americans were concerned. That the United States government occasionally provided "side-payments" in the same issue area to facilitate a favorable response increased the self-confidence of the Canadians, some of whom had been afflicted with an inferiority complex when they contemplated dealing with the giant.[20]

The sense of weakness in comparison to the United States that underlies Canadian extreme nationalists' protests gets exported abroad, whence it returns as a "fact" to confirm their suspicions.[21] This kind of feedback does not affect those Canadian officials experienced in dealing with the United States government. They understand that the major problem is that the giant's government actually is composed of many quasi sovereignties and that the American span of attention is more attenuated than the Canadian. Thus former Ambassador to the United States and, later, Undersecretary of State for External Affairs A. E. Ritchie told a House of Commons committee that

the American government . . . is the most approachable and the most immovable government in the world. There is no government anywhere which you can get at more readily and to which you can make your point more readily than that of the United States. . . . But it is a government whose views and policies are very difficult to move.[22]

That different, highly uncoordinated parts of the United States government (or state or local governments) deal directly with their counterparts in Canada helps to ensure that issues do get considered on their merits, separate from each other. The more agencies and levels of policy determination involved, the greater the likelihood that Canadian interests are not ignored when they are in fact affected. Both countries may gain from cooperation, but on some issues the less powerful country may hold better cards and gain greater benefits when it skillfully has choosen its strategy.[23] There may be a core area of strong pulling power, but not all the pull is in one direction.[24]

The lack of coordination in the United States government means that Canada, like others, may be forgotten when Treasury or Commerce makes a decision, but the Canadians know better than those from other countries how and where to penetrate the system. And American officials looking at Canada as a whole seldom see it as a threat to United States interests as a whole. Meanwhile, the much smaller and somewhat more coordinated government of Canada can, when it wishes, focus its claims more intensely.[25]

The failure of the United States to respond to a neighbor's desire may sometimes be attributed to the internal noise in the giant's government; this cacophony may also help to explain why only in the case of Brazil did United States officials try to exploit the disparity of influence flowing from unreciprocal penetration by Americans of the other country.[26]

Aside from the question of asymmetrical penetration, it is noteworthy that the Americans asked for many more kinds of cooperation from their neighbors than from the distant middle powers, and they did so much more frequently. Yet the responses from the nearby middle powers were more balanced in number and weight by reciprocal concessions from the United States for the mutual benefit of both the greater and lesser powers. If one is interested in power rather than in communication and "subsystem steering capacity," this study of Canadian-American and Mexican-American issue management should demonstrate that neither neighbor of the United States was a satellite, despite nationalist fears. That it was only in the late 1960s that Canadians and Mexicans began to look at each other to see how they might profit from experience in dealing with their common neighbor becomes all the more strange.

Concomitant with the greatest degree of responsiveness and the most extensive transnational social and economic relations between Canada and the United States has been the growth of the northern neighbor as a distinctive actor on the world scene.[27] Canadian experience can be instructive for the other middle powers, who share the problems of combining cooperation with the the superpower with the maintenance of their autonomy and of coping with a giant who often seems myopic or deaf. What generalizations can we draw from these countries' various efforts to meet these political tasks? Following are some tentative observations on the management of influence and attraction, as exemplified by their experience.

¶A middle power may engage in **joint activities** with the United States despite the partners' unequal ability to exercise influence on each other without greatly altering that asymmetrical relationship. Privately undertaken, joint enterprises can always be controlled by a concerned government. Public joint enterprises are a sign of some specific interdependence, as well as a step towards increasing each of the two countries' dependence on actions of the other.

¶Middle powers' perspectives on their vulnerability to United States power limit **reciprocal exchanges,** while Americans tend to overestimate in their own favor the mutuality of the benefits to be derived from reciprocity. Dealing with the United States in a multilateral context offers opportunities for genuinely mutual benefit while diluting United States influence. The influence of particular domestic groups limits the most obvious kind of reciprocity, trade concessions, which have been of even greater concern to the middle powers than to the United States. Nevertheless, in recent years these powers have greatly increased their bargaining position with respect to certain commodities.

¶Careful **specification** of the terms of desired bargains with the United States protects a middle power, while such a state can avoid undesired arrangements with the more powerful partner by very general agreements to agree. Even general agreements to cooperate vary both as to what is wanted and readiness to respond, as time brings changes in technology and the global configuration of power.

¶**Geographical proximity** to the United States stimulates and enables a middle power to conduct a more independent global foreign policy than that of more distant middle powers attracted to the United States. Closeness promotes freer trade, enhancing the prosperity of both partners. However, it also encourages more direct investment by Americans, which may combine economic benefits with psychological disadvantages resulting from fear of American economic influence. **Cultural distance** limits the readiness of either party to cooperate on security-related matters when one is less developed. Differences in stage of development also slow down the practice of neighborly cooperation in resource and environmental fields, even when the mutual benefits seem obvious, since the middle powers fear the speed and energy of American action.

¶In bargains between a middle power and the United States, influence in one issue area does not extend automatically to influence in another. A middle power can strictly confine **spillover** in practice to further collaboration in the same field. This is one explanation for a middle power's capacity to exercise some influence over actions of the United States; another is that only part of the United States government needs to be influenced.

¶Formal **channels of communication** can reduce the disparity of power in the issue areas for which they are designed if the United States chooses to deal with a middle power through them. Furthermore, they serve to call the attention of the giant to the needs of the smaller power, as well as vice versa. Informal channels, though less authoritative, may nevertheless be more reliable avenues of influence. Both types are more numerous between the United States and neighboring middle powers than between the United States and the other two, reflecting among other things the larger number of matters of common concern.

¶Although problems which can be handled by bureaucrats on a routine, technical basis usually do not pose difficult questions of national influence, the middle power is more likely than the United States to see power aspects in such questions, thus raising them to levels of **high politics** where power status becomes involved. However, once the problems of reciprocal influence have been faced to the satisfaction of both parties, the matter in question can usually be recommitted to technical experts and treated nonpolitically.

¶For **domestic political** reasons, the middle powers cannot easily respond affirmatively to United States initiatives in many fields of common interests. Domestic groups are always present to exploit the fear of unwanted American influence, because the United States is the giant, and such groups have become increasingly influential in reaction to the spread of the multinational corporation. Within the United States, however, relations with the friendly middle powers rarely arouse political concern except on trade matters.

Are these generalizations likely to apply to a wider variety of relations between different categories of powers? They would appear to be relevant primarily in cases of middle powers, those with substantial influence in certain areas but not so important to world politics as second-tier powers. Among such middle powers, they would mainly apply to those countries attracted to and in turn attractive to only one major power and to cases where the expectation of violence or coercion is absent in a complex system of interactions. Thus, relations between the Soviet Union and either Poland or East Germany, to cite two relationships in a different category, would probably not reveal such characteristics. Whether or not some or all of the generalizations could apply to some European middle powers in their relations to the greater friendly states around them, such as Italy or Sweden with respect to Britain, France, or West Germany, awaits further inquiry. Nor can it yet be said how applicable they would be to relations between adjacent middle powers such as Australia and Indonesia.

CONCLUSIONS: POWER AND RESPONSIVENESS

If the relationship between the United States and the four middle powers—
which though not tied closely to other great powers were yet increasingly
not clients of the Western superpower—is not one of continuously increasing attraction on ever broader fronts, how should it be described? Unlike
greater powers, these countries were not rivals of the United States in larger
power struggles nor in competition to influence others. Formerly within
what was generally recognized as the American sphere of influence, Mexico
and Brazil, it is true, have become forthright leaders of third-world countries
and in the process have become even less aligned with United States policy
in important fields than earlier. The interests of Mexicans and Brazilians, as
is also true of those in the two more developed middle powers, involved rivalry with the Americans primarily in the economic sphere; but this competition was basically among private interests in all five countries, interests
that have often sought to use the state to promote their concerns. Nevertheless, the history of the mid-twentieth century indicates that the relationship
of these four countries with the United States constitutes a special form of
interdependence; even if asymmetrical, it reflects a strong pull in both directions, despite intermittent resistance in various issue areas. Cultural ties
make the attraction especially powerful for Canada and Australia. However,
since the lines through which attraction is manifest are essentially transnational, with many of them private rather than official or at levels of government lower than the highest political authorities, the two neighbors of the
superpower reveal a magnetic effect needing no governmental stimulus. In
fact, efforts of nationalists to promote their own influence, which they identify with that of their state, may be pulling against an irresistible attraction in
the opposite direction, even though they are partly responsible for making
their governments more self-consciously assertive in world politics. Despite
these general observations, no propositions about middle powers and the
United States can ring true unless they take note of the issue area involved
and domestic forces within the countries as well as the global system and its
configuration of power at a particular time. Generalizations also should take
heed of the output, which can be favorable to both parties regardless of
whether the process producing it could be called "integrative."

A large number of the objectives sought elsewhere by more purposeful
and conscious efforts to form political communities can be secured by the

United States and its neighbors or even more distant middle powers in a less structured way (and with less acrimony over the organizational framework). But huge asymmetries rule out much formal institutionalization. Nevertheless, experience has shown that despite difference in size, governments have been responsive to each other's needs in many different issue areas. The closer they are, the greater the need and the readier the response. Opportunities to achieve efficiencies and to avoid unnecessary conflict, especially important among neighbors, could be even more effectively exploited with the use of channels of communication, both bilateral and multilateral, that are readily available. These could serve to facilitate appropriate responses and avoid the lag in perception which otherwise permits events to get out of hand and produce inappropriate national responses later. Such channels could also provide the kind of certainty so necessary to stable and trust-inducing relations, which free the members from fears of unpredictable shifts in response.

Although not the same as influencing the outcome of the superpower's policy on an issue of common concern, any participation, if only through advance information, is often politically satisfying to a middle power. The advantages to the superpower of being more responsive are substantial. The giant power tends to be more hard of hearing than its middle-power friends, and a continuing effort to overcome that tendency may not only make for more effective policy in particular issue areas but also should alleviate or at least cloak the power disparities inherent in its relations with the others. The growing self-confidence of all four middle powers, Canada, Australia, Mexico, and Brazil, has proceeded concomitant with greater mutual awareness.

NOTES

FURTHER IDENTIFICATION OF SOME CITED PERIODICALS

GOVERNMENT PUBLICATIONS

Current Notes on International Affairs, mostly cited below as *Current Notes* and renamed in 1973 *Australian Foreign Affairs Record,* is the official bulletin of the Australian Department of Foreign Affairs (earlier named Department of External Affairs). *External Affairs* was the official bulletin of the Canadian Department of External Affairs, and it was superseded by *International Perspectives. Canada Weekly,* formerly *Canadian Weekly Bulletin,* is a Canadian government publication, as is the monthly brochure, *Canada Today. Relatorio* is the annual report of the Ministry of Foreign Relations in Brazil.

NEWSPAPERS

Greenwich Time is published in Greenwich, Connecticut. *Correio de Manhã, Jornal do Brasil,* and *O Globo* are published in Rio de Janeiro; *El Heraldo, Excelsior,* and *The News* are published in Mexico, D.F.

OTHERS

ACSUS Newsletter, renamed *The American Review of Canadian Studies,* is published by the Association for Canadian Studies in the United States; *Latin America* is a newsletter published in London. *Comercio Exterior de México* is published monthly in English by the Banco Nacional de Comercio Exterior in Mexico, D.F. *Behind the Headlines* is a pamphlet series published by the Canadian Institute of International Affairs, which also publishes the monthly professional magazine *International Journal* and the monthly news chronicle *International Canada.* The Australian Institute of International Affairs publishes *The Australian Outlook.* El Colegio de México publishes the scholarly journal *Foro Internacional* three times a year. *Queen's Quarterly* is the scholarly journal of Queen's University,

Kingston, Ont. *Cooperation and Conflict,* the Nordic Journal of International Politics, is published in Stockholm by the Nordic Committee for the Study of International Politics.

ONE *THE GIANT NEXT DOOR AND FAR AWAY*

1. *Canadian Weekly Bulletin,* December 1, 1971.

2. Melbourne: Sun Books, 1966.

3. Alzira Vargas do Amaral Peixoto, *Getulio Vargas, Meu Pai* (Rio de Janeiro: Editora Globo, 1960).

4. For example, cultural distance rather than geographical distance seems to have been one factor influencing the size of the staff and budget of the United States Information Agency in these countries. According to the forty-second semiannual report of the USIA to Congress, made in 1974, out of a total of 1,185 Americans serving on overseas staffs, 38 were in Brazil, 21 in Mexico, 8 in Australia, and 5 in Canada. These figures can be compared to 10 in Britain, 14 in France, 27 in the Federal Republic of Germany, and 28 in Japan (as well as 32 in India, 16 in Yugoslavia, and 13 in Italy). The third largest expenditure, $4,599,000, was budgeted for Brazil (Germany and Japan were higher) and the seventh largest, $2,162,000, for Mexico (South Vietnam was sixth).

5. These observations derive from Robert Dahl's concepts of "influence gap" and a "probabilistic" definition of power, set forth in his *Modern Political Analysis* (Englewood Cliffs: Prentice-Hall, 1964), pp. 41–46 and 53–54.

6. The concept of spillover and its relations to integration are discussed by Ernst Haas in many of his writings, including his article under "International Integration" in the *International Encyclopedia of the Social Sciences* (1968) and his *Beyond the Nation State* (Stanford: Stanford University Press, 1964).

7. Karl W. Deutsch, *The Analysis of International Relations* (Englewood Cliffs: Prentice-Hall, 1968), pp. 80–82.

8. Kal J. Holsti, *International Politics* (Englewood Cliffs: Prentice-Hall, 1967), pp. 203, 486.

9. See Albert Wohlstetter, "Strength, Interest, and New Technologies," in *The Implications of Military Technology in the 1970s,* Adelphi Papers, no. 46 (London: Institute for Strategic Studies, 1968), p. 12.

10. For example, Walker F. Connor, "Myths of Hemispheric, Continental, Regional, and State Unity," *Political Science Quarterly,* December, 1969, pp. 570–71.

11. Richard N. Merritt, "Noncontiguity and Political Integration," in *Linkage Politics,* ed. James Rosenau (New York: Free Press, 1969), pp. 239–41.

12. Herbert Goldhamer, *The Foreign Powers in Latin America* (Princeton: Princeton University Press, 1972), p. 68.

13. Roger W. Cobb and Charles Elder, *International Community: A Regional and Global Study* (New York: Holt, Rinehart and Winston, 1970), pp. 26–28, 88–89, 129–30.

14. Quincy Wright, *A Study of War* (Chicago: University of Chicago Press, 1942), app. 40.

15. See Oran Young, "Professor Russett: Industrious Tailor to a Naked Emperor," *World Politics,* April, 1969, pp. 487–92; and Bruce M. Russett, "The Young Science of International Politics," *World Politics,* October, 1969, pp. 91–92.

16. Joseph S. Nye, Kal J. Holsti, Roger D. Hansen, among others have asserted this point. James N. Rosenau's often cited "Pre-Theories and Theories of Foreign Policy," in *Approaches to Comparative and International Politics,* ed. R. Barry Farrell (Evanston: Northwestern University Press, 1966), pp. 27–92, defined "issue area" by putting somewhat more stress than this study does upon great differences in the allocation of values, but otherwise his use is one which this study and others have followed (pp. 81–82). Before these scholars, Robert A. Dahl was using the concept in his analysis of domestic politics.

TWO *INSIDE THE FOUR MIDDLE POWERS*

1. Further discussion of these countries' economic life will appear in the treatment of trade issues (chap. 6).

2. During 1945–1963 almost 20 percent of Canada's population growth came from immigration; Louis Parai, *Immigration and Emigration of Professional and Skilled Manpower During the Post-War Period* (Ottawa: Queen's Printer, 1965), p. 1. Between 1947 and 1961, almost three-fourths of the increase in the Australian laborforce was due to immigrants; O. H. K. Spate, *Australia* (London: Ernest Benn, 1968), p. 132.

3. W. L. Morton, *The Canadian Identity* (Madison: University of Wisconsin Press, 1961), p. 110. See Everett C. Hughes, "A Sociologist's View," in *The United States and Canada,* ed. John Sloan Dickey (Englewood Cliffs: Prentice-Hall for the American Assembly, 1964), pp. 9–12, on the ways Canadians and Americans are close.

4. In each country, the foreign ministry was called the Department of External Affairs. The Canadians have retained this title; the Australians in 1973 renamed their ministry the Department of Foreign Affairs.

5. Until the late 1960s, the parliamentary committee on foreign affairs in Australia did not have on it members of the Labor party (then in opposition) because of the party's unwillingness to participate. The Australian committee lacked specialized information, did not publish its hearings, and stimulated very little debate. The Canadian House of Commons Committee on External Affairs and National Defence has been accumulating experience in recent years and does conduct illuminating hearings, with government officials (including others in addition to the prime minister, secretary of state or parliamentary secretary) as well as outside experts testifying. It publishes reports of the hearings.

6. *Economic Almanac, 1967–1968* (New York: Macmillan, 1967), p. 499.

7. Agency for International Development, *Gross National Product: Growth Rates and Trend Data* (Washington, May 1, 1974), pp. 13, 14.

8. One observer encapsulated the political and social structure of Brazil as "rather fluid authoritarianism" and that of Mexico as "stable, secretive corporatism"; Douglas A. Chalmers, "The Demystification of Development," in *Changing Latin America,* ed. Douglas A. Chalmers (New York: Academy of Political Science, 1972), p. 121.

9. See Juarez Rubens Brandão Lopes, "Some Basic Developments in Brazilian Society," in *New Perspectives on Brazil,* ed. Eric N. Baklanoff (Nashville: Vanderbilt University Press, 1966), pp. 57–78.

10. A somewhat similar group appeared in Mexico after the Bay of Pigs invasion in Cuba, and an "Independent Canada" movement arose in the late 1960s which had certain parallels to these Latin manifestations. Independence in all three countries meant liberation from American influence.

11. One possible exception to this rule of congressional subserviency occurred when Quadros suddenly resigned after eight months in office, opening the presidency to the suspect Goulart, currently vice-president. To prevent his assuming unbridled power, Congress converted the Brazilian government from the presidential to the parliamentary system. Like many other formal changes in Brazil's official constitution, this one did not last long.

12. For a forthright statement of *dependencia,* see Osvaldo Sunkel, "Big Business and 'Dependencia': A Latin American View," *Foreign Affairs,* April, 1972, pp. 517–31. Among critiques are two passages in Douglas A. Chalmers, ed., *Changing Latin America* (New York: Academy of Political Science, 1972), one by Philippe C. Schmitter, "Paths to Political Development in Latin America," pp. 99–105, the other by Douglas A. Chalmers, "The Demystification of Development," pp. 115–18.

THREE *RELATIONS WITH THE UNITED STATES: THE INTERWAR YEARS*

1. Although as late as 1926 there circulated among Canadian military districts a top-secret-classified "Defence Scheme No. 1," which provided for the possibility of armed attack by the United States, the document reveals more about its author than about current Canadian-American relations; James Eayrs, *The Art of the Possible: Government and Foreign Policy in Canada* (Toronto: University of Toronto Press, 1961), p. 74, citing C. P. Stacey, *Six Years of War* (Ottawa: Queen's Printer, 1955), p. 30.

2. For isolationist policies in Canada and Australia, see J. D. B. Miller, *Britain and the Old Dominions* (London: Chatto & Windus, 1966), pp. 111–12.

3. That Mexican leaders were trying to protect their country from further American intervention by seeking to keep the United States neutral, too, is persuasively argued by P. Edward Haley, *Revolution and Intervention: The Diplomacy of Taft and Wilson with Mexico, 1910–1917* (Cambridge: MIT Press, 1970), pp. 253–65. He points out the usefulness of Germany as a countervailing power to the threat from the north.

4. James Eayrs, "A Low Dishonest Decade: Aspects of Canadian External Policy, 1931–1939," in Hugh L. Keenleyside and others, *Growth of Canadian Policies in External Affairs* (Durham: Duke University Press, 1960), p. 67. This repudiation was in line with the often quoted declaration of Senator Dandurand at the League of Nations Assembly in 1924 that Canada lived "in a fireproof house far from inflammable materials"; J. Bartlet Brebner, *North Atlantic Triangle* (New Haven: Yale University Press, 1945), p. 281; see also Gerald M. Craig, *The United States and Canada* (Cambridge: Harvard University Press, 1968), pp. 185–86.

5. For the four countries' foreign policies in this era, see, in Brazil's case, Pedro Calmon, *Brasil e America* (Rio de Janeiro: Livraria Jose Olympio, 1944), p. 137; Jose Maria Bello, *Historia da República* (São Paulo: Companhia Editora Nacional, 1964), pp. 298–99, 371–72, 383–84; Delgado de Carvalho, *Organização Social e Política Brasileira* (Rio de Janeiro: Editora Fundo de Cultura, 1963), p. 304; *Relatório do Ministro de Estado das Relações Exteriores, Anno de 1935* (Rio de Janeiro: Imprensa Nacional, 1937), vol. 1, p. 8. For Mexico, see Secretaría de Relaciónes Exteriores, *Un Siglo de Relaciónes Internacionales de Mexico* (Mexico, D.F.: Archivo Historico Diplomatico Mexicano, 1935), pp. 441, 445. For Mexico and Brazil, see Stephen Duggan, *The Two Americas* (New York: Scribner, 1934), pp. 198, 202–7, 209–10. For Australia, see E. M. Andrews, *Isolationism and Appeasement in Australia* (Columbia: University of South Carolina Press, 1970), esp. pp. 33, 65, 70. For Canada, see J. Bartlet Brebner, *Canada: A Modern History* (Ann Arbor: University of Michigan Press, 1960), pp. 415–18; and Hugh L. Keenleyside, "Introduction," in Hugh L. Keenleyside and others, *Growth of Cana-*

dian Policies in External Affairs (Durham: Duke University Press, 1960), pp. 9–11; and for both Canada and Australia, Miller, *Old Dominions,* pp. 111–12.

6. The final constitutional tie, right of appeal to the Privy Council, remained until some years after World War II.

7. Gaddis Smith, "Canadian External Affairs During World War I," in Hugh L. Keenleyside and others, *Growth of Canadian Policies in External Affairs* (Durham: Duke University Press, 1960), p. 55.

8. Thereby he opened the way to the Washington conference on naval disarmament; Craig, *United States and Canada,* pp. 187–89; Brebner, *Canada,* pp. 418–20.

9. Mason Wade, "The Roots of the Relationship," in *The United States and Canada,* ed. John Sloan Dickey (Englewood Cliffs: Prentice-Hall for the American Assembly, 1964), pp. 49–50.

10. Alan Watt, *The Evolution of Australian Foreign Policy, 1938–65* (Cambridge: Cambridge University Press, 1967), p. 60; Miller, *Old Dominions,* pp. 111, 203; Thomas B. Millar, *Australia's Foreign Policy* (Sydney: Angus and Robertson, 1968), pp. 2–3; Frank P. Chambers, Christina Phelps Harris, and Charles C. Bayley, *This Age of Conflict* (New York: Harcourt Brace, 1950), p. 339; Brebner, *Canada,* pp. 416–18, 443–44.

11. W. Macmahon Ball, "Australia's Role in Asia," Australian Institute of International Affairs, Eighteenth Milne Memorial Lecture, Melbourne, November 1, 1967, p. 4.

12. *External Affairs,* June, 1966, pp. 240ff.

13. Ibid.; Wade, "Roots." Canada had no legation in the Soviet Union until 1943.

14. Millar, *Australia's Foreign Policy,* pp. 14–22; Watt, *Australian Foreign Policy,* pp. vii–viii, 20–22, 292–93.

15. Bryce Wood, *The Making of the Good Neighbor Policy* (New York: Columbia University Press, 1961), pp. 121–22; Gordon Connell-Smith, *The Inter-American System* (London: Oxford University Press, 1966), pp. 31–32, 86–87, 97.

16. In Portuguese, "Com os Estados Unidos, mas não a reboque"; quoted by Maurício Nabuco, *Algumas Reflexões Sôbre Diplomacia* (Rio de Janeiro: Irmãos Pongetti, 1955), p. 31. Mueller was foreign minister early in the century. See also E. Bradford Burns, *The Unwritten Alliance: Rio Branco and Brazilian-American Relations* (New York: Columbia University Press, 1966), esp. chap. 7; J. O. de Meira Penna, *Política Externa: Segurança & Desenvolvimento* (Rio de Janeiro: Livrario Agir Editôra, 1967), pp. 30–31.

17. Connell-Smith, *Inter-American System,* p. 58.

18. Wood, *Good Neighbor Policy,* pp. 16–21. The arrival of Dwight Morrow as ambassador in 1927 marked the beginning of improved relations.

19. Such a statement is to be found in Department of State, *Foreign Relations of the United States, 1939,* vol. 5, p. 683 (hereafter cited as *Foreign Relations, US*). Officials from both countries not infrequently referred to the adverse effects on domestic politics that would be brought about by the other government's not acceding to a claim. Bargaining between the Mexican and United States governments often was complicated by the internal tension among officials within each country as well as by the tendency of officials to shift blame for difficulties by passing it on to other officials.

20. Brebner, *Canada,* pp. 448–49, 456–58; Brebner, *North Atlantic Triangle,* pp. 292–93, 306–08.

21. Wade, "Roots," p. 50.

22. *Foreign Relations, US, 1934,* vol. 1, pp. 845–74; Brebner, *Canada,* p. 462; Brebner, *North Atlantic Triangle,* pp. 308–9; F. H. Soward, et al., *Canada in World Affairs: the Pre-War Years* (Toronto: Oxford University Press, 1941), pp. 109, 195–99, 207, 212–14.

23. Except for Nazi Germany, Australia was the only country against which President Roosevelt so used his authority under the Reciprocal Trade Agreements Act, but it was a temporary action; Samuel F. Bemis, *The Latin American Policy of the United States* (New York: Harcourt Brace, 1943), p. 303.

24. John G. Crawford, *Australian Trade Policy, 1942–1966* (Canberra: Australian National University Press, 1968), pp. 393–94; Herbert Burton, "The 'Trade Diversion' Episode of the Thirties," *Australian Outlook,* April, 1968, pp. 7–14; O. H. K. Spate, *Australia,* (London: Ernest Benn, 1968), p. 85; D. F. Nicholson, *Australia's Trade Relations: An Outline History of Australia's Overseas Trading Arrangements* (Melbourne: F. W. Cheshire, 1955), pp. 109ff.

25. Thomas E. Skidmore, *Politics in Brazil, 1930–1964: An Experiment in Democracy* (New York: Oxford University Press, 1967), pp. 41–43.

26. *Foreign Relations, US, 1933,* vol. 5, pp. 13ff; Bemis, *Latin American Policy,* p. 440; John D. Wirth, *The Politics of Brazilian Development, 1930–1954* (Stanford: Stanford University Press, 1970), pp. 22–27, 32–36, 43–48.

27. *Foreign Relations, US, 1934,* vol. 5, pp. 385–91; Bemis, *Latin American Policy,* p. 440.

28. One exception was automobiles. These were assembled in Mexico by American manufacturers and it was they who had requested the higher rates; *Foreign Relations, US, 1938,* vol. 5, pp. 773–83; Wood, *Good Neighbor Policy,* p. 224.

29. Howard F. Cline, *The United States and Mexico,* rev. ed. (New York: Atheneum, 1963), pp. 208–9; Bemis, *Latin American Policy,* pp. 214–17; Samuel F. Bemis, *A Diplomatic History of the United States,* 3rd ed. (New York: Henry Holt, 1950), pp. 562–64.

30. Secretaría de Relaciónes Exteriores, *Un Siglo,* p. 452; idem, *Las Relaciónes Internacionales de Mexico, 1935–1956* (Mexico D.F., 1957), p. 20.

31. "Expropriation by Mexico of Agrarian Properties Owned by American Citizens," *American Journal of International Law Supplement,* 1938, pp. 181–207; Bemis, *Latin American Policy,* pp. 216–17.

32. *Foreign Relations, US, 1930,* vol. 3, pp. 476, 492–93; *1933,* vol. 5, p. 808; *1935,* vol. 4, pp. 754ff., 772ff., 782ff.; *1936,* vol. 5, pp. 705, 710–15, 717–19, 729; *1937,* pp. 690–92; *1938,* vol. 5, pp. 657, 660–61, 674–78, 683, 704, 707, 762–77; *1939,* vol. 5, pp. 654–67.

33. Cline, *United States and Mexico,* pp. 229–42; Charles C. Cumberland, *Mexico: The Struggle for Modernity* (New York: Oxford University Press, 1968), pp. 308–17.

34. Secretaría de Relaciónes Exteriores, *Relaciónes Internacionales,* pp. 34–37. The foreign minister commended the "correct attitude of the United States government for limiting itself to diplomatic suggestions that the Mexican Government and the enterprises negotiate among themselves."

35. Both the American and British oil companies had embarked on a vigorous effort over a wide front to prevent the Mexicans from operating the oilfields economically and selling oil. They organized boycotts among potential buyers, tried to prevent Mexico from getting oil tankers or oil-drilling equipment, and instituted cases in American and European courts alleging that certain oil cargoes had been illegally seized; Cline, *United States and Mexico,* pp. 229–38; *Foreign Relations, US, 1938,* vol. 5, pp. 730ff.; *1939,* vol. 5, pp. 668ff.; 676ff.; 703ff.

36. Wood, *Good Neighbor Policy*, chaps. 8, 9; Bemis, *Latin American Policy*, pp. 345–53; Cline, *United States and Mexico*, pp. 239–51. Mexico had broken off diplomatic relations with Britain in 1938 as a result of the expropriation controversy but renewed relations later through President Roosevelt's intervention. Eventually the British got a settlement of their claims, one that was in some ways more favorable than the American settlement, but not until two years after the end of the war; Cline, *United States and Mexico*, pp. 250–51.

FOUR *WORLD WAR II COLLABORATION*

1. F. H. Soward, et al., *Canada in World Affairs: The Pre-War Years* (Toronto: Oxford University Press, 1941), p. 4.

2. Alan Watt, *The Evolution of Australian Foreign Policy, 1938–65* (Cambridge: Cambridge University Press, 1967), esp. p. 109.

3. *Relatório do Ministro de Estado das Relações Exteriores, Anno de 1939* (Rio de Janeiro: Imprensa Nacional, 1943), p. x; hereafter cited as *Relatório*.

4. Department of State, *Foreign Relations of the United States, 1939*, vol. 5, p. 56; hereafter cited as *Foreign Relations, U.S.*

5. R. G. Casey, *Personal Experience, 1939–1946*, pp. 10–11, quoted in Alan Watt, "The Anzus Treaty: Past, Present and Future," *Australian Outlook*, April, 1970, pp. 18–19.

6. Mackenzie King made no overt response to the first hint of cooperation, which President Roosevelt threw out in a speech at Chatauqua in 1936; Mason Wade, "The Roots of the Relationship," in *The United States and Canada*, ed. John Sloan Dickey (Englewood Cliffs: Prentice-Hall for the American Assembly, 1964), p. 51.

7. The most useful sources for Canadian-American wartime collaboration are Charles P. Stacey, *Six Years of War* (Ottawa: Queen's Printer, 1955); and Stanley W. Dziuban, *Military Relations Between the United States and Canada, 1939–1945* (Washington: Office of the Chief of Military History, Department of the Army, 1959). Also useful are Stetson Conn and Byron Fairchild, *The Framework of Hemisphere Defense* (Washington: Office of the Chief of Military History, Department of the Army, 1960), chaps. 14, 15.

8. Dziuban, *Military Relations*, pp. 48–49, 194–96.

9. Gerald M. Craig, *The United States and Canada* (Cambridge: Cambridge University Press, 1968), p. 216.

10. Dziuban, *Military Relations*, pp. 289–95; Conn and Fairchild, *Hemisphere Defense*, p. 391.

11. Dziuban, *Military Relations*, pp. 259–68; Conn and Fairchild, *Hemisphere Defense*, p. 390; Stacey, *Six Years*, pp. 106–7, 501–2, 506, 511–12.

12. And so were individuals from the two countries. About fifteen thousand Americans enlisted in Canadian forces; C. Cecil Lingard and Reginald G. Trotter, *Canada in World Affairs, September 1941 to May 1944* (Toronto: Oxford University Press, 1950), p. 78. After Pearl Harbor, more than twenty-six thousand Canadians served in the United States armed forces; Dziuban, *Military Relations*, p. 242.

13. Conn and Fairchild, *Hemisphere Defense*, pp. 377–83; Dziuban, *Military Relations*, pp. 88–89, 103–6, 110–16, 122; Charles Foulkes, "The Complications of Continental De-

fense," in *Neighbors Taken for Granted,* ed. Livingston T. Merchant (New York: Praeger, 1966).

14. Late in the war, a United States corps served with the First Canadian Army under command of a Canadian general; there was also much teamwork in Europe between Canadian and American units, ground and air; Dziuban, *Military Relations,* p. 241. In 1944, the Canadian government offered to provide forces for the Central and North Pacific. Plans for a force of thirty thousand Canadian volunteers, to be trained in the United States, organized along American lines, and equipped like the Americans, were being implemented when the Japanese surrendered (ibid., pp. 268–72).

15. For Canadian–United States naval cooperation, which antedated entrance of the United States into the war, see William L. Langer and S. Everett Gleason, *The Undeclared War* (New York: Harper, 1953), p. 431; Dziuban, *Military Relations,* pp. 242–55; Conn and Fairchild, *Hemisphere Defense,* pp. 132–33, 388, 390, 399; Lingard and Trotter, *Canada in World Affairs,* p. 78; H. F. Angus, *Canada and the Far East, 1940–1953* (Toronto: University of Toronto Press, 1953), p. 17.

16. Wilfrid Eggleston, *Canada's Nuclear Story* (London: Harrap Research Publications, 1966), chaps. 4, 5, 6; Leslie R. Groves, *Now It Can Be Told* (New York: Harper, 1962), p. 407.

17. Not only did Prime Minister Menzies declare that because Britain was at war, Australia was, too, but also he spent some precious months in Britain, the center of war decisions, only to lose his office in August, 1941, after he returned home.

18. Watt, *Australian Foreign Policy,* p. 55. J. D. B. Miller, *Britain and the Old Dominions* (London: Chatto & Windus, 1966), p. 132, indirectly quotes from John W. Wheeler-Bennett, *King George VI,* the sour comment of Churchill in January, 1942: "From what I know, I fear they will have a very awkward reception in Washington. Access to the supreme power is extremely difficult. It is only granted to few and then in abundant measure."

19. One of them was replaced without advance notice to the Australian government, which had earlier welcomed him and had even proposed him for supreme commander, previous to MacArthur's coming; Paul Hasluck, *The Government and the People, 1942–1945* (Canberra: Australian War Memorial, 1970), pp. 105–11, 115.

20. Ibid., p. 114.

21. Watt, *Australian Foreign Policy,* p. 56; Hasluck, *Government and People,* 29–32, 38, 73ff.

22. Hasluck, *Government and People,* pp. 13, 35, 114, 167, 182–83, 302, 432, 615.

23. Conn and Fairchild, *Hemisphere Defense,* pp. 327–29; Manoel Thomaz Castello Branco, *O Brasil na II Grande Guerra* (Rio de Janeiro: Biblioteca do Exercito, 1960), pp. 123–28.

24. In patrolling the South Atlantic off Brazil's coast, Brazilian air and naval units were eventually coordinated with those of the United States, serving under the general direction of the admiral of the South Atlantic Force. Conn and Fairchild, *Hemisphere Defense,* pp. 119, 321–23, 278, 298–99; Castello Branco, *Brasil,* pp. 87–89.

25. Conn and Fairchild, *Hemisphere Defense,* pp. 355–56, 363; Howard F. Cline, *The United States and Mexico,* rev. ed. (New York: Atheneum, 1963), pp. 277–78; Wesley Frank Craven and James Lea Cate, *The Army Air Forces in World War II* (Harrisburg: Military Publishing Co., 1954), p. 696; *Excelsior,* July 23, 1967. Mexicans rarely refer to their overseas contribution to the Allied cause in World War II; their government had not contemplated any overseas service at the time it declared war on Germany.

26. On the other hand, both Mexicans and Brazilians demanded that American military men who might be helping at air installations or in such other services as surveying *not* wear their uniforms.

27. Conn and Fairchild, *Hemisphere Defense*, pp. 272–302, 305–6, 312–14, 317, 319, 322, 327.

28. Ibid., pp. 361–62.

29. William L. Langer and S. Everett Gleason, *The Challenge to Isolation* (New York: Harper, 1952), p. 703; Dziuban, *Military Relations*, pp. 11–12.

30. Dziuban, *Military Relations*, p. 48.

31. Ibid., pp. 149–55; Langer and Gleason, *Challenge to Isolation*, pp. 429–33, 684–87; idem., *The Undeclared War*, pp. 427–31.

32. Dziuban, *Military Relations*, pp. 170–80; Lester B. Pearson, *Mike: The Memoirs of the Right Honourable Lester B. Pearson* (Toronto: University of Toronto Press, 1972), vol. 1, pp. 189–97. With respect to the controversial American desire to have the Free French ousted from St. Pierre and Miquelon in December, 1941, Pearson was on sufficiently good personal terms with United States Minister J. Pierrepont Moffatt that he could tell the American official emphatically to report to Secretary Hull Canada's adamant opposition; *Mike*, p. 200.

33. As Lester Pearson later put it, the Canadians had to take care to avoid "being squeezed out, not squeezed between"; *Mike*, pp. 211–15.

34. Conn and Fairchild, *Hemisphere Defense*, p. 372.

35. Dziuban, *Military Relations*, p. 49. The unfortified-border provisions of the historic Rush-Bagot treaty had included bans on most armed naval vessels. These prohibitions were progressively relaxed for the duration of the war, first at the instance of one country, then of the other; ibid., pp. 278–80.

36. Conn and Fairchild, *Hemisphere Defense*, pp. 391–403; Dziuban, *Military Relations*, pp. 181–240; Stacey, *Six Years*, pp. 153–58; F. H. Soward, *Canada in World Affairs, From Normandy to Paris, 1944–46* (Toronto: University of Toronto Press, 1950), p. 259; Lingard and Trotter, *Canada in World Affairs*, pp. 67–77.

37. Conn and Fairchild, *Hemisphere Defense*, pp. 391–95, 398–99; Dziuban, *Military Relations*, p. 219; Lingard and Trotter, *Canada in World Affairs*, p. 67.

38. Conn and Fairchild, *Hemisphere Defense*, pp. 405–6.

39. Dziuban, *Military Relations*, pp. 9–10, 281–83; Conn and Fairchild, *Hemisphere Defense*, p. 370.

40. Dziuban, *Military Relations*, p. 281; also Conn and Fairchild, *Hemisphere Defense*, p. 390. Reciprocity could operate in reverse, too. After the United States entered the war, Canada accepted the need to transfer gradually Americans who had been part of the air-training program or in its armed forces to service in the United States, if the individuals so requested; and later similar arrangements were made for Canadians serving in the United States armed forces (Dziuban, *Military Relations*, pp. 274–76).

41. Roger MacGregor Dawson, *Canada in World Affairs: Two Years of War, 1939–41* (Toronto: Oxford University Press, 1943), p. 62; Conn and Fairchild, *Hemisphere Defense*, pp. 369, 387, 391.

42. Lingard and Trotter, *Canada in World Affairs*, p. 85.

43. Ibid., p. 215.

44. Ibid., pp. 86, 197.

45. Trevor R. Reese, *Australia, New Zealand and the United States: a Survey of International Relations* (London: Oxford University Press, 1969), pp. 15–16.

46. Hasluck, *Government and People*, p. 224. He points out that Melbourne and Sydney "knew the Americans chiefly as transient troops while Queensland knew them in much larger numbers as troops in training or in occupation of permanent encampments or quarters. Brisbane . . . and northern coastal towns . . . were possessed by the Americans in a manner and on a scale quite different from that experienced in any other part of Australia."

47. Ibid., p. 621.

48. Dwight D. Eisenhower, *Crusade in Europe* (Garden City: Permabooks, 1952), p. 36.

49. Reese, *Australia, New Zealand*, p. 24; Hasluck, *Government and People*, pp. 566–72.

50. *Foreign Relations, US, 1940*, vol. 5, pp. 59–61.

51. Samuel F. Bemis, *The Latin American Policy of the United States* (New York: Harcourt, Brace, 1943), pp. 347–49; Bryce Wood, *The Making of the Good Neighbor Policy* (New York: Columbia University Press, 1961), 247–59; Samuel F. Bemis, *A Diplomatic History of the United States* (New York: Henry Holt, 1950), pp. 568–69.

52. Conn and Fairchild, *Hemisphere Defense*, pp. 344–47; Bemis, *Diplomatic History*, p. 567.

53. Conn and Fairchild, *Hemisphere Defense*, pp. 258, 348–50, 357–61.

54. Langer and Gleason, *Challenge to Isolation*, p. 620; Conn and Fairchild, *Hemisphere Defense*, pp. 352–54.

55. Conn and Fairchild, *Hemisphere Defense*, pp. 355–56. Peak enrollment of about 165 officers and men was reached in July, 1943. The most important programs were those at the two naval training schools, the Subchaser Training Center at Miami and the Air Training Center at Corpus Christi.

56. Wood, *Good Neighbor Policy*, pp. 411–12.

57. Langer and Gleason, *Undeclared War*, p. 709.

58. Conn and Fairchild, *Hemisphere Defense*, pp. 353–155; Bemis, *Latin American Policy*, pp. 349–51.

59. Department of State, *Bulletin*, August 13, 1944; Secretaría de Relaciónes Exteriores, *Las Relaciónes Internacionales de Mexico, 1935–1956* (Mexico, D.F., 1957), pp. 65–66, 75; Cline, *United States and Mexico*, p. 275.

60. Cline, *United States and Mexico*, p. 276; Department of State, *Bulletin*, January 23, 1943, p. 873; Secretaría de Relaciónes Exteriores, *Relaciónes Internacionales*, p. 86.

61. Secretaría de Relaciónes Exteriores, *Relaciónes Internacionales*, p. 60. Some Mexican troops crossed from Nogales to Tijuana via San Diego on December 9, 1941 (Department of State, *Bulletin*, December 9, 1941, p. 484).

62. *Foreign Relations, US, 1939*, vol. 5, p. 56; ibid., *1940*, vol. 5, pp. 139–43. American fears of internal disorder were one motivation for supplying Mexico with arms; Conn and Fairchild, *Hemisphere Defense*, p. 213.

63. Secretaría de Relaciónes Exteriores, *Relaciónes Internacionales*, pp. 46–47, 59.

64. Conn and Fairchild, *Hemisphere Defense*, pp. 253ff., 266ff., 296; Langer and Gleason, *Undeclared War*, pp. 600–601.

65. Conn and Fairchild, *Hemisphere Defense*, pp. 285, 297.

66. Ibid., pp. 253ff., 296.

67. Ibid., pp. 314–17.

68. Ibid., p. 326.

69. Ibid., pp. 279–83, 293–96, 314–17.

70. Langer and Gleason, *Challenge to Isolation,* pp. 617–18; idem, *Undeclared War,* p. 600; Wood, *Good Neighbor Policy,* pp. 312, 617–18; Conn and Fairchild, *Hemisphere Defense,* pp. 269–72; John D. Wirth, *The Politics of Brazilian Development, 1930–1954* (Stanford: Stanford University Press, 1970), pp. 62–68; Thomas E. Skidmore, *Politics in Brazil, 1930–1964: An Experiment in Democracy* (New York: Oxford University Press, 1967), pp. 44–47; Percy W. Bidwell, *Economic Defense of Latin America* (Boston: World Peace Foundation, 1941), pp. 45–46.

71. Wirth, *Brazilian Development,* pp. 114–18, 244.

72. Bidwell, *Economic Defense,* pp. 44, 75; Langer and Gleason, *Challenge to Isolation,* p. 277; Bemis, *Latin American Policy,* p. 352.

73. Skidmore, *Politics in Brazil,* p. 45; *Relatório, Anno de 1942,* pp. 34ff., 38–42.

74. *Relatório, Anno de 1942,* pp. 34–42.

75. Langer and Gleason, *Challenge to Isolation,* p. 701. The Brazilian government's inertia in protecting itself from subversion was partly due to uncertainty about Hitler's ultimate defeat; Conn and Fairchild, *Hemisphere Defense,* pp. 240, 247–48, 303, 306.

76. From a paper issued by the State Department and the Foreign Economic Administration, quoted in Conn and Fairchild, *Hemisphere Defense,* p. 234.

77. Conn and Fairchild, *Hemisphere Defense,* p. 322.

78. Later, the Americans were willing to play this game too; Secretary Hull was eager in 1944 to send extra war materiel to Brazil for its southern border in order to impress "the present military gang in control of Argentina"; Alfred Vagts, *Defense and Diplomacy* (New York: King's Crown Press, 1956), p. 209, quoting Cordell Hull, *Memoirs,* vol. 2, pp. 1309ff.

79. For Brazilian examples, see Conn and Fairchild, *Hemisphere Defense,* pp. 273–96, 304–12; and for Mexico, ibid., pp. 333–41, 344–47.

80. Cline, *United States and Mexico,* p. 295.

81. Hasluck, *Government and People,* pp. 49, 151, 228, 630; Vincent Massey, *What's Past Is Prologue: The Memoirs of the Right Honourable Vincent Massey, C.H.* (Toronto: Macmillan, 1963), pp. 348–64.

82. Hasluck, *Government and People,* pp. 427–28, 438–39.

83. Ibid., p. 36.

84. Watt, *Australian Foreign Policy,* pp. 51–52; Hasluck, *Government and People,* p. 23.

85. Hasluck, *Government and People,* p. 423.

86. Reese, *Australia, New Zealand,* pp. 32–35; Watt, *Australian Foreign Policy,* pp. 73–77; W. J. Hudson, *Australian Diplomacy* (South Melbourne: Macmillan, 1970), pp. 36–37.

87. Conn and Fairchild, *Hemisphere Defense,* pp. 175, 267.

88. Pedro Calmon, *Brazil e América* (Rio de Janeiro: Livraria José Olympio, 1944), pp. 180–82; Langer and Gleason, *Challenge to Isolation,* pp. 617–18; Estevão Leitão de Carvalho, *Memórias de um Soldado Legalista* (Rio de Janeiro: Emprensa do Exército, 1964),

vol. 3, pp. 371–72, 421; Estevão de Carvalho, *A Serviço do Brasil Na Segunda Guerra Mundial,* 2nd ed. (Rio de Janeiro: Editora a Noite, 1952), pp. 8–24.

89. Thus Canadians made sure "that arrangements entered into for a specific purpose in time of war were not allowed to drift on when their immediate object had been fulfilled and when they might begin to cause embarrassment"; G. P. de T. Glazebrook, *A History of Canadian External Relations,* p. 427, quoted in Conn and Fairchild, *Hemisphere Defense,* p. 404.

90. Robert A. Mackay, *Canadian Foreign Policy, 1945–1954* (Toronto: McClelland and Stewart, 1970), pp. 177–80.

91. Some military officers did learn. The American general who arranged, in the spring of 1943, a touchy project for weather and communications facilities at certain Mexican airfields, involving Mexicans and Americans working together, advised that to ensure success extreme care be taken to select United States personnel not only technically qualified but "also qualified temperamentally to work . . . [in] daily close association with the Mexican personnel"; Conn and Fairchild, *Hemisphere Defense,* pp. 350–51.

92. Dziuban, *Military Relations,* chap. 2; and Charles P. Stacey, "The Canadian-American Joint Board on Defense, 1940–1945," *International Journal,* Spring, 1954.

93. See Dziuban, *Military Relations,* pp. 134–35, for the kinds of parallel channels of communication, so numerous as to make coordination very difficult.

94. Ibid., pp. 72–76.

95. Ibid., pp. 82–85.

96. Soward, *Canada in World Affairs, 1944–46,* pp. 277–78. As Lester Pearson recorded, there were in Washington Canadian counterparts for the staff of all United States war agencies; *Mike,* pp. 206–7.

97. J. D. B. Miller, *Britain and the Old Dominions* (London: Chatto & Windus, 1966), pp. 131–33; Reese, *Australia, New Zealand,* p. 26; Hasluck, *Government and People,* pp. 227–28; Hudson, *Australian Diplomacy,* p. 35; Dziuban, *Military Relations,* p. 84.

98. Watt, *Australian Foreign Policy,* pp. 65–67; Hasluck, *Government and People,* pp. 227–28.

99. Hasluck, *Government and People,* pp. 48, 52–54, 227, 229–30, 474, 630–31.

100. Ibid., pp. 44–45, 473. As Australian Prime Minister Menzies put it, the British prime minister had no conception of the dominions as separate entities, and the more distant the problem from the heart of the Empire, the less he thought of it; Watt, *Australian Foreign Policy,* p. 60, quoting Paul Hasluck, *The Government and the People, 1939–41* (Canberra: Australian War Memorial, 1951), p. 347.

101. And thus caused much unhappiness for Prime Minister Curtin; Hasluck, *Government and People,* pp. 132, 310–11.

102. Ibid., pp. 150–56, 229.

103. Conn and Fairchild, *Hemisphere Defense,* pp. 277, 314, 319.

104. Leitão de Carvalho, *A Serviço do Brasil,* esp. pp. 176–77, 179ff., 187–93, 198–219.

105. Castello Branco, *Brasil,* pp. 123–24.

106. A year earlier a joint board had been established to coordinate the preparation of military facilities there (Conn and Fairchild, *Hemisphere Defense,* pp. 310, 318–19, 326–27.

107. Ibid., pp. 194, 198–200.

108. For example, the Mexican government created an agency to cooperate in repressing the transit of dangerous persons, following the report of the seven-member inter-American emergency advisory committee for political defense, in July, 1943 (Secretaría de Relaciónes Exteriores, *Relaciónes Internacionales*, pp. 72–73). This was the kind of action which the Mexican government would not have taken under direct United States pressure.

109. More than once, the Mexican section drew up a proposal identical to that of the American section and then put it to the latter for approval, perhaps a way of balancing the appearance, if not the substance.

110. Conn and Fairchild, *Hemisphere Defense*, pp. 341–43, 361.

111. Ibid., p. 309.

112. An official report from the foreign ministry remarked that thereby Brazil had "passed from the continental plane to that in which today the great powers deliberate"; *Relatóio, Anno de 1943*, p. xvii.

113. Conn and Fairchild, *Hemisphere Defense*, pp. 194, 285, 287, 299, 328.

114. Hasluck, *Government and People*, pp. 231–33, 236–37, 438–40, 574–76. The Australian government strove to make the Americans "feel at home" and gave them "the run of the house." Prior to the creation of the South-West Pacific Command, the American chief of staff was put "on the same footing as the three Australian Chiefs of Staff as though he were at the head of a fourth arm of the services"; ibid., pp. 230–31.

115. For a time, the Canadian prime minister acted as an intermediary between President Roosevelt and Prime Minister Churchill, thus engaging in very high politics on a world level.

116. Eggleston, *Canada's Nuclear Story*, pp. 64–85; Groves, *Now It Can Be Told*, chap. 9, pp. 125–37. Scientists Vannevar Bush and James Conant shared some of General Groves's exclusivist views on exchange of information.

117. See Department of State, *Bulletin*, August 25, 1943, pp. 122–23, for an example during a Roosevelt visit to Ottawa. In some contrast was the rarity of personal contacts between the American and Mexican heads of state. On a visit to Monterey, Mexico, in April, 1943, the first time in thirty-four years that an American president had met a Mexican president face to face, President Roosevelt said that he looked forward to more neighborly visits; ibid., April 24, 1943, p. 348.

118. Mackay, *Canadian Foreign Policy*, p. 225.

119. Dziuban, *Military Relations*, pp. 33–46; Conn and Fairchild, *Hemisphere Defense*, pp. 375–77, 386; Hugh L. Keenleyside, "The Canada–United States Permanent Joint Board on Defense," *International Journal*, Winter, 1960–61; Stacey, "Joint Board on Defense."

120. For the 1938 soundings, see Mason Wade, "Roots," p. 51.

121. James Eayrs, *The Art of the Possible: Government and Foreign Policy in Canada* (Toronto: University of Toronto Press, 1961), pp. 185–87.

122. Dawson, *Canada in World Affairs*, pp. 73–74.

123. Ibid., p. 173.

124. George F. G. Stanley, *Canada's Soldiers, 1604–1954: The Military History of an Unmilitary People* (Toronto: Macmillan, 1954), pp. 364–75; Soward, *Canada in World Affairs, 1944–46* p. 268.

125. Dziuban, *Military Relations,* p. 340.

126. A few, probably less than two hundred, were eventually permitted at the three air ferrying bases of Natal, Belem, and Recife, in northeast Brazil.

127. Conn and Fairchild, *Hemisphere Defense,* p. 336.

128. Alfonso Arinos de Melo Franco, *Un Estadista da República* (Rio de Janeiro: Livraria José Olympio Editôra, 1955), vol. 3, pp. 1567–68, 1578.

129. Yet Roosevelt explained to American military planners more than once "why President Vargas of Brazil could not leap into action and give us permission to put more troops on the Natal Peninsula." He "had to feel his way—be sure of his ground"; Conn and Fairchild, *Hemisphere Defense,* p. 309, quoting notes of a White House meeting of January 4, 1942.

130. Inevitably, some social friction developed from the presence of very large numbers of American soldiers in Australia; Hasluck, *Government and People,* p. 225.

FIVE *POSTWAR COLLABORATION IN DEFENSE*

1. Dale C. Thompson, *Louis St. Laurent: Canadian* (New York: St. Martin's Press, 1968), p. 181; Robert A. Mackay, *Canadian Foreign Policy, 1945–1954* (Toronto: McClelland and Stewart, 1970), pp. 177–78; Blair Fraser, "Canada: Mediator or Busybody?" in *Canada's Role as a Middle Power* ed. J. King Gordon (Toronto: Canadian Institute of International Affairs, 1966), p. 8.

2. See Adolfo López Mateos, *Presencia Internacional,* (Mexico, D.F., 1963), vol. 1, p. 543.

3. Mario Ojeda Gomez, "Mexico as a Middle Power," in *Canadas Role as a Middle Power,* ed. J. King Gordon (Toronto: Canadian Institute of International Affairs, 1966), p. 127.

4. David Wood, *Armed Forces in Central and South America,* Adelphi Papers, no. 34 (London: International Institute for Strategic Studies, April, 1967), p. 33.

5. *The Military Balance, 1967–1968* (London: International Institute for Strategic Studies, 1967), pp. 20, 27, 33; Alfred Stepan, *The Military in Politics: Changing Patterns in Brazil* (Princeton: Princeton University Press, 1971), p. 26; Joseph E. Loftus, *Latin American Defense Expenditures, 1938–1965* (Santa Monica: Rand Corporation, 1968), pp. 37, 49.

6. *Jornal do Brasil* May 8, 1966.

7. Dean Acheson, *Present at the Creation* (New York: Norton, 1969), pp. 497–98; Senate Committee on Foreign Relations, *United States–Latin American Relations, Post-World War II Political Developments in Latin America: A Study,* 86th Cong., 1st sess. (November 19, 1959), p. 32.

8. Richard N. Rosecrance, *Australian Diplomacy and Japan, 1945–1951* (Melbourne University Press, 1962), chap. 5; Trevor R. Reese, *Australia, New Zealand and the United States: A Survey of International Relations, 1941–1968* (London: Oxford University Press, 1969), pp. 54–55; Alan Watt, *The Evolution of Australian Foreign Policy, 1938–1965* (Cambridge: Cambridge University Press, 1967), pp. 100–101; Alan Watt, *Australian Diplomat* (Sydney: Angus and Robertson, 1972), p. 185; John J. Dedman, "Encounter Over Manus," *Australian Outlook,* August, 1966, pp. 135–53; J. D. B. Miller, *Britain and the Old Dominions* (London: Chatto & Windus, 1966), pp. 171–72.

9. Watt, *Australian Diplomat,* pp. 174–76; Thomas B. Miller, *Australia's Foreign Policy* (Sydney: Angus and Robertson, 1968), pp. 195–96; Rosecrance, *Australian Diplomacy,* p. 184.

10. *Current Notes on International Affairs,* May, 1969, pp. 216, 235, June, 1969, pp. 323–33 (hereafter cited as *Current Notes*); *New York Times,* August 19, 1971.

11. Ian Bellany and James Richardson, "Australian Defence Procurement," in *Problems of Australian Defence,* ed. H. G. Gelber (Melbourne: Oxford University Press, 1970), pp. 253–54, 258; H. G. Gelber, *The Australian-American Alliance, Costs and Benefits* (Baltimore: Penquin Books, 1968), p. 35; Thomas B. Millar, "Partnership in Defence," in *Pacific Orbit: Australian-American Relations Since 1942,* ed. Norman Harper (Melbourne: F. W. Cheshire, 1968), p. 36.

12. For further discussion, see sections on Reciprocity and Domestic Politics.

13. As Prime Minister Trudeau told some school children in the spring of 1971, referring to continental defense, "We don't want to leave that only to the Americans" (*Canadian Weekly Bulletin,* May 12, 1971).

14. James Eayrs, *Northern Approaches: Canada and the Search for Peace* (Toronto: Macmillan, 1961), p. 40. This "geopolitical fatality of position" was underscored by General Jean V. Allard, a former Canadian chief of staff, when he remarked that the day a would-be neutral Canada permitted the United States to defend it unilaterally its neutrality would cease; Twelfth Annual University of Windsor Seminar on Canadian-American Relations, held at Columbia University, New York, November 17, 1970. See a report of his remarks in J. Alex Murray, ed., *Canada: The Unknown Neighbour* (Windsor: University of Windsor Press, 1971), p. 11.

15. F. H. Soward, *Canada in World Affairs, From Normandy to Paris, 1944–1946* (Toronto: University of Toronto Press, 1950), pp. 267ff; Robert A. Spencer, *Canada in World Affairs: From UN To NATO, 1946–1949* (Toronto: Oxford University Press, 1959), pp. 307ff.; Jon B. McLin, *Canada's Changing Defense Policy, 1957–1963* (Baltimore: Johns Hopkins Press, 1967), pp. 11–12; George F. G. Stanley, *Canada's Soldiers, 1604–1954: The Military History of an Unmilitary People* (Toronto: Macmillan, 1954), pp. 370–75.

16. In January, 1973, the two countries agreed that Canada should take over operation and maintenance of most of the Goose Bay facilities and installations, while the United States Air Force would continue to make use of them under lease until 1976; *Canadian Weekly Bulletin,* January 31, 1973; *International Canada,* June, 1973, p. 192.

17. "Canadian Defence Policy in the Nuclear Age," *Behind the Headlines,* May, 1961, p. 5.

18. NADGE (NATO Air Defense Ground Environment) provides a somewhat comparable system of warning and communications for NATO.

19. For example, the United States supplied certain aircraft to Canada to enable the latter to pay the cost of maintaining the Pinetree stations.

20. Melvin A. Conant, *The Long Polar Watch* (New York: Harper, 1962), pp. 39–41; McLin, *Defense Policy,* pp. 27–28; Roger F. Swanson, "NORAD Origins and Operations: Choices for Canada," *International Perspectives,* November–December, 1972, pp. 4–5. The Mid-Canada line was discontinued in 1965, and the Pinetree line was partly discontinued and otherwise absorbed into the contiguous radar coverage.

21. *New York Times,* May 10, 1975.

22. *International Canada,* March, 1973, pp. 104–5, April, 1973, pp. 126–27.

23. *Atlantic Community News,* October, 1967. An extensive discussion of NORAD is given in chapter 3 of McLin, *Defense Policy;* more recent information appears in Swanson, "NORAD."

24. McLin, *Defense Policy,* chap. 7; Robert W. Reford, "Merchant of Death?" *Behind the Headlines,* October, 1968, pp. 16–17; *International Canada,* November, 1971, p. 218, October, 1972, p. 166; John J. Kirton, "The Consequences of Integration: The Case of Defence Production Sharing Arrangements," in *Continental Community? Independence and Integration in North America* ed. Andrew Axline et al. (Toronto: McClelland and Stewart, 1974), pp. 122–24.

25. McLin, *Defense Policy,* p. 192; Kirton, "Consequences of Integration," pp. 126–27.

26. McLin, *Defense Policy,* pp. 61–84, 179–80; Conant, *Polar Watch,* pp. 154–61; Eayrs, *Northern Approaches,* pp. 25ff. A less fortunate attempt to respond to the Canadian government's needs, this one encouraged by members of Congress as well, later turned out to be counterproductive. The languishing BOMARC program, whose threatened extinction had not been discussed with the Canadian government, was extended in part to make good on earlier promises to Canadian officials, with after-effects to be noted below (McLin, *Defense Policy,* 84–100, 95–97).

27. *International Canada,* March, 1973, pp. 104–6, April, 1973, pp. 126–29; Melvin A. Conant, "A Perspective on Defence: the Canada-United States Compact," *Behind the Headlines,* September, 1974, pp. 19–22; *New York Times,* May 8, 1975.

28. *International Canada,* June, 1972, p. 105.

29. Spencer, *Canada in World Affairs,* p. 317; Lord Sherfield, "On the Diplomatic Trail with LBP: Some Episodes, 1930–1972," *International Journal,* Winter, 1973–74, pp. 75–82.

30. The key provisions of the Inter-American Treaty of Reciprocal Assistance signed at Rio de Janeiro on September 2, 1947, that relate to collective security are the members' obligation to interpret an armed attack on one as an armed attack on all and to assist in meeting it, to consult concerning collective measures if there is a threat of armed attack or other danger to the territorial integrity and independence of the American states, and to put into effect specified sanctions by a two-thirds vote.

31. Department of Defense, *Military Assistance and Foreign Military Sales Facts,* March, 1970, p. 13. See also Alfred Stepan, *Military in Politics,* p. 332; David Wood, *Armed Forces,* p. 23. The ten conditions appear in Senate Special Committee to Study the Foreign Aid Program, *Two Studies,* 85th Cong., 1st sess. (March, 1957), p. 162.

32. Department of State, *The Mutual Security Program: Fiscal Year 1961, A Summary Presentation* (1961), pp. 108–19; Senate Committee on Foreign Relations, *United States-Latin American Relations;* Senate Committee on Foreign Relations, *Survey of the Alliance for Progress: The Latin American Military, A Study,* 90th Cong., 1st sess. (October 9, 1967), pp. 28–31.

33. The United States recognized that the island was exclusively Brazilian, the improvements would belong to Brazil, no indemnity would be exacted if permission were terminated, and the agreement was to run for five years but be continued if both countries agreed. *Relatório do Ministro de Estado das Relações Exteriores, Anno de 1957* (Rio de Janeiro: Imprensa Nacional, n.d.), pp. 5, 38; *Anais da Camara Dos Deputados, 1958,* November 28–December 4, 1958, vol. 24, pp. 368–69.

34. Canada's mutual assistance to the allies eventually totaled more than $2 billion, including not only armaments but also training of pilots in Canada. See Harald von Riekhoff, "NATO: To Stay or Not to Stay," in *An Independent Foreign Policy in Canada?* ed. Stephen Clarkson (Toronto: McClelland and Stewart, 1968), pp. 160–72.

35. See Alan Watt, "The ANZUS Treaty: Past, Present and Future," *Australian Outlook,* April, 1970, pp. 22–24; Watt, *Australian Diplomat,* pp. 179–85; Watt, *Australian Foreign Pol-*

icy, pp. 100ff.; Percy Spender, *Exercises in Diplomacy,* (New York: New York University Press, 1969), pp. 34–190; Reese, *Australia, New Zealand,* pp. 52ff.

36. The security treaty between Australia, New Zealand, and the United States signed on September 1, 1951, provided, inter alia, that each would separately and jointly "maintain and develop [its] individual and collective capacity to resist armed attack," consult together when any party believed its territorial integrity, political independence, or security in the Pacific was threatened, and act to meet a common danger according to its constitutional processes.

37. Millar, *Australia's Foreign Policy,* pp. 122–23.

38. Ibid., p. 275.

39. McLin, *Defense Policy,* pp. 12–19, gives a concise summary of Canada's entrance into NATO. For a contemporary account, see William A. Willoughby, "Canada and the North Atlantic Pact," *Virginia Quarterly Review,* September, 1949, pp. 429–42.

40. Millar, *Australia's Foreign Policy,* p. 118.

41. Ibid., p. 33.

42. Peyton V. Lyon, "Beyond NATO?" *International Journal,* Spring, 1974, p. 273.

43. See (Canadian) Ministry of Defence, *White Paper on Defence: Defence in the Seventies* (Ottawa: Queen's Printer, August 1971); see *Armed Forces Journal International,* April, 1973 (which is a special issue on Canada).

44. Reese, *Australia, New Zealand,* pp. 64, 292.

45. Millar, *Australia's Foreign Policy,* pp. 128–29, 297–98.

46. See Alan Watt's description of the conference in *Australian Diplomat,* pp. 22–25.

47. Thomas B. Millar, *Australia's Defence* (Melbourne: Melbourne University Press, 1965), pp. 88–90; Millar, *Australia's Foreign Policy,* p. 128; *Current Notes,* September, 1969, pp. 547–59; Norman Harper, "The American Alliance," in *Pacific Orbit: Australian-American Relations Since 1942,* ed. Norman Harper (Melbourne: F. W. Cheshire, 1968), pp. 15–16; Reese, *Australia, New Zealand,* p. 287; Arthur Burns, "Australia and the Nuclear Balance," in *Problems of Australian Defence,* ed. H. G. Gelber (Melbourne: Oxford University Press, 1970), pp. 144–45, 154–55; *New York Times,* May 4, 1969, November 14, 1970; Colin S. Rubenstein, "Australian Science Policy" (Ph.D. diss., Columbia University, 1973), pp. 133, 190–91; Gordon Greenwood and Norman Harper, *Australia in World Affairs, 1961–1965* (Melbourne: F. W. Cheshire, 1968), pp. 339–43. See the section on Domestic Politics for further developments.

48. Millar, *Australia's Foreign Policy,* pp. 119, 122, 136; J. D. B. Miller, "Problems of Australian Foreign Policy, June–December, 1963," *Australian Journal of Politics and History,* April, 1964, pp. 10–15; Miller, *Old Dominions,* pp. 206–7; Peter King, "Problems of Australian Foreign Policy, January–June 1964," *Australian Journal of Politics and History,* October, 1964, pp. 288–89; Reese, *Australia, New Zealand,* pp. 219–24; Watt, "ANZUS Treaty," p. 29; Robert O'Neill, "Malaysia and Singapore," in *Problems of Australian Defence,* ed. H. G. Gelber (Melbourne: Oxford University Press, 1970), pp. 102, 32), citing Millar, *Australia's Defence,* p. 80, and second edition (1969), pp. 62–63.

49. Watt, "ANZUS Treaty," pp. 33–35. The Whitlam government withdrew the ground forces from Singapore but maintained an air squadron in Malaysia; Peter King, "Whither Whitlam?" *International Journal,* Summer, 1974, pp. 424–25.

50. McLin, *Defense Policy,* p. 189.

51. Peyton V. Lyon, *Canada in World Affairs, 1961–1963* (Toronto: Oxford University Press, 1968), pp. 32–51; McLin, *Defense Policy,* pp. 156–58.

52. For Canada's response during the Berlin crisis, see McLin, *Defense Policy,* pp. 109–10; Lyon, *Canada in World Affairs,* pp. 15–24; Conant, *Polar Watch,* p. 176.

53. Watt, *Australian Foreign Policy,* p. 162.

54. Harper, "American Alliance," p. 14.

55. Reese, *Australia, New Zealand,* pp. 65–67, 201; Watt, *Australian Foreign Policy,* pp. 85, 94, 99–104.

56. Acheson, *Present at the Creation,* p. 502; Spender, *Diplomacy,* p. 64.

57. Spender, *Diplomacy,* p. 147; Watt, *Australian Diplomat,* pp. 179–81.

58. Quoted by Watt, *Australian Foreign Policy,* p. 124, from *Current Notes,* November, 1953, p. 657.

59. Spender, *Diplomacy,* p. 42.

60. On occasion, leaders of the Canadian government defended their political position in Parliament by referring to the ways in which they took part in consultations, as did the secretary of state for external affairs during the 1958 Berlin crisis; House of Commons Standing Committee on External Affairs, *Minutes of Proceedings and Evidence,* March 9, 1959, pp. 19, 23–24 (hereafter cited as Commons External Affairs Committee, *Minutes*).

61. Gerald M. Craig, *The United States and Canada* (Cambridge: Harvard University Press, 1968), p. 227.

62. *International Canada,* February, 1971, pp. 43–44; Bruce Thordarson, *Trudeau and Foreign Policy: A Study in Decision Making* (Toronto: Oxford University Press, 1972), chap. 5, "The NATO Decision," esp. pp. 138–42; *Ottawa Citizen,* March 31, 1971.

63. Charles Foulkes, "The Complications of Continental Defense," in *Neighbors Taken for Granted,* ed. Livingston T. Merchant (New York: Praeger, 1966), p. 101.

64. James Eayrs, *The Art of the Possible: Government and Foreign Policy in Canada* (Toronto: University of Toronto Press, 1961), p. 122, citing *House of Commons Debates,* March 17, 1960, p. 2192.

65. H. G. Gelber, "The U.S.A. and Australia," in *Problems of Australian Defence,* ed. H. G. Gelber (Melbourne: Oxford University Press, 1970), p. 89.

66. Omitted from this section are Mexico, which deliberately tried to keep aloof from the United States in defense matters, and Brazil, where the closest relations were between military officers of the two countries, to be discussed later.

67. Senate Committee on Foreign Relations, *Hearings, United States Policy Toward Europe,* 89th Cong., 2nd sess. (1966), p. 2.

68. Matthew J. Abrams, *The Canada–United States Interparliamentary Group* (Ottawa: Parliamentary Centre for Foreign Affairs and Foreign Trade and Canadian Institute of International Affairs, 1973), pp. 73–74.

69. (Canadian) Department of External Affairs, "The Canada–United States Permanent Joint Board on Defence," *Interparliamentary Group,* Reference Paper no. 116, August, 1965, cited in Abrams, pp. 73–74. See also Arnold Heeney, *The Things That Are Caesar's: Memoirs of a Canadian Public Servant* (Toronto: University of Toronto Press, 1972), pp. 199–200, for his assessment of the board's value, based on his own experience. He says it "enabled short cuts to

be taken in important advice to governments" and praises the "mutual confidence and informality" which developed among the individual members and principal assistants. On the continuing though changing function of the board, see Conant, "Perspective on Defence," pp. 26–29.

70. Conant, *Polar Watch,* p. 159; Spencer, *Canada in World Affairs,* p. 294; *External Affairs,* June, 1949, pp. 23–24; Department of State, *Bulletin,* April 24, 1949, pp. 512, 537.

71. K. J. Holsti and Thomas Allen Levy, "Bilateral Institutions and Transgovernmental Relations Between Canada and the United States," *International Orgainization,* Autumn, 1974, p. 879; Brian Crane, *An Introduction to Canadian Defence Policy* (Toronto: Canadian Institute of International Affairs, 1964), p. 31.

72. Harald von Riekhoff, *NATO: Issues and Prospects* (Toronto: Canadian Institute of International Affairs, 1967), p. 117.

73. Melvin Conant has estimated that about two hundred operational or technical agreements, formal or informal, form the "web of undertakings which links Canada and the United States in North American defence," even though NORAD does not have responsibility for "real planning or procurement"; "Perspective on Defence," pp. 26, 30.

74. Spender, *Diplomacy,* pp. 14–17, 108.

75. Reese, *Australia, New Zealand,* pp. 144–45.

76. Acheson, *Present at the Creation,* pp. 637, 541, 687–89.

77. Philippe Schmitter and others have called the sealing off of a well-functioning organization from expansion into other fields "encapsulation."

78. Ian Bellany and James Richardson, "Australian Defence Procurement," pp. 262–63; *New York Times,* February 2, 1969.

79. Millar, *Australia's Foreign Policy,* p. 132.

80. Ibid., pp. 130, 132.

81. G. St. J. Barclay, "Problems in Australian Foreign Policy, July–December, 1968," *Australian Journal of Politics and History,* April, 1969, pp. 8–9; Millar, *Australia's Foreign Policy,* pp. 130, 134; Bellany and Richardson, "Australian Defence Procurement," pp. 257–58.

82. A similar conclusion was expressed by Millar, *Australia's Foreign Policy,* p. 134. The Canadian decision to adopt the nuclear-armed version of the F-104 in some ways was a similar case; some Canadian experts criticized this choice as unwise.

83. John Duffy, ms. on Canadian science policy, Columbia University, 1970; *Canadian Weekly Bulletin,* August 14, 1968; A. H. Zimmerman, "Defence Research Programs," *Air University Review,* March–April, 1967, pp. 14–21; McLin, *Defense Policy,* pp. 177–78.

84. *Canadian Weekly Bulletin,* July 10, 1968.

85. A. J. Seyler, "Australian Capabilities—Telecommunications and Space," in *Problems of Australian Defence,* ed. H. G. Gelber (Melbourne: Oxford University Press, 1970), pp. 240–41; *Current Notes,* April, 1970, p. 209; *Baltimore Sun,* April 24, 1969.

86. *New York Times,* December 4, 6, 1969.

87. See Lester B. Pearson, *Mike: The Memoirs of the Right Honourable Lester B. Pearson* (Toronto: University of Toronto Press, 1973), vol. 2, chaps. 3, 4.

88. An article somewhat similar to Article 2 was inserted in the Southeast Asia treaty, largely at the prompting of Australia, New Zealand, Britain, and the Philippines (Reese, *Australia,*

New Zealand, p. 176). Although the Australians were more interested in the Colombo Plan, of which they were principal promoters, they made substantial gifts of equipment and services to the Asian members of SEATO, not including weapons or munitions (Watt, *Australian Foreign Policy,* pp. 158–59).

89. Interviews.

90. Interviews.

91. Alfred Vagts, *Defense and Diplomacy* (New York: King's Crown Press, 1956), p. 209.

92. *Canberra Times,* August 13, 1968. This is one example of how Australian-American military relations rub off on New Zealanders, just as Australia–New Zealand military cooperation affects Americans; J. D. B. Miller, "The Mutual and Shared Commitments of Australia and New Zealand," *Australian Outlook,* April, 1968, p. 18.

93. Millar, *Australia's Defence,* pp. 114–15.

94. Ibid., pp. 124–25; D. E. Kennedy, "The Administration of Defence," in *Problems of Australian Defence,* ed. H. G. Gelber (Melbourne: Oxford University Press, 1970), p. 281 and app. p. 308.

95. *New York Times,* November 1, 1970.

96. Department of Defense, *Military Assistance and Foreign Military Sales Facts,* March, 1970, p. 17.

97. Each class toured the United States as a guest of that government; Stepan, *Military in Politics,* pp. 128–31, 232, 239–43, 174–79; Thomas E. Skidmore, *Politics in Brazil, 1930–1964: An Experiment in Democracy* (New York: Oxford University Press, 1967), pp. 325–30. Among the alumni of the Brazilian Expeditionary Force who were associated with the Escola Superior de Guerra were those who led the coup of March, 1964; and Castelo Branco himself was very sympathetic to this particular form of "active internationalism."

98. Edwin Lieuwen, *The United States and the Challenge to Latin American Security,* Ohio State University Pamphlet Series (Columbus: Mershon Center for Education in National Security, April, 1966), p. 71; Skidmore, *Politics in Brazil,* pp. 126–27, 303–9, 321.

99. Stepan, *Military in Politics,* pp. 131, 236, 249–50. Brazil has been host to the largest United States military advisory group in Latin America.

100. Note Hanson Baldwin's article, *New York Times,* February 20, 1967.

101. For example, in 1967, the year of Canada's centennial, the American *Air University Review* carried articles about Canadian defense in five of its six issues. Roger F. Swanson examined these transnational professional ties among the military in his "An Analytical Assessment of the United States–Canadian Defense Issue Area," *International Organization,* Autumn, 1974, pp. 784–88.

102. McLin, *Defense Policy,* p. 39, fn. 10.

103. It did not escape the notice of some parliamentarians that the number of Canadians in the defense establishment who had journeyed professionally to the United States far outweighed those from any civilian agency; Commons External Affairs Committee, *Minutes,* November 20, 1969, pp. 64, 66.

104. Andrew Brewin, *Stand on Guard: The Search for a Canadian Defence Policy* (Toronto: McClelland and Stewart, 1965), p. 85.

105. McLin, *Defense Policy,* p. 58.

106. Millar, *Australia's Foreign Policy,* p. 131.

107. The Liberals, under whom the original arrangements had been made by the military (arrangements which had been checked at various stages by civilian offices up to but not including the cabinet committee on defense), had put off presenting them to Parliament because of the election of 1957, which they lost. They later criticized the new government for sliding into the agreement without the usual consultations with appropriate cabinet and parliamentary groups regarding its political consequences and for appearing to allow the military to control matters which the government should have controlled; Foulkes, "Complications of Defense," pp. 111–16; Commons External Affairs Committee, *Minutes,* November 28, 1957, pp. 20ff., December 5, 1957, pp. 40ff.; McLin, *Defense Policy,* chap. 3. The ineptness of the Diefenbaker government in upholding its side resulted in an extended political tug-of-war over what were mostly procedural matters. When the House of Commons finally approved the agreement, there were only eight votes against it. Ironically, just prior to leaving office ten years later, the Pearson government signed a rewnewal without parliamentary action.

108. Note that the dates of this crisis coincided with those of crises that the United States was experiencing with its French ally and its British ally concerning nuclear arms, NATO, and EEC.

109. Good accounts may be found in McLin, *Defense Policy,* pp. 130–67; Lyon, *Canada in World Affairs,* pp. 72–111, 131–217.

110. *New York Times,* August 25, 1971.

111. *New York Times,* April 1, 1973, March 22, April 2, 1974; *Greenwich Time* (AP dispatch), April 2, 1974; Peter King, "Whither Whitlam?" pp. 424–30; James Richardson, "Australian Foreign Policy Under the Labor Government," *Cooperation and Conflict,* nos. 18–19, 1974, passim. The Australian Labor party government, however, maintained for internal reasons much of the secrecy which they had deplored in the government they succeeded; Desmond Ball, "Pine Gap and Nurrungar: What They Are and What They Do," to be included in Ron Witton and Michael Richards's forthcoming book called *The American Connection.*

112. Conditions for permitting United States facilities on Canadian soil included allowing them only when Canada judged them necessary and could not provide them by itself, suitable arrangements for liaison, Canadian inspection of sites during construction, bids by Canadian contractors and electronic firms on an equal basis with American firms, assumption of operations and manning of stations at Canadian option, preferential treatment for Canadian labor and transport firms, and recognition of Canada's ultimate control (McLin, *Defense Policy,* p. 28).

113. Ibid., pp. 128–30; Conant, *Polar Watch,* p. 95; *New York Times,* August 25, 1971; *External Affairs,* May, 1956, pp. 125, 138–39; James Eayrs, *Canada in World Affairs, October 1955 to June 1957* (Toronto: Oxford University Press, 1959), pp. 143–51; Department of State, *Bulletin,* July 4, 1955, pp. 22–25, June 20, 1955, p. 1020.

114. Robert E. Scott, *Mexican Government in Transition,* rev. ed. (Urbana: University of Illinois Press, 1964), p. 234; Secretaría de Relaciónes Exteriores, *Las Reláciones Internacionales de Mexico, 1935–1956* (Mexico, D.F., 1957) p. 117; Edwin Lieuwen, *Arms and Politics in Latin America,* rev. ed. (New York: Praeger, 1961), pp. 119, 200, 206, 237.

115. *Correio de Manha* April 18, 29, 1953.

116. Vagts, *Defense and Diplomacy,* p. 209.

117. Stepan, *Military in Politics,* pp. 125–26, 210.

SIX ECONOMIC RELATIONS: FOREIGN TRADE

1. See Robert C. Keohane and Joseph S. Nye, Jr., eds., "Transnational Relations and World Politics," *International Organization,* Summer, 1971; and Annette Baker Fox, Alfred O. Hero, Jr. and Joseph S. Nye, Jr., eds., "Canada and the United States: Transnational and Transgovernmental Relations," *International Organization,* Autumn, 1974. This special issue of *International Organization* was published in book form by Columbia University Press in 1976.

2. The period covered by this study does not extend to the time in the mid–1970s when there were further startling shifts in trade patterns, among them the decline in Europe's dependence on importation of most foods. Meanwhile, many industrialized countries began to suffer shortages of raw materials, but those industrialized countries which were exporters of grains and soybeans found their products in great demand. For varying reasons, these changes did not adversely affect the four middle powers, although three—Canada, Australia, and Brazil—began to loom very important in the eyes of Washington as possessors of "commodity power"; *New York Times,* November 17, 1974.

3. The three countries, the United States, Britain, and Japan, rank in reverse order as Australia's main suppliers to their position as customers. These three countries also rank in reverse order as Canada's best customers. The ratio of Canadian imports from the United States to its total imports rose from 69 percent in 1948 to 73 percent in 1968; its exports to the United States rose from about 50 percent of its total exports to about 66 percent; House of Commons Standing Committee on External Affairs and National Defence, *Minutes of Proceedings and Evidence,* July 27, 1970, p. 24; (hereafter cited as Commons External Affairs Committee, *Minutes*). By 1974, the imports figure had dropped back to 69 percent, but the exports figure was 67 percent; *Canada Weekly,* February 5, 1975.

4. John Crawford, "Partnership in Trade," in *Pacific Orbit: Australian-American Relations Since 1942,* ed. Norman Harper (Melbourne: F. W. Cheshire, 1968), p. 55.

5. See also Gordon Greenwood and Norman Harper, eds., *Australia in World Affairs, 1950–1955* (Melbourne: F. W. Cheshire, 1957), p. 149; J.O.N. Perkins, "Recent Trends and Problems in the Trade and Payments of Australia with the U.S.A.," *Australian Outlook,* August, 1968, p. 190; *Official Yearbook of the Commonwealth of Australia* (Canberra: Government Printer, 1970), pp. 302–3, 305, 308.

6. I. A. Litvak and C. J. Maule, "Foreign Investment in Mexico: Some Lessons for Canada," *Behind the Headlines,* July, 1971, p. 3. United States exports to Mexico in 1968 were about one-eighth of those to Canada.

7. Howard F. Cline, *The United States and Mexico,* rev. ed. (New York: Atheneum, 1963), p. 352; First National City Bank, *Mexico, An Economic Survey, 1971* (New York, September, 1971), p. 30.

8. Congress of Mexico, *Memoria de la Cuarta Reunion, Parlamentaria Estados Unidos–Mexico* (Mexico, D.F., 1964), pp. 79–80. In the early 1970s, the percentage was even smaller (3.31 percent in 1973); imports from Canada constituted a little over 25 percent of total United States imports; *Statistical Abstract of the United States, 1974,* pp. 792–95.

9. Government of Mexico advertisement, *New York Times,* January 28, 1972.

10. Imports and exports were almost equal in 1967, but Brazilian exports to the United States far exceeded imports from the United States in 1953, 1955, and 1956. By the 1970s, Brazil's bilateral trade balance with the United States resembled that of the other Middle powers, but meanwhile Canada was at least temporarily enjoying a trade surplus with the United States.

11. Department of State, *United States Foreign Policy, 1969–1970: A Report of the Secretary of State* (1971), p. 23, hereafter cited as *US Foreign Policy*. By 1974 the combined trade had reached forty billion dollars; *Canada Weekly,* February 5, 1975.

12. About 75 percent of American imports from Canada came in free in 1971; Canadian-American Committee, *The New Environment for Canadian-American Relations* [Washington and Montreal, April 6, 1972], pp. 11, 13.

13. Carl E. Beigie, *The Canada–U.S. Automotive Agreement: An Evaluation* (Washington and Montreal: Canadian-American Committee, 1970), pp. 1–7.

14. For the automobile pact, see *ibid.,* esp. pp. 1–7, 11–12, 117, 123–24, 133–34; Michael Barkway, "U.S. Investment in Canada," in *Neighbors Taken for Granted,* ed. Livingston T. Merchant (New York: Praeger, 1966), p. 79; Paul and R. J. Wonnacott, "The Automotive Agreement of 1965," *Canadian Journal of Economics and Political Science,* May, 1967, p. 282; Gerald M. Craig, *The United States and Canada* (Cambridge: Harvard University Press, 1968), p. 271; *Wall Street Journal,* February 14, 1972; *New York Times,* February 11, April 2, 1972; Economic Council of Canada, *Sixth Annual Review, Perspective 1975* (Ottawa: Queen's Printer, 1969), p. 84; *Canadian Weekly Bulletin,* July 9, 19, 1969; William Diebold, Jr., *The United States and the Industrial World* (New York: Praeger, 1972), pp. 81–91; Henrik O. Helmers, D. S. Wood, and B. G. Barrow, "The Canada–U.S. Auto Pact, A Case Study," in *Canadian-American Interdependence: How Much?* ed. R. H. Wagenberg (Windsor: University of Windsor Press, 1970), pp. 79–95.

15. Henrik Helmers's expression in *Canadian-American Interdependence: How Much?* ed. R. H. Wagenberg, p. 79.

16. For the program as it operated up to 1971, see Kenneth W. Dam, *Implementation of Import Quotas: The Case of Oil,* Brookings Institution Reprint 221 (Washington, 1971), and, in general, Edward H. Shaffer, *The Oil Import Program of the United States: An Evaluation* (New York: Praeger, 1968). The oil and gas issues are discussed further under Distance and in chapter 8.

17. Rafael Izquierdo, "Protectionism in Mexico," in *Public Policy and Private Enterprise in Mexico* ed. Raymond Vernon (Cambridge: Harvard University Press, 1964), pp. 243ff.; Dam, *Import Quotas,* pp. 35–36.

18. Ivan L. Head, "The Foreign Policy of the New Canada," *Foreign Affairs,* January, 1972, p. 248. Presumably "minority" meant France, Germany, and Japan. See also *Canadian Weekly Bulletin,* August 21, September 1, October 20, 1971.

19. Canada did retain some small remnants of Commonwealth preferences in its tariff schedules even in the 1960s while simultaneously offering most-favored-nation treatment to countries not so favored by the United States. See Kenneth C. Mackenzie, *Tariff-Making and Trade Policy in the U.S. and Canada* (New York: Praeger, 1968), pp. 60–63.

20. See for example, A. F. W. Plumptre, "Canada and the International Monetary Fund," *International Journal,* Winter, 1970–71, esp. pp. 110, 113–14.

21. *New York Times,* October 12, November 17, 22, 1974; *Canada Weekly,* October 30, 1974, January 8, 1975. In December, Canada imposed export controls on certain livestock and meat to the United States "to protect traditional trade patterns" within the United States quota limitations, pending settlement of the whole issue. The Canadian meat industry also was suffering from Japanese and European restrictions.

22. John G. Crawford, *Australian Trade Policy, 1924–1966* (Canberra: Australian National University Press, 1968), pp. 89ff.; D. F. Nicholson, *Australia's Trade Relations: An Outline History of Australia's Overseas Trading Arrangements* (Melbourne: F. W. Cheshire, 1955), pp. 116ff.; C. W. James, "Foreign Economic Policy of Australia," *Australian Outlook,* September, 1953, pp. 153–63.

23. Perkins, "Trade and Payments," p. 193. Although minerals have challenged agricultural and pastoral commodities as Australia's most valuable exports, the latter, especially meat, remain the most important among United States purchases, which reduces the opportunities for bargaining which might otherwise be available to Australia.

24. *Current Notes on International Affairs,* August, 1971, pp. 435–36; hereafter cited as *Current Notes.*

25. John G. Crawford, "Economic Policies," in *Australia in World Affairs, 1961–1965,* ed. Gordon Greenwood and Norman Harper (Melbourne: F. W. Cheshire, 1968), p. 83; Crawford, "Partnership in Trade," pp. 61–64.

26. Mexico, with the acquiescence of the United States, ended in 1950 the trade agreement which had been concluded during World War II and revised in 1947. The Mexicans desired greater flexibility than they felt they had under such commitments, especially freedom to raise tariffs and impose other barriers which the government desired in its national programs; Cline, *United States and Mexico,* p. 389; Raymond Vernon, *The Dilemma of Mexico's Development: The Roles of the Public and Private Sectors* (Cambridge: Harvard University Press, 1963), pp. 137–40.

27. For example, a tremendous growth in American imports of Mexican textiles in the mid–1960s led the United States in 1967 to seek Mexican agreement to cut them in half. The United States promised to take a somewhat larger amount in subsequent years. Mexico accepted the reduction because, without it, it was likely to be able to export only half the agreed-to amount; *El Heraldo* June 3, 1967; *News,* June 3, 1967. (Canada followed suit on imports of Mexican textiles.) The United States also secured "voluntary" agreement from Brazil in 1969 to curb its cotton-textile exports to the United States.

28. Note the observation of a Mexican business man that "it is so much simpler to trade with the United States. We know the market, the exchange rate is stable, and transportation is easier"; *New York Times,* January 27, 1974.

29. Note the Mexican government's advertisement, *New York Times,* January 28, 1972. Secretary of the Treasury John Connally's reply to the inquiry about the impact of the policy on Latin American states was that the United States had no friends in that area anyway; *New York Times,* August 15, 1971.

30. *Excelsior,* June 27, 1967. Canada was the only other country in the Western Hemisphere having such an agreement with the United States. That same year, the Mexican government had responded to President Charles de Gaulle's attack on the United States dollar by putting its entire $200 million gold reserves on public sale to show confidence in the United States dollar (and its own economy); *News,* December 20, 1967, reprinted in advertisement in *Wall Street Journal,* January 23, 1968.

31. At times the United States has taken almost two-thirds of Brazil's total production; in the 1950s, Brazilian coffee constituted about 40 percent of the entire world output; Speech of United States Ambassador John Moors Cabot to American Chamber of Commerce for Brazil in São Paulo, October 15, 1959.

32. *Relatório do Ministro de Estado das Relações Exteriores, Annó de 1940* (Rio de Janeiro: Imprensa Nacional, 1944), p. 25.

33. W. F. Rowe, *Primary Commodities in International Trade* (Cambridge: Cambridge University Press, 1965), pp. 177–82; Isaiah Frank, "New Perspectives on Trade and Development," *Foreign Affairs*, April, 1967, p. 528; Joseph Short, "American Business and Foreign Policy: Cases in Coffee and Cocoa Regulation" (Ph.D. diss., Columbia University, 1974).

34. Short, "Coffee and Cocoa"; *US Foreign Policy, 1969–1970*, p. 122; Department of State, *Bulletin*, May 26, 1969, p. 455, April 2, 1971, August 30, 1971.

35. In 1974, Brazil joined Colombia, the Ivory Coast and Portugese Angola in a producer's organization, as a result of which Brazil even began to import some coffee in order to keep up the price. These four countries were producing 85 percent of the world's coffee; anticipating supplies exceeding requirements at current prices for the first time in eight years, they intended to manipulate the market to keep prices from falling. They failed. *New York Times*, Feb. 2, July 6, 1974, April 26, 1975.

36. *New York Times*, November 27, 1971.

37. Congress of Mexico, *Memoria de la Cuarta Reunion*, pp. 94–100.

38. *New York Times*, June 23, 1972; *US Foreign Policy, 1969–1970*, p. 64.

39. *Current Notes*, October, 1968, pp. 456–57, November, 1968, p. 493, May, 1969, p. 255; Crawford, *Australian Trade Policy*, pp. 406–10.

40. *International Canada*, March, 1973, pp. 108–9; *Canada Weekly*, January 23, 1974, February 6, 1974.

41. *New York Times*, December 14, 1966.

42. *Canada Weekly*, January 23, 1974.

43. Jean Royer, "Commercial Policies and Techniques," in Economic Council of Canada and Agricultural Economics Research Council of Canada, *Conference on International Trade and Canadian Agriculture* (Ottawa: Queen's Printer, 1966).

44. Francis Masson and J. B. Whitely, *Barriers to Trade Between Canada and the United States* (Washington and Montreal: Canadian-American Committee, 1960), p. 88.

45. Peyton V. Lyon, *Canada in World Affairs, 1961–63* (Toronto: Oxford University Press, 1968), p. 393.

46. The current pipeline went only to Toronto; part of it was south of the border. The two governments had shifted positions more than once on the desirability of a Canadian pipeline to Montreal, with United States officials at one point urging upon a reluctant Canada that such a pipeline would free them from dependence upon overseas oil, which if cut off might have to be replaced from the United States. With the 1973 Arab oil embargo on exports to the United States, the situation was reversed. Even without the pipeline, supplies in Canada suffered little shrinkage because they continued to come from overseas. Although Canada has depended more on imported oil than has the United States, much of it came from Venezuela and Africa, and in 1973 Canada was not on the Arabs' blacklist; *Toronto Globe and Mail*, March 21, 1970, November 9, 1973; *Montreal Star*, November 8, 1973; *Ottawa Citizen*, January 21, 1971; *New York Times*, January 17, September 10, 1973, January 23, 1974. Politics had dominated economic and geographic considerations.

47. *New York Times*, February 2, November 23, December 8, 1974; April 23, November 20, November 21, 1975; *Canada Weekly*, April 2, 9, 1975; *International Canada*, January, 1973,

pp. 13–14, November, 1973, pp. 289–90, 306. See chapter 9, section on Natural Resources for further discussion.

48. Testimony of Under-Secretary of State A. E. Ritchie, Commons, External Affairs Committee, *Minutes,* May 5, 1970, p. 9.

49. *New York Times,* September 28, 1974.

50. *International Canada,* November, 1973, p. 312.

51. *New York Times,* June 5, 1970, October 3, 1971; *Current Notes,* July, 1969, pp. 399–400.

52. Mexico's "single biggest export is pleasure"; Cline, *United States and Mexico,* p. 353.

53. Izquierdo, "Protectionism in Mexico," 247; Donald W. Baerresen, *The Border Industrialization Program of Mexico* (Toronto: Heath Lexington Books, 1971), p. 69. Although general tariffs do not apply there, Mexico has increasingly regulated imports in these zones as well as, with the growth of affluence, in Baja California. Affluence also has created an important flow of Mexican tourists northward, thereby somewhat offsetting the large contribution that foreign tourists have provided Mexico's balance of payments.

54. *New York Times,* July 8, 1966.

55. *Toronto Globe and Mail,* September 14, 16, 17, 1971.

56. Peyton V. Lyon, *The Policy Question* (Toronto: McClelland and Stewart, 1963), p. 110; Craig *United States and Canada,* pp. 249–52.

57. *Canadian Weekly Bulletin,* January 12, 1972; *Toronto Globe and Mail,* April 8, 1972; *International Canada,* December, 1972, p. 242. See Ernest H. Preeg, "Economic Blocs and U.S. Foreign Policy," *International Organization,* Spring, 1974, pp. 239ff, for reasons why the Canadian dollar, even when floating, usually stays close to the American dollar, including the fact that the Canadian dollar reflects similar price trends in the North American market.

58. Bernard Goodman, *Two Dependent Economies: Canada and Australia* (Melbourne: F. W. Cheshire, 1964), pp. 22, 29, 37, 41.

59. Thomas B. Millar, *Australia's Foreign Policy* (Sydney: Angus and Robertson, 1968), pp. 131–32. Even American military procurement in Australia for the Vietnam war was mainly agricultural produce.

60. H. G. Gelber, *The Australian-American Alliance, Costs and Benefits* (Baltimore: Penguin Books, 1968), p. 58.

61. Wilfred Prest, "Economic Policies," in *Australia in World Affairs, 1950–1955,* ed. Gordon Greenwood and Norman Harper (Melbourne: F. W. Cheshire, 1957), pp. 133, 137; Arthur Burns, "Problems of Australian Foreign Policy, July–December, 1967," *Australian Journal of Politics and History,* April, 1968, p. 10; *New York Times,* January 24, 1972; *Current Notes,* August, 1971, pp. 435–36, December, 1971, p. 675; J. D. B. Miller, *Britain and the Old Dominions* (London: Chatto & Windus, 1966), pp. 219–25; Ian Potter, "Capital Inflows and Australia's Defence Commitment," in *Problems of Australian Defence,* ed. H. G. Gelber (Melbourne: Oxford University Press, 1970), pp. 209–10.

62. *New York Times,* September 26, 1974; Prospectus for issue of bonds by Commonwealth of Australia, May, 1975; pp. 14–17. Tariffs were raised again later.

63. Miguel S. Wionczek, "The Latin American Free Trade Association," in *International Political Communities* (Garden City: Doubleday, 1966), p. 319; Joseph Grunwald, Miguel S. Wionczek, and Martin Carnoy, *Latin American Integration and U. S. Policy* (Washington:

Brookings, 1972), passim; Victor L. Urquidi, *Free Trade and Economic Integration in Latin America* (Berkeley: University of California Press, 1964), pp. 71–72; Ernst B. Haas and Philippe C. Schmitter, *The Politics of Economics in Latin American Regionalism,* Social Science Foundation Monograph Series, vol. 3, no. 2 (Denver: University of Denver, 1965), pp. 57–58.

64. Isaiah Frank, "Trade and Development," p. 527; Camara de Senadores, *Memoria de la Segunda Reunion Parlamentaria Estados Unidos–Mexico* (Mexico, D. F., 1963), pp. 26–27.

65. Royer, "Commercial Policies," pp. 215–16; Lincoln Gordon, "Punta del Este Revisited," *Foreign Affairs,* July, 1967, p 632; *New York Times,* November 15, 1969; Department of State news release, Statement by Acting Secretary of State Robert S. Ingersoll, 19th Annual Meeting of Inter-American Economic and Social Council, March 12, 1975.

66. Note Brazilian government's advertisement in *New York Times,* January 25, 1971. The favorable treatment by the United States contrasted with Brazil's small quota for the so-called free market in sugar in 1954, which caused it to withdraw from the International Sugar Agreement for four years. The free market was not large and of little importance to Brazil compared to the American market, where until the mid–1970s the price was higher than the world price.

67. *New York Times,* February 28, 1968.

68. These bilateral institutions are in addition to the many multilateral organizations in which the two countries have played leading roles, such as the International Wheat Council.

69. So successful was the committee that Canada later formed similar groups with Britain, France, and Japan. With the last-named country the United States also formed such a group. The Japanese attended their two North American ministerial committees on succeeding days.

70. See Maureen Appel Molot, "The Elephant, the Mouse, and the Financial Relationship," *Queen's Quarterly,* Spring, 1971, pp. 71–82; Gerald Wright and Maureen Appel Molot, "Capital Movements and Government Control," *International Organization,* Autumn, 1974, pp. 671ff; also A. E. Ritchie's testimony in Commons External Affairs Committee, May 5, 1970, p. 26, for comment on the failure for these contacts to work in the 1963 crisis. Prior to the imposition of the 1965 guidelines, United States officials did consult with their Canadian counterparts.

71. In the informal, personal relationships among counterparts responsible for financial policy, which were then apparently so abruptly severed, "Gentlemanly relations" presupposed that all the participants were gentlemen. For how these relationships were of greater importance than formal institutions, See Maureen Appel Molot, "The Role of Institutions in Canada–United States Relations: The Case of North American Financial Ties," in *Continental Community? Independence and Integration in North America,* ed. Andrew Axline et al. (Toronto: McClelland and Stewart, 1974), pp. 164–93, esp. 176–81.

72. Apparently this group was the model for a more recently established British–North American committee.

73. See Matthew J. Abrams, *The Canada–United States Interparliamentary Group* (Ottawa: Parliamentary Centre for Foreign Affairs and Foreign Trade and Canadian Institute of International Affairs, 1973) and Peter C. Dobell, "The Influence of the United States Congress on Canadian–American Relations," *International Organization,* Autumn, 1974, pp. 925–27.

74. Constant Southworth and W. W. Buchanan, *Changes in Trade Restrictions Between Canada and the United States* (Washington and Montreal: Canadian–American Committee, 1960), p. 6; Ernest H. Preeg, *Traders and Diplomats: An Analysis of the Kennedy Round of Negotia-*

tions *Under the General Agreement on Tariffs and Trade* (Washington: Brookings, 1970), pp. 186–88, 238, 249, 253.

75. Nicholson, *Australia's Trade Relations,* pp. 20ff.; Crawford, *Australian Trade Policy,* pp. 14–15, 390; Wilfred Prest, "Economic Policies," p. 132. Australia eventually received a substantial reduction in the wool tariff, as well as other benefits, during the GATT bargaining.

76. "International Trade Discussions," *Australian Outlook,* March 1948, pp. 42–49; Crawford, "Partnership in Trade," p. 50.

77. John Crawford, "Economic Policies," pp. 204, 218; and Nicholson, *Australia's Trade Relations,* pp. 206–7.

78. See H. W. Arndt, "Australia—Developed, Developing or Midway?" *Australian Journal of Sciences,* December, 1965, pp. 209–15. In the 1965 GATT review, Australia did get an amendment providing a special right to renegotiate bound tariff rates for members which depended largely on a rather small number of primary commodities and which relied on the tariff for important aid in diversifying their economies.

79. Julius Stone, "Problems of Australian Foreign Policy, January–June, 1955," *Australian Journal of Politics and History,* November, 1955, pp. 22–24.

80. Crawford, "Partnership in Trade," p. 58.

81. *Report of the Committee of Economic Enquiry* (Vernon Report) (Canberra: Commonwealth of Australia, May, 1965), vol. 1, pp. 12–31.

82. Arndt, "Australia," pp. 212–13; James H. Polhemus, "Australia and the New States," in *Contemporary Australia: Studies in History, Politics, Economics,* ed. Richard Preston (Durham: Duke University Press, 1969), pp. 410–12.

83. By 1966, however, they had decided to join its Development Assistance Committee, which endeavors to coordinate the foreign-aid programs of the members.

84. Australia has been a member of some international commodity agreements, joined the Economic Commission for Asia and the Far East in 1963, and more recently participated in the Asian Development Bank. The idea of a Pacific free-trade area has not strongly appealed to the Australians any more than it has to Americans. Yet, like the abortive North Atlantic Free Trade Area in Canada's case, it might offer a solution for the odd man out in international economic bargaining. (The same would apply to New Zealand, which has, however, secured more favorable treatment from the United States and the EEC.) Unlike the Americans, the Australians strenuously opposed Britain's entry into the EEC.

85. Jorge Casteñeda, *Mexico and the United Nations* (New York: Manhattan Publishing Co., 1958), pp. 166–70; *News,* June 27, 1967; Antonio Carrillo Flores, "Cooperacion Economica Interamericana," *Foro Internacional,* July–Sepatember, 1960, p. 3.

86. Vernon *Mexico's Development,* pp. 137–40.

87. See, for example, Banco Nacional de Comercio Exterior, *Comercio Exterior de Mexico,* December, 1966, pp. 15–17, February, 1967, p. 19, February, 1968, p. 7, September, 1966, pp. 2, 7, 19–21, November, 1966, pp. 10–12, May, 1971, p. 15.

88. Statement of Foreign Minister Vasco Leitão da Cunha, July 6, 1964, in Ministério das Relações Exteriores, *Textos e Declarações sobre Política Externa, de Abril de 1964 a Abril de 1965* (Rio de Janeiro, 1965), pp. 64–66.

89. See Dale C. Thompson's testimony in Commons External Affairs Committee, *Minutes,* April 28, 1970, pp. 9, 10, 12, 14. An example was the American legislation of 1972 that

created a system of domestic international sales corporations (DISC), embodying preferential taxes. Canadians were greatly concerned about its impact on them. Less substantively important but more shocking was President Nixon's wildly inaccurate remark, made on September 16, 1971, during the monetary crisis, that Japan was the largest customer of the United States.

90. These demands included changes in the special guarantees of the automobile pact, liberalization of Canadian tourist allowances, ending of preferential treatment given by Canada to its defense suppliers, and lowering of some duties still imposed on United States defense materiel.

91. *New York Times,* July 27, 1972; *International Canada,* April, 1972, p. 63; Grant L. Reuber, "What's New About Recent United States Foreign Economic Policy?" *International Journal,* Spring, 1972, esp. pp. 292–97; *Canadian Weekly Bulletin,* December 29, 1971.

92. Izquierdo, "Protectionism in Mexico," p. 254; Robert E. Scott, *Mexican Government in Transition,* rev. ed. (Urbana: University of Illinois Press, 1964), p. 32.

93. *US Foreign Policy, 1969–1970,* p. 122; Murillo Gurgel Valente, "The Participation of Developing Countries in Shipping," *International Conciliation,* March, 1971 (special issue on Shipping and Developing Countries), pp. 29, 34–35, 39–40, 42.

94. See, for example, Irving Brecher and S. S. Reisman, *Canada–United States Economic Relations* (Ottawa: Queen's Printer for Royal Commission on Canada's Economic Prospects, 1957), especially pp. 186–94. Because foreign trade is so much less important in the United States economy, enactment of trade legislation favoring special domestic interests by the lesser power is likely to have far less impact in the United States.

95. Lyon, *Canada in World Affairs,* p. 197.

96. *International Canada,* December, 1971, pp. 233–34; January, 1973, pp. 14–15; April, 1973, p. 125; *New York Times,* July 27, 1972, January 6, 1973; *Wall Street Journal,* January 8, 1973; *Journal of Commerce,* May 29, 1973.

97. Crawford, *Australian Trade Policy,* pp. 66–68 and Crawford, "Partnership in Trade," p. 57; Trevor R. Reese, *Australia, New Zealand and the United States: A Survey of International Relations, 1941–1968* (London: Oxford University Press, 1969), p. 74.

98. *New York Times,* July 13, 1972, April 8, 1973; *Greenwich Time* (AP dispatch), July 12, 1972. With looming shortages in bauxite, of which Australia is an important producer, some American economists have predicted an OPEC-like grouping led by Australia; *New York Times,* January 27, 1974.

99. Raymond Vernon, ed., *Public Policy and Private Enterprise in Mexico* (Cambridge: Harvard University Press, 1964), p. 5.

100. Joseph Short, "Coffee and Cocoa," *New York Times,* December 19, 1970.

101. Jerome Levinson and Juan de Onis, *The Alliance That Lost Its Way* (Chicago: Quadrangle Books, 1970), p. 196; *Jornal do Brasil* editorial, May 7, 1966; *New York Times,* April 9, 1967.

102. Levinson and de Onis, *Alliance Lost Its Way,* p. 196.

SEVEN *ECONOMIC RELATIONS: FOREIGN DIRECT INVESTMENT*

1. Department of State news release, "Special Report: The United States Role in International Investment," January 16, 1974, p. 7. Richard N. Cooper has described foreign direct investment as that "which carries with it decision-making control by the foreign investor. Portfolio investment [is] international investment which involves the purchase of foreign securities or

other financial claims on foreigners without management control" (*The Economics of Inter-dependence: Economic Policy in the Atlantic Community* [New York: McGraw-Hill, 1968], pp. 81–82). Another definition, freer of political implications, is that of Peter B. Kenen, who refers to foreign direct investment as international transactions between related enterprises—parent companies and foreign affiliates—and portfolio investment as transactions in stocks, bonds, bank deposits, and money-market instruments involving independent firms or individuals ("Private International Capital Movements," *International Encyclopedia of the Social Sciences*, pp. 27, 28).

2. From 1948 to 1968, about 85 percent of total Canadian foreign capital requirements, including portfolio investment, was met by Americans. Of nearly fifty manufacturing industries in which in 1967 nonresident ownership was more than 50 percent, those above 90 percent were rubber products, aircraft and parts, motor vehicles and parts, industrial electrical equipment, batteries, petroleum refineries, and soap and cleansers; House of Commons Standing Committee on External Affairs and National Defence, *Minutes of Proceedings and Evidence*, July 13–27, 1970, pp. 26, 40 (hereafter cited as Commons External Affairs Committee, *Minutes*). American investors predominate in many of the mining and smelting industries and in petroleum production. The tapering off of new American investment in Canada in the 1970s suggested that the importation of this capital was no longer so vital in financing Canada's economic growth and that "Canadian perceptions of American economic domination have been rising at a time when the factual basis for concern was actually in decline"; Peyton V. Lyon, "Introduction," in *Continental Community? Independence or Integration in North America*, ed. Andrew Axline et al. (Toronto: McClelland and Stewart, 1974), p. 7.

3. By the end of 1967, Australia had become the fifth most important destination for American direct investment in terms of book value; Donald T. Brash, "Australia as Host to the International Corporation," in *The International Corporation*, ed. Charles P. Kindleberger (Cambridge: MIT Press, 1970), p. 293. The others were, in order of importance, Canada, Britain, Germany, and Venezuela. By 1972, Americans' investment of about $5 billion had made Australia the country with the fourth largest concentration of United States foreign direct investment; Department of State, *United States Foreign Policy, 1972; A Report of the Secretary of State*, p. 364; hereafter cited as *US Foreign Policy*.

4. *Current Notes*, May, 1969, p. 214; Ian Potter, "American Investment in Australia," in *Pacific Orbit: Australian-American Relations Since 1942*, ed. Norman Harper (Melbourne: F. W. Cheshire, 1968), p. 82.

5. *Current Notes*, April, 1969, p. 166.

6. For one comparison of international enterprise in Mexico versus Brazil, see Raymond Vernon, *The Multinational Enterprise and National Security*, Adelphi Papers, no. 74 (London: International Institute for Strategic Studies, January, 1971), pp. 30–31.

7. By 1966, prices in Brazil had risen thirty times from a 1958 base, while in Mexico they had only doubled during the same period; based on figures in *Economic Almanac, 1967–68* (New York, Macmillan, 1967), p. 504. For a few years thereafter, the Brazilian rate of inflation was drastically reduced.

8. Thomas E. Skidmore, *Politics in Brazil, 1930–1964: An Experiment in Democracy* (New York: Oxford University Press, 1967), pp. 173, 178–81.

9. *New York Herald Tribune*, International edition, September 12, 1970; *New York Times*, December 10, 1969.

10. Lester Pearson's minister of finance, Walter Gordon, had sought unsuccessfully in 1963 to institute more drastic measures but ended up with an ineffective tax concession to enterprises with Canadian membership of 25 percent on boards of directors; Gerald M. Craig, *The United States and Canada* (Cambridge: Harvard University Press, 1968), pp. 255–66; and Jack N. Behrman, *National Interests and the Multinational Enterprise: Tensions Among the North Atlantic Countries* (Englewood Cliffs: Prentice-Hall, 1970), p. 138. In September, 1973, the government proposed that federally chartered businesses be required to have 50 percent of their boards of directors Canadians.

11. A large influx of foreign banking institutions in the 1970s revealed that there were sizable loopholes in the restrictions on such activities; *New York Times*, November 11, 1974.

12. That certain kinds of jointness raise problems for the Canadian government was illustrated by the events in a long strike at an American-owned airplane-engine plant in Montreal. The parent company removed some of the machinery from the plant to the United States to fill its orders and maintain its markets until the strike was settled. Government opponents raised both the question of control by outsiders and the fact that the technology involved in the machinery had been developed with the aid of Canadian government funds; *New York Times*, November 16, 1974. For the Foreign Investment Review Act, see discussion in section on Domestic Politics.

13. The Canadian federal government also encouraged provincial governments to time their borrowing appropriately in the United States, purchased Canadian securities held in the United States to offset excess flows, and exchanged borrowed European currencies for American dollars in its reserve holding. As their ministers proclaimed from time to time, "a healthy American dollar means a healthy Canadian dollar"; *New York Times*, January 20, 1969; *Wall Street Journal*, May 14, 1968; *Canadian Weekly Bulletin*, January 12, 1972.

14. On the United States capital restrictions and Canadian reactions, see A. E. Safarian, "Benefits and Costs of Foreign Investment," in *Canadian Economic Problems and Policies* ed. L. H. Officer and L. B. Smith (Toronto: McGraw-Hill, 1970), p. 115; A. E. Safarian, *Foreign Ownership of Canadian Industry* (Toronto: McGraw-Hill, 1966), pp. 27–28, 166–67; 253–56; Bruce MacDonald, "The Issue That Will Not Die," *Behind the Headlines*, June, 1967, p. 13; *External Affairs*, February, 1966, giving Minister of Finance Sharp's explanation to the House of Commons on January 27, 1966; Gerald Clark, *Canada: The Uneasy Neighbor* (New York: David McKay, 1965), pp. 71–73; Craig, *United States and Canada*, p. 266; Gerald Wright and Maureen Appel Molot, "Capital Movements and Government Control," *International Organization*, Autumn, 1974, pp. 675–80.

15. Donald T. Brash, *American Investment in Australian Industry* (Canberra: Australian National University Press, 1966), pp. 44–45; Brash, "Australia as Host," pp. 298–99.

16. D. H. Merry, "The American Impact on Australian Business," in *Pacific Orbit: Australian-American Relations Since 1942*, ed. Norman Harper (Melbourne: F. W. Cheshire, 1968), p. 117.

17. Brash, *American Investment in Australian Industry*, pp. 61, 63, 75, 634; Potter, "Capital Inflows and Australia's Defence Commitment," in *Problems of Australian Defence*, ed. H. G. Gelber (Melbourne: Oxford University Press, 1970), p. 219.

18. *New York Times*, January 25, 1971. The foreign public debt had risen from about 6 percent of GNP in 1958 to nearly 10 percent in January, 1970; *New York Times*, January 26, 1970. See also National City Bank, *Mexico, An Economic Survey*, 1971, p. 30.

19. Howard F. Cline, *The United States and Mexico*, rev. ed. (New York: Atheneum, 1963), p. 348; William O. Freithaler, *Mexico's Foreign Trade and Economic Development* (New York: Praeger, 1968), pp. 122–23. In the second largest industrial center, Monterrey, foreign investment is secondary to the role of the local tightly knit group of wealthy Mexican business-men who run the big enterprises in a highly independent fashion; *New York Times*, October 18, 1974.

20. *Jornal do Brasil*, June 15, 1966, June 17, 1966; *Comercio Exterior de Mexico*, March, 1965, p. 15.

21. Note the diplomatically worded concern expressed by Secretary of State William Rogers in March, 1971, regarding possible Canadian restrictions. Noting a major review by the Canadian government of its policies on foreign investment, the statement in his annual report suggested that if significant new controls or restrictions were to be proposed, "close consultation between the two governments may be needed"; *US Foreign Policy, 1969–1970*, p. 25; *Toronto Globe and Mail*, March 29, 1971.

22. *New York Times*, July 20, August 5, August 11, August 26, December 7, 1973; *Wall Street Journal*, August 13, 1973.

23. R. C. Gates, "Australian Taxation and United States Investment," *Australian Outlook*, December, 1953, pp. 236–37. The other countries with which Australia has special tax agree-ments are Britain, Canada, and New Zealand.

24. In some cases, the practices in an industry were almost revolutionized, as in the case of beef raising and motor-vehicle manufacture (Merry, "Australian Business," p. 110).

25. Jonathan Aitken, *Land of Fortune: A Study of the New Australia* (New York: Atheneum, 1971), pp. 156ff.

26. J. E. Richardson, "American Influence on the Air Transport Industry" in *Contemporary Australia: Studies in History, Politics, Economics*, ed. Richard Preston (Durham: Duke Univer-sity Press, 1969), pp. 535, 537.

27. Brash, *American Investment in Australian Industry*, pp. 33, 136, 202, 288.

28. For advantages, see Ian Potter, "American Investment in Australia," p. 74. Labor govern-ment policy is discussed below in the section on Domestic Politics.

29. Two-thirds of American investment was in manufacturing, a very much smaller percentage being in metallurgical industries and in commerce, Raymond Vernon, *The Dilemma of Mex-ico's Development: The Roles of the Public and Private Sectors* (Cambridge: Harvard Univer-sity Press, 1963), pp. 22–23; Roger D. Hansen, *The Politics of Mexican Development* (Bal-timore: Johns Hopkins University Press, 1971), p. 57; A. Böhrisch and König, *La Politica Mexicana sobre Inversiones Extranjeras* (Mexico, D.F.: El Colegio de Mexico, 1968), pp. 17–18.

30. Böhrisch and König, *La Politica Mexicana*, p. 58; Vernon, *Mexico's Development*, p. 22; I. A. Litvak and C. J. Maule, "Foreign Investment in Mexico, Some Lessons for Canada," *Behind the Headlines*, July, 1971, p. 12.

31. Cline, *United States and Mexico*, p. 379.

32. Freithaler, *Mexico's Foreign Trade*, pp. 71, 77.

33. Böhrisch and König, *La Politica Mexicana*, p. 67; Carlos F. Díaz Alejandro, "Direct Foreign Investment in Latin America," in *The International Corporation*, ed. Charles P. Kin-dleberger (Cambridge: MIT Press, 1970), pp. 324–25.

34. Böhrisch and König, *La Politica Mexicana,* p. 22.

35. Litvak and Maule, "Foreign Investment in Mexico," p. 14.

36. Díaz Alejandro, "Investment in Latin America," p. 334; *New York Times,* May 19, 1972. On the Mexican side, the minister of national properties stated that with the reduced share in American markets that was occurring, there should be a reduced share of earnings to United States investors.

37. Donald W. Baerrsen, *The Border Industralization Program of Mexico* (Toronto: Heath Lexington Books, 1971), passim; *Newsweek,* January 24, 1972; National City Bank *Mexico: An Economic Survey,* September, 1971, pp. 38–39; *New York Times,* March 24, 1972 and May 22, 1975. The picture brightened toward the end of 1975 with the improvement in the United States economy; *Wall Street Journal,* November 21, 1975.

38. March 13, 1966.

39. San Tiago Dantas, *Politica Exterior Independente* (Rio de Janeiro: Editôra Civilização Brasileira, 1962), pp. 229–31; Skidmore, *Politics in Brazil,* pp. 220, 228, 244.

40. Skidmore, *Politics in Brazil,* p. 257; Jerome Levinson and Juan de Onis, *The Alliance That Lost Its Way* (Chicago; Quadrangle Books, 1970), pp. 43–46; Díaz Alejandro, "Investment in Latin America," p. 339. The enormous foreign indebtedness of Brazil at the time gave the United States government the leverage implicit in its willingness to help refinance these financial obligations.

41. *O Globo,* May 9, 1966; *Jornal do Brasil,* May 6, 1966; Skidmore, *Politics in Brazil,* pp. 162, 165. The working-capital guarantee provided that the firm would receive in cruzeiros, when converting its funds back into dollars, an amount which the dollars would then be worth rather than what they had been worth when brought in.

42. Similarly, large sales of United States wheat and other agricultural commodities were a boon to American producers, even, as in the case of wheat, at the expense of Canadian suppliers; See Elmer L. Menzie, "Techniques for the Expansion of Agricultural Exports," in Economic Council of Canada and Agricultural Economics Research Council of Canada, *Conference on International Trade and Canadian Agriculture* (Ottawa: Queen's Printer, 1966), p. 292, for comments on a United States Department of Agriculture study of subsidized sales. Viewed in longer perspective, however, Brazil's development enabled it later to make large purchases in Canada.

43. Levinson and de Onis, *Alliance Lost Its Way,* pp. 133–34. There was precedent for this. The Eisenhower administration, on coming to office, reneged on an earlier arrangement, made under the Joint Brazil–United States Economic Development Commission, to supply aid for approved projects in Brazil. The promised money was turned over to the Export-Import Bank as part of a plan to help Brazil out of the 1953 balance-of-payments predicament created by its large indebtedness to private American creditors; Skidmore, *Politics in Brazil,* p. 117; Charles O. Porter and Robert J. Alexander, *The Struggle for Democracy in Latin America* (New York: Macmillan, 1961), pp. 198–99; Ronald M. Schneider, *The Political System of Brazil* (New York: Columbia University Press, 1971), p. 63.

44. See further discussion under section on Cumulation and Spillover.

45. See Commons External Affairs Committee, *Minutes,* January 20, 1970, pp. 50–51, July 27, 1970, pp. 72ff., for examples. The Merchant-Heeney report in fact recommended that so far as the United States Trading with the Enemy Act was concerned, the United States should recognize this irritant by issuing a kind of general license for American subsidiaries in Canada,

a suggestion which was never implemented so specifically; see this report, titled "Canada and The United States—Principles for Partnership," first published in Department of State, *Bulletin*, August 3, 1965.

46. *Toronto Globe and Mail*, March 21, 1970.

47. *New York Times*, May 4, 1972, January 26, 1975; *Time*, May 15, 1972; Brash, "Australia as Host," pp. 303–10. The Clorox Company's plan to take over the Kiwi shoe-polish enterprise was also frustrated; *New York Times*, September 17, 1972.

48. Potter, "Capital Inflow," p. 219.

49. *New York Times*, December 12, 1972.

50. Potter, "Capital Inflow," pp. 211–19.

51. *New York Times*, November 24, 1972.

52. Marion Davis Berdecio, "The Position of the Canacintra on Foreign Investment," M.A. thesis, Columbia University, 1962, pp. 44, 50; Böhrisch and König, *La Politica Mexicana*, p. 25.

53. Litvak and Maule, "Foreign Investment in Mexico," pp. 7, 9, 14; John Womack, Jr., "The Spoils of the Mexican Revolution," *Foreign Affairs*, July 1970, p. 686; advertisement for Banco Mexicano in *New York Times*, January 28, 1972. As in many other aspects of Mexican government, would-be foreign investors might find what a Mexican businessman once said of the Partido Revolucionario Institucional: "The official party is like a cathedral; you can get whatever you want by going there, praying hard enough and lighting enough candles. But you must know in which chapel to pray"; Robert E. Scott, *Mexican Government in Transition*, rev. ed. (Urbana: University of Illinois Press, 1964), p. 32.

54. *New York Times*, November 24, 1972.

55. Skidmore, *Politics in Brazil*, p. 97; Schneider, *Political System of Brazil*, pp. 56, 63.

56. Skidmore, *Politics in Brazil*, pp. 271–72; *Latin America*, August 25, 1972.

57. Ministério das Relações Exteriores, *Textos e Declarações sobre Política Externa, de Abril de 1964 a Abril de 1965* (Rio de Janeiro, 1965), p. 35; Schneider, *Political System of Brazil*, pp. 150–51.

58. See Robert M. Fowler, "The Impact of American Business," *The Atlantic*, November, 1964, p. 121. The greatest regular amount of news about Canada appears in the *Wall Street Journal* and in the business pages of other newspapers.

59. Brash, *American Investment in Australian Industry*, pp. 108–12.

60. Ibid., pp. 116–18, 286.

61. Ivan White, "American Business in Canada," in *Neighbors Taken for Granted*, ed. Livingston Merchant (New York: Praeger, 1966), pp. 88–89.

62. Lester Brown, "Social Impact of the Green Revolution," *International Conciliation*, January, 1971, p. 40.

63. Sometimes proximity has embarrassed government planners. Leaders feared that Mexican consumers would be discontented with the necessarily limited number of models that their newly decreed Mexican automobile industry could produce, since it was easy for potential buyers to see the variety available to Americans. They dealt with the problem by continuing to import bodies; J. Wilner Sundelson, "U.S. Automotive Investments Abroad," in *The International Corporation*, ed. Charles P. Kindleberger (Cambridge: MIT Press, 1970), pp. 247–48.

64. *Excelsior,* June 28, 1967.

65. The Americans nevertheless had foreign competition. Brazil has concluded "cooperation" agreements that provided some kind of aid with several developed countries, including Japan, Germany, France, Britain, and even the Soviet Union; most of these were not physically much farther away than was the United States.

66. Alfred Stepan, *The Military in Politics: Changing Patterns in Brazil* (Princeton: Princeton University Press, 1971), p. 236. Nor were administrative officers the same; Peter Bell, "Brazilian-American Relations," in *Brazil in the Sixties,* ed. Riordan Roett (Nashville: Vanderbilt University Press, 1972), p. 97.

67. Werner Baer and Mario Henrique Simonsen, "American Capital and Brazilian Nationalism," in *Foreign Investment in Latin America,* ed. Marvin D. Bernstein (New York: Knopf, 1966), p. 281.

68. One instance where the practical outcome favored Canadian interests, too, was the United States government's requirement that Schlitz divest itself of the Labatt Brewery, which it had taken over.

69. Canada, in NATO, was a partner to allied agreements regarding trade with the Soviet Union.

70. Former Ambassador A. E. Ritchie told the House of Commons Standing Committee on External Affairs and National Defence on May 5, 1970, that following the Merchant-Heeney Report, the instances involving foreign-assets control decreased noticeably.

71. *New York Times,* March 9, April 24, 1974; *International Canada,* February, 1974, p. 21; March, 1974, pp. 45–46. The United States government evaded taking an official position, despite a month of Canadian pressure. In the same year, Litton Industries ordered a wholly owned subsidiary in Toronto to cancel a large contract for the sale of office furniture to Cubans because of an adverse reaction from the United States agency responsible for licensing such sales; *New York Times,* December 24, 1974.

72. For some time, the OECD has been studying problems presented by the multinational corporation, but lack of information on particular corporate practices is an obstacle. On the need for multilateral action, see Seymour J. Rubin, "The International Firm and the National Jurisdiction," in *The International Corporation,* ed. Charles P. Kindleberger (Cambridge: MIT Press, 1970), p. 193; Isaiah A. Litvak and Christopher J. Maule, "Canadian–United States Corporate Interface and Transnational Relations," *International Organization,* Autumn, 1974, pp. 721–22; A. E. Safarian, "Foreign Direct Investment From a Canadian Perspective," in *Continental Community? Independence and Integration in North America,* ed. Andrew Axline et al. (Toronto: McClelland and Stewart, 1974), p. 297; Joseph S. Nye, "Multinational Corporations in World Politics," *Foreign Affairs,* October, 1974, pp. 172–75; Grant Reuber, "Canadian Independence in an Asymmetrical World Community," *International Journal,* Autumn, 1974, pp. 554–55.

73. Wolfgang G. Friedman, Oliver J. Lissitzyn, and Richard Crawford Pugh, *International Law: Cases and Materials* (St. Paul: West Publishing Co., 1969), p. 479; Vincent W. Bladen, "Economic Aspects of Foreign Policy," in Hugh L. Keenlyside and others, *Growth of Canadian Policies in External Affairs,* Durham: Duke University Press, 1960), p. 131, fn. 5.

74. *New York Times,* July 6, 1971, *International Canada,* November 11, 1973, p. 309; *Canada Weekly,* October 16, 1974. Some of the objectionable United States practices could be obviated if new Canadian countervailing legislation filled in a vacuum, as noted by Behrman,

Multinational Enterprise, pp. 112–13, 185). It was difficult for the Canadian government to do more than strenuously object when the 1971 wage freeze imposed by the United States government prompted Chrysler and Douglas Aircraft subsidiaries in Canada to declare that they would observe it.

75. Brash, "Australia as Host," pp. 304–5; Behrman, *Multinational Enterprise,* p. 94. The measure was administered in such a way as not to frighten American enterprise away.

76. H. G. Gelber, *The Australian–American Alliance: Costs and Benefits* (Baltimore: Penguin Books, 1968), pp. 140–41; J. O. N. Perkins, "Recent Trends and Problems in the Trade and Payments of Australia with the U.S.A.," *Australian Outlook,* August, 1968, p. 199.

77. Perkins, "Trade and Payments," pp. 197, 202.

78. Skidmore, *Politics in Brazil,* p. 245; Levinson and de Onis, *Alliance Lost Its Way,* p. 191; *Revista Brasileira de Politica Internacional,* September, 1961, p. 114. For a critical overview of United States interventions in the 1960s, see Bell, "Brazilian-American Relations," p. 101.

79. Skidmore, *Politics in Brazil,* p. 245; Levinson and de Onis, *Alliance Lost Its Way,* pp. 143–46.

80. The law specified that in calculating the permissible limits of remittances, profits which had been reinvested could not count as capital; Skidmore, *Politics in Brazil,* p. 227; Werner Baer, *Industrialization and Economic Development in Brazil* (Homewood, Illinois: Dorsey, 1965), pp. 50–61.

81. Skidmore, *Politics in Brazil,* pp. 240–41, 251. Goulart had failed to carry out any of the obligations undertaken in Washington in 1963, which included reducing the budget, undertaking agrarian reform, trimming petroleum and wheat subsidies, and tightening bank credit; James W. Rowe, "Historical Antecedents and the Immediate Setting," in *Political Power In Latin America: Seven Confrontations,* ed. Richard R. Fagen and Wayne A. Cornelius, Jr. (Englewood Cliffs: Prentice-Hall, 1970, p. 170.

82. Ministério Relações Exteriores, *Textos e Declarações,* pp. 60, 64.

83. By 1971, the rate of inflation had dropped to 18 percent, the lowest figure since 1957. From 1962, when amortization and interest on foreign debts equaled 45 percent of Brazil's foreign exports, the outflow for these purposes had dropped to 15 percent by 1967; *New York Times,* January 22, 1968; January 28, 1972; Levinson and de Onis, *Alliance Lost Its Way,* p. 192. The inflation rate was back up to 35 percent by 1974, the foreign debt had risen to $10 billion and was increasing rapidly, and Brazil again had a balance-of-payments problem, but the enormous growth in its economy by that time had provided grounds for more optimistic views on Brazil's capacity to overcome these difficulties; Peter J. Reichard, "The Price of Progress in Brazil," *New Leader,* May 13, 1974; *New York Times,* November 24, 1974; Bruce Handler, "Flying High in Rio," *New York Times Magazine,* June 8, 1975.

84. Levinson and de Onis, *Alliance Lost Its Way,* pp. 101–5, 197–200; *Comercio Exterior de Mexico* March 27, 1967, p. 7; Bell, "Brazilian–American Relations," pp. 95, 98.

85. This agreement followed Canadian protests concerning American antitrust moves in a case where the Canadian government was already conducting its own combines inquiry, protests which were contained in the Canadian minister of justice's speech before a New York State Bar Association meeting, plus formal complaints in Washington; I. A. Litvak and C. J. Maule, "Conflict Resolution and Extraterritoriality," *Journal of Conflict Resolution,* September, 1969, pp. 315–17; Kingman Brewster, *Law and United States Business in Canada* (Washington and Montreal: Canadian–American Committee, 1960), pp. 16–17.

86. Interview, September 20, 1967; also A. E. Ritchie's testimony in Commons External Affairs Committee, Minutes, May 5, 1970, p. 42. See Peter C. Dobell, "The Influence of the United States Congress on Canadian-American Relations," *International Organization*, Autumn, 1974, pp. 922–24, for other examples.

87. He also communicated with leading American companies in Australia to gain information regarding the probable effects of the restrictions; Fred Alexander, "Problems of Australian Foreign Policy, July–December, 1964," *Australian Journal of Politics and History*, April, 1965, p. 216.

88. Reprinted in Brian Fitzpatrick and E. L. Wheelwright, *The Highest Bidder: A Citizen's Guide to Problems of Foreign Investment in Australia* (Melbourne: Lansdowne, 1965), pp. 40–46. The minister of the treasury then went to Washington to develop arguments in personal discussions.

89. Trevor R. Resse, *Australia, New Zealand and the United States: A Survey of International Relations, 1941–1968* (London: Oxford University Press, 1969), p. 227; *Current Notes*, January, 1968, pp. 28–29.

90. Reese, *Australia, New Zealand*, p. 76.

91. David M. Kiefer, "Mexico Strives for Industrial Independence," *Chemical and Engineering News*, December 4, 1969, pp. 98–99; Litvak and Maule, "Foreign Investment in Mexico," p. 11; *International Canada*, March, 1973, p. 109. Mexico took the initiative for the charter of economic rights and duties of states approved by the United Nations General Assembly in 1974 (and which the United States opposed because of imbalance in its terms).

92. *New York Times*, November 28, 30, 1970.

93. Olga Pellicer de Brody, "La Revolución Cubana en Mexico," *Foro Internacional*, April–June, 1968, p. 376–78; *News*, June 27, 1967; *Excelsior*, June 26, 1967.

94. Secretary of State Rusk's remarks in Congress of Mexico, *Memoria de la Cuarta Reunion, Parlamentaria Estados Unidos–Mexico* (Mexico, D. F., 1964), p. 19; Levinson and de Onis, *Alliance Lost Its Way*, p. 225.

95. *Revista Brasileira de Politica Internacional*, January, 1960, pp. 116–21; *Relatório do Ministro de Estado das Relações Exteriores, Annó de 1958* (Rio de Janeiro: Imprensa Nacional), pp. xi, xv; *Annó de 1959*, p. 3; Gordon Connell-Smith, *The Inter-American System* (London: Oxford University Press, 1966), pp. 267–68; 269–71.

96. Levinson and de Onis, *Alliance Lost Its Way*, pp. 123–24, 282ff.; Dale W. Adams, "What Can Underdeveloped Countries Expect from Foreign Aid to Agriculture? A Case Study of Brazil, 1950–70," *Interamerican Economic Affairs*, Summer, 1971, pp. 50ff.

97. John W. Tuthill, "Operation Topsy," *Foreign Policy*, Fall, 1972, pp. 65–66; *Jornal do Brasil*, May 10, 1966. Riordan Roett, *The Politics of Foreign Aid in the Brazilian Northeast* (Nashville: Vanderbilt University Press, 1972), deals in detail with how the United States aid program influenced Brazilian domestic politics in the Northeast.

98. There were 920 Americans in the Rio de Janeiro embassy in June, 1966, and 527 by the end of 1971; AID staffing had been reduced by half, to 208 Americans; Tuthill, "Operation Topsy," p. 85.

99. Ibid., pp. 68–78; *New York Times*, November 25, 1967.

100. Skidmore, *Politics in Brazil*, p. 159.

101. Ibid., pp. 174–82, 194–200, 248–51; Levinson and de Onis, *Alliance Lost Its Way,* pp. 193, 209; Roberto Campos, "Relations Between the United States and Latin America," in *Latin America: Evolution or Explosion?* ed. Mildred Adams (New York: Dodd, 1963), p. 41.

102. *New York Times,* January 22, 1967; *Canadian Weekly Bulletin,* February 3, 1971; A. E. Ritchie testimony to Commons External Affairs Committee, *Minutes,* May 5, 1970; Craig, *United States and Canada,* pp. 267–68; *Toronto Globe and Mail,* January 9, 1971; John Fairweather, "The Mercantile Bank Affair," *Columbia Journal of World Business,* November–December, 1971.

103. Among them is Dr. John Deutsch, in Commons External Affairs Committee, *Minutes,* November 13, 1969, pp. 12–13. Another is A. E. Safarian, who has suggested several alternatives which the Canadian government could follow to avoid the unwanted consequences of foreign direct investment; "Foreign Direct Investment," pp. 281ff.

104. Brash, *American Investment in Australian Industry,* p. 2; Brash, "Australia as Host," pp. 308–10; Potter, "Capital Inflows," p. 210.

105. Vernon, *Mexico's Development,* pp. 25–26. "Each case is decided in deference to the particular circumstances of the interested parties, guided by the elastic and subjective interpretation of the official on duty. . . . The foreign investor is aware of directives currently in effect with no assurance that they will be the same tomorrow"; J. L. Siqueiros, "Administrative Aspects of Foreign Investment in Mexico," *Mexican-American Review,* September, 1969, pp. 48, quoted in Litvak and Maule, "Foreign Investment in Mexico," p. 5.

106. Furthermore, the action became a political instrument by which the government was able to maintain its popularity when caught in the cross fire between Right and Left, as Cuban expropriations were arousing intense hostility in the United States, and some Mexicans were likening the situation to the earlier Mexican oil crisis; Miguel Wionczek, "Electric Power, the Uneasy Partnership," in *Public Policy and Private Enterprise in Mexico,* ed. Raymond Vernon (Cambridge: Harvard University Press, 1970), pp. 75–99; Pellicer de Brody, "La Revolución Cubana," p. 369.

107. *New York Times,* May 19, 1972. See discussion of Mexico above, in section on Reciprocity.

108. Böhrisch and König, *La Politica Mexicana,* p. 29; Litvak and Maule, "Foreign Investment in Mexico," p. 10; Kiefer, "Industrial Independence," p. 92.

109. Böhrisch and König, *La Politica Mexicana,* p. 38; *News,* July 4, 1967.

110. Hansen, *Mexican Development,* pp. 168–70.

111. Skidmore, *Politics in Brazil,* pp. 159–61, 185, 196, 240, 248–51; Philippe Schmitter, *Interest Conflict and Political Change in Brazil* (Stanford: Stanford University Press, 1971), pp. 337, 350–51, 361.

112. This was an allegation against *Reader's Digest* and *Time* and *Life,* among others; *O Globo,* May 9, 1966. For the administrative weaknesses, see Skidmore, *Politics in Brazil,* pp. 185, 197.

113. *New York Times,* May 3, 4, 7, 1972, January 25, 1973; *Time,* May 15, 1972; *International Canada,* May, 1972, pp. 75–82; January, 1973, pp. 17ff.; March, 1973, pp. 96ff.; April, 1973, pp. 134ff.; May, 1973, pp. 160; June, 1973, pp. 174ff.; July–August 1973, pp. 204ff.; November, 1973, p. 308.

114. *International Canada,* January, 1974, p. 10.

115. Department of State, *Bulletin,* August 4, 1958, p. 207.

116. *Current Notes,* September, 1969, pp. 520–24, gives one example.

117. *New York Times,* September 17, 1972; November 13, 1974; January 26, 1975; Peter King, "Whither Whitlam?" *International Journal,* Summer, 1974, pp. 436; *Greenwich Time* (AP dispatch), May 28, 1975.

118. They were the Confederacion de Camares Industriales (CONCAMIN), Confederacion de Comercio (CONCANACO), and Confederacion de Centros Patronales. Berdecio, "Canacintra," p. 3; Böhrisch and König, *La Politica Mexicana,* pp. 43–50; Rafael Izquierdo, "Protectionism in Mexico" in *Public Policy and Private Enterprise in Mexico,* ed. Raymond Vernon (Cambridge: Harvard University Press, 1964), pp. 280–81.

119. Litvak and Maule, "Foreign Investment in Mexico," p. 7.

120. Hansen, *Mexican Development,* p. 189.

121. See Roberto Campos, for example, in *Jornal do Brasil,* April 29, 1966.

122. Stepan, *Military in Politics,* p. 236; and Henry J. Steiner and David M. Trubek, "Brazil—All Power to the Generals," *Foreign Affairs,* April, 1971, p. 478.

123. Skidmore, *Politics in Brazil,* p. 142; Baer and Simonsen, "Brazilian Nationalism," p. 274.

124. They were presumably pharmaceutical companies. Speech reprinted in Richard R. Fagan and Wayne A. Cornelius, Jr., eds., *Political Power in Latin America: Seven Confrontations* (Englewood Cliffs: Prentice-Hall, 1970), pp. 182–86.

125. Stepan, *Military in Politics,* p. 125; Skidmore, *Politics in Brazil,* p. 323; Bell, "Brazilian–American Relations," pp. 87–88, 95.

126. *New York Times,* December 17, 1968. The very day that his predecessor had decreed a new national security law broadening the powers of the military, the United States entered into an agreement which would eventuate in $450 million of credits for importing United States machinery; *New York Times,* March 12, 1967. The gradual alienation is noted in Bell, "Brazilian-American Relations," pp. 96–98.

EIGHT   *GLOBAL ISSUES OF FOREIGN POLICY*

1. At one point in their maneuvers, the Americans did support the Latin American members. *Excelsior,* July 4–5, 1967; see also Arthur Lall, *The UN and the Middle East Crisis, 1967* (New York: Columbia University Press, 1968), chap. 9, "The Latin American Position," esp. pp. 154, 159, 162, 164, 173, 179, 208, 217, 237.

2. Lester B. Pearson, *Mike: the Memoirs of the Right Honourable Lester B. Pearson* (Toronto: University of Toronto Press, 1973), vol. 2, chap. 7; Robert W. Reford, *Canada and Three Crises* (Toronto: Canadian Institute of International Affairs, 1968), pp. 44–50; Donald C. Masters, *Canada in World Affairs, 1953–1955* (Toronto: Oxford University Press, 1959), pp. 99–107; *External Affairs,* vol. 7, no. 4 (1955), p. 127.

3. Dean Acheson, *Present at the Creation* (New York: Norton, 1969), pp. 497–98, describes the differing responses of these two governments, with admiration for their adroitness. For Canada's participation in the Korean War decisions, see Pearson, *Mike,* chaps. 7, 8; Chester A. Ronning, "Canada and the UN," in *Canada's Role as a Middle Power,* ed. J. King Gordon

(Toronto: Canadian Institute of International Affairs, 1966), pp. 37–42; Denis Stairs, *The Diplomacy of Constraint: Canada, the Korean War, and the United States* (Toronto: University of Toronto Press, 1974).

4. John Holmes pointed out that Canadian wheat sales relieved the Chinese of scarce dollars and the Canadians of overplentiful supplies of grain.

5. John W. Holmes, "The Diplomacy of a Middle Power," *The Atlantic,* November, 1964, p. 112, and James Eayrs, *Northern Approaches: Canada and the Search for Peace* (Toronto: Macmillan, 1961), pp. 160–62.

6. *New York Times,* September 11, 15, 1966.

7. J. D. B. Miller, "Problems of Australian Foreign Policy, July–December, 1963," *Australian Journal of Politics and History,* April, 1964, p. 4. Along with New Zealand, Australia sought in 1973 to restrain French nuclear above-ground testing in the Pacific by a suit in the World Court.

8. S. Encel and Allan McKnight, "Bombs, Power Stations, and Proliferation," *Australian Quarterly,* March, 1970; Colin S. Rubenstein, "Science Affairs and Australian Politics," (Ph.D. diss., Columbia University, 1973), pp. 15, 21, 25; H. G. Gelber, "Australia and Nuclear Weapons," in *Security, Order and the Bomb,* ed. Johan Jørgen Holst (Oslo: Universitetasforlaget, 1972), pp. 113–18.

9. Senate Committee on Foreign Relations, *Hearings on Additional Protocol II to the Latin American Nuclear-Free Zone Treaty,* September 22, 1970, 91st Cong., 2nd sess., and February 23, 1971, 92nd Cong., 1st sess. (one vol., 1971), esp. pp. 2–3, 8, 10, 18, 30–31, 34. The United States position on such a zone was at best neutral, and Brazil's footdragging on the Latin American treaty was viewed very tolerantly by American officials. They later became more apprehensive about mounting Brazilian ambitions in the nuclear field.

10. For example, the United States position on the seabed ban of nuclear weapons moved along lines proposed by Canada; *New York Times,* October 24, 1967.

11. Francisco Cuevas Cancino, "Política y Democracia Internacionales," *Foro Internacional,* vol. 1 (1960–61), pp. 306–7; Robert O. Keohane, "Political Influence in the General Assembly," *International Conciliation,* March, 1966; Jorge Castañeda, *Mexico and the United Nations* (New York: Manhattan, 1958), p. 149.

12. On the Mexican and Brazilian voting patterns, see John R. Faust and Charles X. Sansifer, "Mexican Foreign Policy in the U.N.: The Advocacy of Moderation in an Era of Revolution," reprinted in *Latin American International Politics* ed. Carlo Alberto Ortez (Notre Dame: University of Notre Dame Press, 1969), pp. 103, 106; Frederick H. Gareau, *The Cold War, 1947 to 1967: A Quantitative Study* (Denver: University of Denver Monograph Series in World Affairs, 1969), pp. 9–11, 17–19, 25, 31–33, 45–47, 49–51.

13. *New York Times,* November 30, 1966, November 12, 1969.

14. Mexico and Brazil joined the United States in the minority position, which would have made the expulsion of Nationalist China an "important question." Mexico was with the majority in the vote on seating the People's Republic, while Brazil stuck with the United States. The vote was 76 for, 35 against, 17 abstentions; *New York Times,* November 5, 10, 1971.

15. By the early 1970s, Mexico was no longer alone in having diplomatic ties with the Castro government and was being joined by other OAS members in a movement to cease isolating Cuba. Brazil, by then a military dictatorship, was supporting, in the face of changed conditions,

the line maintained so adamantly by the United States for so long. By 1975, the United States had to give up trying to hold the other OAS members in line on this issue.

16. *External Affairs,* December, 1955, p. 129; Eayrs, *Northern Approaches,* p. 162; James Eayrs, *Canada in World Affairs, October 1955 to June 1957* (Toronto: Oxford University Press, 1959), pp. 217–23.

17. House of Commons Standing Committee on External Affairs and National Defence, *Minutes of Proceedings and Evidence,* April 21, 1970, p. 13. See also Masters, *Canada in World Affairs,* pp. 22–25, and Eayrs, *Northern Approaches,* p. 13.

18. Department of State, *United States Foreign Policy, 1969–1970: A Report of the Secretary of State,* p. 121. True, United States Ambassador C. Burke Elbrick had been kidnapped by terrorists in September, 1969. Also without parallel were United States protests over the reported torture of an American businessman (formerly a missionary) in Recife in October, 1974; *New York Times,* October 16, 1974.

19. Quoted in Gough Whitlam, "Beyond Vietnam—Australia's Regional Responsibility" in "Australia's Foreign Policy in the Seventies": Papers read in Australian Institute of International Affairs, North Queensland Branch, mimeographed, 1968, p. 20.

20. See Robert O'Neill, "Australian Military Problems in Vietnam," *Australian Outlook,* April, 1969, pp. 46–57, for the difficulties experienced by Australia in maintaining control over the operations of its own forces in Vietnam.

21. Sir Garfield Barwick at symposium in Australian Institute of Political Science, *Australian Defence and Foreign Policy* (Sydney: Angus and Robertson, 1964), p. 11.

22. See statement of Secretary of State Mitchell Sharp to House of Commons, May 29, 1973 in (Canadian) Department of External Affairs, *Vietnam: Canada's Approach,* May, 1973; *Canada Weekly,* March 8, 1973, April 4, 1973; *Wall Street Journal,* February 27, 1973; W. M. Dobell, "A 'Sow's Ear' in Vietnam," *International Journal,* Summer, 1974, pp. 356–92.

23. See Dean Acheson's acid remarks about unwelcome Canadian nudgings during the Korean War; *Present at the Creation* (New York: Norton, 1969), pp. 696–700. Note also the irate response of President Johnson to Prime Minister Pearson's publicly delivered but gentle suggestion to curb the bombing of North Vietnam, made in Philadelphia in April, 1965. The Canadian leader was not unique in incurring the displeasure of the president for disagreeing with him. From Denis Stairs's close study of Canada in the Korean War, he concluded that although the Canadians could not effectively influence United States behavior, neither did they suffer when their views deviated from their great ally's; "Confronting Uncle Sam: Cuba and Korea," in *An Independent Foreign Policy in Canada?* ed. Stephen Clarkson (Toronto: McClelland and Stewart, 1968), p. 68.

24. *News,* July 3, 1967.

25. Alan Watt, *The Evolution of Australian Foreign Policy,* 1938–65 (Cambridge: Cambridge University Press, 1967), pp. 340–41; Peter Bell, "Brazilian-American Relations" in *Brazil in the Sixties* ed. Riordan Roett (Nashville: Vanderbilt University Press, 1972), p. 93. Of course, these sentiments were quickly derided in the leaders' respective countries.

26. The Australians did secure American reassurance in 1962 that ANZUS obligations covered their island territory; and in 1963 the Australian government believed that it had similar assurance for Australian forces in Malaysia; Trevor R. Reese, *Australia, New Zealand and the United States: A Survey of International Relations, 1941–1968* (London: Oxford University Press, 1969), pp. 219–24; Miller, "Australian Foreign Policy," pp. 14–15; Thomas B. Millar,

Australia's Foreign Policy (Sydney: Angus and Robertson, 1968), pp. 119, 136; Gordon Greenwood and Norman Harper, eds., *Australia in World Affairs, 1961–1965* (Melbourne: F. W. Cheshire, 1968), pp. 333–39.

27. Note Prime Minister Pearson's surprise when, after the Canadian government's agreement to move as quickly as possible to perform a peacekeeping function in Cyprus had eased greatly the United States position in its own efforts to moderate that crisis, President Johnson asked the Canadian leader what he could do for him in return.

28. Keohane, "Political Influence," pp. 17–19.

29. Watt, *Australian Foreign Policy*, pp. 83–91.

30. For their contributions, see Castañeda, *Mexico and United Nations*, pp. 43ff., 151, and *passim;* William T. R. Fox, "The Super Powers at San Francisco," *Review of Politics*, January, 1946, pp. 122, 126–27; Daniel Cheever and Field Haviland, *Organizing for Peace* (Boston: Houghton Mifflin, 1954), pp. 65, 195, 263; C. Delgado de Carvalho, *História Diplomática do Brasil* (São Paolo: Companhia Editora Nacional, 1959), pp. 273, 355.

31. F. H. Soward, *Canada in World Affairs: From Normandy to Paris, 1944–46* (Toronto: University of Toronto Press, 1950), pp. 17ff. The Americans were grateful for their problem-solving style and tendency to beat down doctrinaire and impractical proposals.

32. Maria Ojeda Gomez, "Mexico as a Middle Power," in *Canada's Role as a Middle Power*, ed. J. King Gordon (Toronto: Canadian Institute of International Affairs, 1966), p. 142.

33. Elie Abel, *The Cuban Missile Crisis* (Philadelphia: Lippincott, 1966), pp. 107–8, tells how the Mexican government was informed.

34. It was acquired because Canadian intelligence officers happened to be in Washington at that time and sensed that something very unusual was about to happen, because of the way their American counterparts were suddenly disappearing or not keeping appointments; Reford, *Canada and Three Crises*, pp. 175, 178, 184, 195, 204. The Canadian government was not asked by the State Department to take the measures which were desired by NORAD.

35. *News*, June 20, 1967.

36. Some fellow Australians judged these attempts clumsy and futile. J. D. B. Miller, *Britain and the Old Dominions* (London: Chatto & Windus, 1966), p. 250; Watt, *Australian Foreign Policy*, pp. 232–33 and 308; *Current Notes*, vol. 27, 1956, p. 345; Katherine West, *Power in the Liberal Party: A Study in Australian Politics* (Melbourne: F. W. Cheshire, 1965), p. 259. Menzies had a surer touch at an earlier period, at least with Dean Acheson, who remarks at his skill in getting what he wanted in Washington unostentatiously; *Present at the Creation*, p. 502. Yet his experiences point up the importance of personalities in creating or obliterating distance. All agree that General MacArthur presented an insuperable obstacle to others who wished to have some impact on American policy during the Japanese occupation and the Korean War.

37. *New York Times*, January 12, 1974.

38. The Australian Department of External Affairs official bulletin, *Current Notes on International Affairs* (in 1973 renamed *Australian Foreign Affairs Record*), regularly carries full reprints of the messages and speeches of the American president. One does not look to the Department of State's *Bulletin* for such exposure to Australian official views.

39. Henry S. Albinski, "Australia and the Chinese Strategic Embargo," *Australian Outlook*, vol. 19, 1965, pp. 117–28.

40. *New York Times*, July 6, 1971, September 17, 1972.

41. Reese, *Australia, New Zealand,* p. 163, quoting Casey.

42. *Australian Foreign Policy,* pp. 245–46.

43. As Secretary of State for External Affairs Mitchell Sharp declared on NATO's twenty-fifth anniversary, continuing consultation through NATO "gives us direct and immediate access to the thinking of our allies and an opportunity to bring our own views to their attention"; *Canada Weekly,* April 24, 1974.

44. Nevertheless, after the Cuban missile crisis, which occurred during the following year, Mexico supported the OAS resolution opposing the introduction of nuclear weapons even if provisional use of force was necessary, and it approved the United States action taken to counter the emplacement of missiles in Cuba; Minerva Morales Etzioni, *Majority of One* (Beverly Hills: Sage, 1970), pp. 155, 165, 190, 194; Gordon Connell-Smith, *The Inter-American System* (London: Oxford University Press, 1966), pp. 32–33, 250, 258–59; *Presencia Internacional de Lopez Mateos,* vol. 1, 1962, p. 545; 1963, pp. 131–32.

45. Castañeda, *Mexico and United Nations,* pp. 166–70, 189–90; Jorge Castañeda, "Pan-Americanismo: Posicion do Mexico," *Revista Brasileira de Politica Internacional,* September, 1958, pp. 5–40. From time to time, the Mexicans endeavored to get OAS agencies located elsewhere than in Washington and to have their officers dissociated from dual functions in Washington, the better to keep inter-American activities independent of the United States; William Manger, *Pan America in Crisis: The Future of the OAS* (Washington: Public Affairs Press, 1961), pp. 13, 35; Daniel Cosío Villegas, *American Extremes,* trans. Americo Paredes (Austin: University of Texas Press, 1964), pp. 188–89.

46. When, outside OAS auspices, Secretary of State Henry Kissinger expressed the desire to meet the foreign ministers "informally," Mexico took the lead in providing the meeting place—and also in trying to get a preliminary Latin American consensus on a number of issues of those states' own choosing, not Mr. Kissinger's; *New York Times,* February 19, 1974.

47. Gerald Clark, *Canada: The Uneasy Neighbor* (New York: David McKay, 1965), p. 63.

48. Peyton V. Lyon, *The Policy Question* (Toronto: McClelland and Stewart, 1963), pp. 36, 40; Connell-Smith, *Inter-American System,* pp. 6, 137, 192; J. C. N. Ogelsby, "Canada and the Pan American Union," *International Journal,* Summer, 1969, pp. 571–89; Douglas G. Anglin, "U.S. Opposition to Canadian Membership in the Pan American Union," *International Organization,* Winter, 1961. As a Canadian official, M. Goyer, once said, the United States is a geographical—or geopolitical—entity lying between Canada and Latin America.

49. Thus their vote on anti-Communist resolutions often failed to reflect the Mexicans' misgivings; Castañeda, *Mexico and United Nations,* p. 194. See also Cuevas Cancino, "Politica y Democracia Internacionales," pp. 306–7, for Mexico's conduct in the United Nations; Francisco Cuevas Cancino, "The Foreign Policy of Mexico," in *Foreign Policies in a World of Change,* ed. Joseph E. Black and Kenneth W. Thompson (New York: Harper & Row, 1963), pp. 665–66.

50. Australia has not been on this committee and has showed little interest in its concerns.

51. W. J. Hudson, *Australian Diplomacy* (South Melbourne: Macmillan, 1970), pp. 65–67; *idem, Australia and the Colonial Question at the United Nations* (Sydney: Sydney University Press, 1970), esp. pp. 4–8 and 170–71.

52. Reese, *Australia, New Zealand,* pp. 194–96; Pearson, *Mike,* chapt. 11; Reford, *Canada and Three Crises,* pp. 103ff.

53. Not only was the United States legal commitment under the Southeast Asia treaty more restricted than the other members' commitment, but the Americans used SEATO in much the same way as they used the OAS, namely, to amplify their voice and gain the support of the other members. Because of this attitude and Australia's unhappy participation in the Vietnam war, justified as a SEATO obligation, the Australian government which came to power late in 1972 decided to let the organization "wither away"; *New York Times,* January 22, 23, 1973.

54. Matthew J. Abrams, *The Canada–United States Interparliamentary Group* (Ottawa: Parliamentary Centre for Foreign Affairs and Foreign Trade and Canadian Institute of International Affairs, 1973), pp. 50–56.

55. See Congress of Mexico, *Memoria de la Cuarta Reunion, Parlamentaria Estados Unidos– Mexico* (Mexico, D. F., 1964), pp. 49–51.

56. This chapter does not deal with the question of whether or not issues could be dealt with on lower levels of the bureaucracy. By definition, foreign policy on global issues is high politics, in which opportunities for lower-level bureaucrats to manage differences are minimal compared to those in other issue areas. These global foreign-policy issues are "statecentric" questions involving the position of a particular country in world politics.

57. Eayrs, *Canada in World Affairs,* pp. 153–54, 158–59; Arnold Heeney, *The Things That Are Caesar's: Memoirs of a Canadian Public Servant* (Toronto: University of Toronto Press, 1972), pp. 144–45; Abrams, *Interparliamentary Group,* pp. 9, 10; Gerald M. Craig, *The United States and Canada* (Cambridge: Harvard University Press, 1968), p. 240; Richard P. Stebbins, *United States in World Affairs, 1957* (New York: Random House, 1958), pp. 287, 288; Department of State, *Bulletin,* April 1, 1957, p. 539, April 29, 1957, pp. 694–95; Eayrs, *Northern Approaches,* p. 11.

58. Thus when the foreign minister, San Tiago Dantas, defended his conduct at Punta del Este in 1961, he encountered substantial political opposition; see his *Política Exterior Independente* (Rio de Janeiro: Editôra Civilização Brasileira, 1962), pp. 184–92. Pressure from another direction forced him from office prior to the coup.

59. President Echeverria became even bolder, and among his initiatives he secured the French signature to the Latin American denuclearization treaty, albeit with reservations; *New York Times,* April, 25, 1974. His Latin American moves included public support of Panama's claim to full sovereignty over the Canal Zone; *New York Times,* September 2, 1973.

60. Olga Pellicer de Brody, "Los Grupos Patronales y la Politica Exterior Mexican: Las Relaciones con la Revolucion Cubana," *Foro Internacional,* July–September, 1969, pp. 1–27.

61. The Mexican government's massacre of student demonstrators in 1968 was an outstanding exception to its ordinarily less brutal methods of countering extremist opposition.

62. Thus Lester Pearson declared early in 1956, with respect to recognition, that it was not worth "having a first-class row with the United States over a matter on which public opinion in our own country is strongly divided"; Eayrs, *Canada in World Affairs,* p. 82.

63. The elaborate series of studies culminating in the Trudeau government's *Foreign Policy for Canadians* appeared to mark new departures in many directions. Significantly, there was no separate booklet on relations with the United States (until, under pressure, an addendum was produced two years later).

64. *Canada Weekly,* May 23, 1973.

65. *New York Times,* July 31, 1973. Prime Minister Whitlam told President Nixon that while relations with the United States still were important, Australia had many other concerns else-

where. See also *New York Post,* August 1, 1973; *New York Times,* December 4, 1972, February 24, 1973.

66. *New York Times,* February 27, 1973, March 25, 1974. For some of the changes, see Peter King, "Whither Whitlam?" *International Journal,* Summer, 1974, pp. 422–40; James L. Richardson, "Australian Foreign Policy under the Labor Government," *Cooperation and Conflict,* no. 1, 1974.

NINE *NEIGHBORHOOD ISSUES*

1. Final, because of the rules accepted for future changes in the river's course; *New York Times,* August 22, November 24, 1970.

2. The most nearly complete source on how these three river systems have been handled is Norris Hundley, Jr., *Dividing the Waters: A Century of Controversy between the United States and Mexico* (Berkeley: University of California Press, 1966); it has been heavily relied upon for this study.

3. A major source of information on the Columbia River development is John V. Krutilla, *The Columbia River Treaty: The Economics of an International River Basin Development* (Baltimore: Johns Hopkins Press, 1967).

4. The fullest description of the twists and turns in the course toward agreement is William R. Willoughby, *The St. Lawrence Waterway: A Study in Politics and Diplomacy* (Madison: University of Wisconsin Press, 1961), which takes the story up to 1960 and has been a main source for this study.

5. Willoughby, *St. Lawrence Waterway,* p. 265. The joint agencies were the St. Lawrence River Joint Board of Engineers; the International Joint Commission, the International St. Lawrence River Board of Control, and the International Lake Ontario Board of Engineers.

6. David R. Deener, ed., *Canada–United States Treaty Relations* (Durham: Duke University Press, 1963), p. 64.

7. Dean Acheson, *Present at the Creation* (New York: Norton, 1969), pp. 639–40; Willoughby, *St. Lawrence Waterway,* pp. 217–36; Dale C. Thompson, *Louis St. Laurent: Canadian* (New York: St. Martin's Press, 1968), p. 258.

8. See his testimony before the House of Commons Standing Committee on External Affairs, *Minutes of Proceedings and Evidence,* December 12, 1957, pp. 247–75, December 13, 1957, pp. 284–86; August 11, 1958, pp. 295, 299–301; April 23, 1959, pp. 205ff.; March 11, 1960, p. 146, March 16, 1960, p. 148, March 18, 1960, pp. 165–198, March 23, 1960, pp. 201–16, and March 25, 1960, pp. 219–33 (hereafter cited as Commons External Affairs Committee, *Minutes*).

9. Krutilla, *Columbia River Treaty,* pp. 7, 66, 119–20, 193–95.

10. Gerald M. Craig, *The United States and Canada* (Cambridge: Harvard University Press, 1968), pp. 319–24; Donald Waterfield, *Continental Waterboy* (Toronto: Clark, Irwin, 1970), pp. 28–60, 105, 114, 154–55.

11. James Eayrs, "Sharing a Continent: The Hard Issues," in *The United States and Canada,* ed. John Sloan Dickey (Englewood Cliffs: Prentice-Hall for the American Assembly, 1964), p. 84; Peyton V. Lyon, *Canada in World Affairs, 1961–63* (Toronto: Oxford University Press, 1968), pp. 372ff.

12. In 1972, Bennett's successor and former opponent, New Democratic party leader David Barrett, tried unsuccessfully to get the national government to reopen the agreement; *International Canada,* December, 1972, pp. 226–27. See also Waterfield, *Continental Waterboy,* passim.

13. Krutilla, *Columbia River Treaty,* p. 10; Deener, ed., *Treaty Relations,* p. 58. This is a logical extension of the principle that Mexico insisted upon in the case of the salinity of the Colorado River, that is, that damage done downstream from upstream action should be compensated.

14. *Canadian Weekly Bulletin,* February 10, 1971.

15. About four million people, living mostly in twin cities, populate the border area; two million acres are irrigated by the boundary river; International Boundary and Water Commission, "International Conference on Water for Peace," Mexico City, May 23–31, 1967, multigraphed, p. 1 (hereafter cited as IBWC, "Water for Peace").

16. The canal's flow could be controlled to permit water to be drawn off above the Morelos Dam at Mexico's request; Department of State press release, "United States and Mexico Reach Agreement on Lower Colorado River Salinity Problem," March 22, 1965; IBWC, "Water for Peace," pp. 11–12.

17. Department of State, *United States Foreign Policy, 1972: A Report of the Secretary of State,* pp. 423–24 (hereafter cited as *US Foreign Policy*); *New York Times,* August 31, 1973. The plant may not actually begin to operate, however, until 1979; *New York Times,* June 27, 1974).

18. IBWC, "Water for Peace," p. 12; *New York Times,* February 11, 1967.

19. The United States agreed to be responsible for reimbursing American owners for the value of land (and improvements) that had been on the American side in order to provide clear title for Mexico, while a Mexican bank would purchase the land and structures on it passing to Mexico. The agreed-upon purchase price for the structures could then be subtracted from the cost to the United States for indemnifying the owners of the land; Department of State release, "The Chamizal Settlement," July, 1963; Sheldon B. Liss, *A Century of Disagreement: The Chamizal Conflict, 1864–1964* (Washington: University Press, 1965), esp. pp. 90ff.

20. Hundley, *Dividing the Waters,* pp. 155–56, 168, 172–80.

21. Such rivers were the Souris, St. Croix, and St. John. The same was true for lesser rivers on the Mexican side. For Canadian examples, see Commons External Affairs Committee, *Minutes* March 16, 1960, p. 159, March 28, 1960, pp. 247–48; June 16, 1961, p. 253. See *International Canada,* February, 1974, p. 20; *New York Times,* August 25, 1974, November 17, 1975, for the controversy arising from the Garrison diversion on the Souris in the United States, which aroused Canadian concern. That proximity does not necessarily produce close cooperation between neighbors may be seen in the absence of such amicable arrangements between Brazil and Argentina with respect to the Parana River; see *New York Times,* March 15, 1972, for the ill will arising from Brazil's hydroelectric developments on that river and its failure to consult with affected countries.

22. Hundley, *Dividing the Waters,* p. 150; Acheson, *Present at the Creation,* p. 95.

23. *Canada Weekly,* February 28, 1973.

24. Senator Mansfield called "catalytic" the part played by the Mexico–United States Interparliamentary Group with respect to the settlement of both the Chamizal and the salinity of the Colorado issues; Matthew J. Abrams. *The Canada–United States Interparliamentary Group*

(Ottawa: Parliamentary Centre for Foreign Affairs and Foreign Trade and Canadian Institute of International Affairs, 1973), pp. 111, also 71, 86, 105.

25. The IBWC lacks the quasi-judicial powers of the IJC.

26. For example, the two governments referred to the IJC the reconciling of tourist and electric-power interests at Niagara Falls in the 1950s, and it later was charged with recommending ways to preserve and enhance the beauty of this spectacle when the falls were threatened by natural erosion; A[rnold] D. P. Heeney, "Along the Common Frontier: The International Joint Commission," *Behind the Headlines,* July, 1967, p. 15; Commons External Affairs Committee, *Minutes* December 16, 1957, pp. 308–9; *New York Times,* October 14, 1974. See also L. M. Bloomfield and Gerald F. Fitzgerald, *Boundary Waters Problems of Canada and the United States: The International Joint Commission* (Toronto: Carswell, 1958), p. 64.

27. Bloomfield and Fitzgerald, *Boundary Waters,* pp. 58, 63.

28. Heeney, "Common Frontier," p. 4.

29. See, for example, his testimony before the House of Commons Standing Committee on External Affairs, cited above in n. 8.

30. Willoughby, *St. Lawrence Waterway,* esp. pp. 161–180, 242, 266–67.

31. See Hundley, *Dividing the Waters,* pp. 41–80, 161. Fortunately for Mexico, Senator Tom Connally of Texas, chairman of the Senate Foreign Relations Committee in the early 1940s, wanted a treaty to be accepted by the United States especially for his state's interests.

32. Krutilla, *Columbia River Treaty,* p. 11.

33. Ibid., pp. 190, 202–3.

34. A pilot joint air-pollution sampling program was started in 1972 between El Paso and Ciudad Juarez; Guillermo H. Davila, "Air Pollution Control on the U.S.–Mexican Border: International Considerations," in *Pollution and International Boundaries: United States–Mexican Environmental Problems,* ed. Albert E. Utton (Albuquerque: University of New Mexico Press, 1973), p. 67.

35. A plant serving Nogales, Arizona, and Nogales, Sonora, was constructed, as well as one serving Douglas, Arizona, and Agua Prieta, Sonora. For the latter plant, each country paid a share of the capital costs proportionate to the part of the works required in its territory; for the former plant, which was built on United States territory, payment by each country for operating costs was in proportion to the sewage flows in that country; IBWC, "Water for Peace," pp. 8–9.

36. Ibid., p. 6.

37. Bloomfield and Fitzgerald, *Boundary Waters,* pp. 76–78.

38. See *International Canada,* February, 1970, p. 36; January, 1971, p. 11; February, 1971, p. 35; July–August, 1971, p. 163; April, 1972, p. 64; November 1972, p. 213; *Canadian Weekly Bulletin,* March 4, June 10, July 15, 1970; January 27, June 30, July 7, 1971; May 3, June 14, 1972. *Canada Weekly,* February 21, 1973. *New York Times,* August 26, November 22, 1969; January 25, February 20, April 19, June 24, August 1, November 22, 24, 1970; June 11, 15, 1971; April 9, 16, 1972; October 24, 1973; April 9, 1974. *Ottawa Citizen,* January 11, 15, March 9, 1971. *Toronto Globe and Mail,* March 30, 1971. Department of State, *World Environmental Quality* (1973) says that the Great Lakes program is probably the most far-reaching ever attempted internationally to counter water pollution.

39. Secretary Sharp had earlier told Parliament that Canada had sent diplomatic notes to the United States but not to the Soviet Union when the latter had carried on a similar test because, in addition to Canada's general opposition to further underground testing in the interests of slowing the arms race, his government objected in particular to the Amchitka test for fear of direct effects on Canadians living on the Pacific Coast; *International Canada,* September, 1971, p. 185.

40. *New York Times* editorial, November 7, 1971; *Ottawa Citizen,* March 30, 1971; *Toronto Globe and Mail,* March 30, 1971; *Greenwich Time,* February 3, 1970; February 9, 1970; Peter C. Dobell, *Canada's Search for New Roles: Foreign Policy in the Trudeau Era* (London: Oxford University Press, 1972), pp. 33ff. *Canadian Weekly Bulletin,* July 12, 1972; *International Canada,* February, 1970, p. 33; February, 1971, p. 35; September, 1971, p. 185; October, 1971, p. 199; November, 1971, p. 218; Kal J. Holsti, "The United States and Canada," in *Conflict in World Politics* ed. Steven L. Spiegel and Kenneth N. Waltz (Cambridge: Winthrop, 1971), p. 386.

41. Canadian concern for preserving the Arctic environment is dealt with below.

42. See Donald Milsten, "Arctic Passage—Legal Heavy Weather," *Orbis,* Winter, 1972, pp. 1173–93.

43. Ann L. Hollick, "Canadian-American Relations: Law of the Sea," *International Organization,* Autumn, 1974, pp. 761–67; *Canadian Weekly Bulletin,* April 29, 1970; Department of State, *Bulletin,* May 11, 1970; pp. 610–11; Department of External Affairs press release, "Note to U.S. Government Concerning Control of Arctic Waters," April 16, 1970.

44. *International Canada,* June, 1972, pp. 93–94; July–August, 1972, p. 116.

45. Not even an extraordinary meeting called by the Canadian members of the Canada–United States Interparliamentary Group in July prior to the final action by Congress could prevent the removal of the final legal impediment to the Alaska pipeline route. For references on the trans-Alaska pipeline, see *International Canada,* January, 1971, pp. 12–13; February, 1971, p. 34; March, 1971, pp. 59–65, April, 1971, pp. 92–95, May, 1971, p. 120, July–August, 1971, p. 164, January, 1972, pp. 2–3, March, 1972, pp. 46–47, May, 1972, p. 84, June, 1972, pp. 92–94, October, 1972, p. 188; *New York Times,* August 14, 1970, March 21, June 27, 1972, March 6, 13, April 6, 13, May 22, 26, October 14, 1973 ("That Unstoppable Pipeline" by Thomas M. Brown), February 1, 9, 1974; *Washington Post,* June 10, 1972; *Wall Street Journal,* February 12, 1973; *Greenwich Time,* (AP dispatch), March 27, 1972; *Toronto Globe and Mail,* February 19, March 29, March 30, 1971; *Ottawa Citizen,* February 17, March 1, 5, 15, 1971; *Canada Weekly Bulletin,* July 12, 1972; Environmental Defense Fund, *Annual Report for 1972,* p. 8; Wilderness Society, *Wilderness Report,* May, 1973.

46. F. H. Soward, et al., *Canada in World Affairs: The Pre-War Years* (Toronto: Oxford University Press, 1941), p. 231; Bloomfield and Fitzgerald, *Boundary Waters,* pp. 137–38; William R. Willoughby, "The International Joint Commission and Air Pollution Investigations," *ACSUS Newsletter,* Spring, 1972, pp. 58ff.

47. The commission had already investigated and reported on a narrower case, air pollution in the Detroit River. In its 1960 report, it found the principal cause to be obsolescent vessels plying the narrow waters. The United States government did not immediately follow through on the commission's recommendations; no federal agency had legislative authority to deal with problems of air quality at that time. Nevertheless, some of the IJC proposals were implemented by local authorities.

48. *Canadian Weekly Bulletin,* November 1, 1972; Willoughby, "Air Pollution Investigations," pp. 62–64. Unlike the IJC, the International Boundary and Water Commission's jurisdiction over United States–Mexican boundary problems does not include air pollution; Bill Enriquez, "International Legal Implications of Industrialization Along the Mexican–U.S. Border," in *Pollution and International Boundaries: United States–Mexican Environmental Problems,* ed. Albert E. Utton (Albuquerque: University of New Mexico Press, 1973), p. 97.

49. *Canadian Weekly Bulletin,* October 25, 1972; Elise Nouël, "Fourth Plenary Session of the Committee on the Challenges of Modern Society," *NATO Review,* May–June, 1971, p. 18.

50. Heeney, "Common Frontier," pp. 16–17; General McNaughton's testimony, Commons Committee on External Affairs, *Minutes,* December 16, 1957, p. 311, June 16, Affairs, 1961, p. 244.

51. *Ottawa Citizen,* February 2, 1971; February 6, 1971.

52. An important proportion of issues with which Department of State officials concerned with Canada have had to deal in the 1970s were environmental questions. As an example, see article by Political-Environmental Officer (in the Office of Canadian Affairs) Edward V. Nef, "Environmental Control: A U.S.–Canadian Problem," *ACSUS Newsletter,* Spring, 1972, pp. 68–73.

53. For an excellent, detailed account of the cross pressures, methods of opponents and proponents, and ad hoc alliances formed for dealing with the Chicago diversion bills, see J. Richard Wagner, *Canada's Impact on United States Legislative Processes: The Chicago Diversion Bills,* Research Series, no. 14, (Tucson: University of Arizona Institute of Government Research, 1973); see also Peter Dobell, "The Influence of the United States Congress in Canadian-American Relations," *International Organization,* Autumn, 1974, pp. 912–14, who refers as well to the aid of Representative Thomas O'Brien, friend of Speaker Sam Rayburn and Senator Everett Dirksen. Despite governmental measures, the level of the Great Lakes is difficult to regulate; it was too high for most interests in the 1970s.

54. *Canadian Weekly Bulletin,* June 11, September 24, 1969.

55. Difficulties encountered in working out the regulations were sufficient that the Arctic Water Pollution Prevention Act was not proclaimed until August 2, 1972. No more *Manhattan* voyages took place. On this controversy, see Donald J. Slimman, "The Parting of the Waves: Canada–United States Differences on the Law of the Sea," *Behind the Headlines,* April, 1975, pp. 2–4, 10–13; Dobell, *Canada's Search,* pp. 69–72; Mitchell Sharp's testimony before Commons External Affairs Committee, *Minutes,* May 12, 1970, pp. 12, 17; Maxwell Cohen, "The Arctic and the National Interest," *International Journal,* Winter, 1970/71, pp. 52–81; Department of State, *Bulletin,* May 11, 1970, pp. 610–11; Canadian Consulate General [New York] release, "Summary of the Canadian Note Dated April 16, 1970, to the Government of the United States of America Concerning Control of Arctic Waters"; *Canadian Weekly Bulletin,* April 29, 1970; August 30, 1972; *International Canada,* January, 1970, pp. 6–8; February, 1970, pp. 223–225; July 8, 1972, p. 129; *New York Times,* September 13, October 24, November 12, 1969; February 21, April 5, 10, 16, 18, 20 (editorial), July 11, August 6, 1970. Gerald F. Graham, *Oil and Ice: The Political Economy of Law in the Canadian Arctic,* Occasional Papers (Ottawa: Norman Paterson School of International Affairs, Carleton University, December, 1974), passim.

56. *Canadian Weekly Bulletin,* March 26, 1969.

57. Ibid., March 11, May 20, 1970; January 13, 1971; July 4, 1973; Department of State, *Bulletin,* March 30, 1970, p. 434.

58. Department of State, *Bulletin,* February 1, 1971; *International Canada,* December, 1970, p. 268.

59. *New York Times,* February 16, 1968. President Gustavo Diaz Ordaz, *State of the Union Address,* September 16, 1968 (Mexico, D. F.: Consejo Mexicano de Hombres de Negocios, 1968), p. 25. Mexico concluded a similar one with Japan which helped settle the jurisdictional controversy with Mexico, which since 1935 had claimed territorial seas of nine miles. In 1975, however, Mexico unilaterally declared that its fisheries jurisdiction extended 200 miles to sea.

60. *New York Times,* May 9, 1972; May 12, 1972.

61. For the efforts of the minister of environment and conservation to widen exclusive Canadian fishing rights, see *Canada Weekly,* December 19, 1973, June 27, 1973, August 1, 1973. At the Caracas conference, the United States came closer to the Canadian position on these zones; *Greenwich Time* (AP dispatch), July 12, 1974; *Canada Today,* October 1974, p. 16). Impatient with the protracted United Nations law-of-the-sea negotiations over a 200-mile coastal fishing zone, some American proponents sought unilateral action through congressional legislation, but as of the end of 1975 they had not yet succeeded, because of the influence of competing interests and opposition by the administration, which preferred multilateral measures; *New York Times,* September 21, 1974; December 4, 1975. The Canadians would have conceded to other countries "surplus stocks," to be allocated by the coastal state; *Canada Weekly,* July 17, 1974; March 19, 1975. So would the Americans; Slimman, "Parting of Waves," pp. 14, 17; Department of State special report, "U.N. Law of the Sea Conference, 1974," pp. 3–4.

62. *Canada Weekly Bulletin,* November 13, 1968.

63. *New York Times,* June 29, July 7, 1973; *Wall Street Journal,* November 12, 1975.

64. *New York Times,* May 7, 1972. On this general subject, see Anthony Scott, "Fisheries, Pollution, and Canadian–American Transnational Relations," *International Organization,* Autumn, 1974, pp. 839–44.

65. *International Canada,* September, 1972, p. 148.

66. *Canada Weekly,* June 20, 1973.

67. Dobell, *Canada's Search,* p. 76.

68. Mexico and Brazil were even more strongly pushing their claims.

69. Quoted in Eayrs, "Sharing a Continent," p. 81.

70. A. E. Dal Graver, "The Export of Electricity from Canada," in *Canadian Issues: Essays in Honour of Henry F. Angus* ed. Robert M. Clark (Toronto: University of Toronto Press, 1961), pp. 248–85; Dobell, *Canada's Search,* p. 77; Craig, *United States and Canada,* p. 63. Illustrative of the continental relationship in electric power, Ontario Hydro in March, 1974, contracted to buy three million tons of coal in Pennsylvania; *New York Times,* March 2, 1974.

71. A. E. Ritchie's testimony, Commons External Affairs Committee, *Minutes,* May 5, 1970, p. 13; *New York Times,* December 27, 1971; *The Inch* (Texas Eastern Transmission Corp.) Winter, 1971/72, pp. 3–12. *Canadian Weekly Bulletin,* June 14, 1972, reported the marine geological survey of the Straits of Juan de Fuca.

72. *New York Times,* March 21, 1974; October 28, 1975; *Wall Street Journal,* May 5, 1975. Most of the Canadian gas would eventually be used in Canada. A major Canadian member, one of the originators of the joint study group, withdrew in favor of an all-Canadian pipeline in September, 1974 (*Wall Street Journal,* September 17, 1974).

73. In 1971–72, more than 90 percent of Canadian exports of crude oil, natural gas, other fuels, and electricity went to the United States; of Canada's imports of such heat and energy sources, 23 percent came from the United States; *Canada Weekly,* July 4, 1973.

74. *Ottawa Citizen,* January 16, 1971. Six years later, the pinch was not so much in eastern Canada as in the eastern United States. Canada was exempt from the Arab embargo. Meanwhile, British Columbia, which normally imported much fuel oil from the United States, was suffering.

75. See in chapter 6 the section on Reciprocity.

76. *Canadian Weekly Bulletin,* February 28, 1973; *New York Times,* November 26, 1971, February 15, 1973; *Wall Street Journal,* February 16, 1973.

77. *International Canada,* February, 1970, p. 38.

78. William Calkins, "A Continental Energy Plan," *ACSUS Newsletter,* Autumn, 1971, pp. 17–35; Edward H. Shaffer, *The Oil Import Program of the United States: An Evaluation* (New York: Praeger, 1968), pp. 118–21, 215; *New York Times,* May 31, 1970. Once again, in 1973 positions were reversed when Prime Minister Trudeau inaugurated a plan to build the pipeline to Montreal; *New York Times,* September 30, 1973.

79. *New York Times,* June 18, 1970, December 21, 1971, May 1, 1972, June 23, 1973; *Greenwich Time* (AP dispatch), March 12, 1970.

80. *New York Times,* January 17, 1973. By 1974, in its pamphlet *Current Foreign Policy: The United States and Canada: Facing the Energy Crisis* (December, 1973), the Department of State was pointing out that Americans "frequently forget Canadian oil is not our own."

81. Department of State, *Foreign Relations of the United States, 1948,* vol. 9, pp. 603–9.

82. Kenneth W. Dam, *Implementation of Import Quotas: The Case of Oil,* Reprint 221 (Washington: Brookings, 1971), pp. 35–36.

83. *Greenwich Time* (AP dispatch), December 31, 1973.

84. *Wall Street Journal,* July 27, 1974; *New York Times,* August 15, October 12, 15, 17, 22, 1974; *Greenwich Time,* October 22, 1974.

85. *New York Times,* August 7, 1969.

86. Peter C. Newman, "The Thawing of Canada," *Saturday Review,* March 13, 1971, p. 15; *New York Times,* September 30, October 5, 1970, November 20, 1971; With the energy crisis, the Canadian government also raised the price of exported gas so that it was in line with prices of energy alternatives available to Americans; *New York Times,* October 21, 1974. In the Canadian view (as in the eyes of many American experts), the price of gas in the United States had been held so low that it discouraged new exploration and encouraged wasteful use; Canadian Consulate general release, Speech of Secretary of State for External Affairs to the Center of Inter-American Relations, New York, March 19, 1975. Because of rapidly dwindling supplies, no further major commitment to export gas was made after 1970.

87. Lester B. Pearson's testimony in Commons External Affairs Committee, *Minutes,* April 21, 1970, p. 14.

88. *Wall Street Journal,* September 12, 1972; this unwanted accompaniment helped kill the Mackenzie Valley alternative to the trans-Alaska pipeline.

89. See, for example, *International Canada,* February, 1970, p. 37.

90. *New York Times*, October 24, 1973; Department of State, *Facing the Energy Crisis*, p. 3; *Canada Weekly*, August 20, 1975.

91. A. E. Ritchie's testimony in Commons External Affairs Committee, *Minutes*, May 5, 1970, p. 10.

92. Dale C. Thompson's testimony in Commons External Affairs Committee, *Minutes*, April 28, 1970, p. 65. This knowledgeable observer raised the question of whether the ease of contact and intimacy between Canadian and American officials that brought the former into the decision-making process at low levels in Washington did not in itself create a kind of "continental approach." Was that why Canada was not included in a special meeting called by the State Department late in September, 1974, to discuss with ministers from Britain, France, Germany, and Japan how to deal with the oil crisis? *New York Times*, October 4, 1974.

93. Shaffer, *Oil Import Program*, pp. 108–18, 135–38, 159–63, 177; James Eayrs, *Canada in World Affairs, October 1955 to June 1957* (Toronto: Oxford University Press, 1959), pp. 130–31; Lyon, *Canada in World Affairs, 1961–63*, p. 391; Commons External Affairs Committee, *Minutes*, March 12, 1959, pp. 46–48. See also "Oil Import Controls: Who Needs Them?" in SPAN (Standard Oil of Indiana), Summer, 1969, pp. 12–15; *New York Times*, February 13, 1967, February 21, March 21, 1970; *Wall Street Journal*, March 9, 1970; *Toronto Globe and Mail*, March 21, 1970.

94. The stemming of the flow of crude oil was followed by a sharp increase in gasoline exports. *New York Times*, June 29, 1973.

95. *New York Times*, June 29, 1973; *Journal of Commerce*, May 29, 1973.

96. *New York Times*, September 10, November 18, December 30, 1973; April 16, 1974; *Canada Weekly*, December 26, 1973. That each country should cope by itself with its own energy problems was the message exchanged in August, 1975, at the dedication of the Libby Dam—a product of earlier Canadian-American cooperation.

97. That the United States, which is well endowed with water, the problem being mainly its quality and distribution, should be regarded as thirsty for Canadian water reveals the continental perspective of some American water-resource planners, whose notions stimulate a negative Canadian reaction.

98. Arleigh H. Laycock, "Interbasin Transfer and Canadian Water Exports?" *ACSUS Newsletter*, Spring, 1972, pp. 45–57; Dillon O'Leary, "Canada Guards its Water Against Our Big Thirst," *Reporter*, January 27, 1966, pp. 36–38; *Air Force Journal*, April, 1973, p. 26. *The Living Wilderness*, Winter, 1972/73, pp. 13–24, reprints one chapter, "The Plan to Drain the Yukon," from Richard Bocking, *Canada's Water: For Sale?* (Toronto, 1972).

99. *New York Times*, January 23, 24, March 28, 1974; *Canada Weekly*, December 5, 1973, February 6, 1974.

100. Thompson, *St. Laurent*, pp. 421–25; Craig, *United States and Canada*, p. 236; Blair Fraser, *The Search for Identity: Canada, 1945–1967* (Garden City: Doubleday, 1968), pp. 139–44. Among the opponents' complaints was the fact that the company was American-financed.

101. *Atlantic Community News*, August, 1965, p. 2; *New York Times*, December 23, 1967,; Craig, *United States and Canada* p. 318; *Toronto Globe and Mail*, December 13, 1968; *Wall Street Journal*, November 20, 1967. For a more extensive discussion of Canada's regulation of gas and oil and the earlier pull of continentalism, see John N. McDougall, "Regulation versus

Politics: The National Energy Board and the Mackenzie Valley Pipe Line," in *Continental Community? Independence and Integration in North America*, ed. Andrew Axline et al. (Toronto: McClelland and Stewart, 1974), esp. pp. 254–65. (He opposed an arctic gas pipeline and deplored the alleged lack of "national interest" considerations in earlier energy decisions.

102. Dale Thompson's testimony in Commons External Affairs Committee, *Minutes*, April 28, 1970, p. 38. Ronald G. Atkey, "The Role of the Provinces in International Affairs," *International Journal*, Winter, 1970/71, p. 259; *Canadian Weekly Bulletin*, March 4, 1970.

103. *Canadian Weekly Bulletin*, June 23, 1971.

104. Ibid., February 3, 1971.

105. This does not require propinquity, however; a somewhat similar arrangement between Australia and Canada has been instituted; ibid., March 20, July 10, 1968, October 22, 1969.

106. Donald W. Baerresen, *The Border Industrialization Program of Mexico* (Toronto: Heath Lexington Books, 1971), p. xi.

107. *Canada Weekly*, March 21, 1973; January 29, 1975.

108. *New York Times*, May 4, 1968.

109. John Duffy, ms. on Canadian science policy, Columbia University, 1970.

110. Department of State, *Bulletin*, September 6, 1965, p. 386; "Canada's First Space Satellite," *External Affairs*, January 1963, pp. 2–15; A. E. Gotlieb and C. M. Dalfen, "International Relations and Outer Space: The Politics of Outer Space," *International Journal*, Autumn, 1970, p. 687; *Canadian Weekly Bulletin*, July 2, 1969; *Ottawa Journal*, January 6, 1971; The second Canadian Telesat, under an arrangement with the United States government, was expected to lease, from its surplus capacity, a channel to RCA that could reach areas of the United States near the border; *Canadian Weekly Bulletin*, December 6, 1972; *New York Times*, December 6, 1972). The two governments also are collaborating on Canada's communications-technology satellite, launched early in 1976; *Canada Weekly*, September 25, 1974, January 28, 1976.

111. *Canadian Weekly Bulletin*, June 2, 1971.

112. Edwin Lieuwen, *The United States and the Challenge to Security in Latin America*, Pamphlet Series, No. 4 (Columbus: Mershon Center for Education in National Security, Ohio State University, 1966), p. 13.

113. *Current Notes*, September, 1969, pp. 547–49; December, 1968, January 1969; A. J. Seyler, "Australian Capabilities—Telecommunications and Space," in *Problems of Australian Defence*, ed. H. G. Gelber (Melbourne: Oxford University Press, 1970), pp. 234–35, 239–41.

114. Trevor R. Reese, *Australia, New Zealand and the United States: A Survey of International Relations, 1941–1968* (London: Oxford University Press, 1969), p. 284. Australians have been eager to participate in earth studies made possible by American satellites and proud to have taken part in various space programs; *Current Notes*, May, 1971, for one example.

115. *New York Times*, October 29, 1967. Furthermore, standards for Western Hemisphere immigration are stiffer, and in the administration of the law, rules governing Mexicans have been particularly strict, thus encouraging illegal migration; *New York Times*, June 8, 1975.

116. *New York Times*, August 31, 1970; Dobell, "Influence of Congress," pp. 910–11.

117. Lawrence H. Officer, "Immigration and Emigration," in *Canadian Economic Problems and Policies* ed. Lawrence H. Officer and Lawrence B. Smith, (Toronto: McGraw-Hill, 1970),

pp. 150–55; Louis Parai, *Immigration and Emigration of Professional and Skilled Manpower During the Post-War Period* (Ottawa: Queen's Printer, 1965), pp. 28, 35.

118. *Canadian Weekly Bulletin,* April 23, 1969, April 21, 1971; *New York Times,* April 2, 1972, October 27, 1974. In 1973, there was an even exchange of citizens; about twenty thousand Canadians migrated to the United States, and about the same number of Americans went to Canada; "Immigration," *Canada Today,* January, 1974, p. 1. But in 1973 and 1974, the British again took first place, while Italy dropped to ninth; the United States remained in second place into 1975; *Canada Weekly,* April 16, August 27, 1975.

119. Officer, "Immigration and Emigration" pp. 152–53; *Canada Weekly,* November 6, 1974. In the 1960s, there was little brain drain from Mexico or Brazil to the United States; see George B. Baldwin, "Brain Drain or Overflow?" *Foreign Affairs,* January, 1970, 367, citing study by Charles Kidd. Very large numbers of Americans have retired to Mexico, concentrating especially in Guadalajara.

120. On the braceros, see Richard B. Craig, *The Bracero Program: Interest Groups and Foreign Policy* (Austin: University of Texas Press, 1971), passim; Howard F. Cline, *The United States and Mexico,* rev. ed. (New York: Antheneum, 1963), pp. 391–94. For other references on events since the end of the program, see *Newsweek,* February 14, 1972; *New York Times,* May 12, 1967, October 17, 1971, July 15, 22, 1973, July 15, August 8, 1974. Mexico did have an agreement with Canada for seasonal agricultural workers; *Canada Weekly,* July 10, 1974. There is a legal arrangement for certain kinds of aliens to live and work in the United States, affirmed by the Supreme Court in November, 1974, which has entitled at least 50,000 Mexicans to commute daily to or to reside in the United States while working there, a right which requires about one and a half to two years to acquire legally; *New York Times,* December 2, 1974.

121. *New York Times,* October 17, 1971. Instead of a few hundred legally regulated migrants under the bracero program who did agricultural work which Americans were loath to undertake, hordes of illegal entrants have since 1965 gravitated to cities, where they compete with unemployed American workers.

122. Mexicans called it a "delicate matter," one subject of the conversations between President Echeverria and President Nixon in their meeting in Washington in June, 1972; *New York Times,* May 4, 1973. For a lengthy treatment, see Richard Severo, "The Flight of the Wetbacks," *New York Times Magazine,* March 10, 1974.

123. They included Walter Mondale, Edward Kennedy, and Edmund S. Muskie. French-Canadian woodsmen, brought into Maine on work permits by big timber and land-management companies, have caused friction and undergone harassment from native Maine woodsmen, who are suffering from contemporary methods of organizing woodcutting and blame the Canadians for allegedly keeping their remuneration low; *New York Times,* November 29, 1975.

124. Abrams, *Interparliamentary Group,* pp. 86–87; A. E. Ritchie's testimony in Commons External Affairs Committee, *Minutes,* May 5, 1970, pp. 7, 26.

125. Parai, *Professional and Skilled Manpower,* p. 91; *International Canada,* January, 1970, p. 13; *Canada Weekly Bulletin,* February 18, 1970.

126. A. E. Ritchie's testimony in Commons External Affairs Committee, *Minutes,* May 5, 1970, p. 44; *New York Times,* May 23, 1969, January 1, 1970 and November 15, 1972; *Canadian Weekly Bulletin,* June 4, 1969; *Washington Post,* April 29, 1969. Canadian authorities quickly responded to the public and parliamentary furor aroused when an overzealous rookie of

the Royal Canadian Mounted Police aided in turning over some deserters to American authorities; *New York Times,* January 28, 1970.

127. *New York Times,* November 15, 1969.

128. R. Barry Farrell, *The Making of Canadian Foreign Policy* (Scarborough, Ontario: Prentice-Hall, 1969), p. 69; *New York Times,* May 17, 1971.

129. *New York Times,* March 25, 1967.

130. *New York Times,* December 4, 1971. This was part of a general new treaty replacing an old one covering extraditable offenses; *International Canada,* December, 1971, p. 234. A few years earlier, domestic politics had entered into an extradition case and thus prolonged an ugly trade-union controversy between the two countries involving the Seafarers International Union on the Great Lakes. The United States government, under pressure from the AFL-CIO, refused to extradite the notorious Hal Banks, a Seafarers leader, who had jumped bail in Canada; this was the last phase of a violence-ridden conflict between rival unions that eventually required attention by the highest authorities in the two governments; Stuart A. Jamieson, *Times of Trouble; Labor Unrest and Industrial Conflict in Canada, 1900–1966* (Ottawa: Information Canada, 1968), pp. 87–88; J. H. G. Crispo, *International Unionism: A Canadian-American Experiment* (Toronto: McGraw-Hill, 1966), pp. 19–20, 47–49; William J. Eaton, "The Battle of the Great Lakes," *Reporter,* November 21, 1963, pp. 38–40.

131. *Canada Weekly Bulletin,* June 10, 1970.

132. *Canadian Weekly Bulletin,* October 20, 1971. During the previous year, nearly two million Americans went to Mexico; *New York Times,* March 3, 1969. In 1973, 80 percent of the three million tourists to Mexico were Americans, who with the others spent about one billion dollars there; *New York Times,* January 23, 1974. In 1973, Canadian and American tourists each spent more than one billion dollars in the others' country.

133. State and provincial governments also encourage tourism and also cooperate. For example, Massachusetts and New Brunswick concluded a tourist-trade agreement early in 1974; *Canada Weekly,* January 16, 1974.

134. *New York Times,* August 12, 1970.

135. By contrast, Australians eagerly pursue opportunities for greater contact, which usually has to be contrived. The Portuguese language, far less familiar to Americans than Spanish, helps to protect Brazilians from unwanted cultural adulteration, a concern which in any case would run counter to Brazilian traditions.

136. For motivations of Canadian students, see George Crowley, "Canadian Students in the U.S.," *ACSUS Newsletter,* Spring, 1972, p. 91. By contrast to that of other countries, the differences between Canadian and American higher education are only nuances.

137. Brazilians were twenty-fifth, and Australians were close to them; Institute for International Education, *Open Doors* (New York: 1968), p. 3.

138. Ibid., p. 10. At the end of the decade, however, France superseded Canada, with Mexico in third place; *New York Times,* October 22, 1972.

139. Anthony Scott, "The Recruitment and Migration of Canadian Social Scientists", *Canadian Journal of Economics and Political Science,* November, 1967, p. 502.

140. *New York Times,* October 23, 1972. The number of Americans teaching in Brazil and Mexico in the late 1960s and early 1970s were greater than those in Canada and Australia, perhaps reflecting a greater need for foreign teachers in the less developed countries.

141. Cline, *United States and Mexico*, p. 301. The notoriously large number of American medical students seeking training at the medical school in Guadalajara faced ever tighter rules on the requirements for their degrees, apparently in response to criticism by the American Medical Association (*New York Times*, April 5, 1975.)

142. *New York Times*, June 11, 1972.

143. Congress of Mexico, *Memoria de la Cuarta Reunion, Parlamentaria Estados Unidos–Mexico*, (Mexico, D.F., 1964) p. 133. Fulbright exchanges and subsequent similar programs operated in Brazil and Australia.

144. An unwelcome spillover from discontent in the United States occurred when, at the annual meeting of the African Studies Association in Montreal in 1969, Americans disrupted the proceedings; *New York Times*, October 17, 1969. For "the common market in talent," see Everett Hughes, "A Sociologist's View," in *The United States and Canada*, ed. John Sloan Dickey (Englewood Cliffs: Prentice-Hall for the American Assembly, 1964), pp. 15–18.

145. *Canadian Weekly Bulletin*, March 19, 1969.

146. Examples can be found in *Canadian Weekly Bulletin*, August 30, September 6, 1972, April 18, 1973. It was the other way around after a United States court invalidated a ban on the use of a growth stimulant in livestock production which had been in effect in both countries. Canada then refused to permit the importation of any United States cattle or beef until an agreement was reached under which the United States government would monitor in detail and certify that cattle and beef exported to Canada had not been treated with the banned stimulant; *Canada Weekly*, August 28 and September 4, 1974.

147. *New York Times*, February 26, 1973. This prison was in marked contrast to Mexican prisons made notorious by tales of American drug offenders who experienced them.

148. Blair Fraser, *Search for Identity*, p. 306.

149. *New York Times*, February 15, May 24, 1970.

150. Dobell, *Canada's Search* p. 67. Meanwhile, a giant tower in Toronto was expected to permit Canadians to compete more strongly with local television in Buffalo, as it beamed broadcasts visible south of the border; *Wall Street Journal*, March 4, 1974. A thorough discussion of this question appears in Norman Spector, "Communications and Sovereignty: The Regulation of Cable Television in Canada, 1968–1973," (Ph.D. diss., Columbia University, in preparation).

151. *New York Times*, November 30, 1975.

152. On this issue, see Frazer, *Search for Identity*, p. 307; *Report on Canada–U.S. Relations* (Wahn Report) in Commons External Affairs Committee, *Minutes*, 28th Parl., 2nd sess. (July, 1970), pp. 120–24; *New York Times*, December 10, 1970, January 24, March 29, April 19, 1975; I. A. Litvak and C. J. Maule, *Cultural Sovereignty: The Time and Reader's Digest Case in Canada* (New York: Praeger, 1974), passim; Canadian Consulate General release, Speech of Secretary of State for External Affairs to the World Affairs Council and Northeast Trade Center, Boston, March 20, 1975.

153. *Ottawa Citizen*, March 3, 1971. One former Canadian publisher, Macmillan, has since been bought back by a Canadian firm; Mordecai Richler, "Going Home Again," *New York Times Book Review*, September 1, 1974. French-Canadian publishers have difficulties surviving the pressures of publishing companies in France, and Mexican publishers face stiff competition from those in Spain.

154. See George Crowley, "How to Have Cultural Affairs Without Really Trying," *ACSUS Newsletter*, Spring, 1972, pp. 88–90. The Quebec provincial government has a small office in Louisiana; *Etudes Internationales*, June, 1971, p. 320.

155. *New York Times*, July 18, 1970; May 30, 1971, May 13, 1973.

156. Congress of Mexico, *Memoria de la Cuarta Reunion*, pp. 136–138.

157. For examples of interactions between experts, see Norman Robertson's testimony in Commons External Affairs Committee, *Minutes* March 30, 1960, p. 266; Atkey, "Role of Provinces," pp. 258–60; Kal J. Holsti and Thomas Allen Levy, "Bilateral Institutions and Transgovernmental Relations Between Canada and the United States," *International Organization*, Autumn, 1974, pp. 888–928, 895; Anthony Scott, "Fisheries, Pollution," pp. 832–34; *US Foreign Policy, 1971*, p. 141; *Canadian Weekly Bulletin*, September 3, 1969, September 3, 1970, October 6, 1971; *New York Times*, August 12, 1971, September 17, 1972; *Wall Street Journal*, August 13, 1971.

158. Examples may be found in *Canadian Weekly Bulletin*, March 6, 1968, July 22, 1970, August 4, 1971; *New York Times*, October 21, 1970, January 19, 1972; Dale Thompson's testimony in Commons External Affairs Committee, *Minutes*, April 28, 1970, pp. 37–39; Atkey, "Role of Provinces," p. 259; *US Foreign Policy, 1971*, p. 141.

159. New England communities demanded passenger service along the way, which greatly lengthened the schedule, compared to the older route, which ran directly through New York state; *Greenwich Time* (AP dispatch), June 27, 1972. Within two years, however, the older route was also put into use.

160. About four million air passengers crossed the border in 1973; *New York Times*, September 16, 1973).

161. Air Canada, for example, had landing rights for New York only at Kennedy International Airport, while its competitor, enjoying preclearance, could offer service to La Guardia Airport, which had no customs service.

162. *New York Times*, April 27, 30, September 16, 1973; *Canada Weekly*, October 3, 1973. In May, 1974, the two governments signed three air agreements, called the "biggest international bilateral package ever developed between two countries," the result of negotiations extending over four years; *Canada Weekly*, May 22, 1974.

163. Cline, *United States and Mexico*, pp. 394–96; John A. Yoppins, "Joint Campaign against Foot-and Mouth Disease," in Department of State, *Bulletin*, January–June, 1947, pp. 710–12.

164. For example, a Mexican law banned the production and sale of amphetamines that had been manufactured in Mexico to get around strict United States regulations; *New York Times*, January 23, 1972.

165. See Department of State, *Bulletin*, January 6, 1945, for note of October 19, 1944, from the United States to Mexico and responses of October 26, 1944, and January 11, 1945; *US Foreign Policy, 1969–70*, p. 114; *US Foreign Policy, 1971*, p. 143; Congress of Mexico, *Memoria de la Cuarta Reunion*, pp. 159–69; *New York Times*, September 25, 28, 30, October 1, 3, 10, (Including editorial) 11, 12, 1969, January 17, March 10, 12, May 17, July 14, 26, August 22, 1970, September 17, 1972. G. Gordon Liddy, later involved in the Watergate break-in, was the mastermind behind Operation Intercept.

TEN   *CONCLUSIONS: ATTRACTION AND RESPONSE*

1. "There is an American dimension to nearly every topic discussed in Canada," noted Gerald M. Craig, in *The United States and Canada* (Cambridge: Harvard University Press, 1968), p. 317.

2. Otherwise they would have recognized that the Brazilians followed an "old custom, almost tradition, of Portuguese diplomacy when they could not succeed: to feign, coast along, postpone, in the hope that time would bring modifications which they might be able to exploit"; João Pandiá Calógeras, *A Política Exterior Do Imperio,* vol. 1, *As Origens* (Rio de Janeiro, Imprensa Nacional, 1927), p. 372. In Portuguese, the passage runs: "Era velha indole, quasi tradição, da diplomacia portuguêsa, quando não poedia vencer fingir, ladear, protelar na esperança de dar tempo ao tempe, o que traria modificações de que pudesse aproveitar-se."

3. Stanley Hoffmann, *Gulliver's Troubles, Or the Setting of American Foreign Policy* (New York: McGraw-Hill, 1968), pp. 404–5; *idem*, "Discord in Community," *International Organization,* Summer, 1963, pp. 530–31.

4. I. A. Litvak and C. J. Maule, "Foreign Investment in Mexico: Some Lessons for Canada," *Behind the Headlines,* July, 1971, p. 8.

5. A former Brazilian ambassador to the United States recalled a conversation with President Truman in which he lamented the absence of the kind of influence with the United States government enjoyed by Mexico in obtaining credits; he accepted the president's reply that if Brazil had the representation in the United States Congress [presumably from border states] which was available to Mexico, he could do more for him; Mauricio Nabuco, *Reminiscências Sérias e Frivolas* (Rio de Janeiro: Editoria Pongetti, 1969), pp. 158.

6. "Policy-Making in a World Turned Upside Down," *Foreign Affairs,* January, 1967, p. 211. He went on: "Inter-service rivalries come back through other people's Foreign Ministries after referral and umpiring by interested foreign parties who factor in their own various weights and measures."

7. Note Secretary of State for External Affairs Mitchell Sharp's statement to the House of Commons Standing Committee on External Affairs and National Defence on March 19, 1974, when he commented on the preceding year's developments by observing that the better climate of relations between Canada and the United States was caused partly by "the resiliency of the American economy and by the turn-around in the United States balance of payments"; *Canada Weekly,* April 17, 1974).

8. Kal H. Holsti devised the list and categories; it appeared in "The United States and Canada," in *Conflict in World Politics,* ed. Steven L. Spiegel and Kenneth N. Waltz (Cambridge: Winthrop, 1971), p. 378.

9. Donald Puchala, "Of Blind Men, Elephants and International Integration," mimeographed (Columbia University, September, 1971, p. 11; Philippe Schmitter, "Three Neo-Functional Hypotheses about International Integration," *International Organization,* Winter, 1969, p. 166. Equally plausible is the hypothesis that politicizing a functional issue, if it involves especially scarce resources and the competition for them, might accentuate a nationalistic response, not an integrating one. This was the case with Canada's oil and natural gas.

10. Compare Barbara Haskel's distinction between "distributive" and "expansive" strategies in "Disparities, Strategies, and Opportunity Costs: The Example of Scandinavian Economic Market Negotiations," *International Studies Quarterly,* March, 1974, pp. 5–6. She suggests that the weaker partner concentrates on how to divide a fixed good.

11. For some observations on the effect of extensive technical cooperation on integrative tendencies, see Ernst Haas, *Beyond the Nation State* (Stanford: Stanford University Press, 1964), pp. 48, 409; *idem,* "Uniting of Europe and the Uniting of Latin America," *Journal of Common Market Studies,* June, 1967, pp. 327–328; also Patrick Sewell, *Functionalism and World Politics* (Princeton: Princeton University Press, 1966), p. 53. Roger Hansen has pointed out that where some integration in a particular field has slowed down or stopped, it could be either because, with equilibrium in that area, the "dramatic-political leadership" has turned elsewhere, leaving the field to the technicians, or because those involved are afraid to risk what they have already achieved for a "bird in the bush"; "European Integration: Forward March, Parade Rest, or Dismissed?" *International Organization,* Spring, 1973, p. 239.

12. So common is the use of the telephone that after leaving office, Lester Pearson advised Canadian officials to make a written record of understandings in dealing with Americans by this means; see his testimony in the House of Commons Standing Committee on External Affairs and National Defence, *Minutes of Proceedings and Evidence,* April 21, 1970, p. 12 (hereafter cited as Commons External Affairs Committee, *Minutes*).

13. NORAD may be an important exception. Gerard Pelletier, when secretary of state, once observed that healthy fraternal relations between two countries are enhanced by "maintaining some degree of distance among the adult members"; ("The Canadian Personality in the North American Environment," Associations for Canadian Studies in the United States, Conference on Canadian Studies in the United States, mimeographed, April 18, 1970, p. 15).

14. As Melvin Conant noted, in matters of defense, effective consultation requires a *continuous* flow of information and arrangements for *swift* and *easy* communications; "A Perspective on Defence: The Canada-United States Compact," *Behind the Headlines,* September, 1974, pp. 32–33. Formal institutions can facilitate these.

15. Puchala, "Blind Men, Elephants," pp. 16ff.

16. Stuart Scheingold, "The North Atlantic Area as a Policy Arena," *International Studies Quarterly,* March, 1971, esp. pp. 34, 51–52. See also the statement of Roger Hansen that "sizeable (and equitably distributed) economic gains would result from a common market *coordinated* by sovereign states rather than managed by ceaselessly expanding supranational authorities"; "Regional Integration: Reflections on a Decade of Theoretical Efforts," *World Politics,* January, 1969, p. 256.

17. Cf. Edward Miles, "Organizations and Integration in International Systems," *International Studies Quarterly,* June, 1968, pp. 215ff.

18. In Peyton Lyon's words, that integration which has occurred is "unconscious and involuntary"; "Introduction" in *Continental Community? Independence and Integration in North America,* ed. Andrew Axline et al. (Toronto: McClelland and Stewart, 1974) p. 3.

19. As Daniel Lerner and Morton Gorden pointed out in another context, if the gap between self and reference group (here the United States) is great, frustration and fear are the reaction, while if it is not beyond imaginable grasp, a more positive response due to empathy and emulation are likely; *Euratlantica: Changing Perspectives of the European Elites* (Cambridge: MIT Press, 1969), p. 42.

20. On side-payments and reassurance, see Haskel, "Disparities, Strategies, p. 25.

21. See, for example, Theo Sommer on "Canadianization," i.e., "being pressed into economic subservience to the United States, their autonomy and freedom of choice threatened by dollar diplomacy"; "The Community is Working," *Foreign Affairs,* July, 1973, p. 753.

22. Commons External Affairs Committee *Minutes,* May 5, 1970, p. 7.

23. See Gilbert R. Winham, "Choice and Strategy in Continental Relations," in *Continental Community? Independence and Integration in North America,* ed. Andrew Axline et al. (Toronto: McClelland and Stewart, 1974), pp. 231, 233, 239; Holsti, "United States and Canada," pp. 385, 392, 394.

24. See Joseph S. Nye, "Comparative Regional Integration: Concept and Measurement," *International Organization,* Autumn, 1968, p. 877.

25. Compare a New Zealander's comments: "We little New Zealanders may sometimes despair at the difficulty of influencing that juggernaut of power labelled U.S.A.; I suspect that the same despair must also chill the hearts of countless Americans. In a small country, we can at least reach the ear of our own Prime Minister, and he can speak up. Have we not perhaps as much chance of influencing the Administration as have our opposite numbers in the United States?" sixth of the Sidney Holland Memorial Lectures, 1967, printed as F. L. W. Wood, *New Zealand and the Big Powers* (Wellington, 1967), p. 11.

26. Cf. Karl Kaiser, "Transnational Politics," *International Organization,* Autumn, 1971, p. 813. That the United States government has not more readily exploited its strength further to increase its power is in sharp contrast to the Soviet-Finnish relationship; between that superpower and its democratic neighbor, there is a rather low level of transactions accompanied by some political penetration into the smaller neighbor.

27. One small sign of this emergence is that in 1974 the Soviet institute dealing with United States studies added "Canada" to its title.

INDEX